WHEN THE WORLD WAS BLACK

THE UNTOLD HISTORY OF THE WORLD'S FIRST CIVILIZATIONS

VOLUME TWO OF THE SCIENCE OF SELF

PART TWO: ANCIENT CIVILIZATIONS

SUPREME UNDERSTANDING

Published by Supreme Design Publishing. PO Box 10887, Atlanta, GA 30310.

Although the author and publisher have made every effort to ensure the accuracy and completeness of information contained in this book, we assume no responsibility for errors, inaccuracies, omissions, or any inconsistency herein. Any perceived slights of people, places, or organizations are not intended to be malicious in nature.

Supreme Design Publishing books are printed on long-lasting acid-free paper. When it is available, we choose paper that has been manufactured by environmentally responsible practices. These may include using trees grown in sustainable forests, incorporating recycled paper, minimizing chlorine in bleaching, or recycling the energy produced at the paper mill.

Supreme Design Publishing is also a member of the Tree Neutral™ initiative, which works to offset paper consumption through tree planting.

TreeNeutral

Graphic Design, Layout, Editing, and Typesetting by Proven Publishing
www.ProvenPublishing.com

First Printing 2013

ISBN: 978-1-64007-986-1

LCCN: 2013931006

Wholesale Discounts. Special discounts (up to 55% off of retail) are available on quantity purchases. For details, visit our website, contact us by mail at the address above, Attention: Wholesale Orders, or email us at orders@supremedesignonline.com

Individual Sales. Supreme Design publications are available for retail purchase, or can be requested, at most bookstores. They can also be ordered directly from the Supreme Design Publishing website, at www.SupremeDesignOnline.com

VISIT US ON THE WEB AT WWW.SUPREMEDESIGNONLINE.COM

TABLE OF CONTENTS

INTRODUCTION

BASIC INSTRUCTIONS

"I am apt to suspect the Negroes to be naturally inferior to the white. There never was a civilized nation of any other complexion than white, nor even any individual eminent either in action or speculation. No ingenious manufactures amongst them, no arts, no sciences." – Philosopher David Hume, 1768

Why are ancient Black civilizations important? What do they have to do with us nowadays? Could this information serve as anything more than a source of inspiration? Or are these stories mere reminders of the greatness that once was?

There are actually several reasons why we need a full and accurate story of the Black role in the world's ancient civilizations:

☐ First, public opinion has not changed much since "Enlightenment" philosopher David Hume said the horrible words above over two hundred years ago. It's not simply that people don't know exactly how much Black people gave the world. Instead, many people think Black people gave the world absolutely nothing. This is especially the case when we talk about the world's ancient civilizations.

☐ Second, this history allows us to see how modern civilization came to be. As the ancient world, beginning with the Neolithic Age (around 10,000 years ago), is the foundation for all the civilizations that followed, we can only fully understand the present (and see the future) when we have a clear lens into the past.

☐ Third, the stories of our ancestors are full of lessons that we can extract and apply to our own lives. They were us, and we are them.

☐ Finally, the Black people who we discuss in this book – particularly the amazing people who we call the Anu – were so well-traveled that we may have Anu ancestors no matter where on Earth we hail from. Again, these are our stories.

THE BACKGROUND TO THIS BOOK

In *When the World Was Black, Part One*, we told the story of our earliest human ancestors, the Original People who settled the globe, paving the way for those of us who would come later. These people understood the sciences associated with modern civilization, but lived as close to a "natural way of life" as their environments permitted. By about 20,000 years ago, the world's climates were shifting. Regions that were once hospitable and fertile were quickly becoming incapable of supporting our ancestors' growing communities. Many of our people, long detached from their ancestral homelands, had lost their old traditions or developed new traditions that reflected their new homelands and history.

Few of these people, however, were responding well to this new period of climate change. Others had grown into such large populations that increasing ethnic diversity and the competition for natural resources resulted in a new era of "inter-tribal" conflicts.

In a world that once knew nothing of theft, deceit, and murder, these social ills were becoming increasingly familiar. It wouldn't be until about 6,000 years ago that these issues would reach critical mass, but by 10,000 years ago, even the most peaceful populations saw their survival threatened by dramatic episodes of climate change. This is the period known to geologists and climatologists as the Holocene epoch. This is when nearly everything changed.

This is when the Anu people come into the picture. They were most likely direct descendants of the Original People who first settled the world over 100,000 years before them. They probably didn't call themselves Anu, but that's the best name by which to refer to this cultural community of Black men and women who traveled the world, introducing the sciences and innovations that allowed local communities to transition into the Neolithic Age. These "foreign" traditions made it so that climate change and population growth no longer posed serious threats to their continued peace and survival. Later waves of Anu people, dispersing from the same African homeland, ushered in the rise of sprawling urban civilizations.

This happened in the Near East, Europe, India, Arabia, China, Indonesia, Australia, the Pacific Islands, and in the Americas. These are the stories we'll tell in this book.

WHAT YOU'LL LEARN

In this book, you'll learn about the people who introduced the "Neolithic revolution" to the world. Beginning 15,000 years ago, there was a cultural community of Black people who traveled far and wide, introducing the world to major changes. These changes would pave the way for modern civilization. Specifically, you'll learn about:

- ☐ The little-known history of Egypt, Nubia, the Sahara, and West Africa.
- ☐ The science of the massive stone monuments, temples, and pyramids we find throughout Africa (not just in Egypt!), throughout southern Asia, across the Pacific Ocean, in North and South America, and in Europe.
- ☐ The ancient Black origins of farming, writing, metal-working, pottery, fabric-weaving, modern government, modern trade and economics, and many other features of modern civilization.
- ☐ The story behind the first civilizations of the Americas and if they really did have "Black visitors" long before Columbus.
- ☐ The Black history of ancient China, Japan, and Indonesia.
- ☐ The advanced city-planning used by the Black civilizations of ancient Crete, Egypt, and India, who had sewers, flushing toilets, and aqueducts more than 4,000 years ago.
- ☐ The reason why our ancestors began farming and breeding animals.
- ☐ Why our ancestors were worshipped as Black gods or "immortals" nearly everywhere they went.
- ☐ The paths our ancestors took crossing the Pacific and Atlantic Oceans into the Americas.
- ☐ Ancient Black influences on Native American cultures.
- ☐ The relationships between the civilizations of India and the Near East, and whether these were colonies of Egypt, Ethiopia, or Nubia.
- ☐ The unknown history of the civilizations that once thrived in the Amazon rainforest.
- ☐ The Black civilizations of ancient Europe...and the wars that nearly eliminated them.
- ☐ Why our ancestors traveled the world, teaching civilization.
- ☐ How and why most of these ancient civilizations fell into ruin.
- ☐ What this history can teach us, and how we can apply these lessons to our present and future.

HOW TO READ THIS BOOK

The following guidelines (also found in Part One) should make it easier to read and understand this book:

- ☐ Think of this book like a reference book. It's full of literally thousands of years worth of content. To support many of the arguments we make, I've had to incorporate lots – and I mean lots – of data. Sometimes, this can be overwhelming. The vocabulary isn't always easy either. But here's the first step: relax.
- ☐ You can reread this book as many times as you need to. And unlike *The Science of Self, Volume One*, you don't necessarily have to read

this book from front to back. You can skip around, because this work is meant to be encyclopedic like *The Hood Health Handbook* – a useful reference on over 1,000 different historical topics.

❏ In other words, if you come across a difficult concept, a technical-sounding quote, or a section that simply doesn't catch your interest, skip it. Often, those long block quotes are followed by an explanation in laymen's terms. And what doesn't catch you on your first read might catch your interest on your second read.

❏ However, it might be easiest to understand if you don't skip around too much, because difficult concepts are explained the first time they're mentioned, but not again afterwards.

❏ If you don't feel like keeping a dictionary next to you while you read, there are free dictionary apps for most smartphones, and Dictionary.com is easy to use as well. Wherever we can, we define tough words, but you still might run into a few that you need to clarify. Don't stress! You're improving your vocabulary. Soon, you'll be able to use "anthropometry" in a sentence.

❏ When you read, write in the margins and highlight text as often as you can. You may even want to use one of those colorful sticky-tab bookmarking systems. It's also helpful to keep a notebook where you take notes and record your thoughts.

❏ We always ask that you share our work with others. We appreciate when you take pictures of our books and share them online, or post quotes with credits. SDP lives off word-of-mouth.

❏ At the same time, you may not get great results if you introduce this book to a friend who doesn't like reading. You may need to start with a book like *How to Hustle and Win,* or *Rap, Race, and Revolution*, or *Knowledge of Self*. Those books are better suited for general audiences. This book, like *The Science of Self, Volume One*, is much heavier reading and will be tough for the uninitiated.

❏ Still, carry the book with you. We delay our eBook releases (sometimes for a year or more) for a reason! We want people to bring this knowledge into the REAL world. We love the internet as much as you do, but we're trying to kill all that disconnectedness and "reinvent the world" by bringing our people back together. (You'll get it when you read this book).

❏ So take this book out with you, and let those random conversations begin. You'll be surprised how much good can come from such a small gesture.

❏ If you're in school, you can quote this book in your papers. As much as some people may not "like" the positions we take, my research methodology is sound. Even if my "plain English" presentation isn't your professor's cup of tea, the facts are strong enough to stand on their own.

THE ANCIENT WORLD

BIG CITIES, BIG CHANGES

"A climate of alienation has a profound effect on the Black personality, particularly on the educated Black, who has the opportunity to see how the rest of the world regards him and his people. It often happens that the Black intellectual thus loses confidence in his own potential and that of his race. Often the effect is so crushing that some Blacks, having evidence to the contrary, still find it hard to accept the fact we really were the first to civilize the world." – Cheikh Anta Diop

Where did it all begin? Everything you consider "modern civilization" is not as modern as you'd think. Throughout the ancient world, we can find all of the earmarks of modern civilization in an earlier form. We're talking about everything from architecture and astronomy to pre-fabricated ship-building and zoology. In other words, our ancestors did it all, **long before anyone who developed these ideas within the past 2,000 years**. These include:

- ☐ The introduction of agriculture (farming) and animal domestication (the taming and breeding of animals used for food), which changed the way we eat and survive.
- ☐ Organized urban cities with paved roads, public plazas, and complex sewer and drainage systems, including flushing toilets found over 4,000 years ago in India, Crete, and Egypt.
- ☐ Sophisticated methods for irrigation, many of which are still in use today, like the terraced mountainside farms in Peru, originally built over 3,000 years ago.
- ☐ Written scripts and languages that form the basis for all of today's modern languages – none of which, notably, originated among Europeans.
- ☐ Impressive stonemasonry, where massive stone monuments (made of stones often weighing more than 100 tons) were erected in

astronomically-oriented circles or other symbolic formations. Ancient stone circles are found throughout Africa, Asia, Europe, and the Pacific Islands.

❑ The introduction of advanced practices in ceramics (the making of pottery), metallurgy (the making of metal items), textiles (the weaving of fabric), and home-building, which changed the way we live.

❑ The veneration of ancestors and cultural leaders, commemorated in massive stone tombs, burial mounds, and pyramids. These "manmade mountains" are found throughout Africa, Asia, and the Americas, where they remain a source of awe.

❑ A wealth of cultural traditions that persist into the modern day, including most forms of government, the first written laws, the establishment of social classes, the idea of property ownership and rights, and most of the world's major religious traditions.

So who brought these innovations to the world? Was it the Greeks? The Romans? The Aryans? The Anglo-Saxons? No? None of them? Well, if not white folks, could it have been aliens? No evidence for them either? Perhaps it was people from a "lost continent" like Lemuria, or maybe Atlantis. Well, there's some truth to that, actually. As we explained in Part One, the idea of a "forgotten civilization" like Atlantis was simply a way for Europeans to discuss **a "homeland" they simply did not want to attribute to Africans.**

Ironically, this homeland was historically situated somewhere near the Aswan Dam in Sudan (ancient Nubia). And, like the myths of Atlantis and Lemuria, this area was indeed submerged underwater. Much of this region's history is now buried under the world's largest manmade lake, Lake Nasser. So maybe not Atlanteans or Lemurians but Nubians? That makes a lot more sense. We'll explain all the details as you continue reading..

THE RISE OF CIVILIZATION

In this book, we're exploring the history of these urban civilizations as they're found throughout the ancient world. We'll talk about who built them, as well as how, when, and why they were built. As you read, we want you to keep in mind what you learned in Part One. That is, don't think that this is when civilization STARTED. We didn't "become" civilized within the past 6,000 years. That's part of the lie associated with the way the white historian has been telling *his story*. He seeks to encapsulate everything important within the place and time where he dominated. *His story*, indeed.

In Part One, we showed how recent scholars are trying to fit everything important into the story of the humans who settled Europe 40,000 years ago – hoping to convince the world that these people were their ancestors (they weren't).

In the past, scholars believed that white history didn't go back more than 6,000 years, so they attempted to cram every important development into this window of time. Whatever was simply too old to fit, they called "primitive" "pagan" "crude" and "savage." Amazingly, remnants of this model have survived into the present.

College students are taught that "civilization" emerged in the Near East within the past 10,000 years. None of the history seems Black, suggesting that Blacks had nothing to do with any of it. It's all a lie. Throughout this book, you'll see why.

THE WAY THE STORY IS TOLD

Historians call the period when "civilization" began the Neolithic. It marks the origins of urban civilization throughout most of the world. The Neolithic is a historical period, literally translating to "New Stone Age." It followed the Palaeolithic period and began with the rise of farming and other social changes. But the Neolithic isn't really a specific time period. It's just a set of characteristics that a society can develop.

Typically, the "Neolithic Revolution" was set off by the systemic use of agriculture and animal domestication, and other things like the use of ceramics, textiles, metallurgy, and – once the population had grown enough – urban city planning. For some time, the scientific community said this happened no sooner than 4,000 BC anywhere in the world, and much later throughout Africa and the Americas.

But they were proven wrong. Researchers later found Neolithic cultures appearing in the Near East region known as the Fertile Crescent as early as 10,000 BC, and from there spreading outwards. By 8000 BC, there were early Neolithic cultures in Turkey, Syria and Iraq, followed by southeast Europe by 7000 BC, South Asia by 7000 BC, China by 6500 BC, the Americas by 5800 BC, Central Europe by 5500 BC, and the Philippines by 5000 BC. And this is what mainstream scholars have believed for a while.

But they're STILL wrong. As you've seen in Part One, dozens of sites throughout the world present evidence of agriculture, animal domestication, urbanization, and written language, thousands of years before the dates above.[1] Not to mention, the oldest stuff (even stone) disappears over time, and some of the oldest cities we built are now submerged underwater, eroded by thousands of years of changing weather, or covered under jungles and deserts that haven't even been explored yet.

What we KNOW is that civilization is not something that happened one day. Civilization is US. We bring it wherever we go. For tens of thousands of years, we lived prosperous lives simply by taking the most ecological (nature-based) route possible. We didn't leave behind large buildings and monuments, but we didn't need them then.

"It is pretty well settled that the city is the Negro's great contribution to civilization, for it was in Africa where the first cities grew up." – Emanuel Haldeman-Julius (1889-1951), Author and Publisher

Within the past 50,000 years, our communities have grown and we've often found ourselves needing systems that can support large, settled communities. Historians call this "the rise of civilization." We simply call it the rise of urbanization. Urbanization refers to the forming of heavily populated "inner cities" serving the needs of thousands of people, who typically:

❒ subsist off an agricultural economy, since you can't feed that many people without domesticating plants and animals, and

❒ have at least some form of social hierarchy, since you can't have that many people – often from different lands – without a small group of people who "manage" things.

As you'll see throughout this book, it was not Europeans but Original people who introduced ALL the innovations we associate with modern civilization (or urbanization). Not only did we develop agriculture, animal domestication, city planning, stone masonry and architecture, metal-working, textiles, ceramics, writing, and anything else you can think of...we developed these sciences from *very old roots*.

None of these things were born within the past 10,000 years. They all have roots in things our ancestors* did (but didn't need to do systemically) as far back as two million years ago. When we revived their usage and took them to the next level, we were simply living out the mathematical cycle that exemplified the nature of Original people, the authors of all creation.

ENKI AND THE JAGUAR
THE REASON MOST PYRAMIDS HAVE FLAT TOPS

In the ancient Sumerian myth of Enki and the Jaguar, they describe a

---

* For an explanation of what exactly we mean by "ancestors," see the FAQ in the Appendix of Part One.

Golden Age over 200,000 years ago, when the *na-ag-en*, or "cloud people" descended from the heavens and gave instructions to Enki, a native of the land. The *na-ag-en* are described as *du-ma-ses*, which Hendrick Peterson translates as **"little dark men."** These Africoid people taught Enki the science of pyramid building. They taught him to build the pyramids with flat tops, so they could be used as landing pads for their vehicles, which we can assume were spaceships. Enki taught this knowledge to his people, and they taught it to the people of the world.

This is why Enki's name can be found in the most ancient cultures of the world. In Egypt there is *ankh*, in Nubia there's *Piankhy*, in Cambodia, there's *Angkor Wat*, and in Korea, *kimchee* appears to derive from Enki. This might even be the origin of the curious slang word *honkey*. This could be why it feels good to say "honkey," because you are communing with the ancient cloud people who gave us all our knowledge and sciences.

The myth of Enki and the Jaguar continues to report that the people of Egypt did not heed Enki's instruction and they covered the pyramids (which were originally flat-topped) with a sharp point. This caused great trouble in the heavens, and Egypt was cursed with plagues and pestilence (described in the Bible and every other world myth of the time), as well as domination by the Persians, Romans, and Arabs. Consequently, Egypt was reduced to a broken shell of what it once was. If only they would have left those pyramids flat, imagine what could have been!

REVIEW

What did you think about that history? Pleeeeease tell me your "bogus" alarms went off almost immediately. If they didn't go off in the first LINE (there's no jaguars in the Near East), they should have definitely gone off at some point. If not, I still love you, but please delete your YouTube account, unsubscribe from all those wacky Facebook pages, and read this book AND Volume One of *The Science of Self* from front to back. Like 80 times.

I used this totally ridiculous story to illustrate the kind of "quack" history that serious scholars hate. And I'm talking about Black scholars who fight HARD against the Western mainstream model. They hate this kind of silliness because it makes EVERYTHING contrary to the mainstream look bad. In reality, all "alternative" theories are not made alike. Some are based on good research methodology, while others – like the one above – were pulled straight out of my imagination.

THE SCIENCE OF RESEARCH

People often ask me about how I find all this information. "I read books," they say, "but I never uncover any of the stuff you talk about. Where do you get this stuff? I mean, I know you're not making it up, but HOW do you find it?" So I'm going to answer that question in this book. I'll answer it directly here, but you'll also find bits and pieces of my process throughout the book.

For those who don't know my background, my doctorate is in education, specializing in the field of Curriculum and Instruction. Getting that degree did three things for me:

It taught me how to thoroughly research and investigate theories without bias or flawed methods. I have a Bachelor's degree in History, and I was inducted into an international History Honors Society, but writing a dissertation taught me how to seriously take my theories through a rigorous scientific process.

It strengthened my skills in developing educational curriculum, which is exactly what you find in our books. Those of you who began this journey with How to Hustle and Win will totally understand how it has worked.

Finally, it made people listen to what I had to say. I'm saying a lot of the same stuff I said before I was "Dr." Supreme Understanding, but it seems that more people will listen to me now that there's letters at the end of my name. Fine with me. Thing is, I learned a lot of this from people who never finished high school.

So let's talk about the process I use.

HOW I RESEARCH

☐ For beginners, I read a lot. I mean, a LOT. I don't know how I find time, really. Sometimes that can be bad for you (it's called "analysis paralysis," when you can't stop taking in information, and you never actually do anything with it). But you can't research without reading, and just visiting websites won't do.

☐ You've gotta read books. You can start researching a subject by reading its Wikipedia page, but then you've gotta read the references at the end of the page. You see, people dog out Wikipedia, but Wikipedia is a lot better than it used to be. You can find great summaries of important subjects there, and if you're worried about something being "made up," you should read the sources they cite at the bottom.

☐ By sources, I'm talking about published books and articles in scholarly journals. That's where the real meat and potatoes of research can be found.

- You can find those books online by visiting books.google.com, where many of them have searchable text and you can read almost half of the book. Google Books gives you a link to that book's page on Amazon.com, where you can also read some of the books for free, but you can also buy a used copy for less than half the retail price.
- Many of the used books on Amazon are available for $0.01 plus shipping. Not only that, but Amazon will suggest other books on the same subject. Check out their reviews and ratings to see which one you want to start with.
- You can find journal articles by following the link from the Wikipedia page, or by searching at scholar.google.com where many of them are available for free. If you're willing to do this, you're on your way.
- You've also gotta read works from Black and brown authors dealing with these subjects, so that you don't find yourself led astray and away from your own connection to the subject. For example, if you're studying slavery, you've gotta read *There Is a River* by Vincent Harding, *Black Odyssey* by Nathan Huggins, or *Before the Mayflower* by Lerone Bennett. Light readers might want to check out Julius Lester's *To Be a Slave*. If you want to study economics, you can't skip out on *Blueprint for Black Power* by Amos Wilson. You need to check in with the Black scholars, or the perspective you develop will be Eurocentric by default.

If that's clear so far, we can talk about the way I develop my theories.

HOW I DEVELOP THEORIES

Throughout this book, I'll let you know whenever I don't have mountains of evidence to support a theory. So I'm only proposing it as a theory. I only propose theories when (a) the theory works to resolve questions that haven't been answered (meaning there isn't already a theory that covers everything), (b) the theory fits the available evidence, (c) there's not a lot of evidence suggesting an alternative theory makes more sense.

That's different from a theory that sounds good but unravels when you consider the actual evidence.

Am I always right? I don't expect to be. Theories are meant to be amended, refined, and even discarded if a better theory comes along. As you can imagine, I've discarded more theories than I've proposed.ˑ In fact, this book has been through five major rewrites since I began it several years ago.

ˑ And I've expanded on many theories that have been around far longer than me. I stand on the shoulders of giants, because scholars like John G. Jackson, Ivan Van Sertima, Chancellor Williams, Cheikh Anta Diop, and several others were developing theoretical frameworks for the prehistoric Black past long before me. They're the ones who inspired me to do this work.

I know that this book breaks considerable ground, and that comes with the risks of a theory being later discredited. I'm okay with that. Just know that I'm not the type of author who says, "This is what definitely happened, and I don't really need to prove it to you." And I hope that you learn to become wary of people who approach matters that way. In fact, we're encouraging scientific discussions of the content we're covering in The Science of Self series. By the time you have this book in your hands, you'll be able to check in to www.thescienceofself.com where you'll find a discussion board for every topic (and theory) we've addressed.

HOW NOT TO RESEARCH

To wrap things up, talking about "how to research" requires that I talk to you about how NOT to research. Let's start with some basics.

YouTube is way worse than Wikipedia. People can put up ANYthing on YouTube, and – unlike Wikipedia – nobody else can come in to clean it up. And because of its visual format, it appeals to people who would rather passively absorb information, instead of actively reading and researching on their own. In other words, they're expecting you to be a sucker. So they're not even gonna TRY to prove their points. They just make some bogus claim, add a picture they found, and at least a few people will believe it. I'm convinced that some of this misdirection is intentional and government-funded.

Getting past YouTube, you still have to be wary of the sources you consult. There are books and websites with very obvious agendas – whether it's "White is right" or "Aliens are coming." But sometimes, you can't tell. What about when you are following a path someone else has created with the data, and you don't even know their agenda? You might be following a trail of breadcrumbs, not knowing it's leading you to the oven. For example, I used to consult a few anthropological blogs quite regularly. Even added their RSS feed to my phone via Google Currents (get that if you don't have it, you can subscribe to any news source or website with a blog). I loved all the history, but then I realized that EVERYTHING he discussed leads the discussion out of Africa. In a subtle, scientific way, he was saying all civilization came from outside Africa. But it wasn't until I got heavy into the work of modern African scholars that I realized what he was doing.

The lesson is to be a critical thinker, and to consult multiple sources, at ALL times. As I explained earlier, if a theory doesn't fit the evidence, it may not be a good theory. If you're reading about how "aliens built everything ancient," your "critical thinking" senses should tingle, and you'll ask, "Well what about all the evidence that…" or "The author just said some amazing stuff, but there's no citation and no evidence for his claim!" Nine times out of ten, you'll realize you're reading some flim-flam.

Next, you have to understand that there are multiple strands of evidence required to make a solid case. It's like court. One or two pieces of circumstantial evidence, or hearsay, just won't get you a guilt verdict (well, at least it shouldn't). Need some other clues that a claim is flim-flam? You won't be able to find any research on it in Google Scholar. Before you think about the failures of Western Science, I'ma stop you right there.

If you think the scholarly journals would hide ALL the evidence of some "controversial" claim, then how did I cite over 200 studies in the references section of this book? Obviously, they're not hiding everything. More than likely, there's no research on the subject because the author is making things up as he goes. If you Google a topic, and the only websites that show up are Bibliotecapleyades.net, Pravda.ru, Thetruthbehindthescenes.org, and Disclose.tv, it's probably some flim-flam. And you CAN'T become one of those people who are okay with the flim-flam! As a brother named Universal Shamgaudd would say, "Beware false knowledge, for it is more dangerous than ignorance!"

This is because a person with no knowledge can acquire new knowledge once they see what they're missing. But a person with false knowledge has barriers up. They might even be arrogant in their ignorance, believing they know something (which is actually untrue) and therefore they don't need to learn something different (which is actually the truth).

People who think like this have to change the way their minds process information, because – if you accept ANYthing as truth, or you don't consider ideas outside of your beliefs or preconceived notions – your closed mind will eventually put you in a problematic situation. It's this failure to think critically that gets us in trouble, time after time. That's yet another reason why this book exists.

WHAT MAKES AN OBJECTIVE HISTORIAN?

So what does it take to be objective? According to Justice Charles Gray – who once had to rule on the matter – these seven points are what distinguish an objective historian:

❐ One must treat sources with appropriate reservations;
❐ One must not dismiss counterevidence without scholarly

consideration;

☐ One must be even-handed in her treatment of evidence and eschew "cherry-picking";

☐ One must clearly indicate any speculation;

☐ One must not mistranslate documents or mislead by omitting parts of documents;

☐ One must weigh the authenticity of all accounts, not merely those that contradict her favored view; and

☐ One must take the motives of historical actors into consideration.

Notice that these criteria have nothing to do with what kind of degree you have, or where you went to school. It's all about HOW you do the work. With that said, let's get to it.

WHEN THE WORLD WAS BLACK, PART TWO

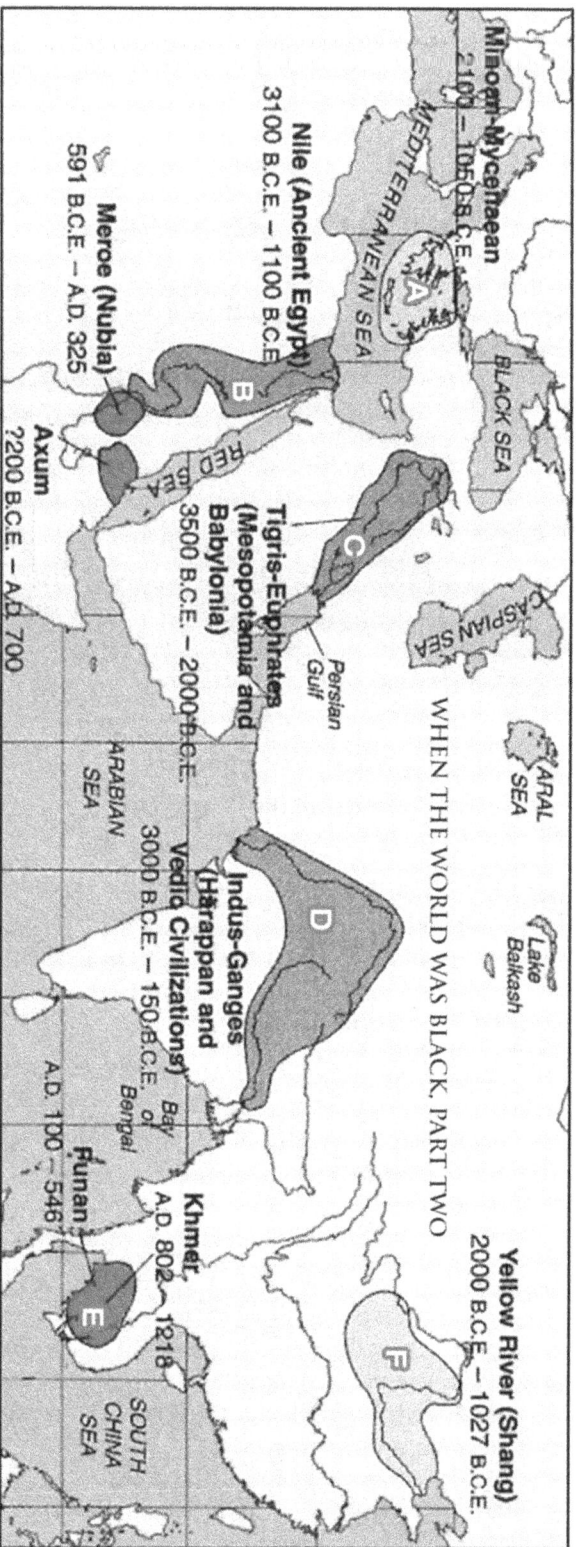

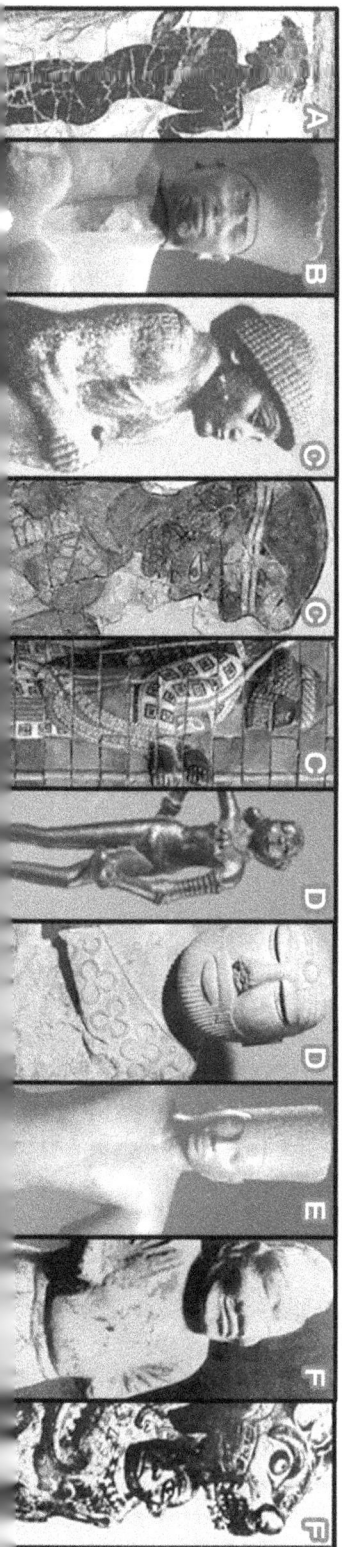

Minoan-Mycenaean
2100 – 1050 B.C.E.

Nile (Ancient Egypt)
3100 B.C.E. – 1100 B.C.E.

Meroe (Nubia)
591 B.C.E. – A.D. 325

Axum
?200 B.C.E. – A.D. 700

Tigris-Euphrates
(Mesopotamia and
Babylonia)
3500 B.C.E. – 2000 B.C.E.

Indus-Ganges
(Harappan and
Vedic Civilizations)
3000 B.C.E. – 150 B.C.E.

Funan
A.D. 100 – 546

Khmer
A.D. 802 – 1218

Yellow River (Shang)
2000 B.C.E. – 1027 B.C.E.

MEDITERRANEAN SEA
BLACK SEA
CASPIAN SEA
ARAL SEA
Lake Baikash
RED SEA
Persian Gulf
ARABIAN SEA
Bay of Bengal
SOUTH CHINA SEA

THE ANU PEOPLE

TEACHERS OF CIVILIZATION

"...There a people, now forgotten, discovered, while others were yet barbarians, the elements of the arts and sciences. A race of men, now rejected from society for their sable skin and frizzled hair, founded on the study of laws of nature, those civil and religious systems which still govern the universe." – Count C.F. Volney, 1793

Rawlinson called them Hamites.

Sergi called them the Mediterranean race.

Haddon called them Eurafrican.

Wells called them the Iberian race.

Huxley called them the Melanochroi.

Baldwin called them Cushites, yet wouldn't admit they came from Africa.

Others have called them the "brown" members of the white race, the "megalithic race," or the "mysterious race" that spread Neolithic culture across the globe.

All of these scholars agreed that these were the people who built all the civilizations of Europe, the Near East, and North Africa. Some traced their presence as far as India, China, and Indonesia.

But who were these people?

The scholars above were hesitant – if not outright dishonest – on the subject of their racial origins. It's been about a century since most of them told their versions of the story. Thanks to the research of the scholars who followed them, we know a great deal more about who these people were. We know they were Black. They were scientific and cultural pioneers. They were revered and even worshipped nearly everywhere they went. Most importantly, they were us. It's only right we learn their story.

THE FATHER OF CIVILIZATION

In 1931, Elijah Muhammad said the Original Man was the "Asiatic Blackman, the maker, the owner, the cream of the Planet Earth, Father of Civilization, and God of the Universe." To some of us, this sounds like "Black Nationalist rhetoric" or "Afrocentric hyperbole." But in 1836, almost a hundred years prior, British historian Godfrey Higgins had said the same thing:

> We have found the Black complexion or something relating to it whenever we have approached the origin of nations…In short all the…deities were black. They remained as they were first…in very ancient times.[2]

Black scholar William Henry Ferris also explored these themes in his massive 1911 work *The African Abroad*.[3] We've covered much of what it means to be the "Original Man" in Part One of this volume, and what it means to be "the maker" of the Planet Earth and "God of the Universe" in *The Science of Self, Volume One*. In this book, we're exploring what it means for the Black man to be the "Father of Civilization."

Let's begin by talking about the Cushites. In *Pre-historic Nations*, historian John Denison Baldwin writes:

> The Cushite race appeared first in the work of civilization. That this has not always been distinctly perceived is due chiefly to the fact that the first grand ages of that race are so distant from us in time, so far beyond the great nations of antiquity commonly mentioned in our ancient histories, that their most indelible traces have long been too much obscured by the waste of time to be readily comprehended by superficial observation.[4]

In other words, the Cushites were the authors of civilization, at a time so long ago that it's not always easy to see their influence. When Baldwin wrote *Pre-historic Nations* in 1869, historians were still attempting to fit all of the world's civilizations into the past 6,000 years. This was because James Usher, a prominent Anglican Archbishop, had developed a chronology that "proved" the Biblical Adam was born in 4004 BC.

As C'BS Alife Allah has noted, "Scientists of the time struggled to fit all the accomplishments of the Nile Valley (and other ancient civilizations) into this window of time after 4,000 BC." Some continue to abbreviate the origins of civilization in this way, even today. But, as Baldwin continues:

> Neither Usher's chronology, nor the little country known to the Greeks and Romans as Phoenicia, will suffice to explain that mighty

and wide-spread influence of the Cushite race in human affairs, whose traces are still visible from Farther India to Norway.[5]

In other words, not only did the Cushites begin building the civilizations of the world long before the recognized timelines, they spread this science across the world, far beyond where we'd expect them to be.

WHO WERE THE CUSHITES?

Before the era of racial classification by means of physical measurements, European historians classified people based on the assumed territories of Biblical populations. Following the mythical flood that eliminated the original people of the planet, the descendants of Noah are assumed to have fathered everyone living in the Near East. Noah's son Ham represented Black people,* but his sons are spread throughout Africa and Asia, suggesting **that the authors of Genesis were knowledgeable of a "Black belt" stretching from Africa to perhaps India.†** These Hamites were thought to have fathered the Black people of Arabia.

One of Ham's sons, Cush was associated with Ethiopia or Nubia. As the Greeks did with Ethiopia, the writers of the Bible associated Cush with a variety of places. As Henry Welsford noted in 1845:

> In the Old Testament Cush appears sometimes to signify Persia, sometimes Mesopotamia, sometimes Arabia, and sometimes Ethiopia in Africa. In the English version Cush is rendered by Ethiopia in every instance, though very different countries, separated from each other by an immense distance, are clearly intended to be spoken of.[6]

In *Pre-historic Nations* Baldwin wrote that the Cushites were the authors of all modern civilization:

> In our researches into the beginnings of culture in the oldest nations mentioned in history, we perceive that they did not originate civilization. It preceded their existence, and came from an older people. They gave it new forms, each developing an individuality of its own; but it came originally from abroad. On this point tradition is uniform and explicit. In Eastern Africa, the civilizers proceeded from the south toward the Mediterranean, creating the countries in the valley of the Nile. The traditions of inner Asia bring civilization

---

* The name Ham may derive from Kham, or Kam, meaning Black.

† While it is "nice" to think the descendants of Noah or the "12 Tribes of Israel" (there are actually 13) could represent people as far and wide as the Japanese and the Cherokee, we now know the writers of Genesis were only aware of people and events within a 100-mile radius of the Near Eastern sites they wrote from. To think otherwise is a stretch of the imagination.

from the south, and connect its origin with the shores of the Erythraean Sea, meaning the Arabian shores of the Indian Ocean and the Persian Gulf; and these traditions are confirmed by inscriptions found in the old ruins of Chaldea. These inscriptions reveal also the fact that the first civilizers were neither Semites nor Aryans, but a "third race," which ethnic and linguistic investigators have been slow to recognise. [7]

So who was the "mysterious race" that authored the world's civilizations? As you noted at the beginning of this chapter, historians have called these people by many different names. Most of them were simply euphemisms, or code words, for Black people outside Africa, and tell us nothing particularly helpful regarding the time and place these people moved throughout the world.

To some extent, the anthropologists attempted to specify what "Eurafricans," "Melanochroi," and "Mediterranean" people looked like, but none of it was written in stone. If there was a dark-skinned people who founded an ancient civilization, they somehow found their racial home in one of these categories. Again, just euphemisms for Black people.

Thus, anthropologists like Giuseppe Sergi could dedicate entire books to *The Mediterranean Race* and their contributions to ancient Europe, Africa, and the Near East. If everyone knew Sergi was talking about Black people (which he was), he'd have been in serious trouble (which is what eventually happened). Meanwhile, historians who drew on the Bible used classifications like "Hamite" and "Cushite" to identify the world's ancient Black populations. This is why Baldwin, a student of Biblical history, described these people as Cushites.

As we continue digging into their history, we'll see that the people we should call Cushites weren't actually the first, but one of the last waves of Black people to reintroduce civilization to the ancient world.

So let's work backwards and see if we can trace these people back to their origins. The Cushitic languages of Ethiopia and Southern Arabia are members of an important and close-knit family known as the Afro-Asiatic language family. It's called Afro-Asiatic because it has branches in Africa and Asia (mostly in the Near East and Arabia). In order to understand who these people are, where they came from, and where they went from there, we have to familiarize ourselves with the meaning of Afro-Asiatic.

MADAGASCAR

THE AFRO-ASIATIC LANGUAGE FAMILY

About 15,000 years ago, near the site of the Nubian Complex where their ancestors had established the blueprint for civilization 100,000 years prior – a distinct group of Black men and women developed a cultural community that spoke a unique variant of their ancestral African language. This language family is now known to most linguists as Afro-Asiatic.

Like Semitic and Indo-European, Afro-Asiatic is not a "racial type" but a linguistic group. As the name implies, it's a linguistic group that stretches across northeast Africa and into Arabia and the Near East, with descendants and infusions into regions even further beyond, including Europe and India.[*]

The Afro-Asiatic language family includes the languages of Ethiopia, the Berber languages of North Africa, the Hausa language of northern Nigeria, other languages as far south as northern Tanzania, as well as Arabic, Hebrew, and Ancient Egyptian. As you can see, most of the Afro-Asiatic languages are found in Africa. And it is from Africa that we get all the languages of the Middle East.

The earliest written evidence of an Afro-Asiatic language is found in pictographs from the Nile Valley dating back to 4000 BC. However, Ancient Egyptian developed long after Afro-Asiatic, which was spoken at least 10,000 years ago. According to Christopher Ehret, the original Afro-Asiatic language (known to linguists as "Proto-Afro-Asiatic") was spoken in its homeland of Northeast Africa by at least 11,000 BC and possibly as early as 16,000 BC.

WHAT DO WE CALL THEM?

"Homer and Herodotus call all the peoples of the Sudan, Egypt, Arabia, Palestine and Western Asia and India Ethiopians." – Sir E. A. Wallis Budge, History of Ethiopia, Vol. I

As much as we'd like to simply call these people Cushites or Ethiopians, that would oversimplify things. As we noted above, the people known as Cushites represent one of their last waves of expansion, but not the totality of their history. In our chapter on the Nile Valley, we'll explore when the empire known as Cush began expanding around 4,000 years ago. But the ancestors of the Cushites

---

[*] Of course, white populations have had a few thousand years to adopt and/or influence Afro-Asiatic and its descendants, but we have enough evidence to know that it begins as a Black language family. See "An Introduction to Linguistics" for more details.

had been traveling the world, laying down the foundations of modern civilization over 10,000 years before that.

So what do we call this community of people? At every period, they radiated from the region we call the "root of civilization." That is, the point where Northeast Africa meets Southern Arabia. And at every period, these people are unmistakably Black. The old historians might have called them by a dozen different euphemisms, but even they couldn't successfully conceal their Blackness.

But simply calling them "Black" won't help us distinguish them from the Black populations that preceded them. Calling them "Original People" doesn't help distinguish them from their ancestors 100,000 years ago. So let's consider our options.

THE ASIATIC BLACK MAN AND WOMAN

Elijah Muhammad called them Asiatic, as in "the Asiatic Blackman." Noble Drew Ali also used "Asiatic," while Henry Gladwin wrote of "Asiatic Negroids." For students of Egyptian history, the notion of "Asiatics" can be off-putting. Chancellor Williams and countless others have described the oppressive relationships that "Asiatic" people had with the Native Egyptians and other African people. But, as with the Arabs, these people weren't the *Original* Asiatic people. In fact, when those ancient records speak of "Asiatic" people, they're really only referring to white people (and sometimes mixed people) in the Near East.

These people came into being literally over a hundred thousand years after Blacks settled Arabia. In other words, the *Original* Asiatic was Black, and when Egyptian records talk about the barbaric hordes who kept trying to creep in, they were talking about Caucasians or their kin.

What does Asiatic really mean? As C'BS ALife explains in *The Science of Self, Volume One*:

> Asiatic is another term referencing a collective global identity for Original People. It is derived from Asia which, although Latinized, is the oldest placename still in usage for that part of the planet (older than Africa, Europe, etc.) Asia appears to come from the Black Akkadian word Asu which means to "to go outside" or "to ascend," referring to the direction of the sun at sunrise. As such, this refers to viewing the eastern horizon and thus the whole planet. Essentially, it is one of the first "global" concepts. As we'll see in Volume Two, "Asiatic" also emphasizes the continuity of Black civilizations across the Red Sea (similar to the term introduced by Dr. Wesley Muhammad, "Afrabia").

Asiatic works as a linguistic, geographic, and ontological identity. What do I mean by ontological identity? "Ontology" is the study of the nature of being, existence, or reality, often used in the same sense as "metaphysics." So I'm referring back to the connection between Man and Mind that we explained in *Volume One*. Five Percenters often use "Asiatic" to refer to the connection between the Mind and the Black body. For example, in a plus lesson circulated in the 90s, Azmar Blackseed Allah writes:

> The Original Man is the root of civilization. Asia [as in "Asiatic"] is the largest of the Earth's continents. Atic [means] the Mind, a storage place for the knowledge [as in an "attic"].

In the oral tradition, the Mind is the seat of logic and mathematical order, and the body is home to feeling, instinct, and emotion. In *The Monstrous Races in Medieval Art and Thought*, John Block Friedman says much of the same about Asia and the Attic:

> For the Greeks, the East or things Asian were extreme with respect to the mean, and we often find an aesthetic polarity between things Attic and Asian. Asia represented emotion, redundance, and formal disorder, whereas Athens and the Attic represented moderation, control, and formal balance.[8]

In *Volume Three*, we'll revisit the nature of the Self, exploring the duality of identity that manifests itself in the two hemispheres of the brain, and countless other relationships.

For now, we can foresee how the use of "Asiatic," even "Asiatic Black People" could be confusing for many readers. Especially considering that Mongoloid people, whose early history we explore in Part One, will also factor into discussions of history during this period.

AFRASIAN, AFRASAN, AFRO-SAMURAI?

In the beginning of this chapter, we listed more than a half dozen different names used by scholars of the past to describe these people without admitting too overtly that they were Black. As Andrew Lancaster notes, modern scholars have also struggled with this issue:

> It should be mentioned that a range of names are used in the literature for the Afroasiatic language group, often intended to emphasize particular points of view, which can be quite important when it comes to this particular language group. Commonly used alternative terms are "Hamito-Semitic" (now sometimes considered to have racist connotations, and therefore out of use in recent literature), the collapsed form "Afrasian"; and "Afrasan," a name chosen to de-emphasize Asia, and make it more clear that the group is mainly found in Africa.[9]

After careful consideration, we've elected to use the name "Anu."

THE ANU PEOPLE

In *The Making of Egypt,* Sir William Flinders Petrie wrote:

> [B]elonging to the north and east, there is the aboriginal race of the
> Anu, or Aunu, people (written with three pillars), who became a part
> of the historic inhabitants. The subject ramifies too doubtfully if we
> include all single-pillar names, but looking for the Aunu, written
> with the three pillars, we find that they occupied Southern Egypt
> and Nubia, and the name is also applied in Sinai and Libya.[10]

The name Anu is found throughout Egypt. It is found east of the
Nile Valley, in Libya to the west, and in both Upper and Lower
Egypt. In *Ancient Egypt, the Light of the World,* Gerald Massey says,
"There was a southern Annu and a northern Annu in Egypt," and
adds that Diodorus reported that the city of Annu (Heliopolis) was
"accounted by its inhabitants to be the oldest city in Egypt."

Among the Egyptians, Anu was considered the place where heaven
and earth met, and stone poles were erected to mark this axis mundi.
For some, Anu was meant to be a reproduction of the celestial (or
"heavenly") Anu. Sometimes Anu was rendered as the place where
"two earths met," suggesting that the people of two lands met there,
with some special significance attached to this convergence.

In fact, as Runoko Rashidi reports:

> The Egyptians titled two of their most important cities Annu:
> Hermonthis, in the south, and Heliopolis/On, in the north, where
> Re was the most important deity, and where the best educated of
> the Egyptians received their instruction.

The name Anu is also found throughout Mesopotamia, as well as in
Arabia. Drusilla Dunjee Houston has said, "The ancient inhabitants
of Arabia Petrae were of the `Anu' of the 'Old Race' of Egypt."
Cheikh Anta Diop has added, "The Anu were the first Blacks to
inhabit Egypt. A number of them remained in Arabia Petraea
throughout Egyptian history."

In *Black Women in Antiquity,* Runoko Rashidi notes that the
deification of Anu is even found in the earliest traditions of Ireland
(where Egyptians may have once settled). He adds:

> The fragments of Manetho say that Osarseph himself, who later
> changed his name to Moses, was a native of Northern Annu. In the
> Egyptian eschatology, Anu was the abode of the resurrected spirit
> of the physical dead.

In other words, the Anu people were of considerable significance anywhere Afro-Asiatic languages came to be spoken. In fact, not only Osarseph (possibly the historical counterpart to the Biblical Moses) an Egyptian, he was one of the Anu.

The early religious significance of the Anu may explain why Anu became one of the highest deities of the ancient Mesopotamians. Among the Sumerians, Anu was the god of heaven, the lord of constellations, and the king of gods, spirits and demons, dwelling in the highest heavenly regions.*

WHO WERE THE ANU?

In *Great Black Leaders: Ancient and Modern*, Wayne Chandler says Anu was "the term utilized by the first blacks, the oldest blacks to describe themselves as a race." He cites renowned Egyptologist Abbe Émile Amélineau, who said the first Black race to occupy Egypt went by the name Anu. According to Amélineau:

> These Anu were agricultural people, raising cattle on a large scale along the Nile, shutting themselves up in walled cities for defensive purposes. To this people we can attribute, without fear of error, the most ancient Egyptian books, The Book of the Dead and the Texts of the Pyramids, consequently, all the myths or religious teachings. I would add almost all the philosophical systems then known and still called Egyptian.

> They evidently knew the crafts necessary for any civilization and were familiar with the tools those trades required. They knew how to use metals, at least elementary metals. They made the earliest attempts at writing, for the whole Egyptian tradition attributes this art to Thoth, the great Hermes an Anu like Osiris, who is called Onian in Chapter XV of The Book of the Dead and in the Texts of the Pyramids.

> Certainly the people already knew the principal arts; it left proof of this in the architecture of the tombs at Abydos, especially the tomb of Osiris and in those sepulchers objects have been found bearing unmistakable stamp of their origin, such as carved ivory, or a little head of a Nubian girl found in a tomb near that of Osiris, or the small wooden or ivory receptacles in the form of a feline head – all documents published in the first volume of my Fouilles d'Abydos.

In other words, the Anu were the authors of ancient civilization.

WHERE DID THE ANU COME FROM?

In *Great Black Leaders: Ancient and Modern*, Runoko Rashidi reports:

> Now, the Egyptians of the historic epoch called their immediate

---

* For more on the theology of the Anu, see *Black God*, a forthcoming work from Supreme Design Publishing, to be released in the Summer of 2013.

predecessors the Anu, of which the Anti Seti were the inhabitants of Nubia who lived on the banks of the Nile.

In 1908, the Smithsonian published a paper by Edouard Naville discussing the ancient Egyptians as a native African people. He reported:

> I believe the name of the prehistoric Egyptians has been preserved. They are called the Anu. The sign An, with which their name is written, means a pillar, a column of stone or wood, or, even as Brugsch translates, a heap of stones. According to Brugsch also, their name Anu, or, in the latter inscriptions Anti…applied to the Kushite nations occupying the land between the Nile and the Red Sea.
>
> But we find them much earlier; they often occur at Anu Ta Khent, the Anu of Lower Nubia and of Khent Hunnefer, the southern part of Nubia. An inscription in the Temple of Deir el Bahari speaks of the Anu of Khent, Lower Nubia, of Khent Hunnefer, Upper Nubia, and of Setet, which, in the texts of the Pyramids is clearly the land of the goddesses Sati and Anqet, the land and islands of the cataracts." The Anu are found much farther north. In the inscriptions of Sinai we see the King Khufu striking the Anu, the inhabitants of the mountains who are evidently the population he conquered when he invaded the peninsula.[11]

The "striking down of the Anu" might suggest that the Anu were foreign to the Nile Valley. Naville counters this notion:

> The land of Egypt is often called the two lands of An, so that we can trace the name of An, not only among the neighboring nations of Egypt, but in the country itself, from an early antiquity. Evidently this name – the two lands of An – for Egypt, is a remainder of the old native stock before the conquest…I conclude, from what has been discovered lately, that they were the native stock occupying the valley of the Nile, and that they had been conquered by invaders, who very soon amalgamated so completely with their subjects that they formed one single people.

It seems the original Anu people were native to Nubia, and some of the Anu authored the founding of Egypt's first dynasties, but – by the time of Khufu – Anu-descended populations from the Near East were coming back to Egypt with intentions of taking over. The consolidation of these populations made the Egyptians, once again, a "single people." Sounds like the way America absorbed its foreign white minorities, right? Except this was the Black version.[*] Amélineau discussed the difficult implications of this knowledge:

---

[*] They were not alone in this practice. Historically, there have been hundreds of ethnic communities of Original people who, like the Iroquois, engaged heavily in the large-scale absorbtion of minorities.

The conclusion to be drawn from these considerations is that the conquered Anu people guided its conquerors at least along some of the paths to civilization and the arts. This conclusion, as can readily be seen, is most important for the history of human civilization and the history of religion. It clearly follows from what has been stated earlier: Egyptian civilization is not of Asiatic, but of African origin, of Negroid origin, however paradoxical this may seem.

This was a tough pill to swallow for them, you know:

We are not accustomed, in fact, to endow the Black or related races with too much intelligence, or even with enough intelligence to make the first discoveries necessary for civilization. Yet, there is not a single tribe inhabiting the African interior that has not possessed and does not still possess at least one of those first discoveries.

Amélineau says these Anu "came slowly down the Nile and founded the cities of Esneh, Erment, and Heliopolis." Before they did this, it is safe to suggest that these people also settled Libya, Arabia, Mesopotamia, and the Levant. Some sources have traced the Anu as far as India. We know these migrations must have predated the founding of ancient Egypt – which was authored in great part by Anu people – because instances of the name Anu are just as old in the Near East as they are in the Nile Valley.

In other words, people from the Egypt/Sudan border area, known anciently as Nubia, dispersed several thousand years ago, ultimately helping found the earliest civilizations of the Nile, the Near East, and Arabia. In all these places, the name An, Anu, or Ani, is prominent.

I don't know if the founders of this population were always known as Anu. Cheikh Anta Diop theorized that "Anu" may simply mean "man" But we don't know what name these people used 15,000 years ago. They could have called themselves anything: Anu, Ani, An, Al, Ala, Ara, Ama, etc. It would take a massive project in comparative linguistics to arrive at any degree of certainty.

For the purposes of this book, however, I'm content with calling them the Anu people. By using this name, we can avoid the confusion associated with ALL of the cultural names and language families associated with the Anu people over the past 15,000 years.

STONE CIRCLES

Afrasiatic people erected stone circles everywhere they went. We know the thousands of stone circles in Europe were not the work of modern Europeans because European legends say the builders of these circles were Black. Also, there are thousands of ancient stone circles in Africa as well, although they are ignored. Would anyone believe that Europeans somehow built those?

STONE CIRCLES ACROSS EUROPE

SCOTLAND

NORWAY

SPAIN

IRELAND

STONEHENGE BRITAIN

WASSU STONE CIRCLES SENEGAL AND GAMBIA

ARABIA

INDIA

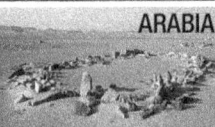

OSHORO STONE CIRCLE HOKKAIDO, JAPAN

BOUAR MEGALITHS CENTRAL AFRICAN REPUBLIC

MZORA STONE CIRCLE MOROCCO

NABTA PLAYA EGYPT'S WESTERN DESERT

The reign of the Anu was most important historical and cultural phase of recent history. Before them, the most important significant movement were that of the Original People who came together to conquer the Neanderthals and allow humans to thrive across Eurasia. The Anu did something a little different, yet not entirely. They introduced the fundaments of modern civilization to indigenous people throughout the world. **This book documents where they went, what they did, how and why they did it, and who they ultimately became.**

POOR RIGHTEOUS TEACHERS

In the same curriculum we quoted at the beginning of this chapter, Elijah Muhammad says "civilize means to teach knowledge and wisdom to all the human families of the planet Earth." As we'll see throughout this book, the people identified with the Afro-Asiatic language family are the ones who did this work between 15,000 and 4,000 years ago. They took their knowledge to the world.

TO ALL THE HUMAN FAMILIES OF THE PLANET EARTH

The people who are the subject of this book did not remain restricted to the Afro-Asiatic *urheimat* (or homeland). They traveled far and wide beyond the shores of Northeast Africa, eventually teaching much of the globe their culture. The cultural innovations we associate with the "Neolithic Revolution," such as agriculture, animal domestication, urban housing, metallurgy, and ceramics – well, those began where the Afro-Asiatic language family began. And that cultural package traveled wherever the speakers of those languages traveled.

As John Baldwin explains regarding his "Cushites":

> The Cushites occupied India, Western Asia to the Mediterranean, and extensive regions in Africa. In this period they brought to full development that knowledge of astronomy and of other sciences, fragments of which have come down to us through the nations they created and by which they were succeeded. The vast commercial system by which they brought together "the ends of the earth" was created, and that unrivaled eminence in maritime and manufacturing skill was developed, which the Phoenicians retained down to the time of the Hellenes and the Romans. In this period were the grandest ages of the great empire of Ethiopia, or Cusha-dwipa.[12]

But did these people literally go EVERYWHERE in the world? It's certainly possible, but their culture also spread to distant societies even when Afro-Asiatic speakers weren't present in that society (yet).

This can all be explained through processes known as diffusion.

AN INTRODUCTION TO DIFFUSION

If you've heard the word "diffusion," most likely it's been related to one of those scented oil things that diffuses good smelling particles throughout the air in your room. When we're talking about history or anthropology, cultural diffusion is kinda the same concept.

Cultural diffusion is the spread of cultural items (such as ideas, styles, religions, technologies, languages etc.) between different people or cultures.[13] You can see diffusion when you look at, for example, how easily slang can spread from the West Coast to the East Coast, or how wearing gold teeth spread from the South to the North. Historically, most scholars can accept that agriculture spread from the Near East to the rest of Asia within the last 10,000 years. They don't mind tracing ceramics, metal-working, other technologies, as well as a gang of languages, back to that *same region*.

But when someone says metalworking started in Africa – that's when the idea of diffusion (from THAT center) becomes a problem – even if it's someone as credible and renowned as the "Father of American Anthropology," Franz Boas.

There are several different models for how diffusion occurs:

❒ Expansion diffusion: an idea or innovation that develops in a source area and remains strong there, while also spreading outward to other areas. (Example: Eating sushi has spread far and wide, but is still firmly rooted in Japan.)

❒ Relocation diffusion: an idea or innovation that migrates into new areas, leaving behind its origin or source. (Example: When white people started using Black slang that nobody Black uses anymore.)

❒ Hierarchical diffusion: an idea or innovation that spreads by moving from larger to smaller places, often with little regard to the distance between places, and often imposed by people in power. (Example: When Western capitalism and government was imposed on indigenous nations in Africa.)

❒ Contagious diffusion: an idea or innovation based on person-to-person contact within a given population. (Example: When Europeans missionaries taught Christian ideas to indigenous leaders in Asia, Africa, Australia, and the Americas.)

There's also hyperdiffusion, the idea that nearly everything can be traced back to one root. In 1911, anthropologist Grafton Elliot Smith embraced this model when he asserted that copper-working spread from Egypt to the rest of the world, along with the erection of stone monuments (known as megalithic culture), ceramics (pottery), written language, and everything else that made "civilization" what it was.[14]

William James Perry elaborated on this theory by using ethnographic data to assert that Egyptian migrants and traders brought civilization to the world. But then it started becoming clear that the people who built Egyptian civilization were Black! And other scholars were going so far as to trace all civilization back to Ethiopia!

That's when it was time to switch gears! And that's when folks like Lord Raglan, author of *How Came Civilization*, came to fame proposing that all culture and civilization had come from Mesopotamia instead of Egypt.[15] This model survived for a while, but then it started to become clear that the first Mesopotamians were Black too.

So European scholars gradually abandoned this model of diffusion, while others worked on establishing the root of civilization in Anatolia, which still seemed pretty white by comparison. I'm not saying that hyperdiffusionism is true, only that the first hyperdiffusionists were tracing everything back to us.

Through proper research, we can trace many of the world's traditions back to older traditions. Often, the similarities are too strong to be coincidence (meaning it's unlikely they came up with the exact same thing on their own). If you were a teacher grading papers, you would know that somebody had copied off somebody. When we see similarities across the entire "cultural complex" of two societies, this tells us that they either came from the same root, or one (usually the older one) influenced the other.

In addition to the different ways diffusion occurs, there are two types of diffusion: cultural diffusion and demic diffusion.

- ❐ Demic diffusion is when the people who know the culture physically expand their nation or empire. That is, the people themselves are traveling and teaching. Often, we'll find genetic traces, cultural artifacts that were made to look like them, and legends or myths describing their endeavors.

- ❐ Cultural diffusion is different. The people themselves don't have to spread, just their ideas. It's sometimes known as memetic diffusion.* For example, brothers from South and Central Asia brought Buddhism to China and Japan about 2,000 years ago, but Buddhism's explosive growth there was memetic, rather than the

---

* A "meme" is a unit of cultural information or information pattern, such as a cultural practice or idea, that is transmitted verbally or by repeated action from one mind to another. In laymen's terms, a meme is an idea that spreads rapidly, like a virus. Today, many memes spread online.

WHO BUILT ALL THESE PYRAMIDS?

 INDONESIA
 MEXICO
 EGYPT
 SUDAN
 GUATEMALA
 MALI

MAURITIUS, NW AFRICA

NUBIAN PYRAMIDS, SUDAN

NSUDE PYRAMIDS, NIGERIA

FUNERARY PYRAMID, CHINA

MAHAIATEA PYRAMID, TAHITI

Cambodia   Guatemala

CANARY ISLANDS, NW AFRCA

LIKE THE SPHINX, IS THIS FACE IN ANGKOR WAT A CLUE TO WHO BUILT THE NEARBY STRUCTURES?

THE EVOLUTION OF THE EGYPTIAN PYRAMID: FROM SAQQARA TO GIZA

 2700 BC
 2630 BC
 2600 BC
 2575 BC
 2560 BC

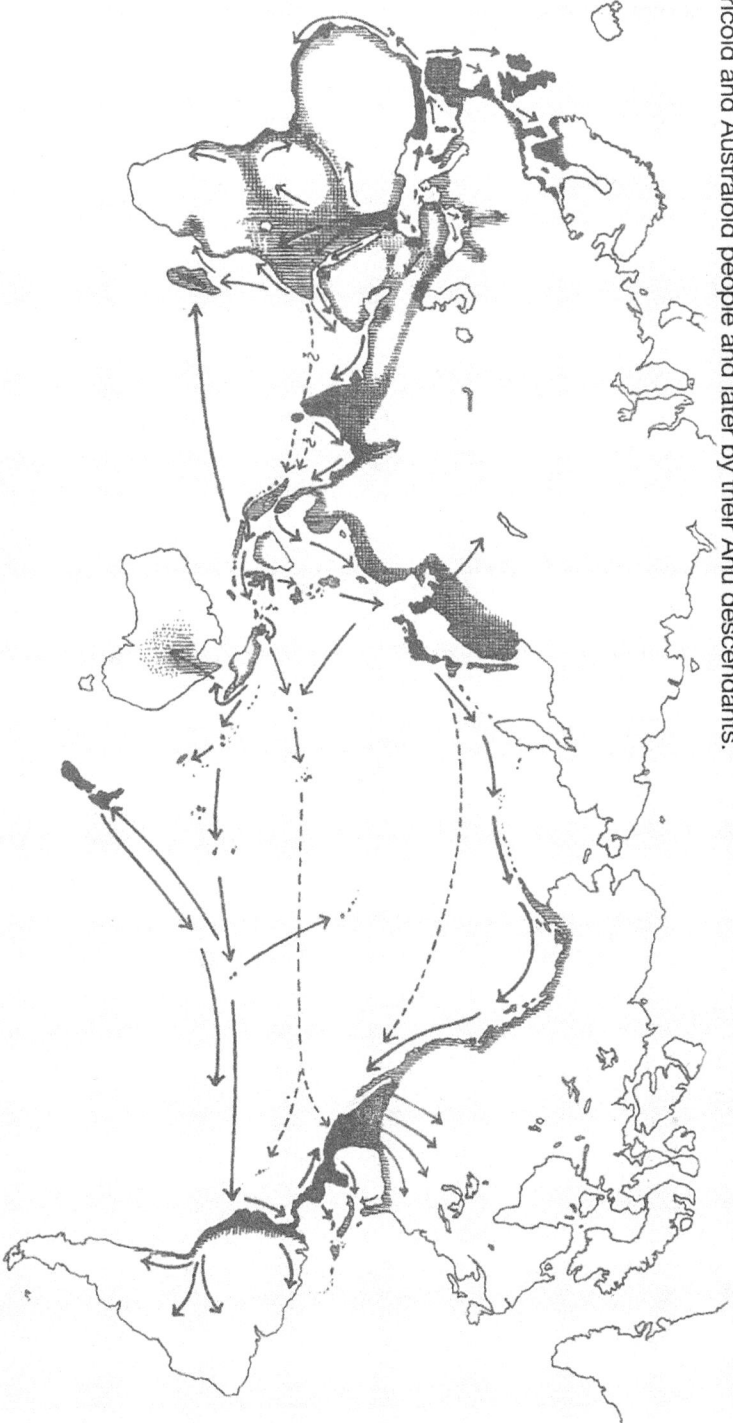

This map comes from Grafton Elliot Smith's 1929 book, *The Migrations of Early Culture*. Smith denied the Blackness of the people who introduced the "heliolithic cultural complex" to the world. Yet he gave us nearly the same map we use elsewhere in this book for the spread of the Anu Cultural Complex. These people, without a doubt, were Black people. These maps correspond with the most dark-skinned people in the world, even today. This is the famous "black belt" originally settled by Africoid and Australoid people and later by their Anu descendants.

Map 2—An attempt to represent roughly the areas more directly affected by the "heliolithic" culture-complex, with arrows to indicate the hypothetical routes taken in the migrations of the culture-bearers who were responsible for its diffusion.

result of a natural increase of the original Buddhist population.

In the real world, few other cultural complexes spread the way Buddhism did among the Original people of Asia. In recent years, comparable examples include the Five Percent and Hip Hop culture. **Six thousand years ago, the best examples would be the Anu Cultural Complex**. Wherever Anu people did not physically go (and that must have been a short list of places, as they traveled all over the world), their culture still influenced local populations this way.

Thus, in examining our past, we find that the most rapid phase of cultural change came from the people who are the subject of this book. They traveled far and wide, changing the way the entire world works in the span of less than 15,000 years. The Original People began laying down the foundations over 100,000 years ago. Long after most of these Original People had been marginalized and forgotten, Anu people – coming from the same geographic and genetic origins – built a new world on top of this foundation.

THE ANU CULTURAL COMPLEX

We've talked quite a bit about the cultural complex they introduced to the world, but haven't been very specific as to what that entails. We'll get into specific when we discuss their presence in various regions, but let's get an idea of the big picture: What, you might ask, are some of the common features of Anu civilization?

Here's what I've noticed about everywhere they've gone. Unlike their hunter-gatherer ancestors who preferred pure democracies with no social stratification, Anu people created social orders. Like their ancestors, they worked to develop a culture of freedom, justice, and equality, but they had to do so in a very different time, with very different circumstances.

They drew on the traditions of their ancestors and *institutionalized* them. They did so through the introduction of institutions like pastoralism (animal husbandry), agriculture (farming), finance, record-keeping, organized theology, and even monument-building. This is how they organized people, many of whom were quite disorganized when they arrived.

The resultant social changes were so dramatic and permeated every area of society so deeply that this phase of cultural change is known as the "Neolithic Revolution." It was Anu people who introduced the Neolithic Age to the prehistoric cultures of the world. For most historians, *the Neolithic marks the birth of modern civilization as we know it.*

These changes weren't always rapid, but Anu people pursued efficiency. For example, they took plant and animal domestication to new heights, systemically breeding new strains within a quarter of the time it took their hunter-gatherer ancestors, and then spreading these practices throughout the world, wherever climate change and population growth were creating food shortages.

Unlike their hunter-gatherer ancestors who preferred to leave nature as nature was, Anu people sought to "remake the Earth." In addition to bioengineering plants and animals, they redirected rivers, created systems to convert arid land to fertile soil, and essentially **made their own hills and mountains**. To do this, they pioneered stonemasonry. They drilled, cut, transported, and erected massive stone and brick monuments and structures everywhere they went.

Thus, wherever we find Anu people, we find more than their languages. To keep things memorable, we'll use an acronym – based on the familiar name AFROASIATIC – for these common cultural elements:

- Astronomy
- Farming
- Religion (a formal theological complex, including priesthoods and the introduction of the cemetery)
- Ownership of Property
- Animal Domestication
- Social Stratification
- Introduction of Metallurgy
- Architecture and Megalithic Construction
- Textiles and Ceramics
- Introduction of Written Language
- Cities (Urbanization)

HOW FAR DID THEY SPREAD?

You wouldn't expect Northern Europe to provide us with mountains of evidence for an ancient Anu presence. But it's there. The genetic, linguistic, skeletal, and archaeological evidence all point to a wave of Anu settlers before (and during) the coming of white Europeans. In Britain alone, the coastal community of Carnac is home to over 3,000 standing stone pillars, erected when Anu people dominated the area between 4500 and 2500 BC.

The menhirs of Northern Europe replicate the obelisks of ancient Egypt, and the stone circle at Stonehenge replicates the circles found at Nabta Playa, Senegambia, and South Arabia. They were all built with the same designs and the same technique. There's no way to get around the fact they were all built by the same people.

Of course, in Europe, Anu populations were much smaller than in the Near East, where things were getting quite congested by comparison. As Anu populations grew in Africa and Asia, they built urban settlements to accommodate the influx of settlers, effectively creating the **first "melting pot" civilizations** of Black and brown people from throughout the ancient world.

In these civilizations, hierarchies emerged. Wherever Anu people came to govern non-Anu people, the Anu became the first elites. The division of labor and other forms of specialization led to social classes and other formal partitions in what were once egalitarian societies. Universal shamanism gave way to priesthoods and magician classes. Some supported the local rulers, while those that didn't were made outcasts.

It was in this environment that new theological traditions emerged. This is why British historian Godfrey Higgins says **all the deities of the world's religions began as Black men and women**, and why Greek historian Diodorus Sicilus reported that all of the religious practices of the world could be traced back to the Ethiopians.[*]

Traces of their linguistic presence help us determine where the speakers went, and genetic evidence helps "triangulate" this data. As we'll see in this text, these people were the ones who introduced modern civilization to the ancient Near East, Europe, India, East Asia, Australia, the Pacific Islands, and the Americas. They were the ones who built the big urban cities and massive stone monuments. They were the ones who spread agriculture and animal domestication. They weren't the first to come up with these sciences, just the ones who systemically spread the ideas far and wide, with incredible consistency – **almost as if they had a curriculum to teach the rest of the human families of the planet Earth.**

---

[*] For more on this, see *Black God*, a forthcoming work from Supreme Design Publishing, to be released in the Summer of 2013.

WHAT DID ANU PEOPLE LOOK LIKE?

In *The Negro and the White Man*, Wesley John Gaines writes about the Anu people:

> The blacks were a fundamental element in the origin, not only of the primitive races of Southern Europe, but of the civilized races of antiquity as well. History may be said to begin in ancient Egypt, and recede into the dim past, just as far as records and inscriptions lend us light. Still in the Nile valley we find a civilization that has drawn from all succeeding ages expressions of wonder and admiration.
>
> Surely these ancient Egyptians were a remarkable people; but who were they? The ruling tribes are called Hamites – the sunburnt family, according to Dr. Winchell; of Nigritic origin, says Canon Rawlinson. But back of these ruling Hamites were a light-headed people – gay, good-natured, pleasant, sportive, witty, droll, amorous – such are the descriptive terms used in telling the story of these primitive tribes, who, Dr. Taylor says, lived peaceably in those regions for two thousand years before the advent of the Asiatic invaders.
>
> Suggestive as they may seem, such terms are truly descriptive of the inhabitants whom we would expect to find in the Nile valley in ancient times. **They were probably as purely Nigritic as are the great mass of our own Africo-Americans.**[16]

In other words, the Anu people were just as Black as Black Americans. Ah! So what more do you want? Seriously, there's obviously more to the story, but it's not simple or straightforward.

You see, when you find Anu populations throughout the world, they all look Black, but they don't all look the same. Why? The first Anu people may have been pretty diverse on their own (especially if they emerged in East Africa, where diversity is high), but – more importantly – they blended with the established populations everywhere they went.

That is, unlike the Toba survivors who – as a majority – displaced the Original People everywhere they went, or Caucasians, who – as a minority – sought to strategically annihilate or enslave everyone everywhere they went, the Anu people – again a minority like the first wave of Original People who became the DBP – chose neither of those routes.

In discussing the Anu, Wesley John Gaines quotes Professor Willis

Boughton, who wrote:

> Old races have often been supplanted by those of inferior culture,
> but of superior energy. More often, however, by fusion of different
> racial types, and by the mingling of various tribes and peoples, have
> been evolved new races, superior to any of the original types.[17]

Instead, Anu migrants came to distant communities of people who
had long since been removed from their foundational cultures. They
taught them, led them, and eventually merged with them. This is why
Anu people in China look like Black Chinese. Perhaps there were
some Chinese-looking traits in the diversity of the early Anu
population, but it's more likely (considering we don't find those types
represented everywhere in the ancient world) that those communities
arose from Anu people "blending in."

So there isn't much to distinguish Anu-speaking people from their
dark-skinned neighbors on a physical level, especially since any local
population could "become" Anu by adopting their language and
culture. Sometimes the migrants associated with spreading Anu
culture have coarse or wavy hair and narrow noses that resemble
some East Africans and Indians, but not always. And they're nearly
always "long-headed" with "tropical" proportions, but so are most
Black people. There is, however, one set of features that makes Anu
migrants tend to stand out from other people around the world,
including other Black populations.

Anu people are typically more "gracilized" than their peers in any
given time period, meaning they are slender, lean, or "slightly-built,"
depending on which words you like best. This is odd, considering
that the rest of the world – that is, among Africoid and Australoid
populations – was dominated by the most "robust" segments of
these populations. In other words, the rest of world leaned towards a
stronger build. But Anu people weren't built like that.

So what made them stand apart, and what allowed them to stand
their ground despite competition from these brawny folks to the east
and west? It seems that *knowledge* may have been what set them apart.
In many cases, Anu people blended with hardier local populations to
produce a stronger next generation of Anu descendants in that area.

For example, the Anu people of East Africa were Nilotes, who are
typically well-built but slender. But, in order to colonize the Near
East, they got with the Kebarans, a more "robust" and "weathered"
population. No clue what I'm talking about? It's time for you to learn
about the Natufians.

THE ANCIENT NILE VALLEY

The ancient Egyptians were not a monolithic Black people, but a diverse assembly of Black

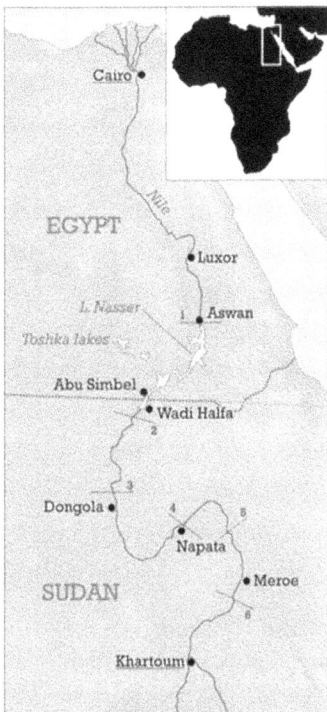

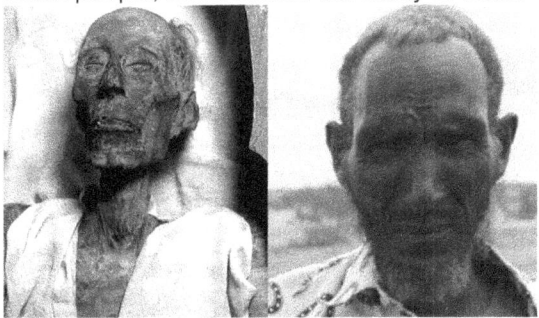

people from the Nile and Sahara regions. They built a unique African civilization that is world-renowned for its cultural and scientific accomplishments, such as the first prosthetic limbs and massive obelisks.

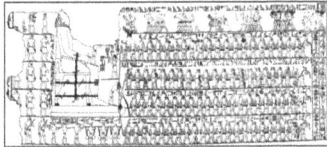

EGYPT

Cairo

Luxor

L. Nasser

Aswan

Toshka lakes

Abu Simbel

Wadi Halfa

Dongola

Napata

SUDAN

Meroe

Khartoum

Nile

SETI I

SAMBURU WARRIOR

THE QUARRYING AND ERECTION OF OBELISKS

NATIONAL GEOGRAPHIC

Great Western Drought

The Black Pharaohs

CONQUERORS OF ANCIENT EGYPT

QUEEN OF PUNT

DJOSER

MENTUHOTEP II

THE NILE VALLEY

THE ORIGINS OF ANCIENT EGYPT

"The history of Egypt is a science in itself. Before the reign of the first recorded king, five thousand years or more before Christ, there had already existed in Egypt a culture and art arising by long evolution from the days of Paleolithic man, among a distinctly Negroid people." – W.E.B. Du Bois

The Nile River is the longest river in the world. It begins in the mountains of East Africa and stretches over 4,000 miles until it flows out into the Mediterranean Sea to the North. The most fertile stretch of this river is concentrated between northern Sudan (ancient Nubia) and southern Egypt. This is the area typically known as the Nile Valley.

About 5,000 years ago, the Nile Valley saw the rise of a royal dynasty that unified separate kingdoms and quickly became an ancient empire. Its inhabitants called it by many names, including KMT (meaning "the Black land"), but most of us know this civilization by the name it was given by its greatest admirers, the ancient Greeks. They called this Black land Egypt.

Within the first 1500 years of a unified Egyptian civilization, they established so many of the foundational elements of modern European civilization that we can rightly say that there would be no such thing as Greece or Rome if it wasn't for ancient Egypt. And the Greeks and Romans knew as much. Just as later European empires would trace themselves back to their Greco-Roman roots, the Greeks and Romans both acknowledged their debt to ancient Egypt.

But just as they say "Rome wasn't built in a day," ancient Egypt didn't just "pop up" around 3,000 BC. In fact, the people who eventually unified the cultures of the Nile Valley had been developing the foundations of this civilization for thousands of years. According to the Egyptians themselves, their history goes back at least 10,000 years. By some accounts, the grandeur of Dynastic Egypt does not represent the apex of their civilization, but their decline!

Who were the people who laid the foundations of ancient Egyptian civilization? What were they doing before the time of the first dynasties? What did they build, and how did they do it? And what happened to them when Egypt fell? These are the questions we'll answer in this chapter.

THE WONDERS OF ANCIENT EGYPT
WHAT DID THE EGYPTIANS BUILD?

I mean, where do we start? This topic alone could consume an entire book. Some of these accomplishments include the following:

- ❏ They developed one of the earliest writing systems in the world, a pictographic language known today as hieroglyphics.
- ❏ They mummified their dead using practices that would impress a modern forensic expert.
- ❏ They built a series of monumental pyramids that are larger than anywhere else in the world.
- ❏ They made tremendous advances in the fields of medicine and surgery, including the use of prosthetic limbs, brain surgery, and tumor removal.
- ❏ They erected hundreds of monumental structures like the Temple of Karnak.
- ❏ They were meticulous record-keepers, documenting hundreds of myths, traditions, and historical accounts.
- ❏ They invented the 365-day calendar, the clock, the lock, and many other important inventions still used today.

They also invented the ventilator, paper, black ink, toothpaste, cosmetics, wigs, ox-drawn plows, and even scissors. They may have invented the earliest version of chess, baseball, bowling, and billiards. They pioneered maritime culture and shipbuilding (including pre-fabricated ships!), trained master stonemasons, and became experts in astronomy. To top it all off, they carved insanely large statues of themselves, like the Sphinx and the colossal statues at Abu Simbel.

Obviously, Egypt was a phenomenal civilization. But we have to be clear. We can't promote the Western-influenced idea that Egypt was the only place where such fantastic developments occurred. Egypt is certainly one of the better documented of ancient Black civilizations, so we don't hear as much about other great Black civilizations.

But we should. Because studying the GLOBAL advent of Black civilization shows us that genius is not about geography, but about identity. In fact, at the height of dynastic Egypt, their scribes reported that this period was actually the DECLINE of their civilization. This is because the period of pre-dynastic Egypt (and the indigenous Nile Valley culture that preceded it) was a time of even greater prosperity, equality, and happiness…although perhaps with less monuments and social complexity.

For example, the people of the Nile Valley had done quite a lot before the rise of the dynasties. We know they built mobile homes and shelters at least 30,000 years ago, pioneered mining (and geology) at least 60,000 years ago,* and even appear to have **mastered chemistry and other sciences.**

WERE THE EGYPTIANS BLACK?

Now, onto the million dollar question! Were the ancient Egyptians Black? Seriously…why is this still up for debate? The arguments showing that ancient Egypt was a Black civilization are endless, covering a broad range of topics and fields. From anthropological remains to the depiction of individuals in artwork, to the descriptions provided by ancient eye-witnesses and the writings of a number of modern authors, there is substantial proof to conclude that, YES, the dynastic Egyptians were, *for the most part*, a Black people.

I say "for the most part" because, following the invasion of a group of whites starting around 3500 BC, dynastic Egypt always contained within it small numbers of whites and mixed people. Then again, after 2000 BC, it absorbed another wave of white invaders, the Hyksos, some of whom eventually became its rulers (in a chain of events that marked the decline of Egyptian civilization). By the time the ancient Greeks were reporting on the Egyptians, there had been several waves of white people through the empire.

Yet the Greeks still said the Egyptians were Black, and most likely descended from Ethiopia! It's only later, under the Persians, Greeks and Romans, that Egypt integrated large numbers of whites (which further contributed to its downfall), and ushered in a final domination by the Arabs who dominate Egypt today.

For several thousand years before the events above, Egypt was a Black civilization. What's our evidence? Well, where do we begin? In 1787, French nobleman and historian Count Constantin de Volney

---

* See "The Origin of the Home" and "The Origins of Mining" in *Black People Invented Everything*, coming in Summer 2013.

published a report of his recent travels through Syria and Egypt. Upon seeing the people in Egypt,⋅ who appear to have the "true face of a mulatto," Volney questioned the race of the ancient Egyptians – who most scholars said were Caucasian. He reported:

> [W]hen I visited the Sphinx, its appearance gave me the key to the riddle. On seeing that head, typically Negro in all its features, I remembered the remarkable passage where Herodotus says: "As for me, I judge the Colchians to be a colony of the Egyptians because, like them, they are black with woolly hair…"
>
> In other words, the ancient Egyptians were true Negroes of the same type as all native-born Africans. That being so, we can see how their blood, mixed for several centuries with that of the Romans and Greeks, must have lost the intensity of its original color, while retaining nonetheless the imprint of its original mold.[18]

And Herodotus wasn't the only ancient writer who described the Egyptians as black. There are numerous references to this fact made by Aristotle, Lucian, Appolodorus, Aeschylus, Achilles Tatius of Alexandria, Strabo, Diodorus of Sicily, Diogenes Laertius, and Ammianus Marcellinus (and this list is not exhaustive).[19] These writers all viewed the Egyptians with their own eyes, and had no qualms with telling it like it is.

THAT'S WHEN THEY CENSOR YOU

By 1791 Volney – having had some time to process – reported in his work *The Ruins, or Meditation on the Revolutions of Empires and the Law of Nature* that all the available evidence said to him that the Egyptians must have been "true Negroes of the same type as all native-born Africans." When it was republished in America as *Ruins of Empire*, this content – along with several other pages describing the Black foundations of ancient civilization – were cut out of the book!

Volney became a critic of European colonialism, American slavery, the genocide of Native Americans, and even Christian missionary work among Black and brown people (which he described as an agent of European domination). And he championed the people of Africa, saying it was Black people who invented all arts and sciences while Europeans were still savages, and lamented that the people who Europe was most indebted to were now its most persecuted and despised.

One of the omitted sections discussed the ancient kingdom of

⋅ If only Volney had seem some of the indigenous people, like the Nuer (also known as the Nei Ti Naath, roughly meaning "Original People"), who still live right along the Nile's river basin, who are so dark they could be called "blue-black."

This is the lie  This is how

HATSHEPSUT

they showed  we portrayed

THUTMOSE III

the world.  ourselves.

SETI I

Ethiopia, and the ruins of Thebes in Egypt, which he said was **one of its colonies:**

> There a people, now forgotten, discovered, while others were yet barbarians, the elements of the arts and sciences. A race of men, now rejected from society for their sable skin and frizzled hair, founded on the study of the laws of nature, those civil and religious systems which still govern the universe.[20]

In the centuries that followed, other Europeans announced the same conclusions, including Volney,* Gerald Massey, Godfrey Higgins, Gaston Maspero, A.E. Amélineau, and a few others.

These accounts aren't the only evidence we have either. Sculptures of kings, queens, various influential figures, and even the gods of Egypt, depict Black features, are carved from Black stone, or both. Egyptologist Cheikh Anta Diop, in *African Origin of Civilization* said that evidence from Egyptian human images from both pre-dynastic periods and early dynasties, when clear, showed that the people were African. For starters, the Egyptians constantly portrayed themselves with Black or brown skin, never in the skin tones they used to represent whites or Semites.

Tragically, **much of the evidence has been obscured, painted over, hidden, destroyed, or vandalized**. Manu Ampim has devoted considerable time to documenting the fraudulent "whitening" of Egyptian imagery in his series at www.manuampim.com. Ampim describes a long history of forgeries, fakes, and intentional alterations to artifacts that evoke ideas of a Black Egypt.

If you ever look at any images from Egypt, it's not hard to spot the missing noses, most of them broken off by the butts of European rifles. You'll also notice that many of the dark-skinned paintings have been scraped off the walls or bleached. Some of this was also done by archaeologists who pretended to be concerned with revealing the past (while really concealing it).

While archaeologists like Petrie and Guy Brunton dug up the Nile Valley, artists like Brunton's wife Winifred documented their finds in highly subjective sketches and portraits. In fact, Winifred Brunton became famous by painting "lifelike renditions" of ancient Egyptian rulers, where they look almost entirely European – in stark contrast to the paintings that were made by the ancient Egyptians

---

* Sadly, a little-known fact about the celebrated Volney is that even *he* had to recant his views. After enduring endless critique for his claims of a Black Egypt, in 1814 he published a "corrected" version of his theory in his *New Researches on Ancient History.*

DID YOU KNOW?
The "good gods" were always depicted as Black, while the "bad gods" were portrayed with red skin or other coloring. While these gods could symbolize the forces of nature, Diop says they may have also been men who sprang from the Egyptian race itself and were deified as national heroes. Godfrey Higgins noted in his 1833 work *Anacalypsis* that all of the gods and goddesses of Greece were Black, apparently because they were derived from the Black divinities of Egypt. Ausar (or Osiris), one of the chief deities of the Egyptian pantheon, was called "Lord of the Perfect Black."[21]

themselves...as well as the theories of "Negroid" origins proposed by Flinders Petrie and Guy Brunton themselves.[*]

THE BLACK LAND

Egypt was known to its inhabitants as KMT (pronounced Kemet), which derives from **Kam, meaning Black**. According to the British Egyptologist, Gerald Massey:

Egypt is often called Kam, the Black Land, and Kam does signify black; the name probably applied to the earliest inhabitants whose type is the Kam or Ham of the Hebrew writers.[22]

KMT literally means "the Black land," or "land of the Blacks." This term does not refer to the black soil deposited by the Nile, but to the inhabitants themselves, as the hieroglyphic representation of the word KMT ends in a symbol denoting a nation, which implies that the name was not meant to describe simply the land itself, but instead that formulated upon it.

"The evidence of language also connects Egypt with Africa and the Negro race rather than with Asia, while religious ceremonies and social customs all go to strengthen this evidence." – W.E.B. Du Bois, The Negro

From the Egyptians' conception of the divine, to their social institutions, their practice of divine kingship, and a number of other customs and traditions, it is clear that Egypt was a Black civilization. According to Frazier, who first popularized the concept of totemism, there exists no such belief or practice among any white peoples. However, both continental Africans and Egyptians share a religious tradition involving the worship of deities represented in animal form. These and other cultural facets and values are common, showing an obvious link.

But when all this evidence still isn't enough, then we have to dig up

---

[*] Brunton was the wife of British Egyptologist Guy Brunton, who excavated with Sir Flinders Petrie. She explained that her celebrated portraits were made just as Michaelangelo did in painting the Christ: "The artist ponders on the faces of those best known to him, comparing them with those of mere acquaintancies, and trying to account for likenesses of form by similarities in character." In other words, "Which of my white friends do I believe this strong, dignified Egyptian ruler must have looked like?"

dead bodies. Cheikh Anta Diop was one of the few Black scientists to conduct such tests. In *The African Origin of Civilization*, he discusses his own findings, as well as a review of the many studies that were done by others. Some of the specific findings include:

❏ Evidence from physical anthropology showed that pre-dynastic skulls were Africoid.

❏ A process Diop invented to measure the amount of melanin in the skin of mummies clearly showed the mummies he examined had high levels of melanin.

❏ Bone evidence showed that the people of Egypt were Africoid.[23]

In summary, in tests of bodily bone structure, face structure, head shape, dental structure, hair texture, blood type, melanin content, race-specific disease, and genetic markers unique to Black people, the results always indicated a majority Black population in Egypt.[24]

ARE YOU SATISFIED?

Now let me ask you a question…Are you satisfied with that explanation? That is, are you satisfied with the proposal that the Egyptians were predominantly Black people? If so, what are your thoughts on all the images (and mummies) with straight hair and thin noses? If you're not familiar with any of these images, you probably haven't studied Egypt yet. That's cool. If you *do* claim to have studied ancient Egypt but can't talk about the fact that pre-Dynastic remains look a lot more "African" than many Dynastic remains, *you're missing something.*

You see, we can't be satisfied with simple explanations for complicated historical phenomena. We can't cover our eyes and act like Egyptian paintings don't show the Egyptians as brown and the Nubians as much darker. We know that the light-skinned Princess Neferititi was a foreigner (actually she was a "gift" from Persia), and "red-haired" people in Egypt were typically remnants of a small invasion of whites from outside its borders, but we can't act like *all* the Egyptians depicted themselves the same as the black-skinned Nubians they called *Nehesi*. So what gives? *Was Egypt Black or not?*

W.E.B. Du Bois discussed the diversity of ancient Egypt by describing the roles played by Nubians to the south meeting with other Anu people who had been long-settled further north. These people he called the Mediterranean race:

> The ethnic history of Northeast Africa would seem, therefore, to have been this: predynastic Egypt was settled by Negroes from Ethiopia. They were of varied type: the broad-nosed, woolly-haired type to which the word "Negro" is sometimes confined; the black,

curly-haired, sharper featured type, which must be considered an equally Negroid variation. These Negroes met and mingled with the invading Mediterranean race from North Africa and Asia. Thus the blood of the sallower race spread south and that of the darker race north. Black priests appear in Crete three thousand years before Christ, and Arabia is to this day thoroughly permeated with Negro blood. Perhaps, as Chamberlain says, "one of the prime reasons why no civilization of the type of that of the Nile arose in other parts of the continent, if such a thing were at all possible, was that Egypt acted as a sort of channel by which the genius of Negro-land was drafted off into the service of Mediterranean and Asiatic culture.[25]

In other words, there was a difference between the people of Upper and Lower Egypt, and these two populations converged to form Dynastic Egypt.

Both the "Mediterraneans" and the Nubians were Anu people. Yet the Nubians were a fresh wave of expansion from the Root of Civilization (circa 4000-2000 BC), while the people further north had left the root thousands of years prior, and may have been related to the Natufians. Some of the people further north looked different from the people further south.

But just because Nubia was generally more dark-skinned and wooly-haired, and the people of Egypt possessed a more diverse array of complexions and hair types, there's no evidence to suggest that Egypt was predominantly non-African or non-Black.

African anthropologist S.O.Y. Keita has written extensively against the idea that the Egyptians weren't Black because many of them had wavy hair and narrow noses:

> In general, this restricted view presents all tropical Africans with narrower noses and faces as being related to or descended from external, ultimately non-African peoples. However, narrow-faced, narrow-nosed populations have long been resident in Saharo tropical Africa... and their origin need not be sought elsewhere. These traits are also indigenous. The variability in tropical Africa is expectedly naturally high. Given their longstanding presence, narrow noses and faces cannot be deemed `non-African.'[26]

Keita goes on to cite several studies of ancient Egyptians that note their characteristically "tropical" or "African" body plan. He adds that anthropometric studies have shown that ancient Egyptians are closer to U.S. Blacks than to American or European whites.

In Dr. Emile Massoulard's *Historie et protohistorie d'Egypte*, she notes that the Naqada skeletons are consistent enough to represent a "Naqada race." This race, she says, has "Negroid" characteristics across most of the head and face, but a narrow "Germanic" nose.[27] Such features, as we note elsewhere, aren't evidence of foreign origin, but are well within the diverse range of features found among East African people.

Echoing the sentiments of Diop and Keita on African diversity in the Nile Valley, Egyptologist Frank Yurco has noted:

> Certainly there was some foreign admixture, but basically a homogeneous African population had lived in the Nile Valley from ancient to modern times…[The] Badarian people, who developed the earliest Predynastic Egyptian culture, already exhibited the mix of North African and Sub-Saharan physical traits that have typified Egyptians ever since…The peoples of Egypt, the Sudan, and much of East African Ethiopia and Somalia are now generally regarded as a Nilotic continuity, with widely ranging physical features (complexions light to dark, various hair and craniofacial types) but with powerful common cultural traits…[28]

An important 1999 report on the physical anthropology of the ancient Egyptians concludes:

> There is now a sufficient body of evidence from modern studies of skeletal remains to indicate that the ancient Egyptians, especially southern Egyptians, exhibited physical characteristics that are within the range of variation for ancient and modern indigenous peoples of the Sahara and tropical Africa. In general, the inhabitants of Upper Egypt and Nubia had the greatest biological affinity to people of the Sahara and more southerly areas.[29]

In other words, the ancient Egyptians were a DIVERSE Black civilization, made up of Black people who did not all look alike.

A QUICK NOTE ON AMATEUR EGYPTOLOGY

Before we get any deeper, I've got to express how important it is that you don't take anything on face value from ANY book talking about ancient civilizations, particularly Egypt. As Jimmy Dunn notes in *Tour Egypt*:

> Reading older histories (even a few decades) of Egypt and newer versions can certainly cause layman considerable consternation. Breakthroughs in Egyptology are likely to even accelerate. New imaging tools and methods of exploration, along with the general use of computers and sophisticated databases will likely increase our knowledge of ancient Egypt dramatically in the coming years. And while the Internet is a viable tool for the dissemination of the knowledge, unfortunately it is so often also a media of crackpots

and simply the uninformed. So it is very important that readers beware, and use a good amount of intelligent judgment on what information can be trusted, and what cannot be.

In other words, just because someone said it in a lecture, showed it in a video, or wrote it in a book, **doesn't mean it's true.**

What we know about the ancient world is constantly changing, yet many pseudo-scholars have presented themselves as "experts" on these stories in order to exploit them for profit. Some don't even TRY to stick to the facts. They'll tell you the people of Egypt came from Nigeria, Bethlehem, Atlantis, or Mississippi…and they built the pyramids 35,000 years ago using telekinesis or alien technology. **With not one piece of evidence that makes sense.**

Personally, I don't consider myself an expert on any of these subjects. I'm just a dedicated student. And I'm constantly learning and revising. So read critically and research on your own. More importantly, beware of extraordinary claims that don't offer extraordinary evidence. I'm not as concerned with the foul-intentioned people who come up with these lies as I am with the well-intentioned people who believe them without question. For more on THAT subject, refer back to "What is Science?" in *The Science of Self, Volume One.*

THE STORY OF THE SPHINX

As an example of the flim-flam that is sometimes associated with ancient Black history (and rarely with other history), I thought we could discuss the Sphinx. For beginners, the Sphinx clearly represents the Black face of the people who built ancient Egypt.

In *From West Africa to Palestine*, renowned scholar Edward Wilmot Blyden reported:

> Her features are decidedly of the African or Negro type, with 'expanded nostrils.' If, then, the Sphinx was placed here—looking out in majestic and mysterious silence over the empty plain where once stood the great city of Memphis in all its pride and glory, as an 'emblematic representation of the king'—is not the inference clear as to the peculiar type or race to which that king belonged?"[30]

And this was written in 1873, so it was quite revolutionary for Blyden – a Black man working in Liberia to bring together continental Africans and Blacks in America – to make such a bold declaration.

Following his footsteps, W.E.B. Du Bois reported in 1915:

> The great Sphinx at Gizeh, so familiar to all the world, the Sphinxes of Tanis, the statue from the Fayum, the statue of the Esquiline at Rome, and the Colossi of Bubastis all represent black, full-blooded

Negroes and are described by Petrie as "having high cheek bones, flat cheeks, both in one plane, a massive nose, firm projecting lips, and thick hair, with an austere and almost savage expression of power."[31]

So who built the Sphinx? And when? These are important questions. There is evidence that the Sphinx – which was known to the Egyptians as the *Her-Em-Akhet* (or "Heru of the Horizon") – is older than most Egyptologist will admit. Studies have suggested that the Sphinx could not have been built 2500 BC, but was more likely constructed between 7500-5000 BC. This seems feasible, as the Sphinx bears obvious signs of erosion caused by levels of rainfall that haven't occurred in Egypt since over 7,000 years ago. And it could be even older, depending on how long it takes to erode material in that way. There haven't been any peer-reviewed studies to make that case, however.

Either way, the Sphinx "could" have been built over 7,000 years ago. But it is UNLIKELY that the Sphinx was built 99,000 years ago using magic powers. And that it actually used to get up and carry us around. But I'm sure that somebody could do a YouTube video saying that and people would share and repost like it's a cute cat picture. Don't be one of those people. We owe it to ourselves to not study our own history with half-hearted effort.

Despite all the lies and fabrications out there, there are ways to get to the truth, or at least a lot closer to it than we are now. This book teaches you many of those ways. Central to those methods is learning how events occurred in chronological order, so you can tell when something sounds anachronistic, or out of its place or time.

As you read this book, you'll also come to appreciate the different "phases" of history our ancestors have gone through, and how one thing led to another. Learning this will also give you **insight into the way the future is being built.** So let's look into how the Nile Valley civilization came to be.

THE NILE VALLEY IS OLDER THAN EGYPT

Egyptian civilization didn't emerge in 3000 BC, as the mainstream version of history suggests. It didn't even start in 4000 BC, as some alternative histories suggest. While 3200 BC is about the time when King Narmer united the two kingdoms of the region to become a united empire, Nile Valley civilization is much older than this unification.

Let's talk about the period commonly known as pre-dynastic Egypt.* The founder of pre-dynastic Nile Valley archaeology was William Finders Petrie, whose excavations at important pre-dynastic sites like Naqada unearthed hundreds of graves. Other archaeologists have only refined and extended his research. It was Petrie who, a century ago, established the basic principles of pre-dynastic archaeology, and worked out a dating method that is still used today. And Petrie recognized Egypt as Black-owned and operated, tracing its origins further south into Africa.

Yet despite how important Petrie was in their field, Egyptologists washed their hands of him for this claim. They've countered that the first Egyptians came from ANYWHERE but deeper within Africa. They pointed everywhere, from the Mediterranean to the Near East to the Far East to Atlantis to outer space. Anything but Africa.

WHERE DID THE EGYPTIANS COME FROM?
THE PALEOLITHIC NILE VALLEY

In Part One, you read about the settling of the Nile Valley. Until the introduction of agriculture, settlements along the desert and valley shared the same culture. After agriculture came to the region, a more "elite" group of farmers and traders emerged along the area that would become Upper Egypt.

PRE-DYNASTIC CULTURES

This is where archaeologists uncovered the pre-dynastic site of Naqada. In its earliest phase, it did extensive trade with sites in Nubia and Ethiopia. The two predynastic phases at Naqada are called the Amratian (4400-3500 BC) and Gerzean (3500-3200 BC) cultures.

At al-Badari, another southern site along the Nile, archaeologists found evidence of another important predynastic culture. The

---

* Narmer established the first dynasty, so everything after that is considered dynastic Egypt.

Badarian culture (4400-4000 BC) was based on farming, hunting, and mining. They were the first to farm systemically in the area, growing barley, wheat, and flax. The Badarians were scientists, a fact we can determine based on the advanced chemical knowledge they used simply to produce cosmetics. They also mined copper, manufactured glass, made pottery, wove linen fabrics, established cemeteries, began stonemasonry, and domesticated animals.[32] As you can see, they had many of the elements later developed in ancient Egyptian civilization.

Where did the Badarians come from? Skull studies suggest the Badarians came from further south, and resembled indigenous Africans.[33] And this is what Egyptologist Alan Gardiner had to say about all the predynastic remains he examined:

They...were long-headed – dolicoceph-alic is the learned term – and below even medium stature, but Negroid features are often to be observed. Whatever may be said of the northerners, it is safe to describe the dwellers in Upper Egypt as of essentially African stock, a character always retained despite alien influences brought to bear on them from time to time.[34]

In other words, they were Black, Black, **Black**.

THE ETHIOPIAN EMPIRE?

Scholars like Rawlinson, Volney, Higgins, and others used to describe Ethiopia, or Kush, as an empire, with colonies in the Near East, India, and beyond. Like the ancient Greeks, they thought that ancient Egypt was a colony of the ancient Ethiopian empire, which eventually became an empire of its own.

There's quite some evidence to suggest that wave of people leaving the old "root of civilization" in East Africa could have branched out and brought new developments to the rest of the globe.

Yet unlike the civilizations they built further north (Sumer, Anatolia, etc.), ancient Egypt was unique because of its theological character:

> Egyptian contact in the 4th millennium BC with SW Asia is undeniable, but the effect of this contact on state formation is Egypt is less clear...The unified state which emerged in Egypt in the 3rd millennium B.C...was unlike the polities in Mesopotamia, the Levant, northern Syria, or Early Bronze Age Palestine – in sociopolitical organization, material culture, and belief system.[36]

In other words, Egyptian civilization was different from the civilizations of the ancient Near East. This was because, unlike their neighbors to their north, they were still in close contact with their southern ancestors. In *Wonderful Ethiopians of the Ancient Cushite Empire*, Drusilla Dunjee Houston writes:

> The Greeks also said that Egyptians derived their civilization and religion from Ethiopia. "Egyptian religion was not an original conception, for three thousand years ago she had lost all true sense of its real meaning among even the priesthood." (Budge, *Osiris and the Egyptian Resurrection*) Yet Egyptian forms of worship are understood and practiced among the Ethiopians of Nubia today. The common people of Egypt never truly understood their religion, this was why it so easily became debased.
>
> Ptolemaic writers said that Egypt was formed of the mud carried down, from Ethiopia, that Ethiopians were the first men that ever lived, the only truly autochthonous race and the first to institute the worship of the gods and the rites of sacrifice. Egypt itself was a colony of Ethiopia and the laws and script of both lands were naturally the same; but the hieroglyphic script was more widely known to the vulgar in Ethiopia than in Egypt. (Diodorus Siculus, bk. iii, ch. 3.) This knowledge of writing was universal in Ethiopia but was confined to the priestly classes alone in Egypt. This was because the Egyptian priesthood was Ethiopian.

According to Diodorus:

> The Ethiopians conceive themselves to be of greater antiquity than any other nation: and it is probable that, born under the sun's path, its warmth may have ripened them earlier than other men [translation: they're very Black]. They suppose themselves also to be the inventors of divine worship, of festivals, of solemn assemblies, of sacrifices, and every other religious practice...[They] affirm that the Egyptians are one of their colonies, and that the Delta, which was formerly sea, became land by the conglomeration of the earth of the higher country which was washed down by the Nile.[37]

As C.F. Volney explains, there are hundreds of ancient reports of this kind, all saying the same thing – that Egypt was a colony of the South:

> It would be easy to multiply citations upon this subject; from all

which it follows, that we have the strongest reasons to believe that the country neighboring to the tropic was the cradle of the sciences, and of consequence that the first learned nation was a nation of Blacks; for it is incontrovertible, that, by the term Ethiopians, the ancients meant to represent a people of black complexion, thick lips, and woolly hair. I am therefore inclined to believe, that the inhabitants of Lower Egypt were originally a foreign colony...of different tribes of savages, originally shepherds and fishermen, who, by degrees formed themselves into a nation, and who, by nature and descent,ʹ were enemies of the Thebans, by whom they were no doubt despised and treated as barbarians. [38]

A southern origin explains why Upper Egypt was the head of Egyptian civilization, as well as where its "religious" character came from. According to Lucian:

The Ethiopians were the first who invented the science of the stars, and gave names to the planets, not at random and without meaning, but descriptive of the qualities which they conceived them to possess; and it was from them that this art passed, still in an imperfect state, to the Egyptians. [39]

In Volume Three, we'll explain – with some help from C.F. Volney – how our ancestors' ingenious science of astronomy gradually transformed into organized religion. Much of this happened in Ancient Egypt (which then gave birth to the religions of ancient Greece and Rome), but it also happened wherever our astronomical ancestors settled.

THEY DIDN'T EXACTLY COME FROM ETHIOPIA

All these ancient writers said the Egyptian civilization came from Ethiopia. Here's something that can make this "Ethiopian origin" theory a little easier to process: This southern empire was only called "Ethiopia" by the Greeks and other outsiders. As you saw in the above quote from Diodorus, the Greeks believed the Ethiopians had spent the longest "ripening" in the Sun, which is where this name came from. It's Greek for "burnt face" (*ethio:* burnt + *ops:* face). Naturally, that wasn't what the "Ethiopians" called themselves.

So, when ancient writers talked about "Ethiopia," they weren't necessarily talking about a specific place that matches up with modern Ethiopia. As Volney noted above, "by the term Ethiopians, the ancients meant to represent a people of black complexion, thick lips, and woolly hair." "Ethiopian" was a general label for all the

---

ʹ Did Volney know he was talking about white folks when he says the savage barbarians who settled the north were the "natural enemies" of the Black people of the south? In Volume Four, we'll see why it seems he did.

Black people south of Egypt.

The earliest name we have for the region immediately south of Egypt is *Ta Seti* (or "Land of the Bow," for its expert archers). Later it was known as Nubia or Kush. Only later did Greek writers call the entire area Ethiopia. Today, this area is known as the Sudan (which comes from the Arabic *Bilād as-Sūdān* or "Land of the Blacks"). Many of the people of Sudan still consider themselves Nubians.

WHO WERE THE NUBIANS?

"Everywhere mankind was seeking where knowledge and mastery and magic power might reside; everywhere individual men were willing, honestly or dishonestly, to rule, to direct, or to be the magic beings who would reconcile the confusions of the community." – H. G. Wells, The Outline of History

When modern historians talk about the Nubians, they're talking about the same people who Bible-based scholars called 'Cushites' and who the Greek historians called Ethiopians. Obviously, Ethiopian was not indigenous, but neither was Nubian (or "Nuba"). These names all came from outsiders.

I'd prefer to use the name "Kushite" for these people, as "Kush" appears to be the only indigenous name they ever used for themselves. However, I'll be quoting from sources that might call them Nubians, Ethiopians, or even the people of ancient Sudan. I'll typically use "Nubian" to avoid confusion. Try not to let the name changes throw you off!

All of these names refer to the people who lived in what is now Sudan. They were one of the last waves of Anu people to disperse from the root. The Nubians (or Cushites) were a Black people who radiated throughout Africa, Asia, and Europe around 5,000 years ago, building their civilizations everywhere they went.

In 1905, Flora Louisa Shaw wrote:

> When the history of Negroland comes to be written in detail, it may be found that the kingdoms lying towards the eastern end of the Soudan were the home of races who inspired, rather than of races who received, the traditions of civilisation associated, for us, with the name of ancient Egypt. For they cover on, either side of the Upper Nile between the latitudes of 10 and 17, territories in which are found monuments more ancient than the oldest Egyptian monuments. If this should prove to be the case, and the civilised world be forced to recognise in a black people the fount of its original enlightenment, it may happen that we shall have to revise entirely our view of the black races and regard those who now exist as the decadent representatives of an almost forgotten era, rather than as the embryonic possibility of an era yet to come.[40]

In other words, Africans – the Nubians/Cushites in particular – were the original authors of all civilization, even before the rise of Dynastic Egypt.

And Shaw, of course, wasn't the first to say this. In German historian Arnold Heeren's 1832 work *Historical Researches into the Politics, Intercourse, and Trade of the Carthaginians, Ethiopians, and Egyptians,* he writes:

> In Nubia and Ethiopia, stupendous, numerous and primeval monuments proclaim so loudly a civilization contemporary to, aye, earlier than that of Egypt that it may be conjectured with the greatest confidence that the arts, science and religion descended from Nubia to the lower country of Mizraim; that civilization descended the Nile, built Memphis, and finally sometime later, wrested by colonization the Delta from the sea.
>
> The monuments, though eloquent, are not the only grounds upon which this conclusion has been reached. The fame of the Ethiopians was widespread in ancient history. Herodotus describes them as the "tallest, the most beautiful and long-lived of human races, and before Herodotus, Homer in even more flattering language described them as "the most just of men; the favorites of the gods." The annals of all the great early nations of Asia Minor are full of them. The Mosaic records allude to them frequently; but while they are described as the most powerful, the most just, and the most beautiful of the human race, they are constantly spoken of as black, and there seems to be no other conclusion to be drawn than that at that remote period of history the leading race of the western world was a black race.
>
> When we reflect that this black race flourished within the very latitudes of Africa which European nations are now engaged in opening to modern civilization, a great interest is added to the study of their possible descendants.
>
> The ancient civilization of Egypt spread, as we know, from south to north, and without venturing to accept or to reject the assumption of some learned writers that it came originally by the way of the

---

* In most books, this quote is wrongly attributed to "Lady Lugard," or Flora Louisa Shaw. I always attempt to trace my quotes back to their primary sources, but when I found Shaw's book *A Tropical Dependency*, I learned that she wasn't the author of these words. She quotes this passage in her book, but so do other authors, like William Henry Ferris, who quoted the same words in his 1911 *The African Abroad.* So how did all the contemporary books end up with the same wrong attribution? It seems the earliest text to feature the mistake was John G. Jackson's *Ethiopia and the Origin of Civilization.* Everyone else quoted Jackson's version, never stopping to check the source. Just goes to show you: We, the authors, are not infallible! You've gotta read and question and explore on your own! This is why I plan to republish all of these old books, so you can dig into the source material on your own.

Arabian Gulf from India, there is seemingly no doubt that the earliest center of civilization in Africa was the country watered by the upper Nile, which was known by the name of Ethiopia to the ancients and which fixed the limits of habitation of the higher races of the Soudan.

Monuments of which a more or less consecutive chain can be traced from Nubia to the Straits of Bab-el-Mandeb point to the existence, in this territory, at a period of great antiquity, of a people possessing many of the arts of a relatively high civilization.

In other words, these Black men and women were the fathers and mothers of modern civilization, including ancient Egypt. The Nubians also invented many of the things that historians now attribute to the ancient Egyptians, such as antibiotics and the waterwheel. The further you go back in time, the more familiar people were with the greatness of the Nubians. In the 6th century AD, Stephen of Byzantium wrote an important geographical dictionary titled *Ethnica*, where he says, "Ethiopia was the first established country on earth; and the Ethiopians were the first who introduced the worship of the gods, and who established laws."

By "Ethiopians," of course, he was referring to the Nubians. When we mention them, we're talking about another phase of Anu diffusion across the ancient world.

ETHIOPIA, EAST AND WEST

"The Ethiopians were considered as occupying all the south coasts of both Asia and Africa...This is an ancient opinion of the Greeks." – Greek historian Ephorus (circa 340 BC)

While we're considering the consensus of ancient historians regarding the greatness of the "Ethiopian Empire" (which was really the Nubian or Kushite Empire), we should also look at what they had to say about the *extent* of this empire. To many Greek writers, "Ethiopian" simply meant what we would mean if we said "African" or "Negroid" nowadays. This is why it was so easy for the Greeks to see the people of India as the Eastern Ethiopians. In *Ethiopia and the Origin of Civilization*, John G. Jackson says:

> In modern geography the name Ethiopia is confined to the country known as Abyssinia, an extensive territory in East Africa. In ancient times Ethiopia extended over vast domains in both Africa and Asia.

According to the renowned Egyptologist Sir E. A. Wallis Budge, in his *History of Ethiopia*:

It seems certain that classical historians and geographers called the whole region from India to Egypt, both countries inclusive, by the name of Ethiopia, and in consequence they regarded all the dark-skinned and black peoples who inhabited it as Ethiopians. Mention is made of Eastern and Western Ethiopians and it is probable that the Easterners were Asiatics and the Westerners Africans.[41]

Budge adds, "Homer and Herodotus call all the peoples of the Sudan, Egypt, Arabia, Palestine and Western Asia and India Ethiopians."[42] Think about that: The forefathers of European history (Homer and Herodotus) said Black people were the primary people of Africa and Asia.

There are dozens of other Greeks and Romans who said the same things, so we won't quote too many more. According to Greek historian Strabo (64 BC – 24 AD):

I assert that the ancient Greeks, in the same way as they classed all the northern nations with which they were familiar as Scythians, etc., so, I affirm, they designated as Ethiopia the whole of the southern countries toward the ocean.

In other words, all of the places where Black people lived in ancient times (along the coasts of Asia, Arabia, and Africa) were considered Ethiopia. Strabo continues:

If the moderns have confined the appellation Ethiopians to those only who dwell near Egypt, this must not be allowed to interfere with the meaning of the ancients.

And these Black communities didn't just disappear with the Greeks. In the 9th century AD, there was a prolific Arab scholar living in what is now Iraq, named Al-Jahiz. He was one of the foremost authors and scientists of his time. In fact, he proposed the Darwinian theory of evolution almost 1,000 years before Darwin did. In his lifetime, he wrote over 200 books, many of them covering scientific subjects. In other words, he knew his stuff.

Commissioned to research the history of Black people, Al-Jahiz, a Black man himself, ended up writing a book titled *Al-Fakhar al-Sudan min al-Abyadh*, which translates to *The Superiority of the Blacks over the Whites*. In it, he says:

The blacks include the Zanj [East Africa], Ethiopians, the people of Fazzan [Libya], the Berbers, the Copts, and Nubians, the people of

Zaghawa [Chad and Sudan], Marw [Central Asia], Sind [Pakistan] and India, Qamar [Lebanon] and Dabila [Algeria], China, and Masin [Afghanistan]. There is more sea than land, and the islands in the seas between China and Africa are full of blacks, such as Ceylon, Kalah, Amal, Zabij, and their islands, as far as India, China, Kabul, and those shores...

Think about that. As late as the 9th century, it was a known fact that Black communities survived across nearly all of Asia. These people were not the descendants of the East African slave trade, but the remnants of an ancient phase of diffusion from Nubia.

"ALL WISE AND RIGHTEOUS"

Over 2700 years ago, it was the Greek poet Homer who said:

The Ethiopians, utmost of mankind,

These eastward situate, those towards the west

The second line is somewhat cryptic, and could mean "In the east as they are in the west" or perhaps something else. What's clear is that Homer recognized Ethiopians in the east and west, and considered these Black people the "utmost of mankind" or the "furthest of men." That's a topic we'll explore in Volume Three, but think about it for a minute.

Homer (like many others who came after him) heaped praises on the advanced civilization of the Ethiopians, not simply for having mastery of all the sciences, but for their unparalleled righteousness. He called them the "blameless Ethiopians" and said they regularly feasted with the Greek gods (who Godfrey Higgins says were all Black as well).

Over 2,000 years later, Stephanus of Byzantium reiterated that the Ethiopians were "loved by the gods because of their justice," adding:

Juniper frequently leaves heaven and feasts with them because of their justice and the equity of their customs. For the Ethiopians are said to be the justest of men and for that reason the gods leave their abode frequently to visit them.[43]

Al-Jahiz too, in his *Book of the Superiority of the Blacks over the Whites,* explains why the Black people of East Africa were the most righteous and generous people of their time. What does this tell us?

QUESTIONS TO CONSIDER

What was so special about the Nubians? We know they left their Nile Valley homeland and spread far and wide, just like the Anu populations who came before them. Black historian Drusilla Dunjee Houston said the climate of this region...

...was favorable to the nurturing and development of a high type of civilization and produced an Ethiopian so superior to the later types, that they were called by the ancients, "the handsomest men of the primeval world."[44]

Wherever they went, they were revered and often deified.

But why? How? Because they spoke a more ancestral Anu language than the people they encountered, were they better prepared to communicate with the communities they traveled to? Did they look like the ancestral populations of these communities, and "inherit" some sort of reverence that way?

Were they trading highly prized commodities like jade, obsidian, cowry shells, or gold? Did they introduce domesticated food products like millet, effectively saving some people from hunger (after all, the climate was changing and food sources were becoming scarce)? Did their knowledge of metallurgy and ceramics grant them the same receptions the first European traders receive when they brought glass beads and iron pots?

Did they come wearing face paint and other forms of ornamentation (shell beads, scarification, etc.) that made them stand out? The designs worn by the Nuba of Kau are simply breathtaking. Were their women considered the ideals of feminine beauty in the ancient world? The Venus Figurines would suggest so.

Were they taller, stronger, more agile? The fact that the Olmec heads may represent Black elites who were both rulers AND ballplayers suggests so, as do ancient legends of Blacks who could fly, disappear, and move mountains.

Were their cosmologies more comprehensive? That is, did they appear to know more about the history of the world's people and places? Or was it more explanatory of natural phenomena? That is, were they better able to "predict" future events because of their understanding of the workings of nature? Were they seen as diviners and gods because of this ability?

If shamans were the first social class to become distinguished from the rest of the population (before rulers and priesthoods), they must have been pretty socially isolated. If shamans retained a greater degree of "racial purity" as a result, they would understandable be "Blacker" than the rest of their communities over time. And this is true. In most communities, the shamans and priests look "Blacker" than everyone else.

In fact, once "pure-blooded" Black people were no longer around – shamans and priests often began painting themselves black. Would the high social status of such shamans afford reverence to a Black population of migrants who all appeared to share some degree of access to the shamanic gift? After all, indigenous Black people (in Africa, India, Australia, etc.) didn't make such sharp distinctions between who had it and who didn't, while the rest of the world drew clear lines between the theological elite (who had access to the divine) and the masses who didn't.

THE NUBIAN ORIGINS OF ANCIENT EGYPT

The Nubians played a significant role in the founding on ancient Egypt. As Petrie notes in *The Making of Egypt*:

> A breath of life came from the Sudan. This southern source was likewise the inspiration of…the 1st, 2nd (Anu), 3rd [Sudanese], 4th, 5th, 12th [Sudanese] dynasties…

In other words, Africans from the south were foundational in Egypt's early dynasties. For the sake of simplicity, we'll call them Nubians. It was Petrie's conviction that there was a "peaceful," if not united, rule all over Egypt and Nubia during the entire pre-dynastic period, that Nubians were the source of the Nile Valley's first dynasties, and that dynastic Egypt remained predominantly Nubian in its formative years.[45]

Later studies have confirmed Petrie's theory. Anthropological and archaeological research indicates that predynastic Nubia and Naqada were ethnically and culturally identical, simultaneously evolving systems of pharaonic kingship by 3300 BC. These systems, along with trade and agriculture, would play a formative role in the rise of dynastic Egypt's first rulers.

In fact, cranial and dental studies of predynastic burials from Naqada reveal that the "elite" members of this society were from further south than others buried in the area. These elites came from Nubia.[46] In other words, Nubians were in high-ranking positions when Upper and Lower Egypt were brought together to form the first dynasties.

WHICH WAY DOES THE NILE FLOW?

The Nile River flows from south to north, beginning in the mountains of East Africa and ending at the Delta region of northern Egypt. This made people from the north (mostly Europeans) believe that it flowed "backwards," as they couldn't imagine the source of the magnificent Nile, the world's longest river, actually being deeper within Africa.

Before the dynastic period, Egyptian cultures were split into two

DID YOU KNOW?
Technically, the Nile has two beginning spots. The White Nile is formed at Lake No in Sudan and the Blue Nile originates from Lake Tana in Ethiopia. The two rivers meet near the city of Khartoum in Sudan.

regions, known as Upper and Lower Egypt. Which name do you think represents the South? Give yourself two points if you guessed Upper Egypt. The northern part was Lower Egypt. It can get confusing if you don't remember this part.

"Upper" Egypt means the upper end of the Nile River, or the southside. And the southside, undeniably African in character, was where it all started. Upper Egypt was the fertile food-producing region from which the dynasties sprung. It's where we find the Badarians and every pre-dynastic culture that matters. And the Badarians weren't some nomadic group of African vagabonds. They were heavily into trade. We know this because they had:

- ❐ basalt vases from the Delta region or the Northwest
- ❐ elephant ivory from the South
- ❐ copper from the North
- ❐ shells from the Red Sea shores
- ❐ turquoise from Sinai
- ❐ pottery from all over (north, west, east, and south)[47]

But as Myra Wysinger notes:

> The problem in most books – it regards the unification of the Two Lands as the start of Egyptian history. Of course it is not – by then they had developed glass, silver, bronze in limited amounts, shells, all of these show us: (1) that they had traded regularly and deliberately for some time; (2) that they knew exactly where to go, how to get there, and what they would find when they got there; (3) they had developed (or learned of) new technologies from their overseas contacts.[48]

In other words, as Toby Wilkinson argues in *Early Dynastic Egypt*, Upper Egypt had everything it needed. This southern area had no trouble providing the resources or leadership necessary to support a growing population of urban settlers. Meanwhile, Lower (northern) Egypt was thinly settled as late as the New Kingdom (1550 BC). Until then, this area's most important function was as a grazing area for cattle.[49]

WHY DID UPPER AND LOWER EGYPT COME TOGETHER?

So why did Upper and Lower Egypt **come together as one** around 3200 BC? Thanks to its northern location and access to water, Lower Egypt was trading with the people of Palestine and the Sumerians.[50] From the predynastic period up to the New Kingdom, the true

> **DID YOU KNOW?**
> The Great Pyramid of Giza was a staggering 481 feet tall - the equivalent of a 40-story building. It was made of 2.3 million blocks of limestone and granite, some weighing 100 tons.
> It was originally cased in white limestone, which would make it shine brightly when reflecting the daytime sunlight. Despite what the "ancient aliens" crowd alleges, Giza did not emerge out of nowhere. There was a steady succession of improving pyramid designs, beginning with burial pits, followed by burial chambers known as mastabas, then earthen mounds to cover these burial chambers, then stone mounds, then stepped pyramids, then a failed "Bent Pyramid," and THEN the "true pyramid" with sloped sides.
> Also, there is no evidence that any of the pyramids were built by "slave labor" and certainly not by some unreported group of Hebrews. Instead, thousands of farmers who needed a source of food and income during the off-season came to the pyramids to work.

importance of Lower Egypt was the ease of trade routes to Asia. This is why the trade leaders of Upper Egypt (like the Badarians) wanted to expand their political empire to include Lower Egypt in order to better control these connections.[51]

This is when King Narmer rose to power. Petrie, in his book *The Making of Egypt*, wrote that the first king of Egypt (Narmer, sometimes called Menes) had strong Black features, characteristic of the people who dominated that period. He affirmed:

> [T]his dynasty, the first to give Egyptian civilization its almost definitive form and expression, was of Sudanese Nubian origin. The equally Negroid features of the protodynastic face of Tera Neter and those of the first king to unify the valley, also prove that this is the only valid hypothesis. Similarly, the Negroid features of the Fourth Dynasty Pharaohs, the builders of the great pyramids, confirm this.

Diop also cites the obvious "Africoid" features of the early Egyptian royalty, such as Narmer, Djoser, Khufu, Mentuhotep II, Senuswret, Ahmose Nefertari, and Amenhotep I.

After Narmer, the kings of Egypt are not well-known until the reign of Djoser (or Zoser) in the 3rd dynasty (c. 2687 BC). By his time, however, all the technological elements of the Egyptian civilization were already in place. Zoser, whose features are undeniably Black, is certainly worthy of researching. He was called *Netjerikhet* (literally "godbody") by his contemporaries. He is most famous for commissioning his high priest Imhotep to engineer the construction of the step pyramid at Sakkara, widely recognized as **the world's first large-scale, cut-stone construction**.

In the 4th dynasty (c. 2580 BC), Khufu (also known as Cheops) was responsible for construction of the Great Pyramid at Giza. Diop described him as "a Cameroon type." Around 2100 BC, Mentuhotep

II founded the 11th Dynasty. He (again) reunited Egypt and established the capital at Thebes. And things were looking good for a while. *Until the Hyksos came.*

THOSE WHO CAME TO DESTROY

The pale-skinned Hyksos appeared in Egypt around 1800 BC, during the 11th dynasty. They were nobodies at first, but they studied, planned, and strategically began their climb to power. By the 13th dynasty, they were in control of the Delta in the north.

The 13th dynasty collapsed following a string of suspiciously short-lived and ineffective kings. By the 15th Dynasty, the Hyksos had risen to power, ruling all of Lower Egypt. Yet as we noted earlier, Lower Egypt was essentially the most undesirable real estate in the Nile Valley at the time. As W.E.B. Du Bois explains in *The Negro*:

> [W]hen the dread Hyksos appeared, Ethiopia became both a physical and cultural refuge for conquered Egypt. The legitimate Pharaohs moved to Thebes, nearer the boundaries of Ethiopia, and from here, under Negroid rulers, Lower Egypt was redeemed.

That's when the Hyksos set their eyes on the south. They were attempting to take over Upper Egypt when Seqenenre Tao II, one of the Black Theban kings of the 17th Dynasty, took them to war. He ultimately lost his life in battle, fighting to the death to protect Black Egypt.

In 1550 BC, his son Ahmose I went back to war and – with the help of the Nubians – conquered the Hyksos, exiling them from Egypt, chasing them all the way into Palestine, restoring Theban rule over the whole of Egypt, and reestablishing control of Nubia and Canaan.

They promptly absorbed Nubians into the imperial hierarchy, ushering in the 18th Dynasty and making Egypt a sprawling empire again. Egypt's New Kingdom **covered nearly a million square miles and as much as five million people.**

Yet there were problems with absorbing new people (other than the Nubians). When the New Kingdom finally disintegrated around 1070

BC, Nubia became an independent kingdom known as Kush. According to Petrie, "Decay continued in a divided kingdom; Egypt seemed hopeless until a fresh Ethiopian invasion stimulated it, as in earlier instances."[52]

This happened in the 25th dynasty (760-656 BC), also known as the Nubian Dynasty or Kushite Empire. Nubian rulers reunited Egypt, bringing it back to a scale not seen since the dawn of New Kingdom.

Clearly the histories of the Egyptians and Nubians were inseparably intertwined. But did the Egyptians originally come from Nubia, or somewhere even further south?

THE MYSTERIOUS HOMELAND OF PUNT

The people of Egypt often spoke of a place called Punt (or *Ta Netjer*, meaning "Land of the Gods").[53] Egyptologists like Jon White,[54] Sir Flinders Petrie,[55] and E.A. Wallis Budge[56] say the Egyptians saw this land as their ancestral homeland.

The most descriptive account of Punt comes from Egyptian records of Queen Hatshepsut's expedition to the area, where they met with Punt's King Perehu and Queen Eti. The stone relief portrays her as obese, with massive hips and thighs, but a "normal" waistline. But she wasn't obese. The Egyptian artist was more likely astounded by Queen Eti's distinctly African steatopygia. Like the Queen, most of the goods they traded were **distinctly African**.

The evidence suggests that Punt was somewhere south of Nubia, possibly in the Horn of Africa (a region that includes modern-day Eritrea, Djibouti, Ethiopia and Somalia), but some scholars argue that it was in Arabia or the Near East. Unfortunately for Eurocentrists hoping to make Punt (and thus their Egyptian descendants) "non-African," Punt is as "Afro-Asiatic" as it gets. In *The Ethiopians*, historian Richard Pankhurst explains:

> [Punt] has been identified with territory on both the Arabian and African coasts. Consideration of the articles which the Egyptians obtained from Punt...leads us to suppose that the term Punt probably applied more to African than Arabian territory.[57]

Most of the evidence suggests that Punt was situated right at the tip of the Horn of Africa, with settlements across the water as well. That is, **Punt wasn't limited to one side of the Red Sea, but covered both sides, across east Africa and southern Arabia, with the cultural emphasis on the African side.**

In 2010, a research team from the University of California Santa Cruz confirmed this theory when they identified the most likely

ANCIENT KERMA

Kerma is an ancient civilization in Nubia that once rivaled ancient Egypt in its development. It had an urban city structure by 2400 BC, but was originally settled about 20,000 years ago.

The deffufa are massive manmade mud-brick temples found throughout ancient Nubia. One deffufa, at Kerma, once stood over 60 feet tall and had over three stories. It was surrounded by a boundary wall. Inside was a complex network of chambers connected by passageways. A nearby deffufa, standing two stories tall, was surrounded by 30,000 tumuli or burial mounds.

location of Punt. They announced that Punt was "a sort of circumscribed region that includes eastern Ethiopia and all of Eritrea," but may have been headquartered in the Red Sea itself. They narrowed down its location to a set of islands named Massawa.[58] Archaeologist Judith Weingarten adds:

> Massawa is the so-called 'pearl of the Red Sea'. The town is located on two islands – absolutely perfect for a trading post, combining as it does, safety and accessibility. It should be clear by now that Punt was an early African trade emporium, not only trading its own products but other products of Africa, and probably Arabian frankincense as well. So an island location fits very well.[59]

An island location also supports the idea that Punt extended to the other side of the Red Sea in Arabia, from where they stocked frankincense, myrrh, and other goods not readily found in Africa. In our section on Arabia, we'll talk about how the founders of ancient Egypt and ancient Arabia shared the same Anu ancestors.

WHERE'S KERMA? IS THAT A PLACE?

How many ancient African civilizations do we really learn about? If you think about it, the only one older than 1000 BC (that we learn about in school) is ancient Egypt, and they do their best to distance Egypt from Africa – even though it's obviously IN Africa. But, as you've probably realized by now, there are so many more!

For example, have you ever heard of Kerma? No, not Kermit. Never mind, I'll tell you. Kerma was an early African civilization situated in the area of present-day Sudan. It became organized as a Nubian state by about 3000 BC, but Kerma gets special attention from archaeologists because it rivaled Egypt in its development by 1600 BC. In other words, Kerma was kind of a big deal.

Archaeological evidence of human occupation in the Kerma Basin goes back to a very early date, spanning tens of thousands of years. 20,000 years ago, residents of the area built natural shelters, such as hollowed-out trunks of acacia trees covered with roofs woven from clay-coated and painted palm fibers.

This method of building huts is actually a practice that persists among some Africans today. This early phase of settlement is when the ancestors of the Anu people began coming together as a culture, not far from the sites their ancestors established for the Nubian Complex over 100,000 years before.

By 7500 BC, the remains become more noteworthy: semi-buried dwellings, various objects and tools, one of the two oldest cemeteries ever found in Africa, and the oldest evidence of cattle domestication yet found in the Nile Valley. In other words, Nubian culture provided the source for ancient Egyptian culture.

SUBMERGING ANCIENT NUBIA

Unfortunately, it's unlikely we'll ever know much more about the Nubians, because most of the primary archaeological sites now lie under 250 feet of water, at the bottom of Lake Nasser. And this is a literal "cover-up" as Lake Nasser is a man-made lake. At approximately 500 square miles, it's actually the second largest man-made lake on Earth.

During the construction of Lake Nasser, over 150,000 Nubians and Sudanese were forced to relocate, and over 45 Nubian villages were washed away along the banks of the Nile. They saved 23 Nubian monuments, but there's no way to know how many temples and tombs were lost. Myra Wysinger laments:

> Because of the creation of the Aswan High Dam, the world will never have an opportunity to study the full impact Africans from the southern Nile Valley had on the development of ancient Egypt and subsequent civilizations.[60]

NABTA PLAYA

Linguist Christopher Ehret has established that the people who settled Egypt came from the south, from where they introduced domesticated cattle, pottery, and the Afro-Asiatic language family, long before any of these things made their way into the Middle East.[61] Regarding the southern origins of the ancient Egyptians, Christopher Ehret writes:

> Ancient Egyptian civilization was, in ways and to an extent usually not recognized, fundamentally African. The evidence of both language and culture reveals these African roots.[62]

Ehret traces these roots back to a region stretching from the Sudan (Nubia) to Somalia in the Horn of Africa (Punt).[63] But there's another region we can't ignore: Nabta Playa.

Nabta Playa is situated in Egypt's Western Desert, about 60 miles west of southern Egypt. It was a highly advanced civilization, predating dynastic Egypt, during a time when the Sahara was not a desert. This is why the site is known as Nabta Playa, "playa" meaning temporary lake. By 7,000 BC, the people of Nabta Playa had:

- above-ground and below-ground stone construction
- villages designed in pre-planned, geometric arrangements
- deep wells that held water throughout the year
- a plant-based diet, consisting mostly of wild fruit, legumes, millets, sorghum and tubers
- food stored in ceramics adorned by complicated painted patterns possibly created using combs made from fish bone
- one of the world's oldest astronomical observatories, predating Stonehenge[65]

THE NABTA PLAYA STONE CIRCLE

The people of Nabta Playa erected a stone circle that predated Stonehenge. Astrophysicist Thomas G. Brophy says the Nabta megaliths were aligned with the stars of Orion's belt in 6400 BC and 4900 BC, matching the radio-carbon dating of campfires around the circle. In other words, they laid out these stones to track the stars. Brophy wrote: "The designers of the megaliths had a basic understanding of physics, and knowledge of astronomy that rivaled or surpassed ours today."[66]

Brophy also suggested the megaliths showed a representation of the Milky Way as it was in 17,500 BC and maps of Orion at 16,500 BC but used these to support his argument for alien intervention.[67] Of course, the archaeological record shows no evidence of habitation this far back, nor of any outside contact – alien or otherwise – and cranial studies show that they were clearly African,[68] while genetic analysis of their remains proves they most likely came from the Sudan.[69] **They simply weren't there 18,000 years ago, and they certainly weren't aliens.**

The Anu people who settled Nabta Playa 9,000 BC accomplished quite a lot:

- They were among the first humans to practice animal husbandry, at least 11,000 years ago.[70]

☐ They had domesticated cattle by at least 8000 BC, long before anywhere else had domesticated animals

☐ Around the same time, they were making some of the earliest pottery found on the planet.* By 7500 BC, they had established extensive pottery traditions with the wavy-line motif (at first modeled upon African gourds), long before the Near East adopted ceramics (from them).

☐ They domesticated wheat and barley around 7000 BC, long before plant domestication was known in the Near East

☐ They were building storage pits to contain domesticated sorghum and millet by 6000 BC, long before...you get it.

They did all these things long before the techniques made their way east. So do you think these innovations came from the Near East? Probably not! The spread of such techniques came from within Africa, from the same root that other Anu people (such as the Nubians) later dispersed from.

Furthermore, the Nabta Playa people didn't die off or disappear. When their homeland began drying up (it is now Egypt's Western Desert), around 4000 BC, they made moves. It appears that at least some of the people of Nabta Playa went east to resettle the Nile Valley.

THE SAHARANS

Other Saharans from even further west may have come to the Nile as well. This would explain linguistic traces of Nilo-Saharan languages in ancient Egyptian and Cushitic.[71] As Egyptologist Frank Yurco notes:

> Climatic cycles acted as a pump, alternately attracting African peoples onto the Sahara, then expelling them as the aridity returned. Specialists in predynastic archaeology have recently proposed that the last climate-driven expulsion impelled the Saharans...into the Nile Valley ca. 5000-4500 BCE, where they intermingled with indigenous hunter-fisher-gatherer people already there. Such was the origin of the distinct Egyptian populace, with its mix of agriculture/pastoralism and hunting/fishing.
>
> The resulting Badarian people, who developed the earliest Predynastic Egyptian culture, already exhibited the mix of North African and Sub-Saharan physical traits that have typified Egyptians ever since...

---

* Its unique style is known to archaeologists as the "dotted wavy-line" style (archaeologists aren't very creative with naming stuff), and it is found everywhere the Nilo-Saharan culture can be found.

Language research suggests that this Saharan-Nilotic population became speakers of the Afro-Asiatic languages…In summary we may say that Egypt was a distinct North African culture rooted in the Nile Valley and on the Sahara.[72]

In fact, the artists who created the amazing cave paintings in the Sahara may have been the ones who upgraded Egyptian art from simple carvings and lines (during the pre-dynastic period) to full-color frescoes (after dynastic Egypt brings together all its separate communities).[73]

NO OUTSIDE HELP NEEDED

Evidently, Black people from all along the Nile and all across the Sahara came together about 5,000 years ago to build what we now know as ancient Egypt. That's quite a lot of communities coming together to make this thing happen. But what was the contribution from the Near Eastern side? After six years of research, a U.S.-based Nile Valley study group concluded:

> State formation in the ancient Nile Valley does not appear to have taken the sudden form suggested by the influx or inspiration of a Dynastic Mediterranean or Mesopotamian race. Instead, material evidence indicates that the indigenous peoples evolved the state gradually, in a slowly phased process suggesting a degree of regional integration well before the 1st Dynasty.[74]

In other words, dozens of communities across Upper Egypt and Nubia came together as a confederation of sorts, ultimately united by the Egyptian government of 3200 BC. Before the 1st Dynasty, there had been up to ten indigenous rulers throughout the Nile Valley area.[75] None of the leadership was Near Eastern. As with the Natufians, the "knowledge" came from the African side, leaving little for the Near Easterners to contribute in terms of cultural influence.*

As the Egyptians consolidated, the extent of their empire gradually expanded to cover larger stretches of the north. This is reflected in their myths, which recall a migration coming from the south. In fact, according to Cheikh Anta Diop, not only was Ausar (Osiris) once a real historical personality, he is the one credited with leading the ancestors of the Egyptians out of Nubia. Diop, a reputable historian, anthropologist, and physicist, even declared that Ausar's actual head was preserved in a canopic jar discovered at Abydos![76]

When Upper Egypt absorbed Lower Egypt, it shifted the genes (and

---

* Don't get me wrong. Every time Africans left the Root of Civilization to settle in the Near East, they introduced the best and brightest ideas. But after a few thousand years of isolation from the Root, they were no longer innovating.

features) of the average Egyptian citizen away from the Nubian default. Once foreigners (like the Hyksos and the Assyrians) began invading the Nile Valley in larger numbers, things shifted even more. These are periods when rulers from the south (i.e. the "Nubian Pharaohs") returned to prominence as "restorationists" or "unifiers" against such outside threats.[77]

In *Pre-Colonial Africa*, Robert July concludes:

Some have argued that various early Egyptians like the Badarians probably migrated northward from Nubia, while others see a wide-ranging movement of peoples across the breadth of the Sahara before the onset of desiccation. Whatever may be the origins of any particular people or civilization, however, it seems reasonably certain that the predynastic communities of the Nile valley were essentially indigenous in culture, drawing little inspiration from sources outside the continent during the several centuries directly preceding the onset of historical times...[78]

In other words, when dynastic Egypt emerged, it wasn't just one group of people who made it happen....but it was definitely all Black people. As you've seen, Nile Valley civilization was built by Black people from all over the area. To be totally clear, the high civilization of ancient Egypt is the result of an indigenous Black Diaspora consolidating and cooperating.

Thus, Nile Valley Civilization was, for thousands of years, characterized by diverse groups of Original people coming together along that fertile and fortuitous stretch of African soil, led by Anu People from the Root of Civilization. *They were uniters, not dividers.*

WHERE DID THE EGYPTIANS GO?

Clearly, Egypt is no longer a predominantly Black nation. (Sorry if you didn't notice until I said that.) So what happened? Did the Black people of the ancient Nile Valley simply disappear? Were they wiped out by conquering hordes of whites and Arabs? Or were they absorbed into the present-day population?

One thing is for sure: They didn't disappear. It's true that the several waves of white invaders ultimately unseated Black power in Egypt, beginning with the dreaded Temehu (c. 3500 BC), followed by another period of conquest by the Hyksos (1700 BC), then by the Assyrians (671 BC), then the Persians (525 BC), then the Greeks (305 BC), and then the Romans (30 BC). **When the Arabs came seven centuries later, they weren't conquering Black Egypt. That had already been done.**

But many of the people who remained living along the Nile Valley still retained traces of the old blood. Volney remarked on this when he visited Egypt in the 1700s and saw traces of Black heritage in the puffy lips and broad noses of the Copts. If Volney had ventured further south, he would see that the Nubians were *still Nubian.* That is, the people of the Sudan are just as Black now as they were then. But did everyone north of Nubia get "mixed up" in the race-mixing that has dominated Egyptian history since the Roman conquest?

Not exactly. You have to keep in mind that Nile Valley culture formed along the Nile River. In other words, they were comfortable with the idea of getting from one place to another by waterways. And, as we noted in Part One, our ancestors' maritime capabilities go back hundreds of thousands of years. So it's no surprise that many (but not all) of the earliest Nile Valley settlers were ship-builders and sailors.[81]

PRE-FABRICATED SHIPS

In the chapter on South America, we talked about the possibility that the massive stone blocks found at early sites in the Andes were "prefabricated." In other words, they were made according to a template. This theory has also been proposed for the limestone blocks used in ancient Egyptian construction. We now have clear evidence that the science of prefabrication was known to the ancient Egyptians at least 4500 years ago.

This conclusion is based on the remains of Khufu's massive "Sun Ship," which was found in an underground storage chamber at the base of the Great Pyramid in 1954. The 142-foot long vessel was completely dismantled into 1,224 components, but not as if it had been torn apart. Instead, the pieces were ready for reassembly. In 2011, archaeologists began excavating another ship nearby. Turns out this ship was another Sun Ship, with its pieces laid out the same way. As Rossella Lorenzi of *Discovery News* reports:

ANCIENT TRADE AND SAILING

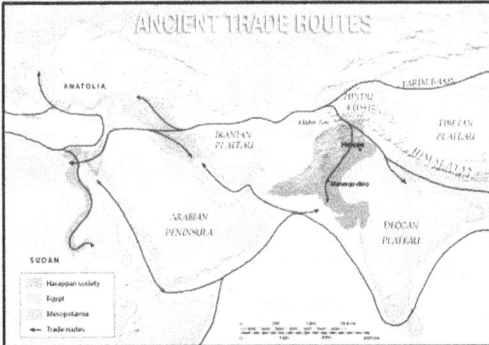

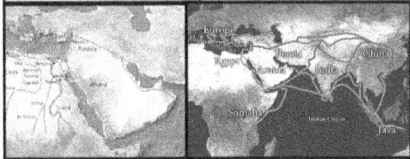

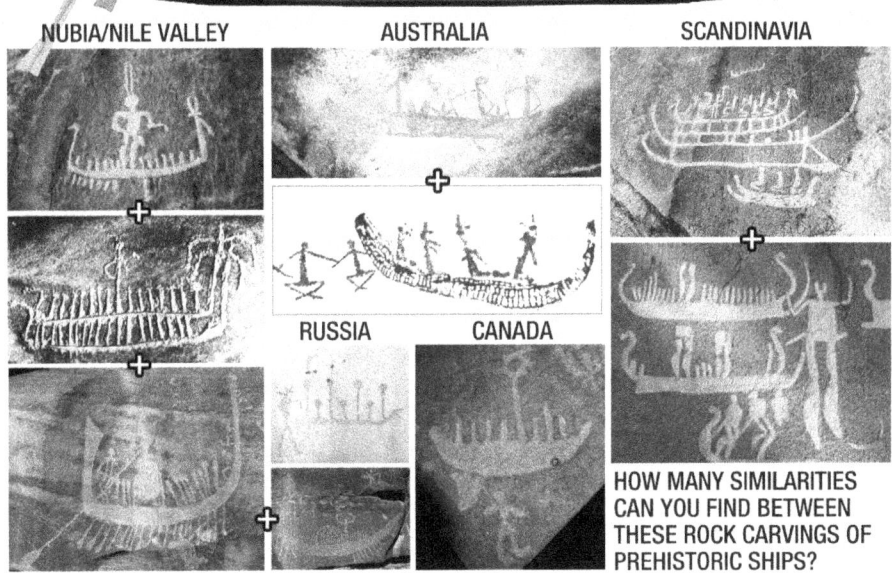

ANCIENT TRADE ROUTES

KHUFU'S SHIP REASSEMBLED

BOAT COMPARISON - TO SCALE
(WHICH DO YOU THINK CARRIED MORE MEN?)

COLUMBUS'S PINTA - 66 FT LONG

KHUFU'S SUN SHIP - 143 FT LONG

KHUFU'S SECOND SHIP

NUBIA/NILE VALLEY   AUSTRALIA   SCANDINAVIA

RUSSIA   CANADA

HOW MANY SIMILARITIES
CAN YOU FIND BETWEEN
THESE ROCK CARVINGS OF
PREHISTORIC SHIPS?

The ships were stored like Ikea furniture – **pre-fabricated and ready for assembly and stacked in a sequence that basically led to the vessel's finished form.**[82]

Imagine that. Boats twice as big as Columbus' renowned Santa Maria…packed away in storage boxes like they were bookcases from IKEA! Considering that the second Sun Ship was only discovered recently thanks to electromagnetic radar, it's reasonable to wonder, "Just how many more ships were built this way?"

THE OLDEST BOAT ON THE NILE

The earliest evidence for an ancient boat on the Nile is found in a piece of rock art that dates to about 7000 BC in Khartoum, Sudan.[83] It looks similar to boats from rock engravings in Nubia as well as the boats painted on walls and pottery at Predynastic Egyptian sites.[84] Clearly, the Egyptians and Nubians were comfortable sailing. It's quite possible that the ancient Nubians did more sailing than the later Egyptians.

Ancient expeditions led by Nubians or Egyptians would account for the presence of Afro-Asiatic DNA in the oldest settlements of coastal Europe, as well as along the eastern shores of North and South America, which predate the emergence of the North African Phoenicians, who became famous for their maritime exploits.

ANCIENT WEST AFRICA

"If your people came from West Africa and you know more about Kemet than West Africa…you might be disrespecting your ancestors. I mean, it's better than only knowing about Benjamin Franklin and Thomas Jefferson…but you're still missin somethin." – Supreme Understanding, via Facebook

When we learn about the civilizations of West Africa, we encounter glorious examples like Mali, Songhai, ancient Ghana, and Benin. On their own, these civilizations are amazing, and everyone should know about the wealth and generosity of King Mansa Musa (literally the richest man history has ever known),[85] the salt trade of the Tuaregs, the world-famous learning center in Timbuktu, the bronze sculptures of Benin, and the Ifá divination system of the Yoruba (all of which we'll revisit in a future volume). But most of these examples emerged within the past 2,000 years, leaving many of us wondering, "Well, **what was happening in West Africa before 500 BC?**"

It's unfortunate how little we know about the people of prehistoric West Africa. In recent years, a few scientists have attempted to change that. Peter Breunig's recent excavation of the Nok culture's settlement in the Nigerian highlands revealed that they smelted iron

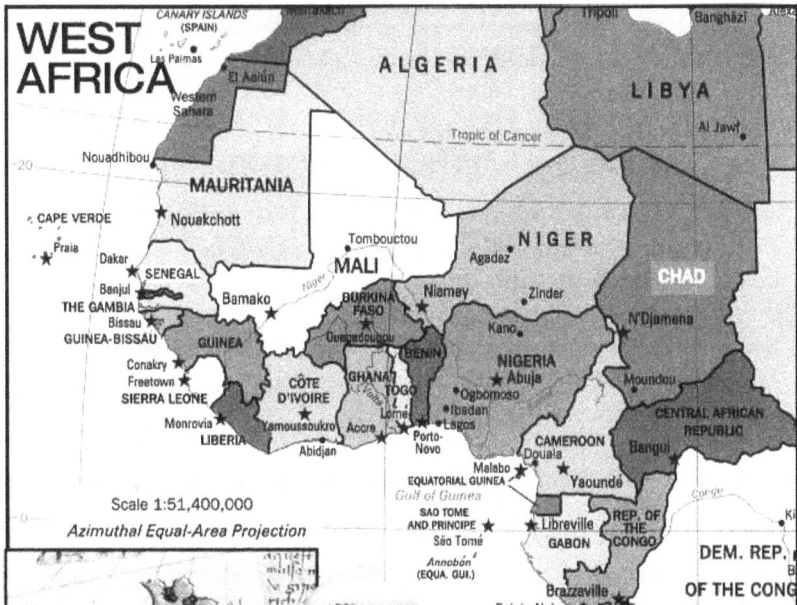

WEST AFRICA

Scale 1:51,400,000
Azimuthal Equal-Area Projection

KING MANSA MUSA

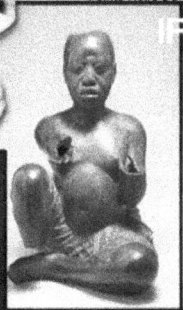

IFE

NOK

DUFUNA CANOE

SENEGAMBIA

SENEGAMBIA

NIGERIA

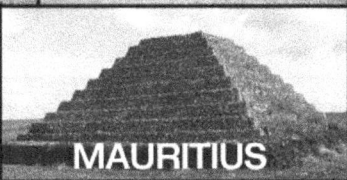

MAURITIUS

tools and mass-produced clay statues over 2,500 years ago. While these technologies were impressive enough, they weren't quite as old as the culture that fished the seas of West Africa 8,000 years ago.

THE MARITIME CULTURE OF ANCIENT NIGERIA

In 1987, a Fulani herdsman discovered a boat now known as the Dufuna Canoe, near the River Yobe in Nigeria. The nearly jet black canoe, carved from African mahogany, was over 8000 years old, making it the oldest boat in Africa and third oldest dugout boat in the world. There are older dugouts from Pesse, Netherlands, and Noyen-sur-Seine, France, but Breunig outranked the Dufuna boat in style over European finds of similar age:

> The bow and stern are both carefully worked to points, giving the boat a notably more elegant form [compared to] the dugout made of conifer wood from Pesse in the Netherlands, whose blunt ends and thick sides seem crude…[Judging by its stylistic sophistication] it is highly probable that the Dufuna boat does not represent the beginning of a tradition, but had already undergone a long development, and that the origins of water transport in Africa lie even further back in time.

In other words, **Africans were building sophisticated boats long before anyone else.**[*]

In 2002, a Swiss-led team of archaeologists discovered pieces of the oldest African pottery in central Mali. The ceramic fragments are at least 11,400 years old, predating most ancient ceramics from the Middle East and the central and eastern Sahara regions by over a thousand years.[86]

Microlithic stone tools at these early ceramic sites in Mali (as well as sites in Iwo Eleru in western Nigeria, dated to 12,000 years old) are like tools at sites further south in Burkina Faso (over 11,000 years old) and at Shum Laka in Cameroon (up to 30,000 years ago).[87] Until prehistoric West Africa is better studied, bits and pieces of evidence like this are all we can use to establish that EVERY part of Africa was full of thriving societies over 10,000 years ago.

What little evidence we have, however, suggests that the earliest sites of West Africa were peopled by migrants from Central Africa and the Sahara (as it desertified). Some of these people originated in the early Nile Valley. It could have been from the Nile Valley that these Black men and women brought the sciences of metallurgy, fishing, ceramics, agriculture, boat-building, and being all-around awesome.

---

[*] For more on the history of trans-oceanic travel, see *Black People Invented Everything*.

Cave art from the Tin Tazarift Mountains of Algeria reveals that the people of the Sahara were building papyrus boats that resembled those of the later Nile Valley. As we'll explore later in this book, the ocean currents of the Atlanta could easily have carried Africans (whether in papyrus boats or dugout canoes) to the Americas from West Africa, North Africa, or even the Nile Valley.

DID WEST AFRICANS COME FROM THE EAST?

Obviously, our ancestors knew how to get around. But is there any truth to the notion that the people of West Africa, who are the ancestors of most Black people in America and Europe today – were themselves descended from the Black men and women of ancient Egypt?

Let's look at the evidence and see what we find. I'll walk you through the process.

❐ First, we need to establish our theory, or hypothesis. It should be specific and measurable, so we can know when we hit the nail on the head. An ambiguous theory leaves you with no nail to hit.

So the hypothesis is "The West African ancestors of Black Americans came from ancient Egypt." We're not going to assume it's true, even if we want to, even if intuition tells us it should be true, even if someone we respect said so. We're going to think for ourselves.

❐ Now let's figure out how to research it. We're digging into the West African past, so we need to find some sources on West African history. Many of the early sources are racist and biased, but may contain accounts of traditional history told by West Africans themselves.

For example, Samuel Johnson's 1921 *History of the Yoruba* says they considered themselves having descended from Oduduwa, a leader who marched his followers from Mecca to establish a monarchy in Nigeria. But was Johnson getting credible information?

In her 1905 study of pre-colonial North Africa, Flora Louisa Shaw, the white woman who gave Nigeria its name, wrote:

> The tradition of the Zingari, as they are found in Northern Africa, is that they came originally from India. This tradition is to be met with again, though faintly and uncertainly recalled, amongst some of the races of Western Negroland˙ [West Africa].[88]

˙ Shaw's reporting is not without its flaws, obviously. She does, after all, call Africa "Negroland," a convention common at the time of her writing. But Shaw wasn't out to insult Black people. She later writes that the Black people of Subsaharan Africa

Did they really say they'd come from India? Or simply from a distant Black nation to the east? And even if they did, is there a way to verify it beyond these accounts?

These early works may contain first-hand accounts and archaeological evidence, but they won't have modern genetic and linguistic data. So let's look at some more recent sources.

Senegalese scholar Cheikh Anta Diop argued that some of the indigenous people of West Africa hailed from Nile Valley origins and that Muslim West Africans used "Mecca" synonymously with Kemet (ancient Egypt).

In both *Pre-Colonial Black Africa* and *African Origin of Civilization*, Diop describes connections between early West African culture and ancient Nile Valley culture. African historian Amadou Hampâté Bâ has written: "The glory of Kush is quite surely reflected in certain legends of Central and West Africa. The Sao and the Bushongo have legends of the bringing of knowledge by men from the east."[89]

However, this still doesn't mean the two cultures (or people) are synonymous, or that one comes from the other, only that there are commonalities. But we also find many differences.

For example, researching the archaeology of West Africa reveals that the region has no stone temples or pyramids. This could be because the soil and geological resources are quite different in West Africa, so we won't find quarries to hull large stone bricks.

But, even if they could have, anthropological research on ancient West African culture reveals that they weren't structured in a manner conducive to massive pyramid building. That is, they retained the indigenous culture typical of most of Africa before the rise of Egypt. They were egalitarian, not a hierarchical society with a centralized government (like ancient Egypt),* at least not until much

---

were the source of all the world's civilizations, and that, when this was proven, "the civilised world [would] be forced to recognise in a black people the fount of its original enlightenment" and "to revise entirely our view of the black races."

* That's normally the kind of setup you need to mobilize hundreds of peasant laborers (mostly farmers who lacked work during the off season) to take on such a major construction task.

NIGERIA

later in their history.

But if we dig deeper (possibly searching for "West African" and "pyramids") we'll learn of the Nsude Pyramids in Abaja, Nigeria. Ah, so there ARE pyramids! But they're not the same. They're made from mud hardened by sun, and take the form of stacked disks. If anything, these represent a method of construction that must have come BEFORE the stone pyramids of ancient Egypt.

This suggests that the migration out the Sahara (east into the Nile Valley and west into West Africa) predated the building of pyramids at Giza. When we find a lead like this, even if it challenges our hypothesis, we pursue it. We want to see where the trail of evidence leads, not attempt to lead the evidence down a trail we chose in advance. In fact, that's what the European scholars did, and I refuse to do the same. Even if challenges my presumptions, I'll research it.

What you'll learn as you probe further is that the age of the pyramids was preceded by an age of megaliths. If the people of West Africa came from the east before pyramids were erected there, this explains why there are megaliths in Morocco, Senegal, and Gambia. These stone circles and markers resemble Nabta Playa in the Sahara. Archaeology is pointing us to the Sahara as a point of origin.

QUESTIONS TO CONSIDER

Could the people of West Africa have come from the Sahara? Could some of these Saharans also gone east into the Nile Valley? Could the Sahara be the source for both West African and Nile Valley culture?

To answer these questions, we'll need to dig into the most modern data available: linguistics and genetics. By looking at the genes and languages of the people in West Africa, we can see if they trace back to the Nile Valley, the Sahara, or somewhere else. But at least we've found some clues to help us figure it all out.

Piecing together the puzzle won't be easy, but it's a lot more honest than hearing a claim that can't be verified, and then parroting it because it makes you feel good. To dig into the question at hand, we'll need to explore the history of population movement in Africa. We'll have to look at genetics, linguistics, archaeology, plant and animal data, and even the climate.

THE STORY OF AFRICA'S LANGUAGES
WARNING: TECHNICAL STUFF AHEAD!

There are literally thousands of different languages and dialects in Africa. It's the most linguistically diverse region in the world. Thanks to the work of linguists like Joseph Greenberg and Christopher Ehret, we know that these languages can be grouped into four large families. These language families are commonly known as Khoisan, Nilo-Saharan, Niger-Congo, and Afro-Asiatic. Each of these families began with a "proto-language," which was basically the ancestral language that gave birth to dozens of variants.

Each of these languages emerged because – at different points in history – a segment of our ancestral African population split off from its parent group and developed its own distinct variation of the "mother tongue." After all, **Africa is not a static, unchanging place.** It is the most diverse place on Earth, in every way imaginable. Cultural diversity is obvious. But I'm also talking about climatic and environmental diversity, especially over time.

While Europe was still in an Ice Age 50,000 years ago, Africa was warm and inviting. But as the Earth tilted, Europe's ice receded, while Africa became cooler. Between 30,000 and 14,000 years ago, Africa became cool and dry everywhere but the south. In fact, the entire floor of Lake Victoria was dry land. Many areas that were once fertile – like the Sahara and Arabia – became desert.

So, starting about 30,000 years ago, Africans from all over – including some who had migrated back in from Arabia 20,000 years ago – began moving into the fertile Nile Valley.

THE STORY OF THE NILE

Along the Blue Nile stretch of ancient Nubia, in the area now known as Khartoum, Sudan, there a rapid cultural transition began around 16,000 years ago. Until this time, the average size per settlement site was between 400 and 800 square meters. This corresponds with the needs of a community of to 5 to 40 people, the size of a nomadic clan of hunter-gatherers. By 12,000 years ago, settlements had grown to about 12,000 square meters. This suggests that there were now settled communities, thriving off of local resources without having to relocate regularly.

When they developed advanced methods for food storage (like grain silos), the chances of them becoming fully stationary became real. With sedentarism (settled living), they let go of the old birth-control methods found among hunter-gatherer groups to keep the numbers of children low (because a mother in motion can't easily provide for more than two young children keeping in two).

Instead, the married were encouraged to have children (more farmhands), increasing populations more rapidly. Over time, growing populations (identifiable both in terms of bigger settlements and grouped burials) may have absorbed smaller groups, causing the community to replace the family as the most important social unit.[91]

At Wadi Kubbaniya in Upper Egypt, they've found grinding stones and tubers at smalls site dated to almost 18,000 years old. Once enough people settled down to stay, they quickly went from foraging tubers and fishing to collecting wild grain and building more permanent homes. By 12,000 years ago, the people of the Nile – who had come from all over the area – were maintaining permanent cemeteries.

In other words, they transitioned from a nomadic hunter-gatherer lifestyle to a much more settled way of life. These people probably started out in the Blue Nile, near Khartoum. Research John Croft concludes:

> It is clear that the Sudan was one of the main centres of differentiation, which produced the bladelet tradition in both the Maghreb and Egypt, a bladelet tradition that is almost identical in their last phases.[92]

Despite the fact that so many of our Nile Valley ancestors were finally settling down, it appears that some part of this community had other plans. At least one branch of this community intended to keep it moving. They may have left the Sudan over 15,000 years ago. This Nile Valley community migrated through the Delta, through Sinai (where they established the culture known as Mushabian), and ultimately arrived in the Levant about 12,000 BC, where they became the major source of inspiration for the Near Eastern and European Neolithic.*

---

* It seems that only one branch left at a time. Others stayed behind, where they established the next phase of Anu culture. After the Mushabians, other cultures – like the Cushites – left the same region with an updated set of practices.

WHAT ELSE DO WE KNOW ABOUT THESE PEOPLE?

If a population movement began leaving the Root of Civilization over 15,000 years ago, it was too early for their language to have been Afro-Asiatic, which doesn't go back that far. Croft continues, "It could, however, have been a movement of people speaking Proto-Nostratic, thus being the bridge that [Alan] Bomhard and others see between Afro-Asiatic and Nostratic languages." For reasons we explain in *Black People Invented Everything*, we call the "Nostratic" by the name of the people who first spoke it – Anu.

THE NILO-SAHARAN FAMILY

About 12,000 years ago, the Earth's axis shifted again. Everywhere in Africa – outside of southern Africa – got hotter. Africa went from cool and dry to hot and rainy. And we're talking about a LOT of rainfall. This is when Lake Victoria actually became a lake! This is also around the time when the Nilo-Saharan language family arose in eastern Sudan.

Due to the rise in rainfall, floods poured through the Nile Valley and drove its people into nearby plains. The languages of the Nile began splitting into branches now known as the Nilo-Saharan language family. Some of these people moved south, following the Nile into southern Sudan.[93]

Others went west. Between 14,000-8,000 BC, the wetter conditions saw the spread of the Ibero-Maurasian traditions across the coasts of North Africa, from Morocco to northeastern Libya. Around 11,000 years ago, the deserts were receding from border areas like what is now Egypt's Western Desert. This is when the Nilo-Saharans built an important site in the area. This site came to be known as Nabta Playa, and it later plays a role in the making of ancient Egypt.

Then, between about 8,500 BC and 5,500 BC, the entire northern half of Africa, including the Sahara, was wet and fertile again. Nilo-Saharan speakers migrated westward.[94] Based on the spread of their dotted wavy-line pottery, they expanded through the fertile Sahara, and made it as far west as Lake Chad.

As their name suggests, Nilo-Saharan speakers were soon settled all across the Sahara and all along the Nile. Over the next few thousand years, the Nilo-Saharan family flourished, establishing settlements along an east-west route from the Nile River to the Niger River, and along a north-south route from southern Libya down to Khartoum, Sudan, and possibly as far south as Lake Victoria in Tanzania.

THE NIGER-CONGO FAMILY

Nilo-Saharans dispersed along the Sahara and the Sahel, the fertile area strip of Africa just south of the Sahara. Just south of the Sahel, in Central Africa, another set of languages dominate. These people may have broken away from their ancestral community about 10,000 years ago.[95] They developed their own language family, commonly known as Niger-Congo.[*] The oldest speakers can be traced back to the southwestern edge of the Nilo-Saharan territory, around the Niger River's headwaters, near the border of Mali and Guinea in western central Africa.[96]

Robert July, in *A History of the African People*, traces the Niger-Congo people back to the Sahara when it was still fertile. Studies suggest that the ancestors of these people must have ultimately started out in East Africa, near the Central Sudan.[97]

When the Sahara desertified, some of its people went back east, while others went west, penetrating the rain forest, harvesting palm trees, cultivating yams, and clearing forests, perhaps for the domesticated animals they had been herding in the Sahara. According to G.P. Murdock, it was this group of Africans who first brought agriculture to Central Africa over 10,000 years ago.[98][†]

These people gave birth to a new culture that would eventually come to dominate most of Africa, bringing agriculture and other traditions everywhere it went. These people are known to us today as the Bantu. The Bantu languages may have been one of the LAST waves of cultural expansion through Africa, but they are now spread far and wide throughout most of Africa.

The Bantu cultural complex (languages, pottery styles, agricultural practices, and iron technologies) developed around Nigeria or Cameroon about 5,000 years ago, after splitting away from the rest

---

[*] The language family best known as Niger-Congo is now known among many linguists as Niger-Kordofanian. If you're wondering why, don't ask. This book is already technical enough!

[†] Murdock traces the first farmers of Africa to this region because this is where you find the origin of a wide range of native crops now found throughout the continent (sorghum, pearl millet, cow pea, etc.). I'd argue that these Africans were actually improving upon traditions developed by those who settled the area before them. The indigenous people of Central Africa, many of whom now survive as DBP, had introduced the foundational concepts of plant management to the area over 30,000 years ago. These people were preserving traditions of ecology and conservation that go back to the dawn of human history. It was through a merger of these two cultures that African agriculture was born.

of the Niger-Congo family.[99] The proto-Bantu language diverged into several daughter branches, most of which stayed near the Bantu homeland (western-central Africa). One branch left and went further into the savannah, where they could have discovered something that inspired them to begin expanding faster than ever before. About 3,000 years ago, a variety of Bantu languages spread into southern and eastern Africa.[100][101]

THE KHOISAN LANGUAGE FAMILY

Throughout southern and eastern Africa, Bantu speakers either displaced or absorbed the indigenous populations they met. Some, like the pygmies of Central Africa, adopted Bantu languages. Sarah Tishkoff says it looks as if these African pygmies "lost their indigenous language," having once spoken a click language like their Khoisan cousins to the south.[102] Genetically, many African pygmies, like the Ba Aka, look closely related to the Khoisan people of southern Africa. In other words, the Original People of Africa aren't all DBP. Some, like the Khoisan of southern Africa, are taller than most pygmies.

And where did the Khoisan people come from? Linguistic and genetic studies suggest that they originated in eastern Africa, possibly as far north as Ethiopia, before migrating into southern Africa. The East African Hadzabe and Sandawe are some of their closest kin, both genetically and linguistically. Culturally, there are many clues as well. For example, rock art in the Sandawe homeland looks just like the rock art found in southern Africa.[103] **In other words, the San, too, most likely came from East Africa.**

Looking at all of the data together, it seems that all of the African language families dispersed from around the same area. Niger-Congo, the language family that gave birth to the Bantu languages, seems to be the odd one out, having originated near western central Africa or the Sahara. However, the ancestors of this people can also be traced back to the eastern Sudan.

REVIEW

The Anu People didn't just expand into Europe, Asia, and beyond. They also expanded further into Africa. This is where some aspects of ancient Saharan culture came from, as well as some aspects of ancient Central African culture, ancient West African culture, and ancient East African culture.

Some branches of the Anu expansion (marked by Afro-Asiatic speakers) went south into Kenya and Tanzania, while others expanded westwards, towards Chad and Cameroon, where we can still find people speaking Afro-Asiatic languages today. There are other African populations along this westward route who don't speak Afro-Asiatic languages, but who possess genetic signatures (like Y-DNA Haplogroups T and E1b1a) that can be linked to Anu people. Many African cultures could have received small influxes of Anu migrants, especially after the Sahara began desertifiying, compelling many communities to relocate.

From about 20,000 to 10,000 years ago, long before the Arabs came, linguistic evidence suggests Afroasiatic speakers crossed paths with Nilo-Saharans in the stretch known as the Sahel, the fertile corridor crossing Africa just south of the Sahara Desert.[104] While some went west, others went back east. A small contingent of Anu migrants may have been the pioneers of East African metallurgy, which quite literally skipped the stages found elsewhere in the world. (See "The Origins of African Metallurgy" in *Black People Invented Everything*.)

ANU EXPANSION INTO WEST AFRICA: HOW?

Between 10 and 15,000 years ago, Anu people speaking Afro-Asiatic languages dispersed from Northeast Africa and settled into the same areas as the Nilo-Saharans. Did they spread before, after, or during the Nilo-Saharan expansion? At this point, it's unclear. But it does seem that many areas where Nilo-Saharans lived simply adopted the Afro-Asiatic languages and culture.

By 7,000 years ago, these Afro-Asiatic speakers made it to the Lake Chad Basin, where Chadic (an Afro-Asiatic language) replaced Nilo-Saharan.[105] Similarly, the Hausa of Nigeria and Cameroon were once Niger-Congo speakers. But due to this Afro-Asiatic expansion, they now speak Chadic as well.[106] Perhaps Anu people accompanied or trailed the Nilo-Saharan and Niger-Congo expansions, and – along the way – they introduced the sciences of pastoralism, agriculture, ceramics, metallurgy, and written language.

CONCLUSION

So what's my conclusion? It appears the people of West Africa DID come from the east, but saying that the Black people of West Africa are descended from the people of ancient Egypt is not as accurate as saying the Black people of West Africa are descended from the same ROOT as the Black people of ancient Egypt.

This is actually a good way to look at things. Because when we say that, we can rightfully say (via our common roots and current culture):

☐ That we ARE the Black people of ancient Egypt,
☐ That we ARE the Black people of ancient India,
☐ That we ARE the Black people of the Americas,
☐ That we ARE the Black people of ancient Europe, and so on.

But we have to know the HISTORY of how these people and places are connected to each other to understand how they are connected to us. To understand our connection to the Black builders of all the world's civilizations, we have to study the journeys of our ancestors.

THE ANCIENT NEAR EAST

CATAL HUYUK, ANATOLIA

ZIGGURAT AT URUK

URUK, MESOPOTAMIA

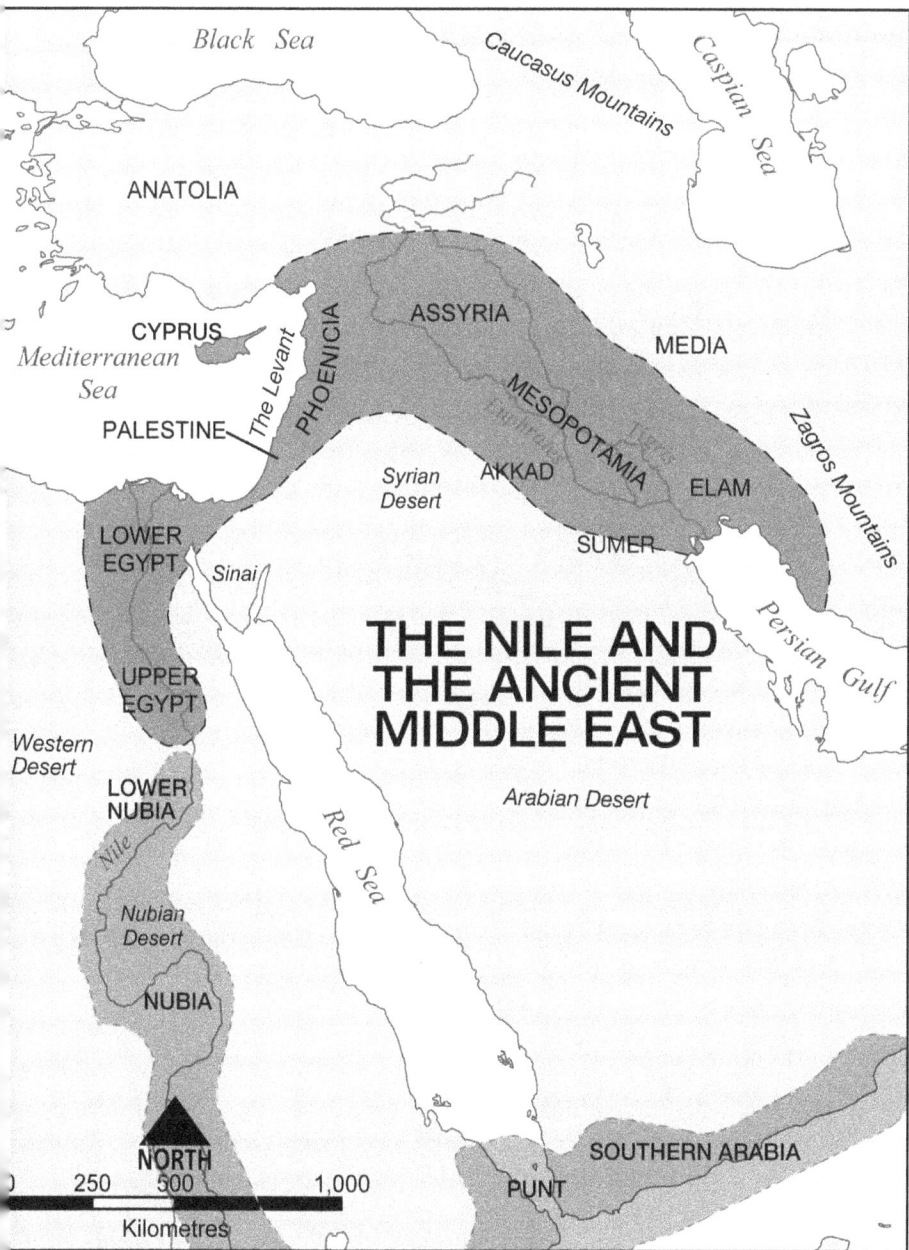

Black Sea

Caucasus Mountains

Caspian Sea

ANATOLIA

CYPRUS

MEDIA

Mediterranean Sea

The Levant

PHOENICIA

ASSYRIA

MESOPOTAMIA

Euphrates

Tigris

Zagros Mountains

PALESTINE

Syrian Desert

AKKAD

ELAM

LOWER EGYPT

Sinai

SUMER

Persian Gulf

THE NILE AND THE ANCIENT MIDDLE EAST

UPPER EGYPT

Western Desert

Arabian Desert

LOWER NUBIA

Nile

Red Sea

Nubian Desert

NUBIA

NORTH

250   500   1,000

Kilometres

SOUTHERN ARABIA

PUNT

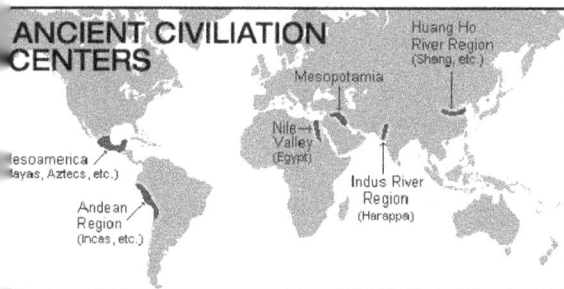

ANCIENT CIVILIATION CENTERS

Huang Ho River Region (Sheng, etc.)

Mesopotamia

Mesoamerica (Mayas, Aztecs, etc.)

Nile Valley (Egypt)

Indus River Region (Harappa)

Andean Region (Incas, etc.)

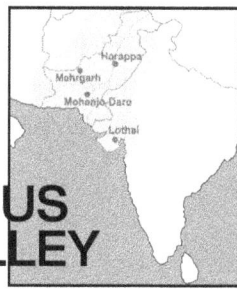

Harappa

Mahrgarh

Mohenjo-Daro

Lothal

INDUS VALLEY

THE ANCIENT NEAR EAST

AKA THE MODERN MIDDLE EAST

"The early inhabitants of South Babylonia were of a cognate race with the primitive colonists both of Arabia and of the African Ethiopia." – Sir Henry Rawlinson

What have you heard about the Ancient Near East? Do you know where it is? It's easy. It's the name archaeologists use for the same region described in the news as the Middle East. It's basically the same area – just a different name used for a different time period.

Historians say the Ancient Near East comprises:

❑ Mesopotamia (modern Iraq and northeastern Syria),
❑ Elam (modern Iran),
❑ Anatolia (modern Turkey),
❑ the Levant (modern Syria, Lebanon, Palestine, Israel, and Jordan),
❑ and (often but not always) ancient Egypt

Archaeologists consider this area the "cradle of civilization." They specifically like to focus on the region that archaeologist James Henry Breasted named "The Fertile Crescent." It's a crescent-shaped region containing the fertile land around the Nile, Tigris, and Euphrates Rivers. These areas were once home to Lower Egypt, Mesopotamia, and the Levant.

These regions might have once been decent farming areas (they're almost all dried up now),[107] but they never contained a "cradle of civilization." They're just the next places we went when our original cradles became overpopulated or started turning to desert. Since Breasted came up with this idea in the early 1900s, modern research has tracked down the roots of Neolithic civilization, and those roots all point further south.

And that's not the only dilemma. We're not a fan of grouping Egypt with the Ancient Near East since it is obviously in Africa and is clearly connected with the indigenous* cultures that preceded it. Of course, if you understand that the geographic boundary between Africa and Arabia was a European invention, and you know that ALL of the first Ancient Near East (ANE) civilizations were Black, you may be comfortable with the grouping. After all, if you examine the linguistic and cultural links between all these neighboring Black civilizations, you'll find plenty.

However, for most ANE historians, taking Egypt out of Africa had nothing to do with explaining cultural commonalities, language, or trade. It was about making Egypt *not African* and *not Black*. We know better.

Anyway, words like "Far East," "Near East," and "Middle East" are ambiguous and can mean anything, depending on how near or far the person is who's labeling the region. Although most modern readers know this area as the Middle East, I'll use "Near East" in this book to avoid confusion with the sources I quote (some sources also call this area Southwest Asia). To be clear, we're focusing on the ancient civilizations that are situated in the modern Middle East, from Turkey to Iran.

This means we're focusing on the history of areas known today as Bahrain, Iran, Iraq, Israel, Palestine, Jordan, Kuwait, Lebanon, Oman, Qatar, Syria, Turkey, the United Arab Emirates, Saudi Arabia, and Yemen. In ancient times, these places were home to the civilizations of Mesopotamia, Elam, Anatolia, South Arabia, and the Levant.

THE LEVANT
SYRIA, LEBANON, PALESTINE, ISRAEL, AND JORDAN

What's the Levant? You know we've got maps all over this book, right? Oh okay, just checking. The area known historically as the Levant includes modern Syria, Lebanon, Palestine, Israel, and Jordan. In other words, it was the part of the ancient Near East where most of the important Biblical stuff happened. In ancient times, this was one of the first destinations for people migrating north out of Africa. As you can imagine, this means that Black people were the first settlers in this area.

When our ancestors first left Africa, many took the southern route

---

* For an explanation of what exactly we mean by "indigenous," see the FAQ in the Appendix of Part One.

from the Horn of Africa across the Red Sea into Southern Arabia. Later migrations took the northern route, traveling up the Nile Valley and then across the Sinai into the Levant. Some of the people who went into Southern Arabia also traveled north into the Levant, where the fantastic conditions (at the time) compelled them to settle down. The first of these migrations began over 100,000 years ago. The Qafzeh and Skhul remains – dated to between 80,000 and 130,000 years ago – are our best evidence that the first settlers in this area were Black people.

THE ANU PEOPLE IN THE LEVANT

The founders of the Anu people came together around 20,000 years ago. They led a similar migration out of Africa around 15,000 years ago. This would be the first of several waves of Anu migration out of (and into) Africa. After an extensive review of the combined archaeological, linguistic, and genetic data, scientists have concluded that migrations between North Africa and the Levant have been ongoing for at least the past 14,000 years.[108] In other words, everything tells us that people were moving back and forth between the Root of Civilization and the Levant, beginning at least 14,000 years ago.

This is why some of the oldest sites in the Near East, including those recognized as "dense settlements" and "proto-cities" are found in the Levant.˙ In the Levant, we find urban housing (houses in pits date back to 12,000 BC in Jordan and Syria), walling (the Wall of Jericho dates back to 8,500 BC), and other evidence of extensive city planning.

Of course, none of this was "new" *per se*. Many of these traditions were simply advanced versions of old traditions established by ancestral populations who'd settled the Levant up to a million years ago. This is why there are sites in the Levant that are over 850,000 years old. And what do we find there? How bout…urban housing, walling, and other evidence of city planning? (See "The Origin of the Home" in *African Origins*)

In this book, we intend to examine what was accomplished by some of our more recent ancestors, the Anu people who introduced urban civilization to the Near East over 10,000 years ago.

˙ Such sites include the Ohalo II site (Israel, 21,000 BC); Mureybet (Syria, 11,000 BC); Ain Mallaha, (Israel, 10,000 - 8200 BC); Jerf el-Ahmar (Syria, 9600 - 8500 BC); and the Wadi Faynan 16 Site (Jordan, 9600 - 8200 BC).

THE ORIGINS OF ANCIENT MESOPOTAMIA

When you learned about ancient civilizations in high school, you might have learned about Ancient Mesopotamia. What do we know about ancient Mesopotamia? Ancient Mesopotamia is the name given to the ancient civilizations that occupied the valley between the Tigris and Euphrates Rivers in what is now known as Iraq.

The first civilization of ancient Mesopotamia was known as Sumer. Reigning over 5,000 years ago, the Sumerians accomplished quite a lot, including:

- [ ] They produced one of the first lunar calendars
- [ ] Their complex system of mathematics gave us our 60 second minute and other important contributions
- [ ] They're were one of the first cultures to invent the wheel and the wagon, as well as the boat sail
- [ ] They had a rich culture, evidenced by a wide array of musical instruments, including harps, drums, tambourines, and pipes.
- [ ] They built massive ziggurats, large temples that resemble stepped pyramids
- [ ] They had the first known codified legal and administrative systems, complete with courts, jails, and government records
- [ ] They developed the cuneiform system of writing, one of the earliest forms of writing known
- [ ] The Sumerian Code of Ur-Nammu was one of the first known law codes, followed by the well-preserved Code of Hammurabi

Many historians consider ancient Sumer the "cradle of civilization" because one of the earliest urban cities in the world, Uruk, developed there between 4100 and 3400 BC. This is also the region where some of the world's earliest writing (cuneiform) emerges, along with major developments in Near Eastern agriculture, animal domestication, metal-working, and city planning.

The Sumerians were followed (over 2000 years later) by other civilizations you might recognize from the Bible, like the Babylonians, the Akkadians, and the Assyrians. These Mesopotamian civilizations are given a LOT of credit in the ancient world (only surpassed by Greece and Rome), mostly because white people find it easier to make these people seem non-Black.

And with good cause, because – by the reign of the Assyrians – they were well on their way to becoming a white empire.* Historian H.G. Wells referred to the civilizations of Egypt, Babylonia and India as a

---

* They were at least halfway there, hence their designation as "Semitic."

"triple system of white man civilizations."[109]

But – as with Egypt and India – these people started out Black. This is the story you haven't been told. But before we can talk about the people of ancient Mesopotamia, we have to backtrack to their ancestors. These people are called the Natufians.

WHO WERE THE NATUFIANS?

"The very ones who claim African people owe a great debt to them for bringing "civilization" to Blacks, are the very ones indebted to those classic African civilizations: their cosmologies, political systems, arts and scientific inquiries." – Asar Imhotep, "African History is World History"

Between 1928 and 1934, archaeologists working in the Levant dug up evidence of cultures far older than the Sumerians. They found settlements dating back up to 45,000 years ago, but the most significant finds belonged to the Natufian culture of approximately 13,000 to 8,500 years ago (when the last Ice Age fully pulled back from the area, allowing new cultures to settle and thrive).

The Natufians had a highly developed culture that made the transition from a hunter-gatherer lifestyle to one of plant cultivation and animal domestication, marking the transitional point between Paleolithic and Neolithic culture in the Near East. This phase was followed by the Ubaid culture of 5500-4000 BC, which would begin transforming into ancient Sumer around 4100 BC. Put simply, the first civilizations in Mesopotamia ultimately trace back to the Natufians. The Natufians ushered in the new era of civilization that would later blossom in the ancient Near East.

THEY WERE BLACK CANNIBALS?

In 1932, the *New York Times* reported on Natufian remains found in Palestine. The article began with a quote from Sir Arthur Keith, who said "They were clearly a Negroid people, with **wide faces, flat noses and long, large heads.**"

Keith connected the "Negroid" Natufians to similar remains from Neolithic Malta (an important island between Sicily and Libya), Aurignacian Europe, Ur in Mesopotamia, and "the prehistoric man of South Africa." The Natufians also appeared to cut their teeth, linking them to the Black settlers of Olmec Mexico, Shang Dynasty China, and many parts of Africa.

But because the Natufian remains looked African, Keith also proposed that they must have been cannibals:

> The Natufians at Shukbah seem to have practiced cannibalism, for it is only by making this supposition that one can explain the cutting and fracturing of bones [of the deceased]...I believe the Shukbah

people ate human brains.

Professor Elliott Smith disputed this theory, saying it was "hardly possible that these people had had Negro blood" nor could they have been cannibals. As if the two went hand-in-hand. When Smith confronted Keith about his "Negroid" claim, he changed his story:

> Sir Arthur speedily corrected him. By the word Negroid he meant merely Negro-like characteristics such as are found throughout Europe and even in Scandinavia.[110]

In other words, the Natufians were white now. If this dude was on *First 48* with a change of story like this, he'd be locked away for life.

ADMIT THEY WERE BLACK? NO, NOT NOWADAYS

No matter how many old books, journals, and papers you find discussing a "Negroid" presence in the Ancient Near East, you won't find modern texts discussing the Blackness of the Mesopotamians. This history has effectively been whitewashed. Yet not because it was proven wrong!

In his 1987 work *Black Folk Here and There*, Black sociologist St. Clair Drake explained the situation succinctly:

> If the early Delta population was Natufian, even Carleton Coon, an anthropologist whose racist statements sometimes embarrassed his colleagues, would concede a Negroid tinge. On one occasion he wrote of Natufians that "the WIDE, LOW VAULTED NOSE, in combination with PROGNATHISM, gives a somewhat negroid cast to the face."

> But he hastened to conclude that these people were really "white", that "these late Natufians represent a basically Mediterranean type with minor Negroid affinities." These same people would probably be classified as "Negroes" in the United States, where such minor Negroid affinities are always enough to tip the scales. In the Middle East, however, they remain "white". Such inconsistencies have evoked charges against the professional taxonomists ranging from hypocrisy to racism, by those Blacks who are aware of their operations. They see a definite attempt to insist that the Neolithic innovators who developed agriculture, pottery, metallurgy, and weaving could not possibly have been what we now call "Negroes."[111]

Several recent studies confirm what historians were suggesting a century ago, that the founders of this civilization were Black.[112] According to J.L. Angel:

> One can identify Negroid traits of nose and prognathism appearing in Natufian latest hunters and in Anatolian and Macedonian first farmers, probably from Nubia via the predecessors of the Badarians and Tasians…[113]

<table>
<tr><td>

DID YOU KNOW?

Egypt and Sumer present interesting case studies in how Europeans approach the race of ancient civilizations. In Egypt, they say the artwork depicts people who look Black, but the human remains don't look African enough... so the people weren't Black. The artwork doesn't matter, only the remains. But in Sumer, the art representing the people doesn't look very African, but the human remains do. There, they say "Just look at the artwork." Now, the remains don't matter!

</td></tr>
</table>

Stuff like this tends to get swept under the rug nowadays. But it's important, because a connection with the predynastic Badarians suggests that a separate arm of the Nubian population who eventually founded Nile Valley Civilization, travelled past their cousins in the Nile and founded a similar civilization along the Tigris and Euphrates Rivers. Anthropologist C.L. Brace has confirmed:

> If the late Pleistocene Natufian sample from Israel is the source from which that Neolithic spread was derived, there was clearly a sub-Saharan African element present of almost equal importance as the Late Prehistoric Eurasian element.[114]

In 2008, a study by Ricaut and Waelkens put the nail in the coffin:

> This northward migration of northeastern African populations carrying sub-Saharan biological elements is concordant with the morphological homogeneity of the Natufian populations, which present morphological affinity with sub-Saharan populations. In addition, the Neolithic revolution was assumed to arise in the late Pleistocene Natufians and subsequently spread into Anatolia and Europe, and the first Anatolian farmers, Neolithic to Bronze Age Mediterraneans and to some degree other Neolithic-Bronze Age Europeans, show morphological affinities with the Natufians (and indirectly with sub-Saharan populations).[115]

In other words, the people who brought civilization into Mesopotamia, Anatolia, and early Europe were Black.

WHERE DID THEY COME FROM?

About 15,000 years ago, a colony of Anu speakers expanded from the root of civilization, spreading north into the Nile Valley and then the Near East (specifically the Levant). In the Levant, they became known as the Natufians, who are considered responsible for introducing the Neolithic to Europe and the Near East, and ultimately for producing one of the world's oldest civilizations in Mesopotamia (while their cousins developed an even older swath of settlements in the Nile Valley into dynastic Egypt).

> *"The Natufian is the turning point between the desert and the sown, between food gatherers and food producers, between wild animal and the domestic." – Archaeologist Gertrude Caton-Thompson, 1969*

The Natufians are considered special in any discussion of the ancient world and its origins. What made them so special? The Natufians were one of the earliest waves of Anu people to leave the root of civilization in East Africa/Arabia and effectively establish a major colony in the Levant. They weren't doing anything the world had never seen before, however. Their Aurignacian ancestors had made the same transition over 30,000 years prior. And later waves of Anu people would repeat this same cycle much later as well.

I'll try to make it a little visual to make it clearer:

People leaving Root (NE Africa/Arabia)		Time arriving in Levant		People already there		Resulting culture
Paleolithic Africans	→	50,000 years ago	+	Paleolithic Asians	→	Aurignacians
Mushabians	→	13,000 years ago	+	Kebarans	→	Natufians
Cushites/Nubians	→	5,000 years ago	+	Natufians	→	Sumerians

QUESTIONS TO CONSIDER

Did Anu people emerge as an outcome of the Aurignacian people's fight with the Neanderthals? Did they come about from the amalgamation of all the Aurignacian people who came together there, from the Levant, from India, perhaps even from Central Asia and China? What role did the war with this campaign play in transforming ancestral populations into Anu people?

The Natufians were the cultural community that resulted from at least two distinct cultures crossing paths in the Levant: The Kebarans and the Mushabians.[116]

WHO WERE THE KEBARANS?

The Kebarans were remnants of the Original People who launched the war with the Neanderthals and won. The Kebarans were descended from the Antelians who came from the Emirians, the same culture that gave birth to the Aurignacian culture in Europe. The ancestors of the Emirians had come to Palestine from the area of the Nubian Complex, possibly by way of Southern Arabia.[117] After more than 30,000 years of settlement in an Ice Age environment, some of the Kebarans had "somewhat cold-adapted" features, which may have made them look quite different from their African ancestors and more like the short, stout people later depicted on some Sumerian statues.* They weren't alone. Throughout Europe,

---

* Tropical body proportions typically come with dark skin, but cold-adapted proportions don't always mean white skin. An easy example is the brown-skinned

many people developed the features anthropologists once called "Cro-Magnon" after thousands of years of living in the cold.

However, there's no evidence that any of the so-called Cro-Magnon populations were white. If nothing else, "Cro-Magnon" was simply another euphemism for prehistoric Black people, only distinct from Africoid and Australoid populations by small variations in facial morphology. And in many cases, these variations are not even "non-African" in appearance, which is why many old discoveries once classified as Negroid were, until recently, reclassified as Cro-Magnon, and why similar remains from recent discoveries (like the Skhul/Qafzeh remains) bear traits anyone with sense would identify as Africoid or Negroid. (See Part One for details)

The Kebarans were no innovators. They are an example of what happens among many populations of Original People who lose touch with the root of civilization. After thousands of years of separation, with no new infusions from this all-important cultural center, the Kebarans were at a cultural standstill. And in many ways, they had actually regressed from the level of innovation introduced by their Aurignacian ancestors.

While Aurignacian people – who constantly received fresh infusions from cultural centers around the world during their campaign against the Neanderthals – were traditionally hunter-gatherers, they also domesticated dogs from wolves, performed surgery, and did a bunch of other stuff the Kebarans could no longer do.

If nothing else, the Kebarans were living semi-sedentary lifestyles. By 18,000 years ago, people in Near East were building permanent homes and showing other signs of a settled culture that would later become the trademark of the Neolithic. But, according to Robert Wenke, the Kebarans weren't likely candidates for the people who would engineer this transition:

> If the Kebaran peoples were doing something that inexorably led their remote descendants to become farmers, it is not obvious in their archaeological traces. Such traces are almost all small concentrations of bones and stone that reflect a people skilled principally in hunting deer and other large grazing animals.[118]

R.O. Fellner adds:

> The transition from the Geometric Kebaran to the Early Natufian culture can be described as the most important cultural change within the Epipalaeolithic of Palestine, as the lifestyle of the Natufian groups differed very substantially from that practiced by

---

Inuit people of Greenland, Alaska, and Canada.

their Geometric Kebaran ancestors.[119]

Ofer Bar-Yosef explains the emergence of the Natufians as follows:

> On the one hand, climatic improvements around 13,000 BP provided a wealth of food resources. On the other hand, contemporaneous population growth in both the steppic and desertic regions made any abrupt, short-term climatic fluctuation a motivation for human groups to achieve control over resources.[120]

Who introduced this science? Bar-Yosef gives credit to the Africans:

> The population overflow from Northeast Africa played a definite role in the establishment of the Natufian adaptation, which in turn led to the emergence of agriculture as a new subsistence system.[121]

These people are known as the Mushabians.

WHO WERE THE MUSHABIANS?

Between 15,000 and 12,000 years ago, the Earth's axis was tilting and the climate was changing. The resultant changes destabilized the settlements of the Nile Valley, and at least one of its communities left the Nile Valley around 14,000 years ago. These Anu-speaking people are known to archaeologists as the Mushabians. We would call them the Anu.

The Mushabians were a distinctly Africoid population, and their contribution is the reason why anthropologists have to concede that at least "part" of the Natufians were African.[122] According to Christopher Ehret, the ancestors of the Natufians were a short-statured African people who expanded from an East African homeland, bringing agriculture and technology into North Africa, the Middle East, and ultimately Europe.[123]

When we trace the Natufians back to their African ancestors, we can see where they learned the science of agriculture. 15,000 years ago, cultures in Ethiopia were harvesting the same wild grasses* that would later become domesticated crops in the Near East.[124] These practices then expanded into North Africa.[125]

So yes, the Natufians may have given birth to birth to modern agriculture, but the seeds came from Egypt and Ethiopia. And I mean that literally, as in the actual grass seeds they cultivated in the Levant were imported from Ethiopia and Sudan.

---

* Before you think we were eating grass like cows, what we mean by grasses are grain-plants like einkorn and emmer, which are older relatives of wheat, a grass that might be more familiar to us. Wheat is actually one of the least nutritious of the cereal grains when compared to the kind of plants the Natufians and other African cultures thrived on.

> **DID YOU KNOW?**
>
> Wadi Kubbaniya is a site west of the Nile Valley in Egypt which has been dated to 18,000 years ago. The site presents the most diverse assemblage of food-plant remains from any "Old World" Paleolithic site in the world, with at least 13 different types of plant foods. Studies of baby poop from the site reveal something very interesting: These people had baby food. They used "fine-ground plant mush" to wean their children off breast milk. "Fine-ground plant mush" is just another way of saying "creamed spinach" or some other kind of vegetable-based baby food, just like the kind we buy (or make) for our own babies!

There are 12,000 year old tools and evidence of crop cultivation in Egypt's Western Desert. Other pre-agricultural sites in the Nile Valley have been dated to 18,000 years ago. This is why the Nilotic Mushabians were the ones who "sparked" the Kebarans into the rapid phase of change known as Natufian culture. These were the people J.L. Angel is talking about when he speaks of an element from Nubia "via the predecessors of the Badarians and Tasians."

This African infusion pushed the Kebarans into a period of rapid cultural change. They quickly birthed a new culture, known as Geometric Kebaran (because now their tools had geometric designs to them).

During this transitional stage, they used identical tool-making techniques to those found in North Africa and sites along the Nile. Archaeologists also found ostrich egg necklaces and fishhooks that look just like those in Africa.[126] In other words, the Kebarans had – like indigenous people in other parts of the world would later do – adopted the earliest dispersal of Anu culture, essentially **becoming the Anu**.

REUNITED

As early as 1901, Guissepi Sergi alluded to an important Nile Valley migration into the Near East, citing its significance in the foundations of both European and Near Easter civilization:

> We have no reason to suppose that the movement of emigration in the east of Africa stopped at the Nile valley; we may suppose that it extended towards the east of Egypt, into Syria and the regions around Syria, and thence into Asia Minor. It is possible that in Syria this immigration encountered the primitive inhabitants, or a population coming from northern Arabia, and mingled with them or subjugated them.[127]

However they came together, the Mushabians and Kebarans mixed and merged and became the Natufians. This was a mix that reproduced the best outcomes of an earlier mix in the area. When our ancestors spread into Asia after mixing with Neanderthals, they picked up the necessary immunities to survive in the most inhospitable locales beyond Afrabia.

Similarly, Nile Valley Mushabians and Eurasian Kebarans made for a perfect couple: One group for the immunities and adaptations needed on a physiological level, and one group for the knowledge and wisdom required on another level altogether. Thus, mind and body came together again, as it did in leading up to the war against the Neanderthals and the settlement of Eurasia.

Since most of the Natufians' culture transferred from the Nile Valley side of this coupling, these people naturally spoke the same Anu language as their Mushabian ancestors. This was the language that later gave birth to the Afro-Asiatic languages of Africa and the Near East, as well as the languages of ancient Sumer and Elam. Linguists call this ancestral language Nostratic, but we call it Anu.

They also continued to look Black, despite what modern scholar may eventually attempt to claim. This was revealed when Sir Arthur Keith first described the Natufian remains in 1932, and it was confirmed when C. Loring Brace analyzed them in 2005.

The genetic data supports this fact as well. As Dana Marniche says:

> New interpretations of biological evolution along the Nile have helped to dispel the myth of the ancient Mediterranean as a type affiliated with modern Europeans or Caucasoids…the perceived lessening of 'Negroid' attributes does not nullify the fact that the ancient type designated 'proto-Mediterranean,' or 'Brown Mediterranean' since the turn of the century, was in no way allied to, nor descended from the type now designated Europoid or Caucasoid. On the contrary, it is today indisputable that the early Mediterraneans-who appear to have been among the first settled agriculturalists of Europe, Africa, and Southwest Asia-were direct genetic and cultural descendents of the Upper Paleolithic hunter of the Nile and North Africa.[128]

The Natufians eventually spread east into Mesopotamia, where their descendants became the Sumerians, and northwest into Europe, where their descendants introduced a sweeping cascade of cultural changes associated with the beginning of Europe's Neolithic period.

These were the people who first introduced farming and animal domestication to Europe, perhaps prepping the environment for a new wave of settlement. Later waves of Anu people introduced metal-working (metallurgy), pottery (ceramics), stonemasonry (megalithic construction), and other sciences.

One branch of the Natufians traveled west into Anatolia, where they brought a similar cultural package. From Anatolia (but perhaps with an infusion from North Africa) they brought these innovations to the island of Cyprus over 10,000 years ago. Again, the things they did (such as importing wild animals to enhance the local food ecology, or clearing out forest areas long before settlements were built) make it seem as if they were simply "paving the way" for a people who would come later.

Of course, this new culture came with its problems. During the hunter-gatherer phase, the first wave of Anu people didn't have a tenth of the problems their farming descendants would experience 5,000 years later. What are we talking about? I'm talking about malnutrition, disease, warfare, social stratification (not just a caste system for different jobs/social roles, but the class divide between the rich and the poor), organized religion (complete with a corrupt priest class), government corruption, and a ton of other issues. In exchange, we got big cities. May not seem like a fair trade when you look at it that way, but it was the only way. (See "The Problem of Civilization" later in this book.)

You see, the world's populations were growing. The more the Earth went through the kind of climate change that made food resources less readily available in many areas, people increasingly adopted agriculture. Meanwhile, people living concentrated along fertile plains and river banks were building urban complexes that were quickly outgrowing the ability to feed their people through simple hunting and gathering. Thus city life (urbanization) and farming (agriculture) emerged hand-in-hand.

In some places, farming came first, in other places, urbanization. This happened all over the world, thanks to the earliest waves of Anu people. Fittingly, later waves of Anu people often came to resolve the issues ushered in by the last period of change. In Volume Four, we'll discuss the most extreme (yet all-encompassing) "solution" introduced by the Anu people around 6000 BC.

WHY FARM?

Between 10,800 and 9500 BC, a severe period of climate change brought a sudden drought to Palestine. This may have been what pushed the Natufian hunter-gathers to get heavy into farming and rely on year-round agriculture. When the Natufians left Palestine, they traveled northeast, arriving in what is now Iraq, where they continued developing the science of farming.

This change led to the agricultural revolution of the Near Eastern Neolithic. The people of the Near East went from collecting wild grasses to cultivating cereal grains and storing the surplus in granaries. They went from a small, highly mobile population to a rapidly-growing, settled community.

But don't get the wrong idea: this wasn't about "progress," because we were doing fine before this. The environment of the Near East basically *demanded* these changes. As the deserts spread around us, we developed Neolithic "civilization" to minimize its negative effects on our people. Not only did we develop agriculture to maintain a steady supply of food for our increasing population, we built homes along well-planned layouts, integrating climate-control technology into their construction.

And this is how Near Eastern civilization was born. It wasn't because some despotic leader told us what to do. We did it because it's what we agreed would work, as a collective. A recent study of Tell Brak, a Sumerian city over 6,000 years old, shows that ancient cities in the Near East did not form because some group rose to power, became a centralized political force, and enforced some new regime, as is commonly believed. Jason Ur, one of the researchers, explained:

> The results of our work show that the existing models for the origins of ancient cities may in fact be flawed. Urbanism does not appear to have originated with a single, powerful ruler or political entity. Instead, it was the organic outgrowth of many groups coming together. [129]

Sound familiar? This is the same way Nile Valley civilization was formed. Why? Because it was the same people doing the forming.

QUESTIONS TO CONSIDER

Was the Neolithic introduced to replace hunter-gatherer cultures that were no longer sufficient in areas that were becoming rapidly desertified? Were the "seeds" of Neolithic resource management born from the meeting between:

❒ 50,000-year-old Aurignacian Ice Age survival techniques in the Near East still practiced by the Kebarans and

❒ 20,000-year-old East African strategies for the "soft management" of wild grasses, recently transported to the Near East by the Mushabians?

WHO WERE THE PHOENICIANS?

Phoenicia was an ancient civilization based on the west coast of modern Lebanon. All their major cities were on the coasts of the Mediterranean. As you can imagine, the Phoenicians were into sailing. Theirs was a maritime culture that specialized in trade and commerce. They established themselves between 3000 and 2300 BC, and spread across the Mediterranean from 1550 to 300 BC.

They later became famous for their precious dye, known in Classical Greece and Rome as "Tyrian purple," which we discussed briefly in *The Science of Self, Volume One*. They were also known for their role in spreading the alphabet from which most modern phonetic alphabets – particularly those in the Near East and Europe – are derived.

The Semitic-speaking Phoenicians enjoyed an almost fraternal relationship with ancient Egypt, as Cheikh Anta Diop states: "Even throughout the most troubled periods of great misfortune, Egypt could count on the Phoenicians as one can more or less count on a brother."

SO WHO WERE THE PHOENICIANS?

And where did they come from? Greek historians such as Strabo and Herodotus said the Phoenicians came from the eastern part of the Arabia peninsula, noting their similar gods, cemeteries, and temples. Today, the Phoenicians are widely thought to have originated from the "Canaanites" who came before them. In the Bible, the Canaanites descend from Canaan, son of Ham. And we all know who Ham represents.

Genetic studies led by Spencer Wells of the Genographic Project established that the ancient Phoenicians and their modern descendants in Lebanon, Syria, Malta, Sicily, and Spain can be associated with two ancestral lineages. One, marked by the m89 mutation, is a Y-DNA lineage at least 40,000 years old. It represents one of the branches of the Original People who left Africa over 100,000 years ago. These people were the first people of the Near East.[130]

The other lineage, Y-DNA haplogroup J2, was more recent. They came to the Levant about 12,000 years ago. These people were present during the construction of some of the area's oldest cities, such as ancient Jericho (c. 8500+ BC), and can be associated with the early Neolithic in the Levant. These people were the Anu. Almost 10,000 years after the Natufians emerged through the interaction between such groups, the Phoenicians were most likely one of the last ancient populations born from this mix.

SO HOW BLACK WERE THEY?

We know that – during the reign of the Phoenicians – the world stage had already opened up to the era of the so-called "Aryan invasions." That is, white people like the Hittites, the Temehu, and the Sea Peoples were no longer gradually working their way into Black civilizations. By 1500 BC, they were simply conquering. Yet the Phoenicians did not become "blacked out through whitewash."

As Spencer Wells explains:

> The Sea Peoples apparently had no significant genetic impact on populations in the Levant. The people living today along the coast where the Sea Peoples would have interbred have very similar Y-chromosome patterns to those living inland. They are basically all one people.[131]

And we know a little bit more about exactly what these people looked like. In his *Les races et L'histoire*, Eugene Pittard says:

> The Phoenicians had nothing in common with the official Jewish type: brachycephal, aquiline or Hittite nose, and so on…Skulls, presumably Phoenicians, have been found west of Syracuse; but these skulls are dolichocephalic and prognathous, with Negroid affinities.

In other words, we have no reason to assume that the ancient Phoenicians were not a Black people.

ANCIENT MESOPOTAMIA
THE BLACK HISTORY OF IRAQ

We know that the people who introduced the Neolithic Age to the Near East, the Natufians, were Black. To be technical, they were an African-centered intellectual infusion into a long-established local community long-removed from the root of civilization. Almost 8,000 years after the Natufians began revolutionizing the cultures of the Near East and Europe, they gave birth to the civilization of ancient Mesopotamia. Again, it appears that a strong Black presence was critical in its rise. This isn't a new theory, nor is it some sort of "Afrocentric myth."

As early as 1911, William Henry Ferris, a Black man, devoted the entire 28th chapter of his phenomenal (yet relatively unknown) work *The African Abroad* to "The Negro in the Babylonian Civilization." Ferris begins this chapter by quoting Joseph P. Widney's *Race Life of the Aryan Peoples*:

> Back in the centuries which are scarcely historic, where history gives indeed only vague hintings, are traces of a widespread primitive civilization, crude, imperfect, garish, barbaric, yet ruling the world of that age from its seats of power in the valleys of the Ganges and the Euphrates and the Nile; and it was of the black races. The first

DID YOU KNOW?
The Mesopotamians built some of the earliest pyramidal structures, called ziggurats. In ancient times these were brightly painted. Since they were constructed of sun-dried mud-brick, there's not much left of them. Ziggurats were massive terraced step-pyramids of successively receding stories or levels. There are 32 ziggurats known in Mesopotamia – 28 in Iraq, 4 in Iran. Notable examples include the Great Ziggurat of Ur near Nasiriyah, Iraq; the Ziggurat of Aqar Quf near Baghdad, Iraq; Chogha Zanbil in Khūzestān, Iran; Sialk near Kashan, Iran, and others. The Sialk ziggurat is the oldest known ziggurat, dating to the early 3rd millennium BC.

Babylon seems to have been built by a Negroid race. The earliest Egyptian civilization seems to have been Negroid. It was in the days before the Semite was known in either land. The black seems to have built up empire, such as it was, by the water of the Ganges before Mongol or Aryan.

Ferris goes on to cite the work of George Rawlinson, who discusses the "Negro race" of the Mesopotamian people in considerable depth in his work, *The Five Oriental Monarchies*. Ferris spends 16 pages of *The African Abroad* detailing the "Negroid" character of the Cushites, the Sumerians, the Babylonians, the Chaldeans, the Susians, the Akkadians, and the other Ethiopian/Hamitic people of the Ancient Near East. He also connects the Black people of Mesopotamia, Egypt, and Ethiopia to the Biblical history of Cush, Ham, and Nimrod.[132]

In 1915, W.E.B. Du Bois published *The Negro*, where he says:

> That Negro peoples were the beginners of civilization along the Ganges, the Euphrates, and the Nile seems proven. Early Babylon was founded by a Negroid race. Hammurabi's code, the most ancient known, says "Anna and Bel called me, Hammurabi the exalted prince, the worshiper of the gods; to cause justice to prevail in the land, to destroy the wicked, to prevent the strong from oppressing the weak, to go forth like the sun over the black-head race, to enlighten the land, and to further the welfare of the people."[133]

WHY HAVEN'T YOU HEARD THIS BEFORE?

If historians admitted that the people of Sumer were Black, there wouldn't be so much debate about whether civilization (agriculture, writing, urbanization, etc.) started in Egypt or Sumer. If historians were to admit that Sumer and Egypt were both Black, they'd find someplace new to claim as the cradle of civilization. Someplace more un-Black. *Like Utah.*

This is because they don't want you to know that **you are the origin of civilization.** Hell, they had a hard enough time admitting that you were the first humans! After it became hard to deny that the first humans were Black Africans, they took the emphasis off "Who is the Original Man?" and put it on "Who is the Father of Civilization?" They keep moving the cheese, so to speak. Every time you realize that you are the origin of something, they say that thing isn't as important as they said it was before.

This is why Black scholarship is essential. In 1985, another esteemed Black historian, John G. Jackson, argued that early Mesopotamia was a Black civilization:

> Before the Chaldean rule in Mesopotamia, there were the empires of the Sumerians, Akkadians, Babylonians and Assyrians. The earliest civilization of Mesopotamia was that of the Sumerians. They are designated in the Assyrio-Babylonian inscriptions as the black-heads or black-faced people, and they are shown on the monuments as beardless and with shaven heads. This easily distinguishes them from the Semitic Babylonians, who are shown with beards and long hair. From the myths and traditions of the Babylonians we learn that their culture came originally from the south. Sir Henry Rawlinson concluded from this and other evidence that the first civilized inhabitants of Sumer and Akkad were immigrants from the African Ethiopia. John D. Baldwin, the American Orientalist, on the other hand, claims that since ancient Arabia was also known as Ethiopia, they could have just as well come from that country.[134]

Here's what makes Jackson's commentary notable: Jackson drew on several sources but acknowledged – like an honest historian – when his sources didn't agree. Although he cites Henry Rawlinson (brother of our often-quoted George Rawlinson) and John Denison Baldwin (author of *Prehistoric Nations*), both of whom presented cases for an Ethiopian origin of the Sumerian leadership (as well as an Egyptian connection[135]), he cites alternate theories, such as those of H.R. Hall, who proposed that Mesopotamia was "civilized" by a Black migration from India

WAS MESOPOTAMIA PART INDIAN?

In 1916, Dr. Hall, representing the Department of Egyptian and Assyrian Antiquities of the British Museum, argued that that the Sumerians were Blacks from the Indus Valley:

> The ethnic type of the Sumerians, so strongly marked in their statues and reliefs, was as different from those of the races which surrounded them as was their language from those of the Semites, Aryans, or others…And it is to this Dravidian ethnic type of India that the ancient Sumerian bears most resemblance, so far as we can judge from his monuments…And it is by no means improbable that the Sumerians were an Indian race which passed, certainly by land, perhaps also by sea, through Persia to the valley of the Two Rivers. It was in the Indian home (perhaps the Indus Valley) that we

suppose for them that their culture developed...On the way they left the seeds of their culture in Elam...There is little doubt that India must have been one of the earliest centers of human civilization, and it seems natural to suppose that the strange **un-Semitic, un-Aryan people** who came from the East to civilize the West were of Indian origin, especially when we see with our own eyes how very Indian the Sumerians were in type.[136]

In light of the linguistic connections between Elamite and Dravidian, as well as the high mobility of the Anu people who carried those languages, it's possible that some of the ancient Sumerians were descendants of an Anu-speaking Black population from India. But genetic studies suggest that a Northeast African origin is more likely for the first Sumerians.*

Either way, the reason why all these ancient civilizations share so much in common is because they were all settled by the same wave of Black people. These are the people we call the Anu. In different historical periods, they established different phases of civilization. In this period, John Denison Baldwin calls them Cushites:

> It seems to me impossible for any free-minded scholar to study the traditions, mythologies, fragmentary records, mouldering monuments, and other remains of the pre-historic ages, and fail to see that the people described in the Hebrew Scriptures as Cushites were the original civilizers of Southwestern Asia; and that, in the deepest antiquity, their influence was established in nearly all the coast regions, from the extreme east to the extreme west of the Old World. This has been repeatedly pointed out with more or less clearness, and it is one of those incontestable facts that must be accepted.[137]

The "Cushite" expansion into Asia explains why so many of the ancient placenames in the Near East (and India) are similar to Kush.

QUESTIONS TO CONSIDER

As we'll see in a future chapter, India was indeed a colony of the same Anu people that colonized Mesopotamia. If you consider how similar some of the statues and figurines from ancient Mesopotamia and the Indus Valley look, is this simply because these civilizations were peopled by similar ethnic types, or do these statues represent elite individuals who actually traveled between these communities?

---

* Either way, we're okay with not being certain. We're open to new discoveries that could shed more light on the subject. And we're prepared to acknowledge when the available data only "suggests" different possibilities, but not enough so that we can come to a fully-informed conclusion. That's the kind of work that can be done by the generation who comes after us.

As we'll see in this book, "elites" were a new but persistent feature of Anu civilizations, and it isn't unlikely that these elite people were frequent travelers. There is enough genetic data, especially in the form of HLA data (which we'll explain later), to suggest that Anu people traveled far and wide, even into the Americas. Could this explain why there are pots in North America bearing faces that look surprisingly similar to statues from the Near East? When we call the Black people of the ancient world our "ancestors," can we interpret this literally? That is, could some of our ancestors literally have traveled all over the world thousands of years ago?

WHEN KUSH BECAME KISH

One of the earliest Sumerian cities was named Kish (c. 3100 BC). Many early historians, like William Henry Ferris, quickly picked up on the name's similarity to the African civilization of Kush, and proposed that Cushites could have colonized Mesopotamia after crossing the Nile Valley.

An Indian study conducted in the 1920s revealed that the remains of Mohenjo-Daro and Harappa looked just like the remains at Mesopotamian sites like Ur, Al-Ubaid, and Kish.[138] The closest modern populations were the Veddahs of India.[139]

In 1931, Buxton and Rice examined 26 Sumerian skulls and identified 17 Eurafricans, five Mediterraneans/Australoids, and four "broad-headed Armenoids."[140] Buxton and Rice described the Eurafrican remains as having strong Australoid traits:

> The forehead was retreating and the brow ridges were always prominent, the cheek bones were rather broad and the nose also was broad, in some case inclining to extreme platyrrhine…There can be no doubt that this type is that which has been described by Sergi, Giuffrida-Ruggeri, and Fleure, and named the Eurafrican type…[141]

In other words, Black folks. In 1933, T.K. Penniman studied 14 skulls from Kish, and identified eight as dolichocephalic (long-headed) or "Eurafrican." Only two were brachycephalic (broad-headed) and four were unknown, suggesting the dominant element at Kish, as late as 3000 BC, was still Black. Some may have been more

Australoid, and others more Africoid, but most were Black.*
Penniman said the Eurafrican skulls resembled those of Neolithic
Egypt.[142]

WHAT'S A EURAFRICAN? OR A MEDITERRANEAN?

And why use these terms? For one thing, early anthropologists
attempted to split remains into distinct classifications based on
sometimes small differences. But few scholars, then or now, could
reasonably explain the specific distinction between a Mediterranean
and a Eurafrican. In other words, it was really about using different
euphemisms that didn't clearly suggest that these people were Black.

As the foundational civilization of the Ancient Near East, European
scholars saw great significance in the emergence of Sumer and its
bearing on the "origin of civilization" mythos. So they fought long
and hard to construct a white identity for these culture-bearers.

They produced mountains of "evidence" to show that the
Sumerians, Akkadians, Babylonians, and Assyrians were all white
people, or – when the evidence was undeniable – brown-skinned
white people.

THE BLACK-HEADED PEOPLE

We know that the Sumerians referred to themselves as *ùĝ saĝ gíg-ga*,
meaning "the black-headed people,"[143] and that can't refer to hair
color in a region where everyone naturally has black hair. But it
would also be unnecessary to self-identify as black-skinned unless we
were now in the company of people without the same complexion.

In fact, this is what the records suggest. The *saĝ gíg-ga* name appears
at a time when a new group of people come into the area, ushering
in great trouble for the Original people of the region. For some
reason, the Ubaid culture ends abruptly after 4,000 BC when these
"Armenoid types" first show up in the mix of remains. These are the
broad-headed minority from the excavations we mentioned earlier.
They're the people who William Henry Ferris calls Semites when he
says:

> The early history of Sumer and Akkad is dominated by the racial
> conflict between Semites and Sumerians, in the course of which the
> latter were gradually worsted. The foundation of the Babylonian
> monarchy marks the close of the political career of the Sumerians
> as a race, although, as we have seen, their cultural achievements long

---

* But the broad-headed remains also tell us that a new minority was coming into the
region. We'll get back to them in a minute.

survived them in the later civilization of western Asia.

Thus, ancient Mesopotamia started out Black, but when white folks came, the Sumerians fell victim. At urban centers like Ur, Eridu, Uruk, and Kish, the original Black Sumerians developed the foundations of Near Eastern civilization. They formalized the practice of writing to make property ownership and other announcements clear to strangers. As it happened elsewhere, pictographs gradually evolved into written symbols, known here as cuneiform. They later built stone monuments and temples, the most famous being the Ziggurat of Ur, built around 2100 BC. Sounds impressive enough. Yet, by this time, Sumerian civilization was fast approaching its decline. Why? The *others* had arrived.

THE OTHERS

"The population of both Upper and Lower Mesopotamia in prehistoric times belonged to the brown or Mediterranean race. While this basic stock persisted in historical times especially in the south, it became increasingly mixed especially with broad-headed Armenoid peoples from the northeastern mountains owing to the recurrent incursions of mountain tribes into the plain." – Historian William Langer[144]

They started out as the insignificant minorities that show up in cities after 3500 BC. But by 2500 BC, there are hundreds busts of Sumerian "elites" with gleaming blue eyes. These people may have been the broad-headed minority found at Sumerian sites circa 3000 BC.

Before long, these people had become the rulers of Sumer. The later empires of Mesopotamia (the Akkadians, the Babylonians, and the Assyrians) became increasingly dominated by white rule and white settlers. By 656 BC, the predominantly white Assyrians were an unstoppable force, wreaking havoc on the Black world they emerged from.

They overthrew the Twenty-fifth dynasty of Egypt and conquered Egypt, Babylonia, Elam, Armenia, Media, Persia, Phoenicia/Canaan, Syria, Arabia, Israel, Judah, Edom, Moab, Samarra, Cyprus, Chaldea, and dozens of other nations. Determined to destroy the Black world, they took special pains to drive the Ethiopians and Nubians from Egypt. We'll fully explore the story of this ancient racial conflict in Volume Four.

ANCIENT ELAM
THE BLACK HISTORY OF IRAN

The area now known as Iran was once home to a civilization known as Elam. Just east of ancient Mesopotamia and the Sumerian

Empire, the Elamite Empire reigned for thousands of years before Iran became home to ancient Media, Parthia, and Persia. Susa is one of the oldest-known cities in the region, with evidence of Neolithic settlements by 7200 BC and a more urbanized structure by 4200 BC.

The people of Elam had a system of government that had checks and balances, thousands of years before Americans pretended they did. They also erected Chogha Zanbil, one of the best preserved ziggurats in the world, and one of the few ziggurats outside of Mesopotamia. They also built significant mounds such as Haft Tepe[145] and Giyan Tepe. Elamites even created the world's oldest known backgammon set.[146]

According to Runoko Rashidi:

Elam was the first civilization of Iran (formerly called Persia), and shared Sumer's eastern border. Diop points to the Africoid presence in early Elam, focusing especially on the region's artistic and sculptural remains identified by Marcel Dieulafoy from his late nineteenth century excavations at Susa. The district of Susa was generally thought by the ancients to be the residence and capital city of Memnon – the illustrious Black warrior-king. The heroic story of Memnon – his courage and prowess at the siege of Troy – was one of the most widely circulated and celebrated of antiquity.

The history of the ancient Elamite Empire begins at Susa, where several Neolithic communities were brought together under one rule.[148] Susa began its history as a colony of the Sumerians of Uruk, but they soon forged their independence. The history of the rivalry between Elam and the Sumerian empire is an early example of a colony seeking independence, even at risk of war, thousands of years before American settlers attempted to break away from British rule. Around 2700 BC, Susa went to war with Kish.[149]

Because of Susa's reputation, all of Elam later came to be known as Susiana. Field reports:

Susiana contains traces of a dark-skinned population which, from the monuments, indicates a pre-Dravidian, or possibly an Ulotrichous [woolly-haired] stock. [150]

When Henry Field reviewed the anthropological literature on Iran in 1939, he found undeniable evidence of ancient Black presence dating back to the earliest periods of settlement.[151]

The clearest evidence can be found at Susa, the ancient capital of Elam. The Black presence here was so strong that even modern Susians (people living in the town of Shush), are "distinct from all other Persian types" and "have the shortest and broadest noses in Iran." Field says the ancestors of these people belonged to an "Irano-Mediterraneus group" (essentially the Mediterranean race of Iran). When he looked at their remains, Field said their "flat and open nose, thick lips, black hair and eyes" reminded him of the aboriginal Black people of India.[152]

Woolly hair and wide noses can be seen in Assyrian artwork depicting the Elamites:

> According to Quatrefages and Hamy the Negroid type which occurs in Assyrian reliefs represents the primitive element of Susiana, whose inhabitants are probably **a mixture of Kuchite and Negro**. The nose is relatively flat with dilated nares, the malars prominent, the lips thick, conforming to a **well-known type**. There may be a relationship with the Hubbashee (Habbashi) of Makran and Laristan recorded by Hamilton Smith. Is this the same people who introduced the prototype of the **Negro Buddhas of India?** [153]

One of the most notable of these ancient reliefs is the Victory Stele of Naram-Sin, the third Akkadian king. According to Dr. Wesley Muhammad, the stele depicts Naram-Sin's military victory over a "Negrito" people in the Zagros Mountains plain of Iran.

In *The Negro in the New World*, Sir Harry Hamilton Johnston writes:

> The Elamites of Mesopotamia appear to have been a negroid people with kinky hair, and to have transmitted this racial type to the Jews and Syrians. There is a curliness of the hair, together with a negro eye and full lips, in the portraiture of Assyria which conveys the idea of an evident negro element in Babylonia.[154]

Josiah Conder also noted an ancient Cushite presence connecting Persia and India:

> In confirmation of this view of the ancient affinity between the Persians and the Indians, it deserves to be remarked, that one of the countries peopled by the descendants of Cush, was evidently in Persia. Josephus speaks of Cutha, which is supposed to be the same as Cushan, as a region of Persia bordering on Media; and the prophet Isaiah speaks of a Cush in connexion with Elam and

Shinar.[155]

Meanwhile, other anthropologists report a distinct "Negrito," or DBP, presence at the earliest levels:

> Both Dieulafoy and de Morgan believed that there was a very ancient occupation of the Susian plain by Negritos who were probably the original inhabitants. Negritos do appear on ancient bas-reliefs. Dark populations are found in Bashagird and Sarhad [Baluchistan]. Maybe that country was **originally peopled by Negritos, the Anarikoi or non-Aryans of the Greeks, who probably stretched along the northern shores of the Persian Gulf to India**.[156]

No matter which way you make sense of the data, the evidence tells us that the people of Iran were originally a Black people, and later a "blended" people with strong Black roots. Only later did non-Black racial elements enter the mix.[157]

As Ella Sykes notes in her 1921 *A History of Persia*, short-statured Black people were the original inhabitants of Elam, but hill districts to the north and east have "no Negroid trace. Therefore there were two elements in Susiana or Elam, as borne out by Strabo and Herodotus."[158]

Who were these new racial elements and where did they come from? The non-Black elements were clearly a late influx of minorities. A full-scale migration of "Iranic" tribes came in the late second millennium BC, ushering in the Bronze Age collapse and the "Aryanization" of ancient Iran. 2,000 years after Black people dominated ancient Elam, they were nearly annihilated by these invaders. Yet, as President Mahmoud Ahmadinejad would gladly acknowledge, the Original people of Iran have not disappeared, even though the original Black features have been repressed.

Henry Field theorized that a mix of ancient Black and white elements gave birth to the people of Iran. He concluded, "Susiana was formerly occupied by a black population, ancestors of the Negroes of India, who were Negritos" and modern Suslans "are hybrid Negritos."[159]

THE ELAMO-DRAVIDIAN CONNECTION

In some of the previous quotes, you may have noted a few references to the Black people of India. Modern studies have found strong evidence for a link between the ancient Dravidians and the ancient Elamites. Not only did they do trade with each other, they spoke closely-related branches of the same Anu language family.[160] I'll explain.

THE ANCIENT NEAR EAST

The Ancient Near East was settled in prehistoric times by Black people (See Skhul/Qafzeh remains), and later "re-settled" by an influx of Blacks about 12,000 years ago. About 6,000 years ago, whites began settling the area.

GUDEA, KING OF SUMER

ELAMITE VASE

SABEAN MALE

ELAMITE/PERSIAN WARRIORS

RECONSTRUCTION OF QAFZEH REMAINS

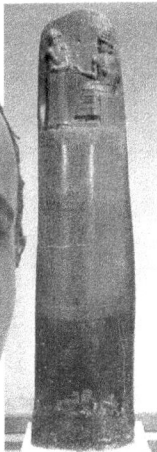

CODE OF HAMMURABI

MESOPOTAMIAN PRIEST (C. 2000 BC)

CUNEIFORM

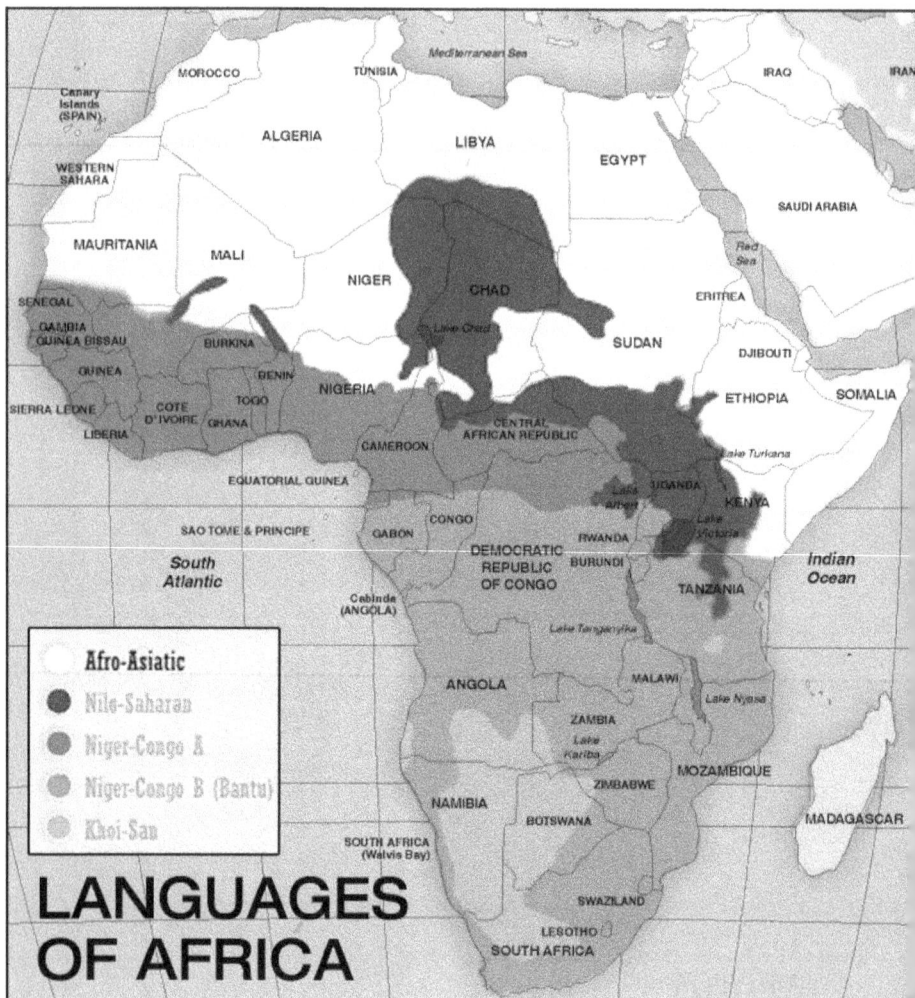

LANGUAGES
OF AFRICA

Legend:
- Afro-Asiatic
- Nile-Saharan
- Niger-Congo A
- Niger-Congo B (Bantu)
- Khoi-San

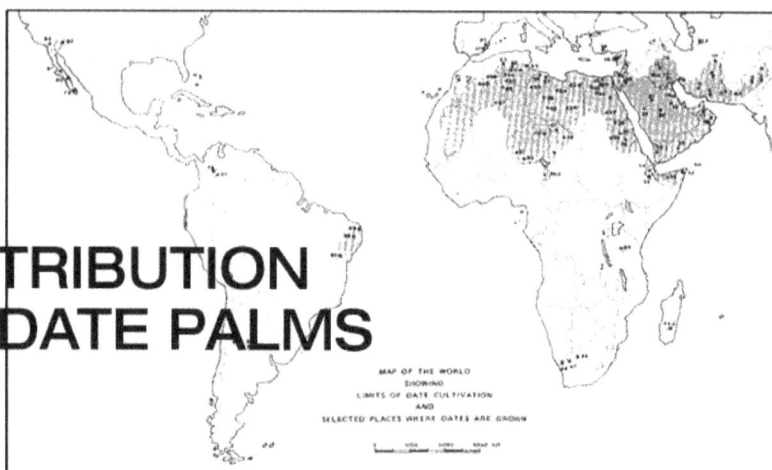

DISTRIBUTION
OF DATE PALMS

MAP OF THE WORLD
SHOWING
LIMITS OF DATE CULTIVATION
AND
SELECTED PLACES WHERE DATES ARE GROWN

Afro-Asiatic is closely related to both the Dravidian languages of India and Sumerian languages like Elamite. This means there was an ancestral language that gave birth to Afro-Asiatic, Dravidian, and Elamite (as well as the indigenous languages of Easter Island and a dozen other culturally connected locales). This proto-language, which also gave birth to Indo-European, was spoken by the Anu people who were around before Mesopotamia, Elam and the Indus Valley Civilizations were established.[161]

This ancient connection is made even clearer by the fact that the native Tamil (Dravidian) name for the South Asian state of Sri Lanka is *Eelam*. *Eelam* also denotes palm trees, which abound in Sri Lanka, India, and the Persian Gulf (where we find Elam). Palm trees occur in Elamite art, including the earliest depictions of the god *Inshushinak*, the protector of the Elamites, after whom the city of Susa was named.

THE BLACK HISTORY OF THE DATE PALM
WHAT DO PALM TREES HAVE TO DO WITH IT?

Palm trees aren't just a Miami/Cali thing. An entire book could be written on the connections between palm trees and the Original people of the Neolithic!

Date palm trees typically grow in areas settled historically by the earliest waves of Anu Black colonists.[162] Their fruits (dates) were crucial to these migrations. As W.H. Barrifield writes:

> Few plant species have developed into an agricultural crop so closely connected with human life as has the date palm. One could go as far as to say that, had the date palm not existed, the expansion of the human race into the hot and barren parts of the "old" world would have been much more restricted.[163]

Barrifield continues:

> The exact origin or gene centre of the date palm has been lost in history…but references to date palms have also been found in Ancient Egypt, and there seems to be a consensus that the earliest form of date palm cultivation coincided with the oldest civilizations and originated in North-East Africa, stretching north east into the delta of the Euphrates and Tigris. From there date palms have spread either purposely or accidentally.[164]

We should probably trace them back further than ancient Egypt, all the way back to the Anu people of Nubia. According to Dr. Arif Gamal of UC Berkeley:

> The essence of the Nubian culture evolves around the "date palm".

Those of you who have looked into pictures or films and saw palm dates on both banks of the Nile, should know that these are not floristic growths that went out of control nor ornaments left to proliferate at will nor botanical species with the sole purpose for a picture perfect horizon. They are property, and very important property at that. They are the Nubian stocks, bonds and long term investment.[165]

They must have first been cultivated at least 9,000 years ago, as there is evidence of date cultivation in eastern Arabia by 6000 BC and in Mehrgarh (Pakistan) by 7,000 BC. If the practice spread from North-East Africa, it had to leave the root of civilization with the Anu colonists who swept out across the globe between 20,000 to 10,000 years ago.

And the spread of the date palm was no accident or coincidence. It was by design. Anu people were the ancient world's leaders in plant cultivation. They brought their staple crops with them everywhere they went. Dates are high calorie energy sources with a long shelf life, making them a perfect food for people in migration. *Plus they're delicious.*

African, Arab, and Indian cultures alike have prized them for as long as they remember, and use them to produce sugar, wine, vinegar, animal feed, cosmetics, and other needed products. Anu people also employed the leaves and wood of these trees to build their homes and crafts, a practice still found in many parts of Africa and India.

This is why date palms are found across a "wide belt from the Atlantic Ocean through the Sahara, the Arabian Peninsula, into Iran and the Indus Valley in Pakistan," **the same belt settled by the Anu migrations of the Neolithic.**[166] In fact, the earliest date palms in Europe are found in Spain, Italy, and coastal sites in Northern Europe, all areas settled by Anu colonists.

ANCIENT ANATOLIA
THE BLACK HISTORY OF TURKEY

Ever heard of Anatolia? You may have heard of the city of Troy, which was one of Anatolia's trade centers about 3,500 years ago. If you watched the movie Troy, don't be mad that all the actors were white. The Trojans were a white tribe that came into the region around 1900 BC, around the same time as another white tribe known as the Hittites. Ultimately, the Trojans were "sacked" by Greeks in the Trojan War, around 1250 BC. Not long after, the Hittites were also destroyed by another horde of whites from Anatolia's coasts, known as the Sea Peoples.

Yet the history of Anatolia does not begin with Troy! Instead, the rise and fall of Troy marked the END of ancient Anatolia, a civilization that goes back over 10,000 years.

Anatolia is situated in what is now Turkey. It is now recognized as home to some of the oldest Neolithic sites. These sites include *Gobekli Tepe* (9500 BC), *Karahan Tepe* (9000 BC), and *Nevali Cori* (8400 BC). But none have gotten as much attention as *Catal Huyuk* (7500 BC). Catal Huyuk was built atop two massive mounds southeast of the present-day city of Konya, with a river channel passing between the mounds to facilitate the emergence of early farming.*

With a population of up to 10,000 people living on eastern mound alone, it's no surprise that Catal Huyuk is widely recognized as the earliest major city in the world. The entire settlement of Catal Huyuk was composed of domestic buildings. There are no obvious public buildings. The lack of differentiation between homes suggests that the people still lived an egalitarian (equal) lifestyle. The mud-brick houses were clustered in a honeycomb-like maze, with no streets or doorways.

Okay, I'm sure you're wondering how that worked. Turns out the

---

* This layout may have been a reproduction of an older African settlement structure, as we can find nearly the same layout in the Nile Valley city of Meroe. Meroe developed much later, but it is notable how the city was laid out. There is a "royal city" for the hierarchy, but outside of this complex, the rest of the site is made up of two extensive settlement mounds, which were once split by a channel of the Nile River. Only one mound has been excavated. They unearthed red mud-brick housing and public buildings, as well as furnaces for iron smelting and blacksmithing. Little is known beyond this, but one archaeologist mentioned "six large mounds of slag and other debris of iron smelting" at the city's outskirts. See Graham Connah's *African Civilizations: An Archaeological Perspective* for details.

DID YOU KNOW?

It is widely believed that cartography, or map-making, existed long before written language. As we note in *Black People Invented Everything*, the earliest "map" found thus far is a wall painting found when anthropologist James Mellaart was excavating Catal Huyuk in 1963. It is nine feet long and believed to be a map of Catal Huyuk itself, showing the town plan consisting of 80 buildings. It was carbon-dated to about 6,000 BC.[168]

people accessed their homes through entrances in the ceiling! But not like some mole men or anything. They had interior and exterior ladders and stairs. Thus, the "streets" people walked on were actually rooftops. So you can imagine how strong these buildings had to be, to withstand daily foot traffic across the roofs! The ceiling openings also served as the only source of ventilation, letting in fresh air and allowing smoke from open hearths and ovens to escape.

Square-cut wooden ladders (or steep mud-brick stairs) usually occupied the south wall of the main room, along with cooking hearths and ovens. Each main room served as an area for cooking and daily activities, and contained raised platforms that may have been used as tables or furniture.

Most of the furniture however, was likely made from local timber and other organic materials. All interior walls and platforms were plastered to a smooth finish, and most likely painted in colors that have faded with time. The ancient practice of painting buildings in light pastel colors was both aesthetic and ecological. The light colors dissipated heat, keeping cities cool even as the climate became hot.

Some of the larger buildings contain ornate wall murals. Smaller rooms served as closets and storage spaces, and were accessed through low entry openings from main rooms. Yes, we're talking multi-story homes.[167]

All rooms were kept scrupulously clean. Archaeologists identified very little trash or rubbish within the buildings, but found that trash heaps outside the ruins contain sewage and food waste as well as significant amounts of wood ash. In good weather, many daily activities may also have taken place on the rooftops, which formed an open air plaza.

In later periods, large communal ovens were built on these rooftops. In other words, they were barbecuing on the roof. I bet your uncles don't seem so ghetto now, do they? Over time, these houses were renewed by partial demolition and rebuilding on a foundation of rubble – which was how the mounds were built up. Up to 18 levels of settlement have been uncovered.[169]

THE RACE(S) OF CATAL HUYUK

Now for the million dollar question: Were the people of Catal Huyuk Black? Modern archaeologists don't mention the race of Catal Huyuk much nowadays, but it's definitely an important issue for most of us, because Catal Huyuk is considered the oldest major city in the ancient world. Among most laypeople, the assumption is that the people of Catal Huyuk were a "Semitic" people like you'll find throughout the rest of the Near East today. But what does Semitic mean? We'll get back to that. Let's first talk about what the "experts" have said.

Nearly every published book on Catal Huyuk claims the site was populated by "two races" before 4,000 BC. Nearly everyone agreed that dolichocephalic (long-headed) people were the natives of the region. But most claimed that it was an invasion from the northeast of brachycephalic (broad-headed) people who introduced the Copper Age (circa 4,000-3,000 BC), effectively saying that white people introduced civilization to Anatolia.

Even Mellaart, who we mentioned earlier, believed that the arrival of this second race was due credit for the massive urban complex he found at Catal Huyuk. That's pretty much what every source I found was saying, although some sources claimed there were FOUR races (also based on skull types).

But I just wasn't buying it. All of the books seemed to be parroting the same primary sources, a common technique among lazy journalists who refuse to dig for their own sources – and apparently also among lazy historians. So I kept digging.

Ultimately, I came across Tangri, Cameron, and Zias's 1994 racial analysis in the journal *Human Evolution*. Their work is aptly titled "A Reconsideration of 'Races' and their Impact on the Origins of the Chalcolithic in the Levant using Available Anthropological and Archaeological Data."

The authors dismantle the "two race" claim and demonstrate that it was only the Mediterranean (Black) people in the earliest period of Catal Huyuk, with some small migrations after most of the building is done, and that non-Blacks don't come in (in significant numbers) until after 2000 BC. After 2000 BC, the "brachycephalic races" (meaning "white people") arrived en masse.[170]

These white invaders are known by the names of the various ethnic groups they belonged to, such as the Hittites. Before the Hittites came, most of the people of Anatolia were known as the Hatti. Yes,

I know it's confusing. As Johannes Lehmann writes in *The Hittites*:

Present indications are that Proto-Hattian, the language of the original inhabitants, was neither Indo-Germanic nor Semitic nor Caucasian. We appear to be dealing with the autochthonous Anatolian people, since their language appears to bear no relation to that of their neighbors.

P.T. English said that the Hatti language made use of Bantu prefixes, while James Brunson cites reports of an "early African-Hattic king, Pamba, who fought the Akkadian ruler Sargon (2350 BC) for hegemony in Anatolia."[171]

In other words, the Hatti – the Original People of Anatolia – were Black. Yet despite all the evidence, the debate continues. Why? **Because white people NEED the world's first civilization to have been the work of white people.**

ANCIENT ARABIA
WHO WERE THE ORIGINAL ARABS?

In 1869, John Denison Baldwin published *Pre-historic Nations; or, Inquiries concerning some of the great peoples and civilizations of antiquity, and their probable relation to a still older civilization of the Ethiopians or Cushites of Arabia*, (yes, that's how they all titled their books back then). In this book, Baldwin says there was an ancient civilization in Arabia predating the rise of the ancient civilizations of Sumer, Egypt and the Indus Valley. According to Baldwin, these civilizations, as well as that of Ethiopia in Africa, were colonies of the original Cushite Empire in Arabia.

The Cushites, he said, were the original people of Arabia, and essentially the "real" Arabs. Baldwin wrote:

To the Cushite race belongs the oldest and purest Arabian blood, and also that great and very ancient civilization whose ruins abound in almost every district of the country....The south Arabs represent a residue of Hamitic populations which at one time occupied the whole of Arabia.[173]

In his seminal work *Black Arabia*, Dr. Wesley Muhammad addresses many of these controversies, demonstrating that Arabia and Ethiopia shared a common civilization (a cultural complex he names Afrabia), that the first Arabs (and earliest Muslims) were Black until an Aryan takeover around 750 AD, and that most of the classical world (as documented in sources from Europe, China, and India) regarded the Arabs and early Muslims as Black people. **The original Arabs themselves saw dark skin as a marker of authenticity, and considered pale skin as a sign that you weren't a "real" Arab.**

Baldwin, too, distinguished between the Ethiopian forebears of Arabian civilization and the people who would later occupy the region, saying Semitic people "are comparatively modern in Arabia" who have "appropriated the reputation of the old race."[174]

Other writers, however, have found considerable traces of the original Black presence in many modern Arab populations. For example, one early study notes:

> Among these Negroid features which may be counted normal in Arabs are the full, rather everted lips, shortness and width of nose, certain blanks in the bearded areas of the face between the lower lip and chin and on the cheeks; large, luscious, gazelle-like eyes, a dark brown complexion, and a tendency for the hair to grow in ringlets. Often the features of the more Negroid Arabs are derivatives of Dravidian India rather than inheritances of Hamitic Africa. Although the Arab of today is sharply differentiated from the Negro of Africa, yet there must have been a time when both were represented by a single ancestral stock; in no other way can the prevalence of certain Negroid features be accounted for in the natives of Arabia.[175]

Grafton Elliot Smith also noted the connections between the ancestors of the Egyptians and the first Arabians:

> There is a considerable mass of evidence to show that there was a very close resemblance between the proto-Egyptians and the Arabs before either became intermingled with Armenoid racial elements.[176]

In other words, before the white people (Armenoids) came in, these people looked African. In 1948, a British oil survey in Iraq reported:

> In Arabia the first inhabitants were probably a dark-skinned, shortish population intermediate, between the African Hamites and the Dravidians of India and forming a single African Asiatic belt with these.[177]

According to Dana Marniche's "When Arabia Was "Eastern Ethiopia," many of the indigenous people of Arabia retain their African roots. She explains that, to this day, the indigenous people of the Tihama region of southwest Arabia still live in beehive huts common to Ethiopia. As late as the 11th century, "at least the southern Tihama (from Mecca southwards) was called Kus [Kush]."[178] Among the Somali or Bin Sam'al in Africa, the Rahan'ayn and the Mahra, along with several other African tribes, claim descent from tribes of the same name in Arabia.

THE CUSHITES WERE WHITE?

What would Baldwin have thought of all this "Negroid" and "African" talk? Guess what! Baldwin would not have approved! Surprisingly enough (or perhaps not), despite all Baldwin's efforts to introduce an Ethiopian origin of civilization to Arabia, he maintained that the Ethiopians were not Black!

Of course not! If they built civilizations and empires before Europeans arrived, they had to be anything BUT Black. And so Baldwin quotes some mysterious claim made by "students of antiquity" that **"The people of Ethiopia seem to have been of the Caucasian race…meaning white men."**

Oh but of course! He even says that when the Greeks called the Ethiopians "Aethiops" meaning "burnt face" or "black skin," this was "perhaps really a foreign word corrupted." He goes a step further and adds, "The appellation (saying *Ethiops*) had religious significance, but **no reference whatever to complexion.**"

Amazing, huh? And this is the way even the most truthful white historians would make a mess of their message. You'll find this kind of double-talk in most books from the time period. In recent years, they've found new ways to say the same things.

In Julian Baldick's 1998 work *Black God: The Afroasiatic Roots of the Jewish, Christian, and Muslim Religions*, we are introduced to an amazing story: that of the original people of Arabia, who – thousands of years before Prophet Mohammed – revered *Almaqah*, a Black God that later became the prototype for many of the "high gods" of the ancient world, and quite possibly even the god of Mohammedan Islam himself.

Yet throughout this entire book, Baldick never once connects "Black" and "race," choosing, instead, to make the god of the Afro-Asiatic people "black" because he represents a storm cloud! As if storm clouds are pitch black? As if our ancestors didn't understand the weather cycle? As if revering a black storm god makes sense in regions that weren't affected by drought?

How this makes sense to people, I can't imagine. The worst part is this: Almaqah doesn't even represent a storm cloud. Recent studies have concluded that *Almaqah* was a solar deity (or "Sun God") like Egypt's Ra. We'll explore some of these theological connections in *Black God*, a title we'll release in the Summer of 2013. For now, let's trace back to the origin of these *cultural* connections.

THE ORIGINS OF ARABIAN CIVILIZATION

Since the time of the Nubian Complex 130,000 years ago – until as recently as the Abyssinian Empire of 1100 AD, Arabia and Ethiopia have shared cultural complexes and civilizations.*

As John Denison Baldwin has written:

> In the early traditions and literary records of the Greeks, Arabia is described as Ethiopia; and this name was applied to other regions occupied or controlled by the Arabian Cushites…At one time, as the early Greeks say, the term Ethiopia was used to describe not only Arabia, but also Syria, Armenia, and the whole region between the Mediterranean and the Erythraean Sea, which means the Indian Ocean and the Persian Gulf.[179]

It's been this way for quite a while (at least 130,000 years). But why such a strong pattern of continuity between every ancient culture that has emerged along the shores of the Red Sea?

First, the Red Sea is no "great divider" of people. The myth of Moses parting the Red Sea reveals that Africa and Arabia aren't as separate as European geographers would have us to think. In fact, the Red Sea literally does recede and allow for passages via land (a natural occurrence attributed to the God of the Old Testament).

Second, every time Southern Arabia is fertile (classical writers called it *Arabia Felix*, or "Happy Arabia"), it is densely populated by Black folks. Every time things dried up, they either went back to Africa or moved up north into Mesopotamia and Palestine, depending on wherever things looked greener at the time. At this time, as it was many times in the past, East Africa and Arabia were so connected they formed a single cultural complex.

In fact, Africa and the Near East (especially the Arabian Peninsula as far north as the Levant) should be considered a shared cultural and genetic territory. You'd be hard pressed to find evidence that people there ever considered the Red Sea to be any more of a geographic barrier than they did the Great Lakes. Throughout this volume, we talk repeatedly about a "Root of Civilization" that spans across

---

* In fact, if we use the tradition of the ancient Greek historians and recognize India as Eastern Ethiopia, it would render the entire Near East as Central Ethiopia, with Southern Arabia at its epicenter.

Northeast Africa and Southern Arabia (and sometimes expands beyond this territory).

This persistent reuse of this region as a center for population expansions (both into and out of Africa) shows us that Africans did not see themselves as separate from the Black people of the Levant or Arabia. The genetic evidence supports this view, as Middle Eastern genetic samples are missing the same genetic markers as African samples, showing a deep connection that goes back long before the spread of Islam or the Arabian Slave Trade.

This is because of "bidirectional gene flow." For example, around 15,000 years ago, a population from the Near East went into Africa, at the same time that people from Africa went into the Near East.* These populations would cross and their descendants would comprise the bulk of Afro-Asiatic-speaking populations throughout the ancient Near East and Africa.[180]

As Drusilla Dunjee Houston observed in her groundbreaking work on the ancient Cushites:

> Arabia was only separated from old Ethiopia by the Red Sea. We would decide that the "Old Race" of the Upper Nile early sent colonies across the sea, which built up the cities and communities along the opposite Arabian coast. This happening before the founding of Memphis or the colonizing of Chaldea.[181]

We now know that ancient Arabian sites share pottery styles, language, and other cultural elements with sites not just in the Horn of Africa, but further inland, in Kerma and southernmost Egypt. By 2500 BC, ancient Egypt appears to have become involved with this cultural complex, as there was also "a quite regular interchange circuit between Egypt and the southern Red Sea countries."[182]

Scholars like Johann Michaelis and Ernst Rosenmuller have noted that the placename Cush was applied to tracts of country on both sides of the Red Sea in Arabia (Yemen) and in Africa. In 1997, Alessandra Avanzini confirmed that sites on both sides of the Red Sea (in the Tihama region of Yemen and Aden, and in Sudan and Eritrea on the African side) represent **a single cultural complex**. She writes, "These sites share enough ceramic features to be regarded as regional variants of one cultural tradition."

---

* Specifically, Haplogroup J (M267) appears to have arisen in the Middle East over 20,000 years ago and subsequently spread into Africa, possibly accompanied by other lineages, like R1b. Meanwhile, a subclade of haplogroup E (M35) appears to have arisen in eastern Africa around the same time, and subsequently spread to the Middle East and Europe.

The megalithic site of Midamman in Yemen is connected to megalithic sites as far inland as Central Africa.[183] It's quite obvious that the same people built these stone monuments. This cultural complex may have extended as far west as Morocco, where cave paintings depict the same type of people as the rock art of Central Arabia: tall, long-headed pastoralists who art specialist Emmanuel Anati calls "oval headed Negroids."[184]

In 1968, Anati connected these people with the Arabian Cushites of the Old Testament (Genesis 10:6-12; Isaiah 45:14; Jeremiah 46:9; Ezekiel 38:5). The motifs at Arabian sites can also be found as far north as the rock art of Palestine and Anatolia.[185]

Thus, in 1909 Grafton Elliot Smith wrote of how the populations on either side of the Red Sea shared a common heritage:

> It seems probable that the substratum of the whole population of North Africa and Arabia from the Atlantic to the Persian Gulf – if not further east – was originally one racial stock, which, long before the earliest predynastic period in Egypt, had become specialized in physical characteristics and in culture in the various parts of its wide domain, and developed into the Berber, the Egyptian, the Ethiopian Hamitic and the Arab populations.[186]

Later he added that these cultures, after living separated from each other, "had become definitely specialized in structure, in customs and beliefs, long before the dawn of the period known as Predynastic in Egypt."[187]

In Ivan Van Sertima's excellent modern anthology, Golden Age of the Moor, Dana Marniche confirms these early theories:

> Ancient Arabia was occupied by a people far different in appearance than most modern-day occupants. These were a people who once occupied Egypt, who were affiliated with the East African stocks, and who now speak the 'Hamitic' or Semitic languages…In the days of Mohammed and the Roman colonization of Palestine, North Arabia and Africa, the term Arab was much more than a nationality. It specifically referred to peoples whose appearance, customs and language were the same as the nomadic peoples on the African side of the Red Sea.[188]

We'll get back to the period of Roman colonization in a few pages, but here's a question: Who were the common ancestors of the pre-dynastic Egyptians and the ancient Arabians? Who was the "root" from which sprang "the Berber, the Egyptian, the Ethiopian Hamitic and the Arab populations," in fact, "the whole population of North Africa and Arabia from the Atlantic to the Persian Gulf – if not further east"? **The Anu.**

ADITES, JECTANIDES, AND THE CONQUEST OF ARABIA

So what happened to the Black people of Arabia? Long story. Summarizing the research of French archaeologist and Assyriologist François Lenormant, Cheikh Anta Diop explains:

> A Kushite Empire originally existed throughout Arabia. This was the epoch personified by the Adites of Ad, grandsons of Ham, the Biblical ancestor of the Blacks. Cheddade, a son of Ad and builder of the legendary "Earthly Paradise" mentioned in the Koran, belongs to the epoch called that of the "First Adites."

Who were the Adites? In his 1869 *Manual of Ancient History*, Lenormant says:

> The Cushites, the first inhabitants of Arabia, are known in the national traditions by the name of Adites, from their progenitor, who is called Ad, the grandson of Ham.[189]

In other words, the Cushites of Arabia were later known as Adites. John Denison Baldwin proposed that the "Earthly Paradise" Ad (or Aden) was actually the Eden of the Bible.

Then what happened? Diop explains:

> Prior to the eighteenth century BC, only Negros (Kushites, in official terminology) were found in the region of Arabia. Infiltrations before the second millennium were relatively insignificant."...

> This empire was destroyed in the eighteenth century BC by an invasion of coarse, white Jectanide tribes, who apparently came to settle among the Blacks. Before long, however, the indigenous Kushites regained political and cultural control. The first white tribes were completely absorbed by the Kushites. This epoch was called that of the "Second Adites."[190]

Despite disruptions by these "barbarians" (as Diop later calls them), the "Second Adite" generation produced Luqman, the legendary wise man named in the Qur'an. Sources disagree about whether Luqman was a prophet or simply wise above common men. **One thing is for sure: Luqman was Black.**

S'ayeed Bin al-Musayyib reported, "Luqman was a black man from the Sudan of Egypt, and his lips were very large," while Jabir bin `Abdullah said, "He was short with a flat nose, and came from Nubia." The "Second Adite" communities included the Sabaeans and other pre-Islamic cultures settled across southern Arabia and the Ethiopia. They introduced a wealth of linguistic, scientific, and cultural innovations to the region.

THE SABAEANS

The Sabaean culture dominated the Red Sea region (on both shores) from 1000 BC to the 6th century AD. Their alphabet was in use in Yemen, Eritrea, and Ethiopia by around 800 BC, where it later evolved into their Ge'ez alphabet. The name of the Sabaeans and their capital city Saba (meaning "seven") can still be found in derived forms in Africa. For example, the names of the Biblical Queen of Sheba and the Habesha dynasty, as well as Abyssinia (the old name for Ethiopia), all derive from Saba somehow.

As archaeologist Francis Chesney notes:

> It appears that the inhabitants of Arabia and of the eastern parts of Africa, were, in early times, intimately connected; for the Homeritae and the Sabaei, according to Procopius, were one and the same people, being merely separated by the Red Sea; and Meroe itself once bore the name of Saba.[191]

According to Runoko Rashidi, the Sabeans built South Arabia's most enduring technical achievement:

> Serving the South Arabians for more than a thousand years, the Marib Dam is traditionally believed to have been conceived by Lokman, the sage and multi-genius of pre-Islamic South Arabia. In effect, the Dam was an earthen ridge stretching slightly more than 1700 feet across a prominent wadi [valley]. Both sides sloped sharply upward, with the Dam's upstream side fortified by small pebbles established in mortar. The Marib Dam was rebuilt several times by piling more earth and stone onto the existing structure.[*]

Another structure built in this was the Almaqah temple of Wuqro in Tigray, Ethiopia. The Sabaeans first built this temple to the "Sun God" *Almaqah* around 800 BC, but kept adding on over the next several centuries. Matching temples are found in Sabaean sites across Southern Arabia. The Sabaean culture, in many ways, provided some of the foundations for what would later become early Islamic culture.

PRE-ARABIC LANGUAGES

Yet these people didn't speak Arabic. At least not the sort of Arabic people speak nowadays. They spoke languages that belonged to a Semitic branch of the Afro-Asiatic language family that predated the evolution of Arabic and Hebrew. In *Pre-historic Nations*, Baldwin says:

> Heretofore both tradition and the Oriental historians have agreed in saying that in ancient times a language was spoken in Arabia wholly

---

[*] See "The Moundbuilders" to compare building methods used in the Americas.

different from the Arabic of Mahomet.

Baldwin added that relatives of this language were found everywhere the Cushites went:

> It is found, also, in the ruins of Chaldea; and, in remote antiquity, it seems to have been spoken throughout most of Western Asia, and also in Hindustan, where it is probably represented at the present time, in a corrupted form, by the group of languages called Dravidian. It cannot properly be classed in the same family with the Arabic, but is closely related to the old Egyptian.

In 1869, Baldwin was catching the connections that we now associated with the branches of the Afro-Asiatic language family. He says that the oldest traces of this ancient language were quickly being lost to time:

> [I]t is very ancient, existing now only in disentombed inscriptions, in sentences preserved, without history, on the stones and rocks of old ruins, and in fragmentary and obscure communities representing the great pre-historic people by whom it was used. In the terminology of linguistic science, this language is called Ethiopic, Cushite, and sometimes Hamitic.

This language family is now known to linguists as Afro-Asiatic. The Sabaeans were another of the Black Afro-Asiatic populations living outside of Africa.

What happened to them? Lenormant says:

> So long as the empire of the Second Adites lasted, the Jectanides were under the Kushites. But a day came when they felt strong enough to become masters in their turn. Led by Iarob, they attacked the Adites and were able to overcome them. This revolution is usually dated at the beginning of the eighth century BC.[192]

In other words, a group of white foreigners attempted to overthrow Kushite rule around 1700 BC, but were unsuccessful. As they were allowed to stay, they were able to grow in numbers and influence. A thousand years later, the descendants of the first cabal were powerful enough to finish the plans of their forefathers.* They overthrew the Adites, including the Sabaeans.

THE ORIGINS OF SEMITIC PEOPLE

Some of the Adites fled into Sabaean cities in Ethiopia while others remained in Arabia. According to Diop, the Cushites who remained in the Near East and mixed with whites can be associated with the

---

* As we'll document in Volume Four, the same thing happened in China, India, Egypt, and possibly the Americas. In the following chapter, you'll see this story played out in the Nile Valley by the Hyksos.

first "Semitic" people:

> Whether in Mesopotamia, Phoenicia, or Arabia, the Semite, insofar as he is discernible objectively, appears as the product of Negro-White mixture.[193]

What does the word "Semite" mean? We should dig into this one. Throughout this book, you may see the occasional use of the words "Hamitic" or "Semitic." 19th century anthropologists used these words to classify ancient people, often directly in connection to the lineages of the sons of Noah, who were identified with the races of man in the Near East.

- ❐ Ham fathered the Hamites, who represent the southern people (Black people/Africans).
- ❐ Shem fathered the Semites, the middle people (Jews, Arabs, and other Middle Eastern people).
- ❐ And Japheth was identified with the northern people (Europeans).

The Bible factored heavily into early understandings of man and his movements, but later anthropologists continued to use the term Semitic to refer to the language family of Middle Eastern people. In fact, most of these languages are related, but they all derive from Hamitic people. That is, the Semitic language family is the offspring of the Afro-Asiatic language family, which comes from Africa.

One of the final waves of Anu expansion (before the birth of the Moorish empire) was the expansion of Semitic languages. According to Egyptologist Frank Yurco:

> Language research suggests that this Saharan-Nilotic population [in the Nile Valley] became speakers of the Afro-Asiatic languages...Semitic was evidently spoken by Saharans who crossed the Red Sea into Arabia and became ancestors of the Semitic speakers there, possibly around 7000 BC.[194]

The Semitic language family developed in the Circum-Arabian

Pastoral Complex, but rapidly expanded throughout the Near East around the 4th millennium BC, around the time when Black civilizations came into their first contact with whites. The Semitic languages can soon be associated closely with "mixed" populations in the Near East.

It's possible that the Sumerians documented the expansion of Semitic-speaking people as an allegorical "flood" which dispersed ancient peoples across the known world. In the Sumerian version, the word for "flood" is *amaru*, a play on *amurru* or *a-maru*, meaning Semitic peoples. This flood myth was later adopted by early Hebrews and worked into the Book of Genesis.

Many of the people who speak these languages were descended from Black populations, but became "of mixed blood" through centuries of white invasion and domination, beginning around 3000-1500 BC. Contemporary Black scholars have suggested that we understand the word "Semite" in the context of the prefix "semi-" which means "half," as in a half-Black people.

This is not simply a play on words. Genetically and linguistically, most people native to the region come from Black roots. Of course, non-Black people, such as the Ashkenazi Jews, have also adopted Semitic languages in recent years (though many still speak Yiddish). In 1931, German scholar Eugen Georg explained the foundations for this understanding of "Semites" as the mixed children of Black and white populations:

> The first general settlement of the present continents was achieved, apparently, by an extension of the Atlantean races.* The new age that began after the disappearance of Atlantis was marked at first by **the world-wide dominance of Ethiopian representatives of the black race. They were supreme in Africa and Asia.** In Upper Egypt and India they erected mighty religious centers and perfected a technique in the molding of bronze – and they even infiltrated through Southern Europe…

Good stuff, right? Sounds like everything we've been talking about so far. Georg continues:

> During the present era – that is the last 10,000 years – the white race, which is the fifth root race, has come to possess the world.
>
> According to the occult tradition, Semitic peoples developed wherever the immigrating white colonists from the north were subjugated by the black ruling class, and inter-mixture occurred, as

---

* Elsewhere in this book, we discuss how this is simply a euphemism for the Original People who first settled the globe over 100,000 years ago.

in oldest Egypt, Chaldea, Arabia and Phoenicia.[195]

To be clear, anyone can SPEAK a Semitic language. But, in ancient times, the spread of Semitic languages typically accompanied mixed populations. This was true in Mesopotamia, Egypt, and Arabia. Despite this new era of "mixed" populations, Arabia maintained its ties to Africa and their shared opposition to the rise of white power.

THE ROMAN CONQUEST

If it's still somewhat unclear that Arabia and Ethiopia shared a common culture, one need only look at their common enemy for clues. In the *Res Gestae Divi Augusti* (written in the year 14 AD), the Roman emperor Augustus recalls his attempt at conquering the Black people of the Red Sea. To do this, he had to launch dual campaigns:

> I extended the borders of all the provinces of the Roman people which neighbored nations not subject to our rule…By my order and auspices two armies were led at about the same time into Ethiopia and into that part of Arabia which is called Happy, and the troops of each nation of enemies were slaughtered in battle and many towns captured. **They penetrated into Ethiopia all the way to the town Nabata, which is near to Meroe; and into Arabia all the way to the border of the Sabaei,** advancing to the town Mariba. I added Egypt to the rule of the Roman people.[196]

Notice that – in order to conquer Egypt – Augustus had to conquer Arabia. Since this time, the crusades against Black Arabia have been ongoing and relentless. As Wesley Muhammad explains in his research on the Aryanization of Islam, whites FEARED a unification of the world's Black people through Islam ever since it emerged among the Black communities of the Middle East, and even more so when it began spreading further into Africa and Asia.

"Mohammedanism can still give the natives a motive for animosity against Europeans and a unity of which they are otherwise incapable." – Sir Charles Elliott

It's no wonder that renowned Eurocentrist Lothrop Stoddard declared his fears thus in 1920:

> Islam is as yet unknown south of the Zambezi, but white men universally dread the possibility of its appearance, fearing its effect upon the natives. Of course Christianity has made distinct progress in the Dark Continent…In so far as he is Christianized, the negro's savage instincts will be restrained and he will be disposed to acquiesce in white tutelage. In so far as he is Islamized, the negro's warlike propensities will be inflamed, and he will be used as the tool of Arab Pan-Islamism seeking to **drive the white man from Africa** and make the continent its very own.[197]

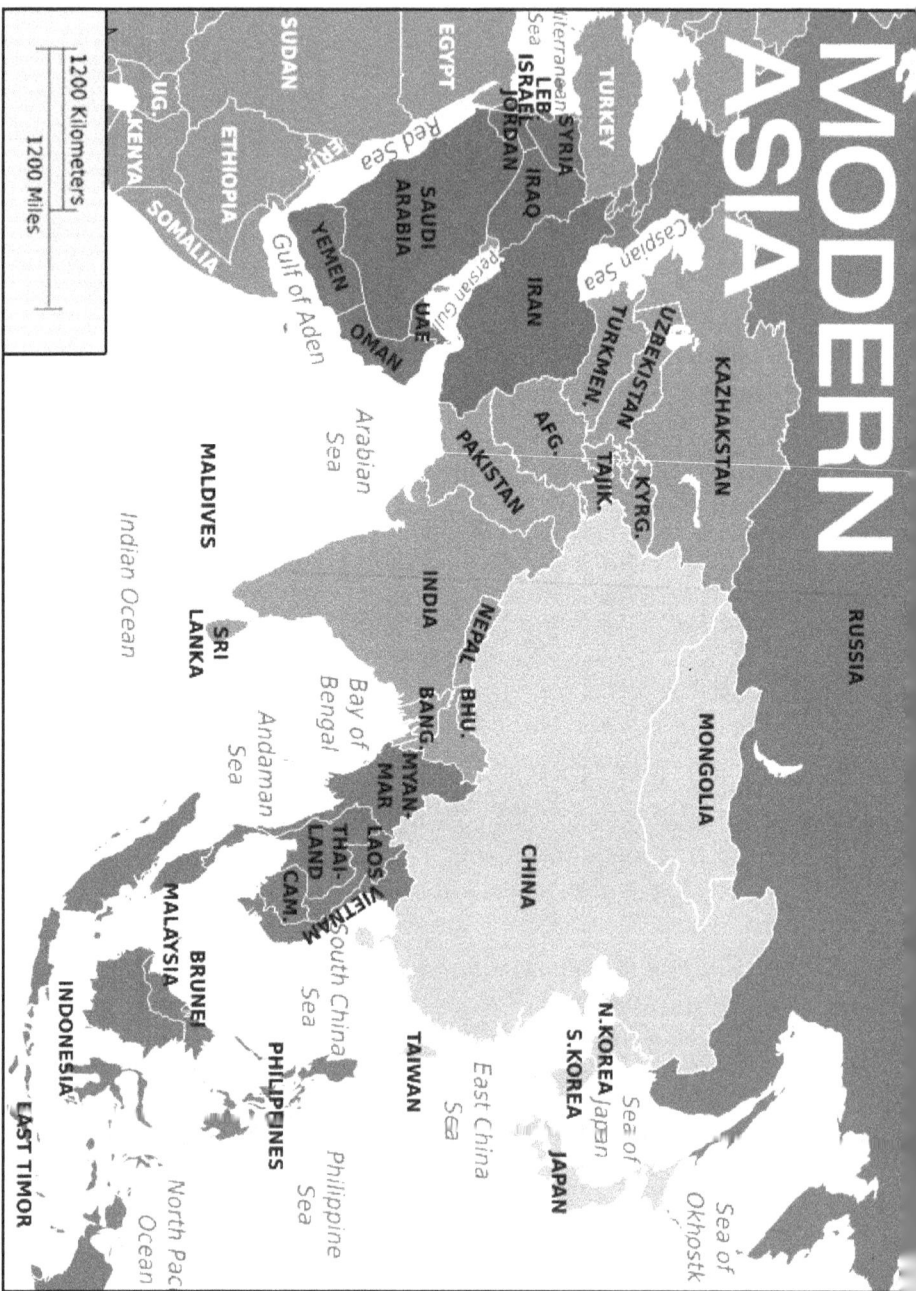

MODERN ASIA

1200 Kilometers

1200 Miles

TURKEY
Mediterranean Sea
SYRIA
LEB.
ISRAEL
JORDAN
IRAQ
IRAN
Caspian Sea
TURKMEN.
UZBEKISTAN
KAZHAKSTAN
TAJIK.
KYRG.
Red Sea
SAUDI ARABIA
YEMEN
UAE
OMAN
Persian Gulf
AFG.
PAKISTAN
Gulf of Aden
EGYPT
SUDAN
ETHIOPIA
SOMALIA
UG.
KENYA

Arabian Sea
MALDIVES
Indian Ocean
INDIA
NEPAL
BHU.
BANG.
SRI LANKA
Bay of Bengal
Andaman Sea
MYAN-MAR
THAI-LAND
LAOS
VIETNAM
CAM.

RUSSIA
MONGOLIA
CHINA
N.KOREA
S.KOREA
JAPAN
Sea of Japan
Sea of Okhostk
East China Sea

TAIWAN
South China Sea
BRUNEI
MALAYSIA
PHILIPPINES
Philippine Sea
North Pacific Ocean
INDONESIA
EAST TIMOR

THE INDUS VALLEY

THE "EASTERN ETHIOPIANS"

"The conflicting claims of Chaldea, India, and Egypt, to the invention of the sciences, are reconciled by the supposition that they were peopled by a common race, a race which appears to have taken the lead among the families of the ancient world, in commerce, civilization, and the arts..." — *Josiah Conder*

The Indus Valley Civilization flourished across modern Pakistan, India, and Afghanistan. At its height, this civilization encompassed a triangular area approximately one thousand miles on each side, making it one of the largest of the world's ancient civilizations. Some of the highlights from this civilization include:

❒ They built polar-aligned pre-planned cities along sophisticated grids.

❒ They paid immense attention to water control, developing a plethora of hydraulic features such as drains, wells, sump pits, sewers, gutters, public baths, and bathrooms, complete with flushing toilets.

❒ They developed a unique and still-undeciphered written script.

❒ They achieved great accuracy in measuring length, mass, and time, being among the first to develop a binary system of uniform weights and measures, as well as the ruler.

❒ They also used this binary measuring system in architectural features such as brick size.

❒ They enjoyed considerable peace and freedom, with no military-related materials, weapons, or fortifications.

❒ They built efficient municipal governments, but without a huge divide between the governors and the people, as there were no palaces, forts, or other types of "power centers."

❒ They were one of the first civilizations to use the wheel in transport, and at Lothal, they built one of the world's first boat docks as well as an early compass.

❒ They also employed advanced metallurgy and the use of curved saws and twisted drills.

❒ They had a massive trade network. For example, they were exporting cotton to their folks in Mesopotamia, Egypt, and East Africa over

4,000 years ago.

The most well-known cities of the Indus Valley civilization are known as Mohenjo-Daro, Harappa, and Lothal. Mohenjo-Daro was first occupied about 3,500 BC. Around 2500 BC, its people built a massive city, constructed almost entirely of kiln-fired bricks. The city was laid out along a grid of intersecting streets like Washington D.C.

There were twelve main streets, with eleven blocks for residential dwellings and a twelfth dominated by the Citadel, or the "government" seat of the elite. There were public baths, entertainment centers, and public plazas. The city of Harappa, about 400 miles away, was built almost identically.

The cities also had sophisticated sewage systems, complete with manhole covers! There were public restrooms on every block, with sewers large enough to walk in (of course, you'd probably have preferred to walk on the paved streets.) They also had flushing toilets leading to enclosed drainage systems made of clay pipes connected to the outside sewers by open brick gutters.

WHO WERE THE PEOPLE WHO BUILT THESE CITIES?

According to Vidya Prakash Tyagi, the Africoid people of India (who later became its "Negritos") were followed by Veddoid/Australoid people. These people were the bulk of the population when the Neolithic Age came to India:

> Veddoid peoples were characterised by gracile body types, dark skin and wavy hair, broad, flat noses and fleshy, protruding lips. They had long heads with low foreheads and prominent eye ridges, thick jaws, large teeth and small chins. The Australoids laid the foundation of Indian civilization. They cultivated rice and vegetables and made sugar from sugarcane. Their languages have survived in the Central and Eastern India. At present this race includes a large number of groups of peoples stretching from Iberia to India. The characteristic type appears in late Natufian times in Palestine and may have been differentiated in the southern steppes of Northern Africa and in Asia, and spread westwards and eastwards.[198]

Studies have established that human remains from Mohenjo-Daro and Harappa were "proto-Australoid," and looked like the skulls of Veddah people still living in India's forest regions.[199] According to the author of *Tribes of India*, Veddoid people, such as the Chenchus and Kadars, "represent a racial type which extends from south Arabia eastwards across India, and as far as parts of the Southeast Asian mainland and Indonesia. Intermixed with other racial types, the Veddoid element is found in most of the tribes of Southern and

Middle India…"[200]* The ancient skulls from Mohenjo-Daro and Harappa also resembled remains from Ur, Kish and Al-Ubaid in ancient Mesopotamia.[201]

Were these the people who introduced Neolithic culture? Did they establish the Indus Valley civilization on their own? Or was there another population in the mix? In his 1937 *Environment, Race, and Migration*, anthropologist Thomas Griffith Taylor tells the story of the people who came long after the earliest migrations into India:

> The Veddah-Australoids were apparently followed into India by the Dravidian peoples who are found in the purest form perhaps in the Southern Indian jungles. Of these are the Kota, Badaga, and Kurumba peoples of the Nilgiri Mountains of South India. They have almost leptorhine [narrow] noses…and are somewhat taller than most of the so-called Dravidians.

Perhaps thanks to their coarse, wavy hair and narrow noses, Thomas Huxley associated these Black-skinned people with the ancient Egyptians who shared these features.[202] Taylor continues:

> It seems probable, as Ruggeri suggests, that the Dravidian language was imposed on aboriginal Veddah types by relatively few invaders of the Kurumba type. These latter were in many ways akin to the Ethiopians of Eastern Africa. It seems likely that the remarkable cultures recently discovered along the Indus at Mohenjo-Daro, Harappa, etc., were developed about 3000 BC by peoples belonging to this Ethiopian (or Mediterranean) race, akin to the Kurumbas of today. These cities were in communication with Sumeria, and in many of its phases their culture excelled the contemporary Egyptian civilization.[203]

In other words, these were the Anu people who built the first urban civilizations across Asia. Later in this chapter, we'll dig deep into the Dravidian languages they brought with them.

LINKS BETWEEN MESOPOTAMIA AND THE INDUS VALLEY

Why did the people of the Indus Valley look just like the people of ancient Mesopotamia? At a symposium on Dravidian civilization, Professor of Asian Studies, Andre F. Sjoberg observed:

> It might be argued that Eastern Africa, the Near East, Iran, and parts of India formed a single culture pool from the Neolithic period onward almost to the beginning of the Christian era, a region

---

* The author continues, "The Veddoid element is absent among the hill tribes of Northeast India, who belong to a racial stratum usually described as Palaeo-Mongoloid, which extends over wide areas of Southeast Asia, including Indonesia and the Philippines." We discuss the Paleo-Mongoloid population of India in Part One.

where ideas and objects traveled back and forth...There is a good deal of archaeological evidence for maritime relations during the first three millennia BC, and perhaps earlier, between the western coast of India and Iran, Mesopotamia, the Eastern Mediterranean, East Africa, Egypt, and parts of Arabia.[204]

This would explain the early trade relationships between the Indus Valley and the Near East. Mesopotamian texts speak of trading with at least two seafaring civilizations – Makkan and Meluha – near the Indus Valley. According to Omar Khan's educational site *Harrappa.com*:

> Ancient Mesopotamian texts speak of trading with at least two seafaring civilizations – Magan and Meluhha – in the neighborhood of South Asia in the third millennium BC This trade was conducted with real financial sophistication in amounts that could involve tons of copper. The Mesopotamians speak of Meluhha as a land of exotic commodities. A wide variety of objects produced in the Indus region have been found at sites in Mesopotamia.[205]

The pictographic script of the Indus Valley is another sign of long-distance connections. The undeciphered script of Rapa Nui (Easter Island) looks surprisingly similar to the script found at Mohenjo-Daro and Harappa, as does the undeciphered script of ancient Elam in the Near East. **In other words, the Anu went everywhere.**

INDIA MEANS BLACK?

According to Drusilla Dunjee Houston, "The name India means black, and Condor thinks that it was employed only to designate the home of the Asiatic Ethiopians."[207] When I attempted to verify this claim (as I do with all my secondary sources) by finding the primary source cited, I couldn't find anything. I didn't want to quote a source I couldn't verify, so I was prepared to drop this reference.

But after digging in a few different directions, I realized that Houston was referring to Josiah Conder (not Condor). And Conder did indeed make such a statement. In fact, Conder wrote that the ancient Cushite Empire extended across India, Persia, Arabia, and Ethiopia, and introduced great advances in all of these regions:

> Some of the tribes of this [Cushite] family were the first navigators. The invention of letters probably originated with them, the

necessity for this medium of intercourse naturally rising out of the extension of commerce; and the first astronomers were probably these adventurous navigators of the southern deep. The conflicting claims of Chaldea, India, and Egypt, to the invention of the sciences, are reconciled by the supposition that they were peopled by a common race, a race which appears to have taken the lead among the families of the ancient world, in commerce, civilization, and the arts...[208]

Houston reports that this Cushite civilization was one of the world's best places to live:

> The villagers united of their own accord to build motes, halls and rest houses. They followed the same plan in building reservoirs, in road mending and park building. There were no landlords and no paupers. There was little if any crime. The people dwelt with open doors. These people occupied a social grade quite above our village folk. They held it degradation to hire. These traits are quite contrary to the nature of the races called Indo-European that peopled western Europe. They were quite contrary to Turanian or Semitic nature as it developed in Asia, but was the nature of Ethiopians and from this foundation of communal life that they laid in southern Europe, in early Chaldea and elsewhere, evolved the foundation and ideals from which the democracies of our times were developed.

> It was by this simple system, as revealed in the communal districts of India – which cannot function perfectly, because of the spirit of exploitation and foreign rule – this system of cooperation, of the Cushite race that built the wonderful temples, palaces and giant engineering works of the past that today bewilder the beholder. The basis of the wonderful achievements of Babylonia, Egypt and Ethiopia was this communal system. It is for the results they gained that we should weigh this system, seemingly impossible to us, for its value. It was by their combined strength that they gained and held world sovereignty for so many thousands of years.[209]

INDUS KUSH?

An expert on Hindu mythology, Francis Wilford said Sanskrit writings describe the extended domains of the ancient Cushite Empire, including records of relations with ancient Egypt. There is even mention of a migration from the Upper Nile into India, representing an ancient wave of settlement.

The Sanskrit *Puranas* divide the known world into seven *dwipas*, or divisions. *Sancha-Dwipa* referred to Africa in general, while *Cusha-Dwipa* was the land of Cush, which extended west from the Nile Valley into the Mediterranean, and east into India.[210] Confirmation of this claim can be found in Baldwin's *Pre-Historic Nations*:

> The old Sanskrit geographers applied the term Cusha-dwipa to very nearly the same regions which the ancient Greeks described as

Ethiopia.

It included Arabia, Asia Minor, Syria from the mouths of the Nile, Armenia, the countries on the Euphrates and Tigris, a large part of the region north of the Persian Gulf, and, finally, an extended region in Africa.

In remote pre-historic times it was the richest, most populous, and most enlightened portion of the world. Cusha-dwipa was in two parts; so, according to Homer and the Greeks, was Ethiopia "divided" into two parts, one being Asiatic and the other African.

All accounts agree in stating that this African Cusha-dwipa was created by emigration from Arabia and from countries connected with it, and it seems to have extended not only northward, but also down the southeastern coast of Africa, and so far into the interior as to include the Sotna-Giri, or Mountains of the Moon, and the lake regions around the sources of the Nile.211

This is probably how the region got the name *Indus Kush*.

ETHIOPIANS IN INDIA?

Following India's original Africoid and Australoid settlers, Thomas Griffith Taylor notes a population in Madras who are "prognathous and with the receding forehead of the Negro rather than of the Veddah."213 These people represent another phase of Black immigration into India. These are the people who Baldwin, Rawlinson, and Drusilla Dunjee Houston called the Cushites of India. Houston says:

> Cushites entering India in primitive ages perhaps found aboriginal Malays. They did not exterminate them but conciliated, civilized and to some extent absorbed them. This was the Ethiopian custom over their wide domains.214

As John Block Friedman notes in *The Monstrous Races in Medieval Art and Thought*, ancient Greek historian Pliny often confused Ethiopia and India because of the similarities between their people:

> In this he was simply following a tradition as old as Homer (Odyssey 1.23-24), who had spoken of two races of "Aithiopes" –

DID YOU KNOW?

In 1870, British anatomist Thomas Huxley, noting that many of the Egyptians did not have woolly hair, theorized that they were related to same type of wavy-haired Black people found throughout ancient India. Huxley said:

"[A]lthough the Egyptian has been much modified by civilization and probably by admixture, he still retains the dark skin, the black, silky, wavy hair, the long skull, the fleshy lips, and broadish alæ of the nose which we know distinguished his remote ancestors, and which cause both him and them to approach the Australian and the "Dasyu" [of India] more nearly than they do any other form of mankind."[217]

meaning "burnt faces," according to popular etymology. Ctesias had actually called Indians Ethiopians, a confusion that continued in both Greek and Latin writers through the Christian period.

Sidonius, for example, spoke of an Indian "like the Ethiopian in hue," and the author of the Greek *Barlaam and Iosaphat* claimed in the preface that his tale came "from the inner land of the Ethiopians, called the land of the Indians." Because of this confusion, "Ethiopia" must be understood in the geographic portions of this study as a vague literary term rather than one denoting a specific place.[215]

THE MIX THAT BECAME ANCIENT INDIA

Both J.H. Hutton and B.S. Guha describe a wave of non-whites who follow the Australoid wave, and can be identified with the Anu people. Like many anthropologists, they call these people "Mediterranean." In Hutton's system, there are "Early Mediterraneans" and "Advanced Mediterraneans":

> The Early Mediterraneans reached South India where their representatives are still found in Karnataka and Tamil Nadu. They are also found in the tribal belt stretching from Gujarat to West Bengal. They have medium stature, brown to black complexion, and slight built.

> The Advanced Mediterraneans...are the early Dravidian people who were associated with the Indus Valley Civilisation. They were the Pre-Aryan people who mingled with the Aryans. They were taller and fairer than the Early Mediterraneans. They spread over Punjab, Haryana, Uttar Pradesh, and Bihar.[216]

For Guha, these people "came to India in successive waves from the Mediterranean region." He identified three sub-groups of Mediterraneans: (a) the Paleo-Mediterranean, (b) the Mediterranean, and (c) the Oriental (or Mongoloid) type. It is only after these people establish urban civilization that anthropologists like Guha and Hutton note the influx of a people they call Aryans.

In other words, Australoid, Africoid, and Paleo-Mongoloid people contributed to the Black population who built the ancient Indus Valley cities of Mohenjo-Daro and Harappa. They were also closely

MEHRGARH, INDUS VALLEY (7500-2500 BC)

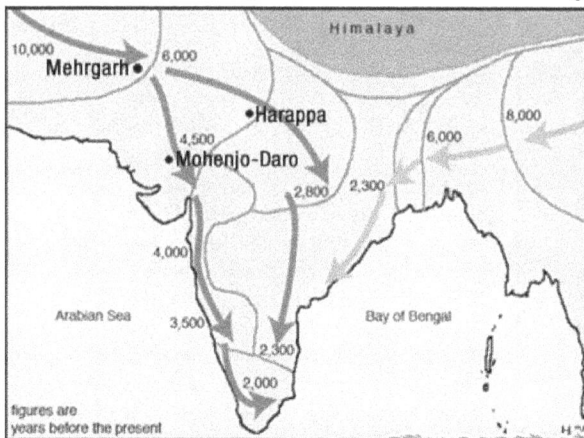

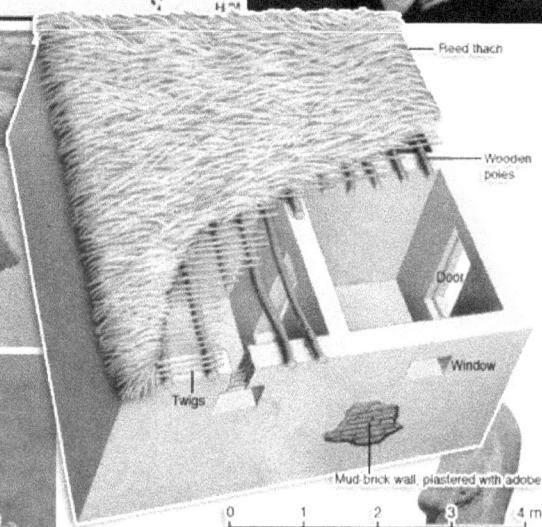

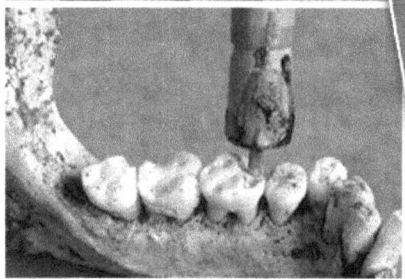

connected to major developments in the Ancient Near East. Much later, these people – together – **would become the diverse array of indigenous people in India today.**

PRE-INDUS VALLEY CIVILIZATIONS

Before the "Cushite" wave of Anu people established the cities of the Indus Valley, Anu people established the cities of Mehrgarh and Cambay.

MEHRGARH

One of the ancient routes from Near East to the Indus Valley crosses the Bolan peak pass of Pakistan. There, the Kachi Plain of once supported a thriving Neolithic civilization known today as Mehrgarh.

Mehrgarh was occupied from 7000 BC to about 2500 BC, predating the Harappan civilization of the Indus Valley further east. One of the most notable finds from this site was that its people had an advanced knowledge of dentistry. As we note in *Black People Invented Everything*, a 2006 study confirmed that the people of Mehrgarh were **drilling teeth 9,000 years ago**, using flint tools that were "surprisingly effective."[218]

The people of Mehrgarh also cultivated cotton as early as 6000 BC, a tradition that would be carried into later Indus Valley civilization. The people of Mehrgarh also grew date palms as early as 7000 BC, a tradition that persisted well into the later Indus Valley civilization.

THE GULF OF CAMBAY

In 2001, another lost city was found underwater in the Gulf of Cambay on the western coast of India. The site's ruins suggested a large urban complex with foundations for massive structures throughout. According to the BBC's report on the site:

> The vast city – which is five miles long and two miles wide – is believed to predate the oldest known remains in the subcontinent by more than 5,000 years. The site was discovered by chance last year by oceanographers from India's National Institute of Ocean Technology, who were conducting a survey of pollution. Using sidescan sonar, which sends a beam of sound waves down to the bottom of the ocean, they identified huge geometrical structures at a depth of 120 feet. Debris recovered from the site – including construction material, pottery, sections of walls, beads, sculpture, and human bones and teeth – has been carbon dated and found to be nearly 9,500 years old.[219]

THE UNDERWATER CITY OF ALEXANDRIA, EGYPT

IMAGINE WHAT ELSE REMAINS UNDISCOVERED

If these artifacts date back to 7500 BC, the Gulf of Cambay civilization would date back to the time of Mehrgarh, another city founded by the first wave of Anu people. According to Rawlinson, a Cushite people was responsible for these early cities:

> Recent linguistic discoveries show that a Cushite race did in the earliest times extend itself along the southern shores of the continents from Abyssinia to India. The whole peninsula of India, the sea coast of Beluchistan [where Mehrgarh is found] and Kerman by the inscriptions belonged to this race.[220]

We can only imagine what else lay beneath the surface.

A QUICK NOTE ON "UNDERWATER CITIES"

Typically, the most extraordinary claims are the least factual. For example, a claim of a "highly-advanced, massive city with giant pyramids" should not be believed if all that the claimant produces is a colorful illustration and three wet bricks. Some researchers claim the existence of a 6,000-year-old sunken city with megalithic ruins in the Yucatan Channel near the western coast of Cuba. However, only computer models have been produced, and no solid evidence has been found (besides a "circumstantial" stone circle found nearby on the coast). Some have said this "city" was the "real Atlantis." Too bad it's probably not a city.

The real stuff is a little more unassuming. For example, there is an underwater cemetery at Windover Pond, near Titusville, Florida. It dates back to 4,900-6,100 BC. What's special is that the bodies are wrapped in a flexible fabric that reveals ancient Indians were weaving plant fibers on looms almost 8,000 years ago.

Dating back to 6900 BC, Atlit-Yam is a pre-pottery Neolithic settlement covering more than 15 square miles of the seafloor just off the Israeli coast. Archaeologists discovered the remains of an urban village where people lived in spacious rectangular stone houses complete with paved floors, courtyards, hearths, storage facilities and wells. A six-foot thick wall running parallel to the channel of an ancient river was probably a levee, indicating increased control over and exploitation of water systems in the Neolithic. A circle of seven upright stones may also have been a megalithic formation like Stonehenge or Nabta Playa.

There are several other sites that are now underwater. One of the most famous is the sunken city of Alexandria, Egypt. Such sites remind us that much of our earliest accomplishments have been lost to the elements over time.

WHO WERE THE DRAVIDIANS?

The Dravidian language family of India emerged a little after the beginning of the South Asian Neolithic around 2500 BC. This is around the time when a new group of Black people appear to have spread into India, which was previously dominated by Australoid peoples. The Dravidian language family is distinct from most neighboring Indo-European languages but also from the older

Austro-Asiatic languages spoken to the east. Its closest relative appears to be the language of ancient Elam.

A few linguists have noted similarities between some Niger-Congo languages (particularly those on the Afro-Asiatic/Niger-Congo boundary area) and the proto-Dravidian language. French linguist Bernard Sargent is one of the principle advocates of the Afro-Dravidian hypothesis, which argues that Dravidian is a derivative of an African language from the Niger-Congo family of languages, and that much of the cultural and technological complex associated with Dravidian culture has African origins. For example, the crops used in early Dravidian agriculture were domesticated in and had their origins the East African Sahel.

Who brought them? The best way to establish such a connection is via genetics. However, tracing genetics is tricky business when it comes to India, where countless migrations have come and gone.

The strongest outside DNA marker in proto-Dravidian sites are from Y-DNA haplogroup T. There is evidence that ancient people carrying haplogroup T were sailing from the Horn of Africa across the Red Sea and Indian Ocean by at least 2500 BC. This suggests that a male-dominated group of Blacks from the root of civilization might have arrived on the coast of India and introduced new crops and technologies over 4,500 years ago.

These people could have emigrated from ancient Nubia (where haplogroup T is still common). Haplogroup T also occurs in Egypt and Mesopotamia at an early date. It's possible that some of these people traveled south into the Horn of Africa, before sailing towards India. It's also possible that they tried their crops in India because they didn't fare so well in Mesopotamia.

As Jared Diamond explains in *Guns, Germs and Steel*, the crops of the East African Sahel wouldn't do well in the Near Eastern Fertile Crescent due to the different climates and seasonal patterns (nor would Near Eastern crops do well in East Africa). But Sahel crops will do well in the monsoon climate of southern India, where the seasonal pattern resembles that of East Africa. **Perhaps this explains why India was such a popular destination for ancient Africans.**

Wherever they came from and why ever they came, we know that it was the Black people of India who built the grand cities of the Indus Valley Civilization, before being subjugated and nearly annihilated by the coalescing of the various Aryan tribes that were working their way into India between 1850 and 1500 BC.

THEN WHAT HAPPENED?

The ancient cities of Mohenjo-Daro and Harappa were continuously occupied until around 1900 BC. Between 1900 and 1500 BC, they were conquered by a slow-creeping foreign invasion of people from Europe. These were white people who came into the Indus Valley in small bands, eventually becoming a strong enough force to overthrow the indigenous population. If their broken and battered skeletons are any indication, it wasn't a peaceful takeover.

We'll get deeper into this event in Volume Four, but the end result of this conquest was a new social structure for India, one where *skin color determined status* (the caste system), and where the native Blacks of India became the *dasas* (or *dasyus*), meaning "Black-skinned slave."

This was in the language of Sanskrit, an Indo-European language that fathered most of the dominant languages of India, including Hindi, Bengali, and several others. As Taylor notes:

> The Aryan-speakers in their invasions about 2000 BC, were mostly opposed by primitive Veddah-Australoid tribes (or Dasyus) with low stature, dark skin, and broad noses. The Bhils and Gonds, in or near the Vindhya hills, who bore the brunt of the Aryan attacks, have just these features. Some of these tribes in Chota-Nagpur still speak the primitive Munda-Kol languages, though the great bulk of the Lower Indian races speak higher languages like Tamil or Telugu of Dravidian type. On the other hand, the Bhils have learnt an Indo-Aryan tongue.[221]

Millions of Indians today (particularly Bengalis including myself) bear *Das* as a surname because we are the direct descendants of the conquered Black people who once built Indian civilization. When I first learned this, I thought "Das" was kind of like a "slave name." But *Das, Dasas,* or *Dasyus* **originally meant "Black enemy."** We were the ones they feared.

Only later, after the conquest and the rewriting of history that followed, did the name come to mean "Black slave." Others were similarly subordinated, but continue to carry the names (and language) of their Dravidian ancestors.*

---

* My daughter Nilani Me'siah Dass carries three histories in her name. Nilani comes from Tamil, a Dravidian language. Dass is the "slave name" Das, to which my father added an "s" in reclaiming the name and rejecting that history. And Me'siah, her middle name, is derived from the way Five Percenters create names. The apostrophe taking the place of the "s" in "Messiah" represents the choice we find in the 19th letter of our Supreme Alphabet, "Self or Savior." When she reaches the age of responsibility, she can either "do her own thing" (self) or be a savior to the world. If

THE ANCIENT INDUS VALLEY
ARTIFACTS AND RECONSTRUCTIONS

PRIEST-KING
(2600-1900 BC)

MOHENJO-DARO
(DIGITAL RECONSTRUCTION)

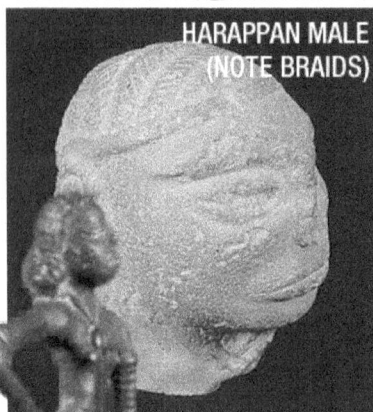

HARAPPAN MALE
(NOTE BRAIDS)

GATEWAY AND SEWER IN HARAPPA
(ARTIST'S RENDERING)

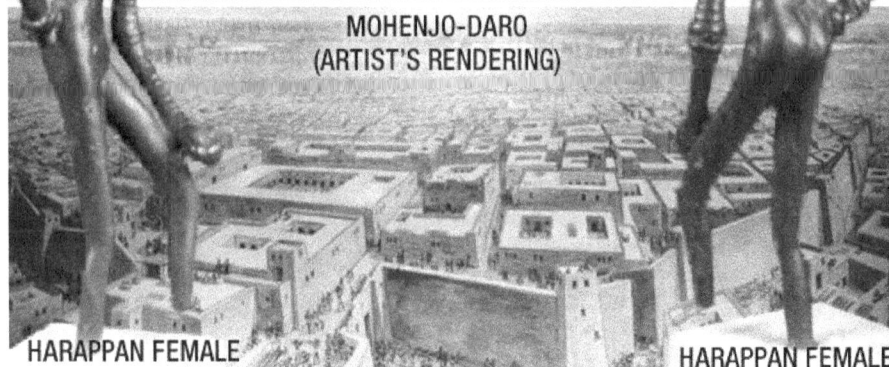

MOHENJO-DARO
(ARTIST'S RENDERING)

HARAPPAN FEMALE

HARAPPAN FEMALE

ADIVASIS
The Aboriginal People of INDIA

The Bison Horn MARIA (Central India)

The people of ORISSA (East India)

The KONDH

The GOND

Back-migrations from the East

The MUNDA of Orissa

The NAGA of Nagaland (Northeast India)

Those who remained became a part of the new era of Indian civilization, one where the "Aryans" ruled and the original Black inhabitants became slaves, servants, or outcasts. Those who weren't absorbed into the new social structure (which took advantage of the existing social stratification, but turned it into a "color system" where whites were now on top) either became "untouchables" or a caste of outcasts.

Others fled to the dense forests and mountains, where they became known as forest tribes. These people have been described as "primitive," "wild," and "savage," but they are the direct descendants of the Black people who built one of the ancient world's most amazing urban civilizations! In light of this disparity, the following quote from Humboldt's *Cosmos* is especially illuminating:

> We will not attempt to decide the question whether the races at present termed savage are all in a condition of original wildness, or whether, as the structure of their languages often allows us to conjecture, many among them may not be tribes that have degenerated into a wild state, remaining as scattered fragments from the wreck of a civilization that was early lost.[222]

Couldn't this conclusion be drawn about many of the world's "broken" people today? Perhaps even us?

Many of these "tribal" people possess oral traditions that record thousands of years of history. These traditions pre-date the Aryan invasion, and can provide us a glimpse into the knowledge and wisdom of India's original Black people – which we can only find in part when we look at later scriptures like the *Puranas* or *Upanishads*. Yet these histories may not survive, because they are not being passed on by today's generation. Within 100 years, many of these unrecorded histories – like that of the Pardhan Gonds of central India – may be gone forever.[223]

In today's India, both groups of indigenous people are allied in a collective resistance movement. So-called tribal people self-identify as *Adivasis*, meaning "original inhabitants," while the "untouchables" call themselves *Dalits*, meaning "broken" people.[224] Dalit activists like B.R. Ambedkar have promoted an African origin for these people, and emphasized a collective struggle against white oppression for Black people throughout the Diaspora. In fact, one resistance movement, known as the Dalit Panthers, has modeled itself explicitly on the platform of the Black Panther Party.[225]

---

that's heavy, relax. We'll get back to the science of names in Volume Three, because they do play a role in determining reality.

TO THE EAST

CHINA, JAPAN, AND SOUTHEAST ASIA

"Archaeological findings from the time of the Shang dynasty give us a different picture. Excavations of the royal tombs at Anyang...have brought out many skeletons...of a Negroid race of people." – Wolfram Eberhard

THE JOURNEY EAST

In the Near East and Europe, Anu people introduced the Neolithic Age, beginning over 10,000 years ago. Another wave of Anu people ushered in the developments of the Bronze Age, and an even later wave of Anu people carried the Iron Age as far east as India. These people were bonded by a common ancestry and point of origin. The leaders of these populations all seem to have dispersed from somewhere near Nubia and the Horn of Africa, the place we've conveniently labeled the "Root of Civilization."

From this center of diffusion, these Black men and women went northwards into Europe, deeper west (and south) into Africa, and eastwards into India. If they carried their culture as far north as the British Isles, it wouldn't make sense to assume that they simply stopped in India and went no further east. In fact, the ancient "Black belt" settled by the Anu people across Asia stretches well into East Asia and beyond.

The Anu people who went east from India appear to have established early cultural centers, ushering in the dawn of China's Neolithic before they brought these settlements together under China's first historical dynasties. They also introduced many of the important cultural developments that we can find in the other places they'd settled before. That is, the developments of the Tigris-Euphrates Valley, the Nile Valley, and the Indus Valley would soon be found near the Yellow River valley of China. In Japan, Korea, and Southeast Asia, similar developments would follow.

ANCIENT CHINA

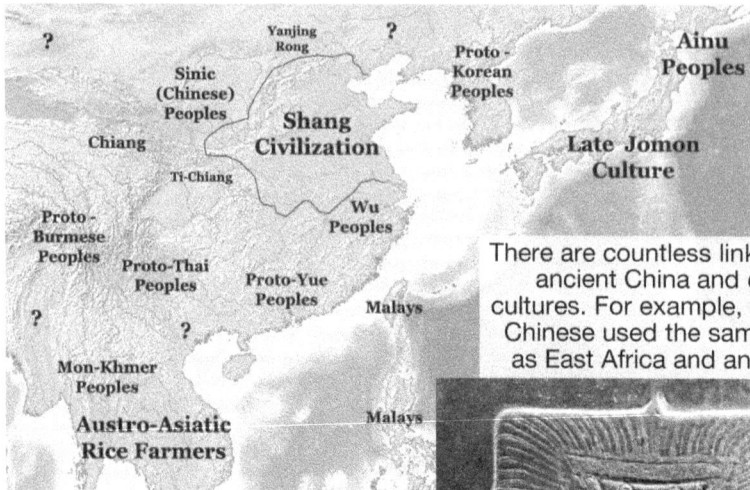

Yanjing
Rong

?

Sinic
(Chinese)
Peoples

Shang
Civilization

Chiang

Ti-Chiang

Wu
Peoples

Proto -
Burmese
Peoples

Proto-Thai
Peoples

Proto-Yue
Peoples

Malays

?

?

Mon-Khmer
Peoples

**Austro-Asiatic
Rice Farmers**

Malays

Proto -
Korean
Peoples

**Ainu
Peoples**

**Late Jomon
Culture**

There are countless links between ancient China and older Black cultures. For example, the ancient Chinese used the same currency as East Africa and ancient India.

What was the significance of the faces found on ritual objects throughout ancient China (center right)? Some say they represent the masks worn by shamans. Others say they were "signatures" of the artisans and metalworkers who crafted these objects. In either case, the earliest examples (bottom) tell us exactly who the faces were meant to portray.

THE BLACK HISTORY OF ANCIENT CHINA

When does Chinese history begin? As you read in Part One of this book, Li Chi's definition for "Chinese" revolves around one's association with Chinese history "from the beginning." In Part One, we thoroughly established that China's first people were Black. Paleolithic China was home to a diverse array of Black cultures, many of whom would survive into the modern day. Thus, **China was Black "from the beginning."**

Yet John T. Meskill's *Introduction to Chinese Civilization* argues: "The verifiable history of the Chinese people begins with the Neolithic period."[226] In other words, they're moving the goal around. For some scholars, the identity of the ORIGINAL Chinese is not as important as the identity of those who founded Chinese civilization. Fair enough. Let's explore it.

Carl Whiting Bishop described the wave of people who displaced China's indigenous Black inhabitants as "the eastern sub-variety of the human type known in the West as the Mediterranean race."[227] By now, we know the "Mediterranean" race is just a euphemism for Black people.[228] Bishop's "Mediterraneans" may refer to the Anu people who expanded throughout Europe and Asia over the last 15,000 years.

From the earliest human settlements to the cultures of the Neolithic, to the formative dynasties of the Xia and Shang, Blacks played the defining role in China, especially in the communities of the south and the eastern shores.

Throughout most of ancient China's cultural centers, the transformation from the Paleolithic to the Neolithic took place around 6000-5000 BC By this time, these Blacks were something of a mixed community (like Egypt and other ancient "metropolitan areas"), composed of several groups, including the DBP, the Australoid people who later populated southeast Asia and Australia, and even a final migration of Anu people identified with "Mediterranean" or "Veddoid" features.

Eventually, this cosmopolitan society would hybridize to form the civilization of the Early Bronze Age, beginning with China's first dynasties. The first three dynasties of ancient China, known as the *San Dai* (Three Dynasties), are the *Xia*, the *Shang* and the *Zhou*. Both the Xia and Shang were once considered mythical dynasties, due to a lack of conclusive archaeological evidence.

Eventually, the historicity of the Shang was verified, along with much of what was claimed in the accounts of later traditional historians.

More recent studies have supported the existence of the Xia. Still, very little is known. Most recently, the 4,000-year-old Lungshan culture of the Central Plains has been said to be identical to Xia.[229] Xia origins, if authentic, may go back to 2205 BC.[230]

The Shang dynasty, China's oldest verified historical dynasty, was predominantly Black. According to Wolfram Eberhard in *China's Minorities: Yesterday and Today*:

Archaeological findings from the time of the Shang dynasty (?-1022 BC), give us a different picture. Excavations of the royal tombs at Anyang…have brought out many skeletons some of which seem to belong to non-Mongol races. Although excavations were done around 1935, the anthropological results have not been fully published, perhaps because the findings were somewhat embarrassing…some preliminary comments about the findings [state evidence] of a Negroid (that is dark-skinned) race of people and of people related to the inhabitants of the South seas (Micronesians).[231]

Before the dynasties, China was home to dozens of Neolithic cultures. For example, the prehistoric Chinese site of Jiahu was settled from 7,000 to 5,800 BC. Jiahu was surrounded by a moat and covered an area of 55,000 square meters_.[233] Most of the site has still not yet been excavated. The people of Jiahu cultivated foxtail millet and rice, buried their dead with pottery and tortoise shells, and left behind delicate flutes made from crane wing bones. Most of them, like other prehistoric flutes, were pentatonic.[234] These cultural practices match with the practices of Black populations in India and the Near East.

Traditional history asserts that the succession of the first three dynasties was entirely sequential and linear, but recent research has shown that each dynasty simply represented a local rulership coming to power. That is, the Shang had already become a powerful political entity when it finally overthrew the neighboring Xia regime around 1766 BC.[235]

Like the Shang, the communities associated with the Xia were predominantly Black. When the Zhou conquered the Shang, it spelled the end of Black power in China. We'll tell that story in a minute.

THEY CAME FROM THE WEST

Chinese scholars often assert that all of China's ancient developments were native-born, with no outside influences. In many cases, foreign traditions (like the domestication of the dog) were repeated in China in such a way that these practices seem to be independent innovations, but most of these sciences were introduced from elsewhere.

Between the Neolithic and Early Bronze Age, major developments were introduced to China, including significant advances in pottery, writing, metallurgy, agriculture, and religious and political thought. Li Chi, one of the foremost early archaeologists of China, outlined six groups of cultural traits distinguishing the Shang period from the pre-Shang remains at Anyang (in Xiaotun, specifically):

❒ New development of ceramic industry
❒ Employment of bronze to cast tools, weapons, and sacrificial vessels
❒ The presence of a highly developed writing system
❒ Chamber burials and human sacrifices
❒ Use of chariots
❒ Advanced stone carvings[236]

Many of these cultural advances don't have clear precursors in the region. That is, there's no evidence for a older form of these practices in the area.[237] Some of them, like metallurgy appeared in China already fully developed. As Li Chi notes, "an earlier background must be postulated in order to explain the stage of development which the bronze of Xiaotun attained."[238]

Li adds that written records might have arrived in the Yellow River valley from the Near East.[239] Many domesticated animals were also introduced to China from the West. C.W. Bishop counts among these:

❒ the sheep and goat (from the mountains of the Near East)
❒ the ass (from northeast Africa)
❒ the ox (from the Near East, and in western and southern China it is mixed with Indian strains)
❒ the water-buffalo (likely from India)

Many plants also made the journey east. Though rice originated in south China, its cultivation may have arrived even earlier from India,

Did You Know?

As Robert Bailey notes in the 2012 *365 Days of Real Black History Calendar*: "Black people developed the first martial arts. One of the earliest papyrus scrolls from Egypt shows a system of attacks and takedowns that has yet to be further explored...The Nuba of Sudan in Africa practiced a form of martial arts over 2,800 years before Christ. There are no other records any-where in the world of such a long and unbroken tradition. The earliest known image of Nubian wrestling can be found on a wall painting in the Egyptian tomb of Tyanen, circa 1410 B.C...

Kung fu was introduced to China by a Black Buddhist monk from India named Boddhi-dharma around 520 AD. Buddhism's recognized founder was also a Black Indian, named Siddhartha. Statues depict him with a broad nose and pepper-corn hair. Many martial arts were introduced to Asia and Europe by Blacks."

while wheat, clearly the staple crop in the early north, is indigenous to the Near East.[240] And there are many other connections that suggest that diffusion from the west was an ongoing process, with elements consistently being brought in by migratory waves of incoming settlers.

For one, peoples of the Neolithic Lungshan culture, most likely the *Tai* and *Yao*, lived on mounds formed by building repeatedly over earlier settlements, in entirely the same manner as did the inhabitants of the mounds of the ancient Near East. These people are identified with the "Black Pottery" culture, a type which Wolfram Eberhard noted also occurred in the Near East.[241]

Meanwhile, copper objects appeared with increasing frequency towards the end of the late Neolithic, until a developed metallurgy ushered in the Bronze Age during the reign of the early Shang dynasty.[242] Li placed the Near East at the origin of Chinese metallurgy and the sudden advent of distinctive bronze vessels, the large tombs and human sacrifices, and, of course, the introduction of the chariot.[243]

Li Chi notes a clear similarity between jar covers from Jemdet Nasr (in southern Mesopotamia), Mohenjo-Daro (in the Indus Valley) and Xiaotun (near the capital of Shang China).[244] L. Carrington Goodrich, Professor of Chinese at Columbia University, linked prehistoric vessels in China to identical artifacts in the Near East and India. Goodrich added:

> Possibly for exchange purposes, and also as a decoration and a charm, these men of the Stone Age began to use the cowry, a little shell that may have come originally from so distant a place as the Maldive Islands southwest of the Indian peninsula.[245]

The cowry shell was used as currency from the end of the Xia dynasty and was in use until bronze imitation shells appeared near the end of the Shang dynasty.[246]

PYRAMIDS IN CHINA?

Throughout China, archaeologists and explorers have noted the presence of several structures that resemble pyramids. Some of these have been confirmed as pyramidal burial mounds (center right), while others have never been excavated. Others have been photographed but never investigated (top right). Still others look like grassy hills with unnaturally sharp angles or flat tops. Are they just hills or are these ancient earthen pyramids (like those in the Americas), camouflaged by millennia of plant growth, weather, and erosion?

This is not a new idea. Mesopotamian influence in China by 2700 BC was noted by Ling Shun-Sheng, who also claimed periods of influence at about 1000 BC and 500-200 BC[247]

And these theories are confirmed by the genetic and skeletal evidence. Long after China's first Black settlers (over 20,000 years ago) are a distant memory, new waves of Black settlers repeatedly appear in Chinese burials. One of the biggest influxes of Black skeletons occurs during the formation of the Shang Dynasty. Another fact to consider: The presence of pyramids.

PYRAMIDS IN THE FAR EAST?

A 1947 article in the *Rocky Mountain News* entitled "Few Tourists Will Gaze on Pyramid Nest in China" reported that an American army aviator has discovered a large earthen pyramid in a remote region of western China while flying over the region of Shensi province.

According to the article, American scientists who had been in the area conjectured that the pyramid rose over one-thousand feet, or more than twice the height of the Egyptian pyramids.[248] Though the claim was disputed, the Chinese pyramids did prove to be, like their Egyptian counterparts, tombs for the ancient noble dead. Many of these pyramids are even flat-topped with small temples situated at their highest points, like the famous temple of Sakkara in Egypt and the models of the ancient Americas.

German researcher Hartwig Hausdorf photographed several of these pyramids, some of which were estimated to be at least 4,500 years old (clearly before the Zhou era), during his 1994 trip to the Forbidden Zone of the Shensi province. Hausdorf reported that there were over a hundred such pyramids, mostly made from clay turned nearly stone hard. Most, however, are now damaged by erosion or farming. There exists one said to be as large as the Great Pyramid of Giza, while another, in Shandong, is approximately fifty feet tall and actually constructed of stone.

CLUES FROM THE CHINESE LANGUAGE

According to traditional Chinese historians, the origin of the Chinese script can be attributed to the ancient scribe *Cang jie*.[249] One legend says *Cang jie* "saw a divine being whose face had unusual features," in imitation of which *Cang jie* created the earliest written characters. Afterwards, "millet rained from heaven and the spirits howled every night to lament the leakage of the divine secret of writing."[250]

Of course, such legends only symbolize and simplify, as most myths do, the development of one of the oldest living languages of the world, Chinese. But is there some significance to the "unusual" man who introduced writing, and presumably the cultivation of millet, to the Chinese? In what other societies were pictographic writing and cultivated millet in place before they appear in ancient China?

The earliest forms of Chinese writing were pictographic characters. These are most prominent in the oracle bone inscriptions of the early Shang period (c. 1300 BC), but there are older pictographs on Neolithic pottery shards from the south (c. 2800 BC). Over several stages, the archaic Chinese language evolved into Old Chinese, which then grew into Modern Chinese.*

The most notable inscriptions from the ancient period are depictions and identifications of people, classes and clan-names. The common people (or "multitudes") of the late Shang were typically identified by the terms *zhong* ("the many") and *ren* ("the men"). *Zhong* first appeared on Shang oracle bones as a sign depicting three *ren* (men) under the sun .[251]

This ideogram suggests a people, who like the classical Ethiopians, may have seemed "burnt by the sun" in the eyes of outsiders. One could also draw an agricultural connection (i.e. the working class of farmers who toil under the sun). Of the *zhong* and the commoners the symbol represented, Cheng Te-K'un has observed that, "In later periods, the common people were called *li min*, literally the brown people."[252]

TWO OF THE PRIMARY TERMS DENOTING BLACKNESS

The term *li min* continues to signify "the multitude" and "the common people" even in Modern Chinese. It is made of the characters *li* , meaning "black" (not brown) and *min* , meaning "people." **Thus it is more appropriately translated as "the black people."**

If you check a Chinese language dictionary, the same character used here for *li* also designates the aborigines of Hainan, who we discussed earlier. This is no coincidence. Another term for the

---

* Even older writing may have been composed on strips of wood, bamboo reed, and other materials which, unfortunately, would not survive millennia of decomposition.

common people is *li miao* 黎苗 , *miao* 苗 being the same character used to represent the indigenous Miao peoples of southern China. Also denoting blackness, the term *li hei* 黎黑 is a composite of the two primary Chinese terms for black, *li* 黎 and *hei* 黑. [253]

Hei 黑, used in the words *hei zhong*, 黑種 "Black race," or *hei ren*, 黑人 "Blackman," [254] is also found in characters such as *xia* 點, meaning "smart; clever; shrewd," as well as a number of terms related to study, teaching, tattooing, and alchemy. [255]

The alternative name for the Miao-dominated town of Kweichow was *Chien (Qian)* 黔, which also meant "black." This same character, which makes use of the *hei* character, was combined with *li* to form *qian li* 黔黎, which too designates "the common people," much as *qian shu* 黔首 means "the people; the multitude." [256]

Thus, it is appears that the majority population of China in its earliest periods – the so-called "commoners" or "multitudes" – were by and large regarded as "Black" by those who had assumed power.

Not only do Chinese words offer us clues into the ethnicity of the ancient Chinese, we can find a wealth of insight in the history of Chinese language itself. Both Old and Modern Chinese are members of the large Sino-Tibetan language family, which was introduced by the earliest wave of Anu settlers.

The development of the Chinese language was also heavily influenced by Austro-Asiatic languages in the south. [257] The non-Chinese speaking, pre-imperial *Yi* people of the east, and other pre-Han southern state of *Yue*, were Austro-Asiatic.* The modern Austro-Asiatic family includes the *Miao-Yao*, the *Mons*, the *Khmers*, the *Sakai*, and the *Semangs*. As you may remember from earlier sections, **these people were the Black folks of the ancient Far East**.

WHAT DOES AUSTRO-ASIATIC MEAN?

Austro-Asiatic is one half of the Austric language family. Austro-Asiatic refers to the Austric languages spoken in mainland Asia, and the Austronesian languages spoken in the islands of Oceania. In

---

* Chinese also had Indo-European influences in the north. We'll discuss the Indo-European factors in Volume Four.

DID THE CHINESE GO TO MESOAMERICA?

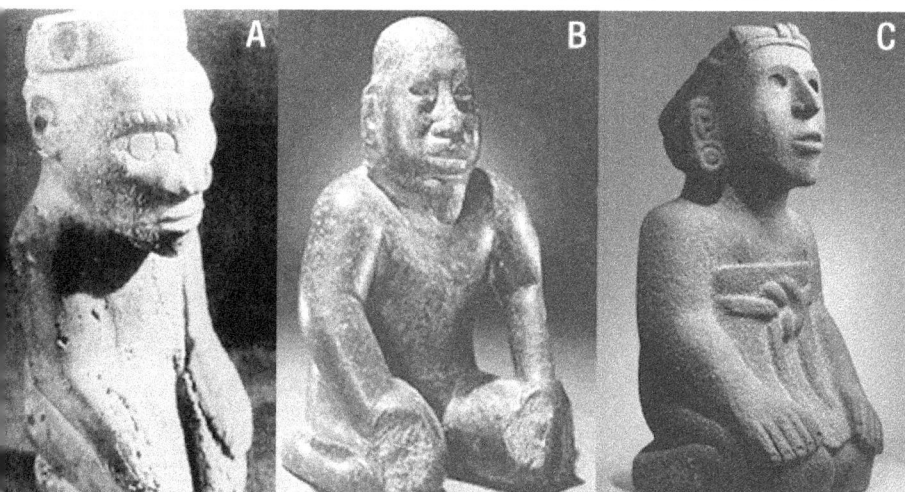

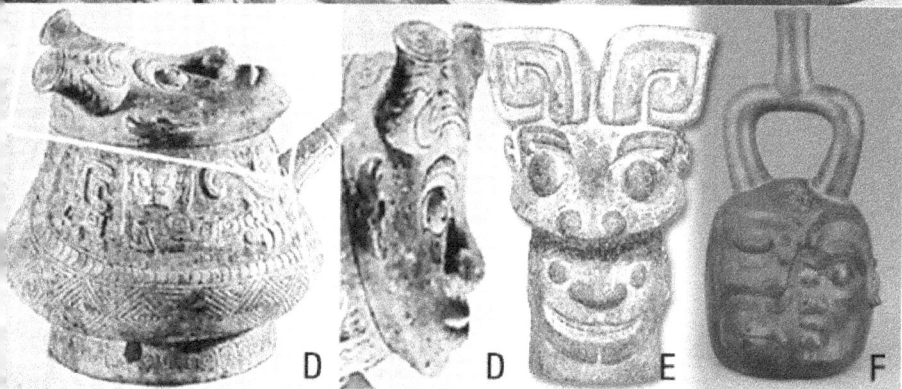

A   B   C

D   D   E   F

Can you guess which sculptures, pots, and masks come from ancient China, and which ones come from ancient Mesoamerica? If its not immediately obvious, it's because there are many connections between the two cultures. Both depicted men in the same squatting and kneeling postures, prized jade and obsidian, had vessels (pots) with Black faces, built burial mounds and earthen pyramids, and had shamans who wore realistic face masks (often with Black features) or stylized masks that exaggerated Black features.

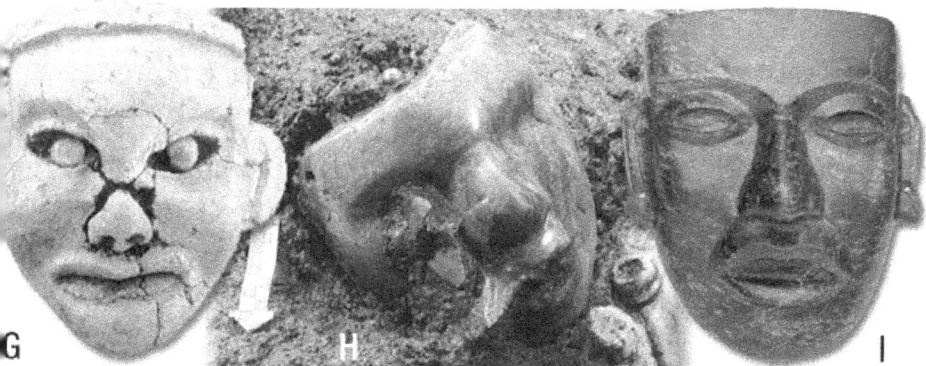

G   H   I

ANSWERS AT WWW.WHENTHEWORLDWASBLACK.COM

PHILIPPINES

general, Austric speakers, wherever they are found, have the following features:

Short to medium stature

Fair to very dark complexion. Generally brown-colored.

Mesorrhinne nose, with greater breadth than length

Slight prognathism, or full lips

Dark, thick, coarse hair

Slight but sinewy build[258]

In other words, they look like Black people. In fact, when Negroid skulls were found at several sites in ancient Sumer, they were used to "prove" that the yet-unclassified Sumerian language must have belonged to the Austric family.[259] Linguist Paul Kekai Manansula says of the Austric family:

Austric also refers to a cultural and "racial" group…The Austric-speaking people do not all belong to one homogenous racial grouping, yet there is definitely a predominant type to be found. Some Austric speakers are Negritos and Oceanic Negroids like the Aetas of the Philippines, the Melanesians and some of the Austronesian speaking peoples of New Guinea. Most Austrics, though, are basically a fusion of three primary races: Mongoloid, Austroloid and Oceanic Negroid.[260]

In other words, the Austro-Asiatic languages (particularly the Austric ones), were mostly spoken by indigenous Black populations that predated the Anu migrations. Austronesian languages evolved among later migrations that sailed from East Asia to the Pacific Islands within the past 5,000 years.

THEN WHAT HAPPENED?

Up to this point, it looks like China was a predominantly Black society. So what happened? With the invasion of foreign westerners, foremost of which was the Zhou (around 1500 BC), these native populations were driven out or absorbed.

When driven out, many followed the same route taken by previous migrations, which swept across the southeast and the Pacific to populate Australia and Melanesia, and to a lesser extent the smaller islands such as Hainan, Taiwan and Japan.

When absorbed, nomadic white populations descending originally from the western steppes, in their miscegenation with the Black base population, produced the intermediate complexion to be found in most Chinese. As we noted earlier, Mongoloid features could have evolved as by-product of natural selection or genetic drift, but the lighter complexions of many East Asians was a change that came much later in their history. As anthropologist Cheikh Anta Diop says in Civilization or Barbarism, the pale complexions of many Chinese are the result of white admixture into an ancient Black population.

And the homogeneity? Since the onset of Zhou reign, the face of China has drastically changed to reflect the "yellow" type associated with the modern Han, who only recently grew (exponentially) to comprise ninety percent of the modern Chinese population. The remaining one-tenth of China is a mix of various ethnic groups.

Lost somewhere in this mix are the traces of remote aboriginal populations descended from these original Blacks. While there are likely very few, if any, true examples of the "pure" type remaining in China today, the "Negroid" and "Negrito" type can be found in mixed measure in several populations throughout southeast Asia, including China, especially in the south.

The racial change that swept the countryside after the Zhou conquest of 1500 BC was followed by another period transformation when the Han Dynasty began in 206 BC. Each of these conquests drastically changed the face of what the majority of Chinese people looked like. As mainland Chinese expanded into other regions, like Thailand and Taiwan, the people there began to look more Chinese as well. **So who are the Chinese? They are Original People.**

ANCIENT JAPAN

We don't know if the Anu ever physically settled in Japan, or if the Original People who first populated Japan were its final wave of Black settlers. The Original People of Japan, who we discussed in Part One, maintained a hunter-gatherer culture for thousands of years, until an influx of rice-farmers introduced agriculture and the first proto-Japanese language.[261] These people came only about 2400 years ago, long after the Anu had made their rounds. They were the Yayoi, a Mongoloid people who also settled Korea. Today most Japanese are part Yayoi and part Jōmon.

The Jōmon are more closely related to the Original People of Japan. They were typically hunter-gatherers, but – about 10,000 years ago – they began developing ceramics, practicing an organic sort of "pre-agriculture," and doing a few other things that remind of us the Anu Cultural Complex. So did the Anu successfully establish themselves, or their culture, in Japan? If so, their influence would explain the megalithic circle found at Hokkaido…and the suspected "pyramids" found underwater near the coast of Yonaguni.

UNDERWATER PYRAMIDS?

In 1958, a Japanese dive tour operator discovered a massive stone structure underwater near the southern coast of Yonaguni Island, the western-most island of Japan.

Marine geologist Masaki Kimura investigated the claim and confirmed the existence of 600-foot wide, 88-foot tall structure. "The largest structure looks like a complicated, monolithic, stepped pyramid that rises from a depth of 25 meters [82 feet]," Kimura told *National Geographic* in 2007.

There are eight anomalous, underwater sites found to date, but debates continue about whether they were entirely manmade, entirely natural, or natural formations "remade" by man. Recent photographs suggest that the structures at Yonaguni weren't shaped like a pyramid, but more like the plaza/temple complexes found in the ancient Americas or the Near East.

This Japanese "ziggurat" appeared to be part of a larger complex of several underwater structures in the area, complete with ramps, steps, and terraces, all sharply carved at angles that are unlikely in natural formations. There is other evidence supporting the theory that they are manmade.

For example, one black has a row of small holes that appear to be an abandoned attempt to split off a section of the rock with wooden wedges, a common Anu technique.* Other parts of the structure suggest they were carved from bedrock using technology similar to that used to carve the terraces of the Andes.

The structures haven't been conclusively dated or analyzed, but are thought to be from somewhere between 5,000 to 12,000 years old. At this time, sea levels could have been low enough for these

---

* They'd fill these holes with wooden wedges, which they'd then soak in water. As the wood expanded, the poles would split the rock along the row of holes. This technique was used in ancient Egypt, Neolithic Europe, and the pre-Columbian Andes, and just about anywhere else Anu people brought megalithic culture.

THE PHILIPPINES

LATER EMIGRANTS WITH
AN INDIGENOUS "GUARD"

structures to be on dry land. About 10,000 BC, Yonaguni was the southern end of a land bridge that connected Taiwan, Ryūkyū, Japan, and East Asia. This theory is supported by evidence of stalactites and stalagmites in submerged cave. Stalactites and stalagmites can only form above water.

TAIWAN

In Part One, we talked about the "Little Black People" who preceded Taiwan's aborigines. These Black people – who survived until about 100 years ago as Taiwan's DBP – settled the area at least 40,000 years ago, which is when we find the first evidence of human remains on the island. These people, associated with the Changpin culture, were hunter-gatherers, living like Original People everywhere else at the time.[262]

By 6,000 years ago, another culture penetrated the island. The Tapenkeng culture, as it is known, was characterized by the advent of agriculture, and it overlapped the late Changpin culture (40,000-3,000 BC). In other words, a new people came into the region with a new culture, but the old settlers (and their culture) weren't "replaced" or wiped out.

These people became some of the world's first rice farmers. They also made cord-marked pottery, fishing nets made from hemp rope, and stone axes, arrowheads, and net-sinkers, as well as some of the most significant megalithic monuments in the Pacific area.[263] One stone pillar, known as the Beinan Monolith, is a massive upright stone with holes drilled at the top for astronomical alignments.[264] In other words, these people brought the Anu Cultural Complex to Taiwan. Much of the data suggests that Taiwan was the starting point for ancient migrations to the Philippines, Indonesia, and other Pacific islands. These migrations reached as far as the Americas.

Like the Anu elsewhere, they crafted thousands of items from stone and jade. They also grew millet – a hardy grain domesticated by dozens of ancient communities from West Africa to East Asia – from which they invented millet wine, the local version of the wine recipe they enjoyed everywhere else they went. In the Andes region of South America, they made this drink with a new staple grain, maize.[265] They stored their rice and millet in raised granaries like those found in the Near East and Nile Valley. The Anu of Taiwan also cultivated hemp, and were soon using cannabis for its medicinal properties (e.g. as a sedative for medical procedures) and for its narcotic properties in shamanism.[266]

QUESTIONS TO CONSIDER

We know that "Little Black People" were still around about 100 years ago, because the Saisiyat aborigines remember them well. Were these people were the descendants of the Original People who first settled Taiwan over 40,000 years, or were they were simply descendants of the Anu? Or did the Anu somehow "merge" into the local population of Black settlers that preceded them – as they had done in other regions? Was this mixed population the origin of Taiwan's DBP?

However they came to be, we can be certain that Black people were still in Taiwan when – about 4,000 years ago – the ancestors of the today's "aboriginals" settled there. This may be why Taiwan's aborigines – who could trace most of their ancestry to a Paleo-Mongoloid population – retain some of the "Black features" associated with the Anu or DBP.

In other words, Taiwan's "aboriginals" weren't its first people, nor even its second. But, today, they are the people in most closely related to the Original Black people who settled and civilized this area. And this is why they are under attack.

SOUTHEAST ASIA

Pasemah is a district in South Sumatra, Indonesia. About 2500 years ago, the area around Pasemah's present-day capital Pagar Alam was home to what Ian Campbell has called "a highly developed indigenous culture that carved and erected large stone monuments." Campbell continues:

> These monuments include groups and avenues of upright stones, stone blocks with hollowed, cup-like mortars, troughs with human heads and figures carved on them, terraced platforms, three-legged 'dolmen' of uncertain function, stone burial chambers, and many dynamic stone carvings of humans and animals.[267]

In other words, we're looking at evidence of the Anu Cultural Complex. This phase is also associated with the beginning of the Early Metal Age, which "correlates with the introduction of new technologies and trade items into the Indo-Malaysian archipelago."

What's so special about the ancient culture of Pasemah? In 1932, Van der Hoop published an extensive study on this megalithic culture, where he established their connections with the bronze-working Dong Son culture of northern Vietnam. He also discussed the importance of their stone tombs:

> The stone cists [graves] formed one of the most gratifying finds in the Pasemah. From their situation, one may positively conclude that they belong to the same culture as the other megaliths and that they alone can perhaps contribute something towards unveiling the secret of the race to which the megalith builders belonged.[268]

In other words, all of these ancient cultures were connected. We can also find many of these features in ancient Taiwan. Although very little has been done to excavate these graves, there's other evidence for the "secret race" that introduced this culture. Campbell reports on the discovery of human figures drawn in rock carvings near these tombs:

> The general form of the figure's face is short and broad. From comparison with other Pasemah carved figures, it is evident that the figure is male, and his armour shows that he is a **warrior**. His large, **round, bulging eyes**, short, **broad nose,** wide mouth, **thick lips** (as wide at the corners as in the middle), large ears, and strong, broad, **projecting jaw** are characteristic of carved human figures from Pasemah. These features, which "express strength and resolution – to say the least" [according to another scholar], were once thought to indicate members of a **negroid** race.[269]

In other words, these were *undeniably* pictures of Black people. Then again, perhaps not *undeniably*. **Because white folks will deny even the obvious!** Thus Campbell argues that these figures were actually NOT Negroid, but their features are simply, and I quote:

> ...stylistic conventions similar to those used in Javanese and Balinese *wayang* figures with the aim of indicating a *kasar* ('unrefined') personality. [270]

Ridiculous. "Unrefined," huh? At least we know that such figures are "characteristic" of the area, and they're also found in Java and Bali. As Chancellor Williams keenly observed, even when they lie we can find the truths hidden between the lines.

There may even be some connection between these people and cultures far beyond Southeast Asia. Campbell says of one: "The most striking part of the figure is the head-dress. There is nothing like it on any other Pasemah figure, several of which are depicted wearing close-fitting caps or helmets." In fact, the plumes in the head-dress resemble some depicted in the artwork of ancient Mesoamerica. For what it's worth, it should be noted that the Olmec heads wore "close-fitting caps or helmets," a practice also found among ancient Nubians.

The megalithic culture of Indonesia (as well as related cultures throughout Southeast Asia, including the Dong Son culture of

Vietnam) practiced a custom of urn burials resembling that of Anu populations in the Near East. Indonesia's megalithic culture also featured earth and stone step pyramid structures, like those discovered in Pangguyangan, Cisolok, and Gunung Padang in West Java. The construction of stone pyramids was said to be based on native beliefs that "mountain and high places were the abodes of the ancestors." These people also developed a tradition of carving massive stone heads and faces, such as the Black Buddha carved into a rock wall near a pyramid-shaped temple in Angkor Wat, Cambodia.

WHO WERE THEY?

So who were the Black warriors carved besides the tombs at Pasemah? They were the Anu. Not simply descendants of the "blended communities" that resulted from small numbers of Anu people from the Root of Civilization settling among indigenous populations elsewhere in the world, but the **actual Anu from the Root**. They were few in number, but their teachings spread like wildfire. They came to people who had not been in touch with the Root for thousands of years, and they introduced a new phase of culture that revived much of what these people had lost, while providing solutions for many of the problems that came with the Holocene epoch's climate change. They were the few, the strong, and the brave, long before the Marines took that motto.

GEOGLYPHS AND PETROGLYPHS

A geoglyph is a large design or motif produced on the ground, typically by arranging rocks. A petroglyph is a design made by carving a rock surface.

GIANT OF CERRO UNITAS GEOGLYPH, CHILE

KU-RING-GAI CHASE, AUSTRALIA

PETROGLYPH OF LAKE ONEGA, RUSSIA

It's easy to assume these massive men are "ancient astronauts." But are they? Or are they representations of the Original Man?

Indigenous traditions say they represent shamans, not spacemen. Who should we listen to? The people who made them, or the guy with the wild hair and bad tan on Ancient Aliens?

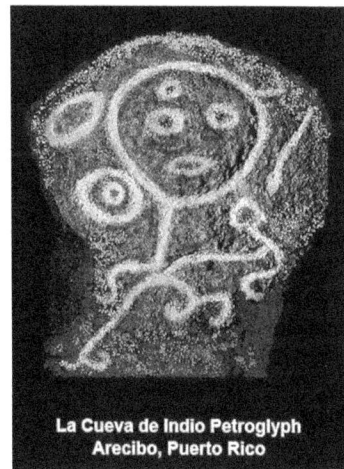

La Cueva de Indio Petroglyph
Arecibo, Puerto Rico

Sweetwater Creek Petroglyph
Douglas County, Georgia

Copper Canyon Petroglyph
El Fuerte, Mexico

MODERN EAST ASIA & OCEANIA

Scale 1:88,000,000

0	500	1000 Kilometers
0	500	1000 Nautical Miles

Miller Cylindrical Projection

Oceans and Seas
- Indian Ocean
- Arabian Sea
- Bay of Bengal
- North Pacific Ocean
- South Pacific Ocean
- Coral Sea
- Tasman Sea
- Philippine Sea

Countries and Places
- KAZAKHSTAN
- MONGOLIA — Ulaanbaatar
- RUSSIA — Vladivostok, Sakhalin, Kuril Islands
- CHINA — Beijing, Xi'an, Shanghai, Guangzhou
- PAKISTAN — Islamabad
- AFG. — Kabul
- UZB.
- INDIA — New Delhi, Bombay, Madras, Katmandu
- NEPAL
- BHUTAN — Thimphu
- BANGLADESH — Dhaka
- BURMA — Rangoon
- SRI LANKA — Colombo
- MALDIVES — Male
- Lake Balkhash — Alma-Ata
- Karachi
- Urumqi
- Cease-Fire Line
- Indian claim Chinese line of control
- Chinese claim
- THAILAND — Bangkok
- LAOS — Vientiane
- VIETNAM — Hanoi
- CAMBODIA — Phnom Penh
- Hong Kong (U.K.)
- Macau (PORT.)
- Taiwan
- Taipei
- MALAYSIA — Kuala Lumpur
- SINGAPORE
- BRUNEI — Bandar Seri Begawan
- INDONESIA — Jakarta, Java, Sumatra, Borneo
- Spratly Islands
- PHILIPPINES — Manila
- Cocos (Keeling) Islands (AUSTL.)
- Christmas Island (AUST.)
- British Indian Ocean Territory (U.K.) — Diego Garcia
- AUSTRALIA — Canberra, Perth, Darwin, Sydney, Brisbane, Tasmania
- Ashmore and Cartier Islands (AUSTL.)
- Coral Sea Islands (AUSTL.)
- PAPUA NEW GUINEA — Port Moresby
- JAPAN — Tokyo, Osaka
- N. KOREA — Pyongyang
- S. KOREA — Seoul
- Demarcation Line
- Guam (U.S.)
- Saipan
- Northern Mariana Islands (U.S.)
- FEDERATED STATES OF MICRONESIA — Kolonia
- Trust Territory of the Pacific Is. [Palau] (U.S.) — Koror
- Wake Island (U.S.)
- MARSHALL ISLANDS — Majuro
- NAURU — Yaren
- KIRIBATI — Tarawa
- TUVALU — Funafuti
- SOLOMON ISLANDS — Honiara
- VANUATU — Port-Vila
- New Caledonia (FR.)
- Norfolk Island (AUSTL.)
- FIJI — Suva
- Wallis and Futuna (FR.)
- W. SAMOA — Apia
- Amer. Samoa (U.S.)
- Tokelau (N.Z.)
- TONGA — Nuku'alofa
- Niue (N.Z.)
- Cook Islands (N.Z.)
- French Polynesia (FR.)
- Pitcairn Islands (U.K.)
- Howland Island (U.S.)
- Baker Island (U.S.)
- Jarvis Island (U.S.)
- Kingman Reef (U.S.)
- Palmyra Atoll (U.S.)
- Johnston Atoll (U.S.)
- Midway Islands (U.S.)
- Hawaiian Islands — Honolulu
- UNITED STATES — San Francisco, Seattle
- Aleutian Islands (U.S.)
- NEW ZEALAND — Wellington, Auckland, Christchurch
- Chatham Islands (N.Z.)
- Auckland Islands (N.Z.)
- French Southern and Antarctic Lands (FR.) — Île Amsterdam, Île Saint-Paul, Îles Kerguelen
- Rodrigues (MAURITIUS)
- Tropic of Cancer
- Equator
- Tropic of Capricorn

occupied by SOVIET UNION since 1945 administered by RUSSIA claimed by JAPAN

OCEANIA

FROM AUSTRALIA TO EASTER ISLAND

"As happened in Africa and in South America, the first missionaries to arrive on Easter Island took steps to remove all traces of a dead civilization. At the foot of the statues there were wooden tablets covered with hieroglyphs: these were all burned or dispatched to the Vatican library which houses many secrets." — Louis Pauwels and Jacques Bergier

From the shores of southern China, Taiwan, and Southeast Asia, Black settlers sailed deep into the Pacific Ocean. Some also traveled from the southern shores of India, Sri Lanka, and Southeast Asia to venture into Australia and New Guinea. Others may have embarked from Japan, where ancient artwork depicts the kind of boats you'd need to sail the open seas.

On their boats, these Black settlers carried with them many of the earmarks of Anu civilization, including a wealth of scientific traditions and a cache of domesticated plants and animals. In far too many cases, the evidence for their presence has either slowly faded into ambiguity or it has been intentionally hidden and destroyed.

Many geographers use "Oceania" to describe the part of the Earth centered on the islands of the tropical Pacific Ocean. Oceania includes all of Melanesia, Polynesia, and Micronesia, as well as Australia, New Guinea, and – by some accounts – parts of Malaysia and Southeast Asia. We'll begin with Australia.

AUSTRALIA

Most people don't know that Aboriginal Australia is not entirely monolithic. That is, the Original People of Australia aren't solely descended from a single founder population. Others came. Specifically, the Anu came.

In Part One, we reported on the genetic research that confirmed

Thomas Huxley's theory of an Indian settling of Australia. Recent research has shown that not only was Australia populated by several waves of Australoid people from India beginning over 70,000 years ago, but that another wave of Black people from India sailed into Australia between 8,000 and 5,000 years ago.

They introduced the Australian small tool tradition (or microlith technology), as well as "plant-processing technologies, especially complex detoxification of cycads and the expansion of the Pama-Nyungan language over seven-eighths of Australia."

In other words, several waves of Anu people from India migrated into northern Australia, where they introduced a new tool tradition, new plant-processing technology, and what Nicholas Wade calls "a semi-domesticated dog (the dingo)."[271] That's right, **the famous Australian dingo was brought in by boat from India.** Their scientists had bred the dingo from the Plains Wolf of India.[272] If you know how dangerous a dingo is, you'll be impressed.

It seems that the appearance of these people triggered the "rapid southward expansion" of the speakers of the Pama-Nyungan languages which now dominate Australia. The Pama-Nyungan languages may have originally been spoken by the first wave of Australoid people, and these people may have expanded southward as Anu people came in, but even their languages bear traces of Anu influence. Linguists have noted similarities between these Australian languages and Dravidian.[273]

This connection to the Anu people of India could explain the evidence people use to support the less likely theories involving an ancient Egyptian, Phoenician, Berber, or Caucasian presence in ancient Australia. And these Blacks were apparently quite successful in their undertaking, as they fathered 50% of the lineages in modern Australia.[274]

USING MALARIA TO TRACK MIGRATIONS

It's not easy to make sense of who went where and when, especially when you're talking about things that happened more than 10,000 years ago. I've worked countless hours, looking at multiple forms of evidence, hoping to assemble the most accurate picture possible. Still, I plan to occasionally update this text with corrections and clarifications. If you see "Second Edition" on the cover of this text the next time you see it in a bookstore, you can expect that a few things have changed since the last edition.

But this is what Chancellor Williams was talking about when he mentioned "the long centuries of the great migrations" that "defied periodization in any meaningful sense."

It's easy enough to talk about skeleton remains, but skeletal remains are rare, even more so the further back you go in time. Then there are all the measures that help determine the age of stone artifacts when there are no bones to date. Yet neither of these can tell us much about when one group of people came into an area, and where exactly they went next. Linguistic evidence can help us here, but **what about migrations that happened so long ago that linguistics doesn't help much?**

Unlike our scholars who wrote more than twenty years ago, we now have genetics at our disposal. Learning population genetics, particularly archaeogenetics is critical for anyone seeking to continue this work today. But even DNA lineages and SNP markers aren't enough. They're only a piece to the puzzle.

Elsewhere in the book, we talk about the evidence provided by HLA alleles, the immune system genes that reveal where a population has been, and what kinds of viruses it's been exposed to.

A 2007 analysis of over 3 million genetic mutations from the International HapMap Project sought to identify the strongest examples of recent genetic change in a regional human population. The analysis highlighted three cases in which two genes in a common biological process underwent positive selection in the same population:

> LARGE and DMD, both related to infection by the Lassa virus, in West Africa;
>
> SLC24A5 and SLC45A2, both involved in skin pigmentation in Europe;
>
> EDAR and EDA2R, both involved in development of hair follicles, in Asia.[275]

In Volume Four, we'll explore the implications behind the last two cases, but for now, we'll focus on the first. What does this tell us about the history of Africa? It tells us that the population of West Africa was significantly altered by its environment, right down to the genetic level. Continuing in this vein (no pun intended), we can look specifically at the connections between viruses that have been historically been intertwined with the movements and cultural changes of a Black population.

For example, malaria. With the advent of agriculture in Africa, malaria became a significant problem, thanks to humans excessively altering their environments to allow for better plant cultivation, and subsequently increasing the prevalence of a natural defense mechanism in form of *Plasmodium vivax*). To counter this new risk, West African populations went through a rise in genes that reduced the risk of infection by the Plasmodium parasite. These genes remain today, despite the fact they contribute to blood disorders like sickle cell trait, demonstrating how strongly natural selection can influence our genetics.[276]

This strain of malaria spread throughout the Black world around 10,000 years ago (thanks to agriculture), but was in some ways a revival or reawakening of a much older strain of malaria that emerged around the same time as the first human expansion out of Africa.

In Melanesia, there is evidence for a strain of Malaria known as *Plasmodium falciparum*. It's 100,000 years old, and may represent the earliest human migration into Melanesia. At 100,000 years old, it corroborates the mtDNA evidence that suggests some of the people of New Guinea were there before Toba and survived (and are thus older than most human lineages outside Africa today).[277]

In other words, the malaria provides more evidence of the Original People who left the Nubian Complex before the Toba event. These people, in Melanesia, are associated with pygmy populations.

So when and where did the 10,000-year-old Malaria strain come from? Same place. According to researcher Peter Marsh:

> Another expansion of Africans occurred 10,000 years ago bringing a different Malarial strain (Plasmodium Vivax) to Panama and the Western Pacific and may have been responsible for the spread of South American Coconut, Afro/American cotton, African gourd, African Jackbean across the Pacific.[278]

In other words, there was a Black population that dispersed from the SAME tropical region as the Original People about 10,000 years ago. They spread throughout the world, just as their ancestors had done 100,000 years before them. We can actually see some of the places they went (Panama, Western Pacific, South America, etc.) by following the genetic trails of this malarial strain. Marsh continues:

> Plasmodium falciparum appeared in Africa and spread around the world with migrating populations, as much as 100,000 years ago. Both the parasite and the mosquito underwent rapid evolutions about 10,000 years ago, forming Plasmodium vivax, which ranges widely through Asia, Africa, Melanesia and the Americas. Their coincidence with the development of settled agricultural societies in tropical regions seems to be a telling clue to the history of the

disease and the movement of man around the world.[279]

These were the Anu people. This evidence is clear in suggesting that they colonized the Pacific Islands and ultimately reached the west coast of the Americas. There's even some evidence connecting Pacific Island agriculture (which is also over 10,000 years old) back to the Nile Valley.[280] There's other genetic evidence in the form of HLAs. These are example of "alternative" genetic evidence that can fill in the gaps left behind when the DNA Haplogroups don't tell the whole story.

THE MEGALITHS OF THE PACIFIC ISLANDS

Did the Anu people make it into the Pacific Islands? The genetic evidence suggests they did. But how far did they go? And what did they build or establish in these travels? The genetic evidence suggests they actually made all the way to the Americas, meaning their influence extended far beyond Melanesia. What did they build? It looks much of their culture came with them.

In 1907, J. Macmillan Brown announced that there was a "definite megalithic track across the Old World from the Atlantic to the Pacific." Brown reported:

> If we look into the regions where these colossal stones abound, we shall find a clearly marked track across the face of the earth. They are most numerous on the southern shores of the Mediterranean and on the Atlantic coast of Europe. And we may conclude that Mauritania, or the North of Africa, is the probable home of the race that displayed such marvellous engineering skill without metal weapons, wheeled machines, or draught animals, whilst the eastern shore of the Atlantic Ocean was their first and easiest line of migration. Megalithic remains abound in Portugal and Brittany, the British Islands and Scandinavia.* They are not found in Central Europe, or anywhere away from the coasts of its oceans and seas except across the Russian and Asiatic steppes, where they stand as single stones or circles of stones, on the kurgans or mound-graves. And the line of these extends through Southern Siberia past Lake Baikal and through Mongolia and Manchuria. In the valley of the Yalu truncated pyramids take their place, as they do at several others points on the megalithic track.

Brown traces this "megalithic track" – which reminds me of Lothrop Stoddard's prehistoric "black belt" – deep into the Pacific Islands, and ultimately into the stonemason sites of the ancient Americas.

---

* Scandinavia consists of Finland, Norway, and Sweden.

Why did our Anu ancestors carry megalithic culture from East Asia in the west coast of the Americas, rather than across the Atlantic? According to J. Macmillan Brown:

> A section of mankind in early Neolithic times, say from ten to fifteen thousand years ago, migrated northwards from the north of Africa, along the Atlantic coast, and was stopped by the unislanded ocean from going farther west than Ireland.

Brown continues:

> [T]here was no endless archipelago to tempt the handlers of giant stones westward from Europe to America, and the titanic-stone path breaks off on the Irish coast. It is otherwise in Japan. To the south stretched a series of stepping-stones into Polynesia, at first minute as in the Bonin Islands, afterwards in large groups as in the Ladrones and the Carolines farther south. And in the former of these two groups there exist avenues of huge unmortared stone pyramids topped with stone hemispheres, whilst in the latter there exist the colossal walls of a long-deserted Venice built of great basaltic prisms piled one on another without cement.

He's referring here to Nan Madol, an ancient city built on a coral reef in the Caroline Islands. Its highly stratified social system was the earliest known example of such centralized political power in the western Pacific.

The people of Nan Madol built a megalithic stone city...on water. They used approximately 400,000 basalt blocks – quarried from the north side of the island and cut in the shape of six-sided prisms – to build artificial islands. These manmade islands were walled and divided by shallow canals. Some of the ruined walls are still more than 125 feet high and up to 2,580 feet long. The hexagonal blocks range from 12 to 27 feet in length, many weighing more than 10 tons. There are other buildings, now underwater, that connect to the island.

After the Caroline Islands of Micronesia, Brown says "the megalithic route across the Pacific is broken and incontinuous." One reason is because many of these islands are made of coral, and lack a good supply of volcanic stone. But once we reach the hard stone of Samoa, there is an ellipse of giant stone columns resembling Stonehenge. Nearby, there are "gigantic truncated pyramids which are called the tombs of the Tui-Tongas, and the colossal trilithon or gateway composed of three giant stones."[281]

In the Polynesian island of Tahiti, the track picks up again with another "gigantic truncated pyramid." Finally, in the North Island of New Zealand, there is a "miniature Stonehenge, with huge blocks standing six or seven feet above the ground, at Kerikeri, in the Bay of Islands, and another near Ateamuri, to the north of Taupo, consisting of fifty great stones set erect in the earth."[282]

Brown credits this megalithic track to a single race of builders:

> We may also conclude that it was the same race. For a skill like this power of handling enormous slabs of stone in primitive times must have been in truth a mystery, the possession of one type of men. It is not a stage in the evolution of all races. We have none of these structures in the lands of Negroids either in Central and Southern Africa, or in Australia, or in the region of the Papuans. Nor have we any of them in any purely Mongoloid region, such as China or Central Asia, or in the central and [eastern] parts of North and South America.[283]

Brown actually attempts to argue that this wondrous ancient race must have been the Caucasian. We now know that there are megalithic sites throughout Africa, where Anu people settled in the ancient past. But Brown knew better, even in 1907. **All of em knew better.**

Why else would he trace these people back to North Africa? Why else would he acknowledge that "There are no colossal stone erections either through the centre of Europe, a route the Huns and Magyars took, or north to Behring Straits or southwards thence to Central America." Better yet, why else would he report "traces of the Negroid even amongst the upper classes" of these people?

> They must have brought some mixture of negroid blood with them. For the nose in many Polynesians is flattened, though it is never squat and wide-nostrilled; and in not a few islands the flat nose is favoured as the aristocratic…The ideal of beauty is always set by the ruling class, and though the finest type of European faces might, according to all early voyagers, find their match in these islands of the Pacific, these were not the most admired by the dusky races, just as the fair skin that sometimes appears amongst them was not admired.[284]

In other words, they preferred dark skin and wide noses because those were the marks of royalty. Marco Polo noted the same preferences when he visited India. Then the Europeans took over and everything was flipped. You know how it goes.

What do we know so far? The first people of the Pacific Islands were Africoid and then Australoid people. Yet, as Brown reports, from "Melanesia and New Guinea to Samoa, there is a tract of from four to five thousand miles without a trace of this great stone record."[285] This is because the Anu people who built this megalithic culture came long after their predecessors, and didn't settle everywhere they still had an established presence. As a result, we won't find many megaliths in places where Australoid people remained the dominant population.

ISLAND CULTURE
WHY DID PACIFIC ISLANDERS TATTOO THEIR FACES?

Facial tattooing is an ancient tradition that goes back several thousand years before Mike Tyson and Lil Wayne. Many East African people tattoo symbolic patterns on their foreheads and cheeks, as do many indigenous people in Southern India and Southeast Asia.

Along the Pacific, we can find facial tattooing among the Maori, who have established a tradition so rich that European ethnographers marveled at the intricacy of their designs, noting that they could not find two designs that were exactly the same. Their tattoos were like cultural fingerprints. This same tradition is also found among the Ainu of Japan and the Haida of Northwest Canada.

In fact, the women of the Ainu, Maori, and Haida all tattoo their lips to make them look wider and darker, while the men sometimes tattoo their entire face and large portions of their body. It's clear there's a linear connection, but *where does the practice come from*?

According to J. Macmillan Brown, the "aristocracy" of the Pacific Islands had the "brown complexion of South Asia, and in many cases the flat nose of the negroid…and **hence the nose of beauty was flat, and the skin of adults was darkened by tattooing**."

Brown argues that these Negroid people must have been a later wave of conquerors, coming after the Polynesians, rather than an aboriginal people who were conquered. "Had this been the case," he argues, "we should never have found the dark skin and the flattened nose as two main points in the ideal of beauty." As we know the first people of the Pacific were Australoid, and they were most likely followed by people of the Polynesian (or Paleo-Mongoloid) type, this final wave of Negroid people must have been members of the Anu migration that influenced the entire world.

In discussing the megalithic sites found throughout the Pacific Islands, J. Macmillan Brown reveals that the erection of stone monuments and earthen mounds were meant to commemorate the burial sites of the region's founding populations. These people were typically either Anu people or their DBP predecessors:

> The chief thing to guide us in this group is the megalithic habit of

the early inhabitants. There are huge mounds in Ponape at least that are, though unexcavated, clearly ancient burial-places; they are called by the natives "giants' graves." There are, also, old tombs in enclosures inland called the "graves of the little people." There are, in addition to these, colossal stone tables and pillared galleries and megalithic ruins all over the island.

And as in mainland Europe, Asia, and the Americas, the DBP of the Pacific were believed to inhabit the fringes of the lands they once ruled, living on in myths of "little people" who would abduct members of the invading race:

> And the natives have, like those of all the larger forested islands of Micronesia and Polynesia, a great fear of penetrating into the forests or mountains, lest they should encounter the fairies, a clear sign that the remnant of a conquered people took refuge in these more inaccessible haunts and preyed on any of their conquerors that ventured far from their coast centres.[286]

THE REAL NOAH'S ARK!

Anu people carried many of their domesticated animals to new settlements by boat. There's no telling how old this practice was, or how many animals were transferred this way, but we know they sailed into Australia with dingoes over 5,000 years ago, and brought giraffes and other "exotic" animals from East Africa to China as recently as the 13th century. The seafarers who crossed the Pacific Islands into the Americas carried domestic fowls, dogs, pigs, and rats.[287]

These were the first domesticated animals in the Americas. Long before this, the Anu people who settled the Aegean island of Cyprus 12,000 years ago were importing animals like goats, pigs, foxes, and Persian deer just to support the hunting population.[288] Essentially, the Anu tradition of transporting animals to new locations may have served as the basis for the Biblical myth of Noah's Ark.

THE FIRST MEAT SUBSTITUTE

Speaking of animals, the history of the pig in the Pacific Islands is interesting, because swine was – ironically enough – the original "meat substitute." Meat, in this case, referring to human flesh. We're talking about cannibalism. There's very little evidence of cannibalism originating among Black populations, but that didn't stop Europeans from reporting back on "ooga booga" jungle people cooking white explorers and missionaries for dinner.

This may be why J. Macmillan Brown admits that Polynesian people brought cannibalism wherever they went, but he attempts to trace the practice back to the people of Melanesia. Yet there's no evidence

TYPICAL MOAI OF RAPA NUI

NOT ALL MOAI HAVE THIN NOSES

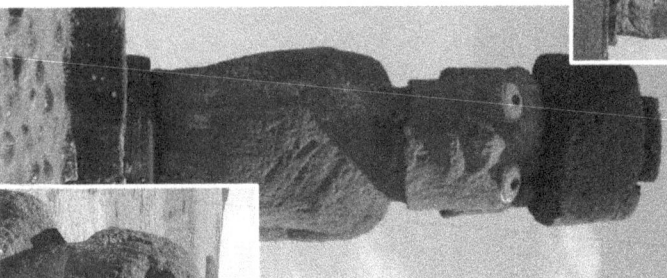

TUKUTURI, A RARE "KNEELING" MOAI WHICH MOAI TYPE CAME FIRST?

RAPA NUI NATIVES

MENHIRS OF TORAJA ISLAND

PALAU OF CAROLINE ISLANDS

NOTE THE SIMILARITIES

of such a practice among the Melanesians, or any Africoid (or Australoid) people anywhere on Earth.

Of cannibalism as a Polynesian tradition, Brown reports:

> It was always sacred to the men, and usually to the aristocrats and warriors. The women as a rule were not allowed to touch human flesh. Only one or two contingents took the pig with them, the others indulging in cannibalism till that animal was introduced into their group.[289]

In other words, somebody, long ago, gave the Polynesians pigs so they'd stop eating people. These people may have been the same Anu people who domesticated the pig first in the Near East, then in Europe, and then again in China, before sailing into the Pacific.

THE "MYSTERY" OF EASTER ISLAND

Wait. Before we begin, let's start by calling this island by its proper name. "Easter Island" was a name white folks invented, and it really has no connection to the island or its people. The indigenous people of this island know it as *Rapa Nui*. Rapa Nui is probably most famous for two things. First, there are the colossal stone heads, known as *moai*. Like the colossal Olmec heads, the giant moai heads of Rapa Nui may look similar, but no two are exactly alike. They appear to represent an elite group of people. John Macmillan Brown writes:

> Taken as a whole they express haughty scorn and imperious will; it is the expression of **victorious warriors and empire-makers**...Though the arrogant and resolute look is given to the faces of all the statues, it is never the same on two faces; every one looks as if it had been intended to be an individual portrait...[290]

Compare these comments with the description of the "strength and resolution" seen in the depictions of the Black warriors at Pasemah in Indonesia, or with any early accounts describing the Olmec heads.

THE MYSTERIES

So who were the people depicted in the moai? Where did they come from? What did they do? And how did they transport these stones? Part of the mystery is that there are no trees on the island. How did they roll these giant stones around without any logs?

Second, there's the mystery of why the island was abandoned and where its people went. You see, they basically disappeared. In *The Science of Self, Volume One*, we explained how a failure to maintain sustainable ecology drove the Rapa Nui civilization to the point of collapse. They DID have trees, it seems, and they used them to build their monuments. Meanwhile, they were domesticating rats as a protein source. This didn't turn out as planned:

> While the natives consumed much of the island's 16 million palm trees, building the ropes and wooden devices used to transport and erect the massive stone heads that are associated with Easter Island, they made efforts to replant as well. However, they couldn't replant fast enough to compensate for the rats, which fed on the seeds, making reforestation nearly impossible. Before long, the island was nearly barren of palm trees, which were key to sustaining Easter's human population.[291]

But that wasn't their end. Just the beginning of their end. Once they were weak, that's when the Dutch came, bringing their diseases and murderous slave raids. "Older explanations essentially blamed the victims for their demise," says archaeologist Patricia McAnany of Boston University, referring to old theories that the 'Easter Islanders had wiped each other out' in tribal warfare. "The island still represents a cautionary tale," she says, "but one of the dangers of invasive species."[292]

By "invasive species" we assume she's either talking about the rats or the Europeans. Either way, the Rapa Nui civilization didn't last. But were the Polynesians the people who brought civilization to Easter Island, or were there people there before them?

Roland Dixon said a "Proto-Negroid" people from Africa "drifted eastward through India to southeastern Asia and thence through Indonesia and Melanesia to Australia, with a long arm stretched out farther through central Polynesia as far as Easter Island."[293]

THE RONGO-RONGO RECORDS

The Rongo-Rongo script of Rapa Nui shares some similarities with that of the Solomon Islands in Melanesia, but no one has firmly established where it came from. In the 1930s, Guillaume de Hevesy connected it to the 4500-year-old script found on stone seals at Mohenjo-Daro and Harappa in the Indus Valley. In *Environment, Race, and Migration*, Thomas Griffith Taylor notes the same similarities.[294]

It is noteworthy that one local legend says:

> The first race invented the Rongo-Rongo writing: they wrote it on stone. Of the four parts of the world that were at one time inhabited by the first race, it is only in Asia that this writing still exists.[295]

Unfortunately, most of Easter Island's history – particularly as written in the Rongo-Rongo language – has been destroyed. Not by time and weather, but by the same people who destroyed almost all of the ancient books of the Mayas, and countless other Black and brown civilizations across the world. Louis Pauwels and Jacques Bergier have said:

> As happened in Africa and in South America, the first missionaries to arrive on Easter Island took steps to remove all traces of a dead civilization. At the foot of the statues there were wooden tablets covered with hieroglyphs: these were all burned or dispatched to the Vatican library which houses many secrets. Was this done to destroy all traces of ancient superstitions, or to remove what could have been evidence of some Unknown Power?[296]

There may only be a few places left in the world where a large number of indigenous written records remain intact or available for study. First, there is ancient Egypt, where the stories are etched in stone. Still, there too, efforts have been made to conceal what those walls reveal. And we should not forget that the grand library of Alexandria was the largest collection of manuscripts in the world and was a great center of learning for 600 years in Egypt...until it was destroyed and burnt down.

Further west lay the libraries of Timbuktu, Mali. These libraries hold from 700,000 to 1,000,000 manuscripts and include the Ahmed Baba Institute, the Mamma Haidara Library, the Fondo Kati, the Al-Wangari Library, the Mohamed Tahar Library, the Maigala Library, the Boularaf Collection, and the Al Kounti Collections. These too, are endangered because territorial fighting in the region has already caused the destruction of hundreds of thousands of manuscripts that had been collected in Timbuktu over the course of centuries. In our chapter on India, we discussed the impending loss of oral traditions among indigenous populations. This is not just in India, but everywhere indigenous people can be found. **Who will preserve our histories?**

EVEN HAWAII?

In his research on the ancient Americas, John Denison Baldwin notes similar ruins in the Hawaiian Islands, where "the masonry is occasionally superior to that found elsewhere," as well as ruins in Hawaii at a hill called Kukii:

> The hill is so regular in its outline that it appears like a work of art, a giant effort of the Mound-Builders. Its general form resembles very much the pyramid of Cholulu in Mexico, and from this fact I felt a great interest in climbing it.[297]

Upon climbing the hill, they discovered that it was entirely manmade, and topped by "great square blocks of hewn stone overgrown by shrubbery." On reaching the summit, they found that "it had been leveled and squared according to the cardinal points, and paved" with two large upright blocks of cut stone erected in an east-west orientation.[298] They also found stone terracing resembling the "polished stones in some of the walls of Tiahuanaco [Tiwanaku], and other ruins in Peru." Baldwin asks:

> By whom and when was this hill terraced and these stones hewn? There is a mystery hanging around this hill which exists nowhere else in the [Hawaiian] Islands. The other structures so numerously scattered over the group are made of rough stone; there is no attempt at a terrace; there is no flight of steps leading to them; there is no hewn or polished stone, nor is there any evidence of the same architectural skill evinced. They are the oldest ruins yet discovered, and were evidently erected by a people considerably advanced in arts, acquainted with the use of metallic instruments, the cardinal points, and some mathematical knowledge. Were they the ancestors of the present Hawaiians, or of a different race that has passed away?[299]

Fifty years after Baldwin asked, A.L. Kroeber answered this question:

> The impression that there is a Negroid strain in the Hawaiians can hardly be escaped. Their resemblance to the less specialized Mongoloids, such as East Indians and American Indians, is even more striking.[300]

The original people of the Polynesian Islands were Black. The evidence is overwhelming that Australoid people traveled far beyond the limits Melanesia. And after Polynesians settled these islands, yet another wave of Anu Black came to these islands, quickly introducing the megalithic Anu Cultural Complex and another "Negroid strain" of physical traits.

SOUTH AMERICA

JUST EAST OF EASTER ISLAND

"Some workers have postulated a "Hispano-African" complex of prospectors in the late third millennium B.C. as a carrier of Near Eastern traits. The trail...seems to lead from Anatolia through the Balkans, Italy, Iberia, North Africa, and the Canary Islands, to the Caribbean, Mesoamerica, Florida, and up the South American rivers." – James Guthrie

They say Brazil has the largest Black population outside Africa. This is true to a certain extent, but only if you narrowly define "Black" within the context of those who were transported around the world by the transatlantic slave trade, also known as the Maafa (or "great tragedy"). Indeed, Brazil has millions and millions of citizens who are the descendants of African slaves. And they have an intensely rich history. You may want to check out a film called *Besouro* to get started.

Now, if we define Black more broadly, India has more people who should be considered Black than anywhere else in the world. We're talking about hundreds of millions of people, most of whom settled there long before any sort of slave trade was invented. But what if I told you that Brazil, too, a Black history that predates slavery? Deep within the Amazon Rainforest, we can find the traces of **Black people who came to South America long before Columbus**.

Meanwhile, on the other side of the continent – in the Andes – we find evidence of yet another ancient Black migration. All things considered – and by all things, I mean the genetic, linguistic, and archaeological data – it is clear that South America received not one, not two, but possibly dozens of Black migrations in its ancient past. These people were highly influential in the history of South America's first civilizations, many of which are still hidden under the cover of the rainforest.

THE LOST CITIES OF THE AMAZON

When you think Amazon, what do you think about? *Jungle, right?*

That's what a lot of archaeologists once thought as well. Just as archaeologists ignore Central Africa in favor of Egypt, in South America, archaeologists ignore the Amazon Basin in favor of the "grand civilizations" of the Incas, the Nazca, and other ancient cultures.

But the Amazon was once rich with prehistoric cultures. When Europeans first sailed into the area in 1540, they reported large, well-populated cities. By 1700, these cities were gone, swallowed up by the jungle. It wasn't until recently that archaeologists reconsidered the possibility that the "jungle tribes" of the Amazon could have once built large, complex civilizations.

In 1542, the Spanish explorer Francisco de Orellano ventured into the Amazon Basin and along the Rio Negro to hunt for the mythical city of El Dorado and its rumored treasure of gold. Instead his expedition found a network of farms, villages, and cities. His chronicles describe large villages, long-range trade networks, governments, and a highly populated Amazon.

More Europeans followed Orellano. By the time the first scientists arrived, those people were gone. So modern scientists assumed that Orellano was mistaken, and there was no great, heavily-populated civilization in the Amazon. *Ever.*

But after years of archaeological finds, it appears Orellano's accounts were just the tip of the iceberg. At more than 100 sites across the Amazon, scientists have unearthed evidence of early civilizations that were far more advanced, far more broadly connected, and far more densely occupied than the small bands of nomadic hunter-gatherers they had predicted.

Anthropologist Michael Heckenberger was studying the Kuikuro people of the Xingu basin in Brazil who he realized had a ruling-class structure far more complex than what would be needed for their small group of just 300 people. He wondered, "Could the region have had a grander past?" When he dug beyond the village borders he found a giant plaza, roads, causeways, canals, and even bridges connecting two large prehistoric settlement clusters.

Each cluster comprised several walled towns, perhaps housing up to 50,000 residents each, with a large plaza that served as both a burial ground for the ruling elite and the hub for ritual ceremonies. Roads going outward in the four cardinal directions led to smaller satellite towns – suburbs basically – many of which were connected to fishponds and agricultural sites.[301]

The ancient sites are about **10 times the size of the local villages there today**. Heckenberger's team uncovered 28 towns, villages and hamlets across roughly 7,700 square miles of present-day forest – **an area bigger than the state of Connecticut**.

The bigger cities featured large plazas, some nearly 500 foot long, and were surrounded by defensive ditches backed by wooden fencing. Heckenberger notes that the fractal organization of these "garden cities" was **better planned than the cities of Medieval Europe:**

> The whole landscape is almost like a latticework, the way it is gridded off…These are far more planned at the regional level than your average medieval town. Here things are oriented at the same angles and distances across the entire landscape.[302]

The people of the Amazon, like the people of West Africa, didn't have much stone to quarry, so they built everything from earth. Surveys of the Amazon have uncovered thousands of acres of raised fields connected by miles of causeways.

They also dug miles of canals for fish-farming, and built mounds to raise their villages above flood level. On the island of Marajo, located at the mouth of the Amazon, they built over 400 massive earthen mounds, including one over with an area of over 50 acres. To construct this, it would require a million cubic yards of dirt!

Archaeologists are now questioning where these people came from and how they were related to the Incas to the west and other civilizations to the north.[303] Anthropologist C.L. Erickson noted that this Pre-Columbian complex of "earth and water" societies was linked together by networks of communication, trade, and alliances.[304]

Tragically, much of the Amazon is being deforested. Although it provides so much of the oxygen we breathe, loggers are tearing down its trees faster than you could imagine. And they're not alone. Companies like McDonalds are clearing its forests to provide pasture land for cheap cattle. Yet this deforestation has revealed something *unexpected*. There was something *hidden* under those trees. In the section on the Andes, you'll learn what archaeologists have been surprised to find.

INDIAN BLACK EARTH

There's another sign of ancient Amazonian civilization left in the earth. It's called *Terra preta de Indio* (Portuguese for "Indian black earth"), a type of soil prized among local farmers. This kind of soil is not natural to the Amazon, where the earth is normally yellowish and nutrient-poor, unfit for growing food crops.

Yet there are these extensive patches of soil that are mysteriously dark, moist, and fertile. These black patches of Earth were actually "made" by the prehistoric people of the Amazon. By devising a way to enrich the soil, the early inhabitants of the Amazon created a foundation for agriculture-based settlements that could support large populations. It's a science known as "**land reclamation**" and Westerners are only recently learning how to do it. *They're learning from us.*

Heckenberger argues that the complex, managed landscapes of this ancient society could serve as a model for sustainable development today. He asks:

> Rather than have the populations that live in the indigenous areas adopt foreign technologies that are not well adapted to the environment, why not use some of these homegrown technologies that were used for a very, very long time in the Amazon basin?

In other words, **our ancestors had it right, yet again.**

WHO WERE THE PEOPLE WHO LIVED IN THE XINGU BASIN?

Wait. Hold up. I've gotta say something that I probably could have said earlier. At this point, some readers may think that I want to "stretch" the facts and assume that Black people simply did *everything, everywhere*...because that's what I want to believe. That's not it. I'm not talking about EVERY indigenous community across South

INDIGENOUS PEOPLE OF THE AMAZON

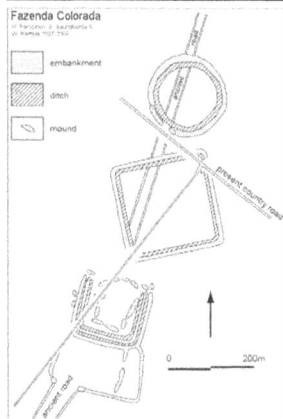

UPPER XINGU REGION

BRAZIL

Brasília

1,000 miles

Fazenda Colorada

embankment

ditch

mound

The geoglyphs were settlements?

KUIKURO WARRIOR

THE ENVIRA

BORORO INDIANS

Many of these people are clearly Mongoloid, but others are not. Also, why does an "uncontacted tribe" like the Envira paint some of their men black? Compare with similar practices of other indigenous Americans.

America. There are hundreds. I'm talking about *specific populations.* And, as you'll soon see, I'm establishing these connections because that's honestly *where the data leads.* Although I know many readers would have been content to read a simple text without all of these technical details, I KNOW there are people who would dismiss everything in this book as "Afrocentric nonsense" unless I laid out all the evidence, even if it sometimes sounds boring or too scientific.

Some people (mostly white people and people related to Stephen from *Django Unchained*) will STILL dismiss all the evidence I've assembled, but that's to be expected. What I set out to do was not to convince the Tea Party, but *to give a future generation of like-minded scholars the ammunition to argue their points solidly.* Let's move on.

THEY WERE BLACK? PROVE IT

Gladly. In the early 1900s, both British anthropologist Thomas Griffith Taylor and French anthropologist Joseph Deniker thought that the "wavy or frizzy" hair of Brazilian indigenous groups like the Korayas of Matto Grosso, the Bakairas of the Xingu River, and some neighboring Arawaks, could be traced back to a race of early Black inhabitants in the Americas.

These scholars weren't alone. Several early explorers reported seeing "Negroes" near South American coasts and in Central America:

> Reports of "Negroes" along the coasts of Panama, Colombia, and Campeche are attributed to Vasco de Balboa (1513), Lopez de Gomara, Alonzo Ponce, Fray Gregoria Garcia, and others. Count (1939), Comas (1956), Vivante (1967), and Van Sertima (1995:66-68, 99-102) give references…De Quatrefages also reported that Charruans on the north bank of the Plata River [in Uruguay, eastern South America] were black. These reports are consistent with other evidence of African or Melanesian presence discussed in the literature of apparent early contacts.[305]

We can add several other names to the above list of eyewitnesses (including Columbus himself), but eyewitness accounts are not all we have. As we noted in Part One, there is significant evidence of African people settling the east coasts of Americas in the prehistoric past. However, most of the genetic evidence for this migration will appear to be remnants of post-Columbian contact via the slave trade.

Nonetheless, there are several genetic markers pointing to African people in the pre-Columbian Amazon, and these markers are often found where markers for post-Columbian contact are absent. We'll discuss just three of these:

❑ The G6PD mutation (related to protection against malaria) suggests that Africans came to the Amazon and then traveled upriver into the Andes.*

☐ The K allele of the Kell system suggests a connection between indigenous people in eastern Brazil and the people of West Africa.†

☐ The Jsa allele points to African people coming to the Amazon, followed by migrations into the Andes and the Caribbean Islands.‡

These genes could have been carried by Anu people traveling across Africa or a more ancient migration. Guthrie discusses the possibility that many of the African settlers of the Americas were Anu people coming across the Atlantic:

> Some workers have postulated a "Hispano-African" complex of prospectors in the late third millennium BC as a carrier of Near Eastern traits. The trail, marked by such items as distinctive pottery (patojos, stirrup-spout vessels, orange wares), figurines, and stamp seals, seems to lead from Anatolia through the Balkans, Italy, Iberia, North Africa, and the Canary Islands, to the Caribbean, Mesoamerica, Florida, and up the South American rivers. This might explain the finding, by Key and others, of a seeming Proto-Anatolian element in Quechua, Aymara, and Uru-Chipaya. Copper mining and shaft tombs seem also to be part of the transmitted complex. The "shaft-tomb complex" was present in Panama, Venezuela, and Peru by 550 B.C. and reached Mexico about 140 B.C. Chadwick proposed two waves of Near-Eastern influence: one about 2000 B.C. and another around 500 B.C. Alcina Franch, de

---

* Among the dark-skinned people of India, Africa, the Near East, Southeast Asia, and Oceania, the presence of the G6PD mutation confers immunity to malaria. It is rare in Australia and America, but the four American samples that have traces of it (the Trio and Wajana people of the lower Amazon, and the Quechua and Aymara people of the Andes) reveal a connection between the Amazon and the Andes, which James Guthrie interprets as "foreign traits," presumably from Africa, being "carried up the rivers [from the Amazon], where they took root in Andean societies."

† The Afro-Asiatic K allele is found in its highest levels in India (14-21%), in Arabia, and in parts of Africa, but Afro-Asiatic migrants appear to have introduced it to northern Europe as well. The only American populations with more than 3% are the Ojibwe (6%), the Ingano of Colombia (6%), and several Ge tribes of Eastern Brazil (6-12%), where the highest American levels are found. Not surprisingly, matching levels are found directly across the Atlantic in Gambia (10%, where the highest West African frequency has been reported. Again, this suggests an African connection with the pre-Columbian Amazon.

‡ The Jsa allele characteristic of African people but also occurs in Asian Negritos. Jsa occurs at high frequencies among the Oyampí and neighboring Wajana of the lower Amazon (25.8% and 24.6%, respectively). It appeared at lower levels in five tribes of a Caribbean cluster (mostly Carib and Arawak people). Jsa was also found in samples of Quechua (1.3%) and Aymara-speakers (0.9%) but was absent from 14 other South American tribes.

Borhegyi, Jett, and others have listed many traits of apparent Near-Eastern origin. A distinctive Peruvian construction method used at Las Haldas, Cerro Sechín, and Chavín de Huantar (1600-800 B.C.), in which large upright orthostats are separated by sections of smaller stones or rubble, is known architecturally as opus africanum, because it is common in North Africa, especially in Tunisia.

In other words, the black earth of the Amazon was produced by an ancient Black civilization,* at least some of whom were clearly environmental scientists. And local scientists say we've seen "no more than a tenth" of what the Amazon forest holds hidden![306]

A QUICK NOTE ON BLACKS IN AMERICA BEFORE SLAVERY
Yes, there were certainly some Africans who crossed the Atlantic before Columbus. This we know. We also know that some of the people Columbus encountered looked African. But what percentage of the indigenous population was West African in origin? The evidence doesn't suggest that the majority of Native Americans were West African, of course. And like the John Hanson myth, this idea negates the role of whites in what they did to African people through the slave trade. It negates the lives of millions of Africans who suffered through the Maafa. I understand some people believe that claiming indigenous is a worthwhile legal tactic, but you can't use secondary source history books to verify your heritage. If you really want to argue for Native American heritage, do it the right way. Get the genealogical and genetic research done.

THEN WHAT HAPPENED?

In August of 2008, *Scientific American* published an article on these findings, titled "Ancient Amazon Actually Highly Urbanized." Journalist David Biello reported:

> The remains of houses and ceramic cooking utensils show that humans occupied these cities for around 1,000 years, from roughly 1,500 years to as recently as 400 years ago. Satellite pictures reveal that during that time, the inhabitants carved roads through the jungle; all plaza villages had a major road that ran northeast to southwest along the summer solstice axis and linked to other settlements as much as three miles away. There were bridges on some of the roads and others had canoe canals running alongside them.

> The remains of the settlements also hint at surrounding large fields of manioc, or cassava (a starchy root that is still a staple part of the Brazilian diet) as well as the earthen dams and artificial ponds of fish farming, still practiced by people who may be the present-day descendants of the Kuikuro. Although such "garden cities," as Heckenberger describes them in Science, do not match the dense urbanism of contemporary Brazilian metropolises such as Rio de

---

* Recent genetic studies supporting a significant infusion of African people into the pre-Columbian Amazon. For details, see the Appendix.

THE ANCIENT ANDES

Caral was one of first urban centers in the Andes. Over 3,000 years later, the Incas reunited many of the people who descended from this community. What did the Incas look like? A well-preserved Inca girl (bottom right) gives us a clue!

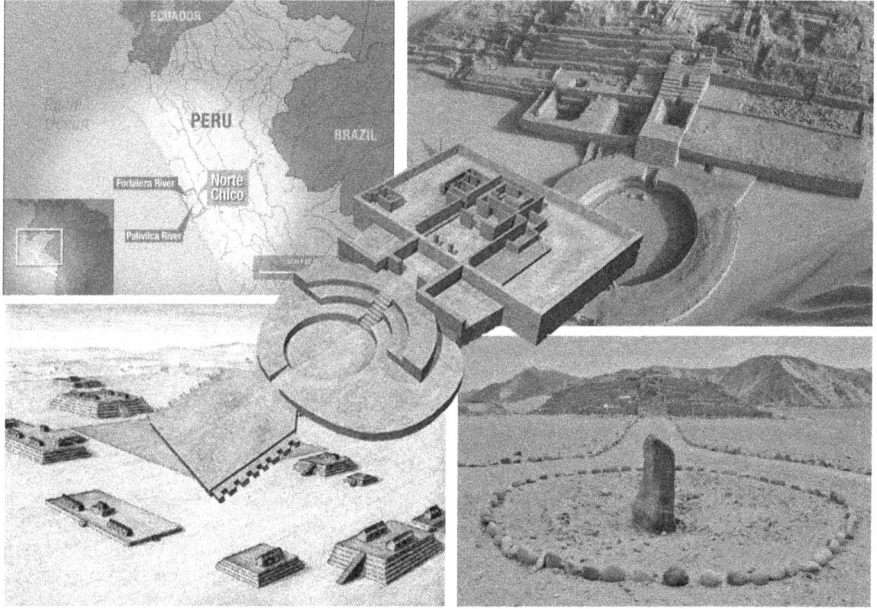

ECUADOR

PERU

BRAZIL

Fortaleza River

Norte Chico

Pativilca River

Caribbean Sea

PANAMA

VENEZUELA

COLOMBIA

ECUADOR

BRAZIL

PERU

PACIFIC OCEAN

BOLIVIA

CHILE

0   1000
kilometers
© CI / CABS
January 2005

ARGENTINA

Equator

Quito
Riobamba
Tomebamba
Tumbes
Solana
Marañón R.
Huancabamba
Chiquitoy   Cajamarca
Chan Chan
Paramonga
Pachacamac
Incawasi
Tombo Colorado

Huanuco
Andahuaylas
Machu Picchu
Oilantaytambo

Amazon R.

SOUTH AMERICA

Pacific Ocean

Ucayali R.

Lake Titicaca

Nazca
Cuzco

Tiahuanaco

Lake Poopó

Paraná R.

Inca Territory

- CE 1230
- CE 1400
- CE 1438-1463
- CE 1463-1471
- CE 1471-1493
- CE-1493-1525
- Inca Road

Sol

Santiago
Talca

Janeiro or São Paulo, they do blend seamlessly into the jungle and maximize use of limited natural resources. They also suggest that the rainforest bears the marks of intense human habitation, rather than being pristine.

In fact, with the disappearance of its citizens, the many plants grown by the people of the Amazon rapidly grew into the dense "jungle" we now associate with the Amazon rainforest. Where did these people go? Biello continues:

> But, ultimately, these cities died; most likely a victim of the diseases brought by European explorers in the early 16th century, according to Heckenberger. Two thirds or more of the original human inhabitants of Brazil are believed to have been killed by such disease, and the forest quickly swallowed the cities they left behind.[307]

Think about that. The Amazon rainforest – with all its ecological diversity – is in great part the result of "garden cities" going untended, meaning that **much of this ecological diversity could have been introduced by the scientists of the ancient Amazon.** And we find almost the same story when we examine the history of the rainforests of Central Africa. These areas both have climates that are conducive to rapid plant growth, but – when they were settled – they looked nothing like the jungles we imagine today.

THE STORY OF THE ANDES

The Andes is the longest continental mountain range in the world. It is a continual range of about 4,300 miles of highlands along the western coast of South America. On average, the lands of the Andes are 13,000 feet above sea level. The Andes extend through seven countries: Venezuela, Colombia, Ecuador, Peru, Bolivia, Chile and Argentina.

Andean Peru is considered one of the world's "cradles of civilization," where indigenous civilization emerged independently and spread outwards. Until recently, historians believed that the history of the Andes began with the Chavín culture of 900 BC, which ultimately gave birth to hundreds of cultures, including the Moche, Wari, and Inca.

But then they uncovered a 5,000 year-old city of pyramids in the Peruvian desert. In 2001, archaeologist Ruth Shady explored the ancient city, now known as Caral. Caral was spread out over 150 acres, and featured an elaborate complex of temples, an amphitheater, plazas and residential buildings. Features like the

WHEN THE WORLD WAS BLACK

DID YOU KNOW?
The Huaca del Sol is an adobe brick temple built by the Moche civilization on the coast of ancient Peru. The pyramidal structure is made of over 130 million adobe bricks and was the largest pre-Columbian adobe structure built in the Americas. The number of different makers' marks on the bricks suggests that over a hundred different communities contributed bricks to its construction. In other words, it was a testament to the extent of the ancient Moche empire. When the Spaniards took over Peru, they actually redirected the flow of the Moche River to run past the base of the Huaca del Sol, just to make it easier for them to loot gold artifacts and other sacred items from the temple. The resulting water damage was immeasurable. It's been estimated that two-thirds of the structure have been lost to erosion and looting. It was originally at least 150 feet tall.

central plaza and **flat-topped pyramids are first seen here,** and then later in most Andean sites.

Like the Incas would do much later, the people of Caral did trade with other cities as far as the Amazon basin, used quipus (knotted cords) to do math and keep records, and enjoyed recreational herb smoking. These laid-back people had no weapons and no evidence of violence or warfare. They fished the waters using cotton nets and farmed the land using a sophisticated irrigation system. By 2600 BC, Caral was a thriving urban complex, around the same time that Egypt's great pyramids were being built.

In fact, there are also six stone platform mounds that resemble pyramids. The largest of these pyramids was terraced with a staircase leading up to an atrium, culminating in a flattened top housing enclosed rooms and a ceremonial fire pit. Between the pyramids, Caral had a central plaza. At a nearby site, a 4200-year-old temple located atop pyramid mound serves as an astronomical observatory, aligned with the summer and winter solstices.

An even older site, known as Sechin Bajo, dates back to 3500 BC. There, archaeologists have found a massive circular plaza and a platform pyramid that may have been 300 feet tall. "Whoever built Sechin Bajo had a good knowledge of architecture and construction." says German archaeologist Peter R. Fuchs. So who built these cities?

To figure it out, we need to look at the bigger picture and work backwards. One thing Shady soon realized was that the cities of Caral and Sechin Bajo were not isolated developments. They were part of a larger cultural complex that extended across the valley. Shady explained:

> The number of urban centers (17) identified in the Supe Valley, and their magnitude, requires a great quantity of surplus labor for their

construction, maintenance, remodeling and burial. If we consider exclusively the productive capacity of this small valley, this investment could not have been realized without the participation of the communities of neighboring valleys.[308]

In other words, there was a massive empire in the Andes long before the Incas unified all the local ethnic groups under one government. Shady regarded the Caral-Supe civilization as the beginning of "5,000 years of cultural identity in Peru."

The discovery of Caral-Supe (also known as the Norte Chico civilization) not only pushed back the timeline of civilization in the Andes, it revealed that the cradle of Andean civilization was not inland (home to the Chavín, and later Inca, civilizations), but at the Peruvian coast.

Now...the next question becomes...where did the people of Caral-Supe come from? The coastal location is a clue. They came from overseas. Then what happened? As Joseph Powell notes in *The First Americans*, in nearly all of South America, including parts of the Amazon, there was a "near instantaneous radiation of people throughout the hemisphere soon after 12,000 years ago."[309] But what kind of people?

THE FIRST PEOPLE OF THE ANDES

The earliest established culture in Peru is known as the Paijan culture. It dates back to about 9,000 BC. This is the time when we find the first bottle gourds and squash being grown in Mexico and Peru. The Paijan remains are extremely long-headed and similar to the earliest human remains from Lagoa Santa sites in Brazil.[310] If you refer back to Part One, that means they looked Black.* These people were mummifying their dead as early as 5000 BC. Many of these mummies revealed evidence of tropical parasites that came from Southeast Asia or Ocean.[311]

However, there's only "limited indication" of human settlement during this early period. Around 3200 BC, the settlements start growing and the people start building communally.[312] By 2600 BC, development moved a little further inland, while still relying on the resources of the coastal areas. This is when they built sites like

---

* At the beginning of the preceramic period in Peru, all the remains are long-headed. Much later during the ceramic period (1000 BC-500 AD), it takes a sharp turn towards bracycephalic because of what Richard Keatinge calls "a massive contribution of Mongoloid-type skulls." This suggests that an influx of Mongoloid people poured into the area, most likely arriving by sea from Polynesia.

Caral.[313]

The Caral-Supe civilization reigned for over 1,000 years, spread to include 20 major residential centers across 700 square miles. The rulers of the Caral-Supe chiefdoms were "almost certainly theocratic, though not brutally so," according to Charles Mann, the author of *1491: New Revelations of the Americas Before Columbus*.[314] **We don't see evidence of bloodshed or human sacrifice, yet the rulers were able to motivate large numbers of their citizens to come together in massive construction projects**. Sound familiar?

Like in Egypt, construction areas show evidence of feasting, which would have included music and alcohol.[315] Caral contains six stone platform mounds – essentially Andean pyramids. All the pyramids were built in one or two phases, which means one of three things:

- ❐ Multiple phase construction was part of the plan
- ❐ They were amended or updated to reflect a new astronomical cycle.
- ❐ New influxes of people added more to the original monuments.

The people of Caral also pioneered the domestication of plants, especially cotton, as well as beans, squashes and guava. This may be the origin of the "three sisters" of the Americas. The rulers maintained large stone warehouses for resources such as cotton, and may have controlled their distribution as part of their position.[316]

They buried their people within their homes, in almost the same way as the pre-ceramic cultures of the Near East. Archaeologists also found ceremonial flutes made from pelican bones, something also found among the oldest civilizations of Asia. These flutes, however, were engraved with the figures of birds and monkeys found in the Amazon, suggesting that at least some of the people of Caral could have come from the Atlantic coast.*

Around 1800 BC, the Caral-Supe civilization began to decline, possibly because its people became disunited and began moving in separate directions. Why? We're not sure. What is clear is that people were leaving. Anthropologist Winifred Creamer adds, "People were moving to more fertile ground and taking their knowledge of irrigation with them."[317]

---

* There's support for this theory in the genetic data. For details, see the Appendix.

The people become fragmented and Andean civilization becomes stagnant until the rise of the next great Peruvian culture, the Chavín, almost a thousand years later. The Chavín were followed by cultures like the Moche, Nazca, Wari, and Tiwanaku (c. 200-1000 AD). All of these cultures, including the Chavín, have considerable evidence of a highly influential Black presence. After the decline of those cultures, however, the Andes became fragmented again.

By the time the Inca rise to power, there were literally hundreds of separate ethnic and linguistic groups living across the Andes. Essentially, the Caral-Supe civilization disappeared around 1800 BC but most of its features – particularly its role as a "great unifier" – were revived by the Incan empire over 3000 years later.

THE COMING OF THE ANU

We've established that the original people of the Andes were Australoid people, who most likely came by sea via the Pacific Islands. But who transitioned these people from a hunter-gatherer lifestyle into a civilization of stonemasons, astronomers, and farmers? It appears that ancient Peru could have been – like ancient Egypt – both a cradle and a melting pot. Black people from East Asia could have brought the practices of moundbuilding and many of their artistic motifs, which look just like the burial mounds and artwork found in Shang Dynasty China. But, like the Olmec civilization in Mexico, Peru was a place where cultures came together.

For example, one study of ancient Peruvian DNA has linked them to people in Ecuador, Colombia, Siberia, Taiwan, and the Ainu of Japan. In response to the Ainu connection, Peruvian archaeologist Luis Chero told the paper *El Comercio*:

> Currently, the DNA results have great value because they can be understood to show that there were people who arrived in these zones from Asia and who then converted these zones into the great culture of the New World.[318]

This is important, because nobody ever objects to the presence of ancient Asians or Europeans in an ancient civilization. It's only when you say "Black people were there" that you have a problem. To be fair, Peru wasn't "all Black" at the time of Caral-Supe, and certainly not by the time of the Incas. The Mongoloid presence was heavy

PYRAMIDS OF THE PERUVIAN ANDES

CARAL (NORTE CHICO, 2600-2000 BC)

RECONSTRUCTION OF CARAL

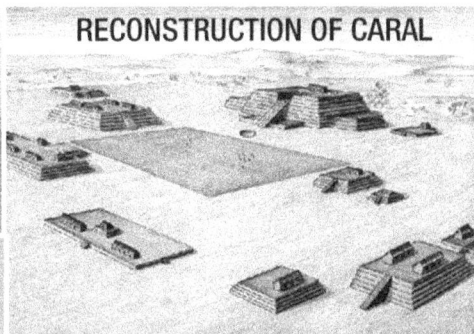

CAHUACHI (NAZCA, 1-500 AD)

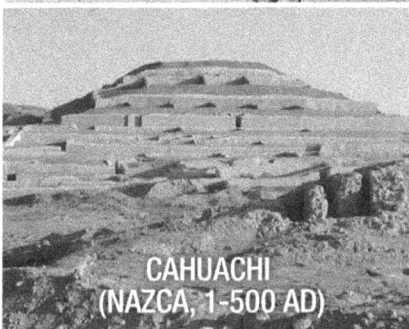

RECONSTRUCTION OF CAHUACHI

Because they were made from mud bricks (and not cut stone), many such pyramids are now in ruins, but artist renderings can show what they may have once looked like.

PIRAMIDE MAYOR (THE GREAT PYRAMID), CARAL

Many pyramid/ plaza complexes were built in a U-shape

CLOSE-UP OF ADOBE BRICKS

HUACA DEL SOL (MOCHE, 100-800 AD)

CEREMONIAL VESSELS OF THE MOCHE

Who do these faces represent? Where are they from? What is their culture? (They came before Columbus, and before Islam, between 100 and 800 AD.)

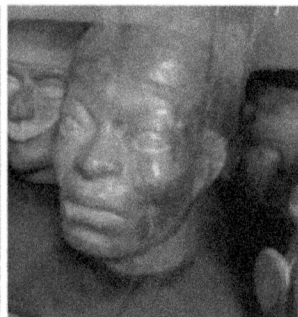

How did these people become so highly revered in this culture? Were they traders? Cultural leaders? Ambassadors of the old empire? Recent immigrants who resembled highly revered immigrants from a time long past?

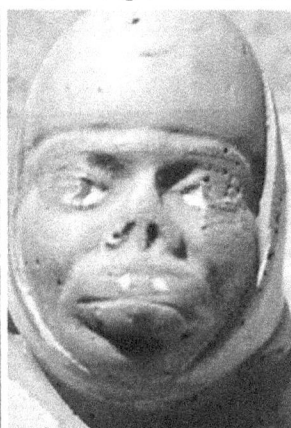

throughout South America at the rise of many of these ancient urban civilizations.

But there's also a Black presence that must have been highly influential. Pottery from the Moche culture (100-800 AD) of Peru's north coast depicts physical features, tattooing, and clothing reminiscent of some North African cultures, and many depict clear "Negroid" facial features. There's a pot from Tiwanaku (around the same time) that appears to bear an inscription referring to North Africa.[319]

An even older pot, cast from a mold of a bottle gourd, depicts a woman with a nose "like that of a negro, and the hair is represented in tufts."[320] These finds accompany skulls that suggest the presence of at least two racial types. One of them: broad-headed like Asians and many Native Americas, the other: long-headed like most Black people.

Where did the Black presence come from? As with the Olmecs, they may have sailed from West Africa into Brazil, where they founded the civilizations of the Amazon before traveling West into the Andes. Or they could have been members of the Black cultures of ancient east Asia, sailing from the coast of China or the islands of the Pacific. In fact, there are some similarities between the stone heads at Easter Island and those found in Peru.

But there's a third possibility, and this is the theory I am proposing throughout this text: The catalyst for the rapid emergence of ancient urban civilization is when two groups of geographically separated Black people come together.

It's what happened in the Nile Valley, where Saharans came together with southerners from Nubia to become the Egyptians. It's what happened in the Gulf of Mexico, where the Black East Asians of the Mokaya met with Nubians (or West Africans) to become the Olmecs. And it appears to be what happened in the Andes, where another group of Black East Asians (most likely coming from the same place as the Mokaya) met with the Africans who landed on Brazil's east coast and migrated across the Amazon to help found the Caral-Supe civilization.

TIWANAKU

Near the coast of Bolivia (just south of Peru), the Andeans built another amazing center, known as Tiwanaku. Andean scholars recognize Tiwanaku (often spelled Tiahuanaco) as one of the most important precursors to the Inca Empire, which would later emerge only a few hundred miles to the north.

Tiwanaku transitioned from an agricultural village in 1500 BC to "a moral and cosmological center to which many people made pilgrimages" between 300 BC and 300 AD.[323] Between 300 AD and 950 AD, it grew into an administrative capital in the region, considered the "center of the world." By 1000 AD, Tiwanaku fell victim to climate change, drought, and overconsumption of natural resources. In 1445 AD, the ninth Inca king absorbed Tiwanaku into the Incan empire.

During its reign, Tiwanaku was an amazing civilization. One of its most outstanding features was the sophistication of its stonemasonry. For example, the Akapana pyramid is over 700 feet wide and 50 feet tall. This means it's almost as wide as the Great Pyramid of Giza in Egypt, but only one-third as tall. Like the Great Pyramid, it also contains hidden tunnels and chambers that they're now using robotic rovers to explore.

North of the Akapana, the Kalasasaya is a large stone-paved courtyard the size of a football field, surrounded by a wall of massive pillars. The largest stone block at Kalasasaya is estimated to weigh 33 tons.[325] The site once served as a ceremonial center and astronomical observatory. **People could use different parts of the court to determine the specific astronomical activities for any date of the year.**

At many of the sites, massive stone gateways are built on artificial mounds, platforms, or sunken courts. One of the most impressive is at Pumapunku, a terraced earthen mound lined with giant stone blocks. In the walls of Pumapunku, each massive stone interlocked with the surrounding stones like a puzzle, forming load-bearing joints that didn't need mortar. And we don't just mean that the sides of the blocks lined up; we're talking about massive stones cut at matching angles so they literally are locked in place.

And many of the joints are so precise that not even a razor blade will fit between the stones.[326] Not only that, but many of the rectangular blocks are cut **so perfectly similar that they suggest mass production.** Even the master stonemason Incas (who came after Tiwanaku) weren't doing that. This is why architectural historian Jean-Pierre Protzen has theorized that the builders of Tiwanaku are the ones who taught later Inca stonemasons some (but not all) of their skills.[327]

On one of the platforms built at Pumapunku, there's a **carved stone slab of red sandstone estimated to weigh over 140 tons.** How did they transport this stone from a quarry near Lake Titicaca over a distance of at least six miles (going up a steep incline all the way), and then up a manmade mound? Archaeologists are still clueless. And while they ponder the possibilities, they continue to find more.

Recent radar surveys and excavations of the area between the Pumapunku and Kalasasaya complexes have revealed an entire world hidden beneath the ground's surface. There are walls and foundations for buildings and compounds, water conduits (basically a stone sewer system), pools or public baths, terraces, residential compounds, and wide areas and paths paved with gravel.

Not only were the city planners working hand-in-hand with the astronomers and stonemasons, Tiwanaku's engineers were constructing **functional irrigation systems, hydraulic mechanisms, and waterproof sewage lines.**

When the Spanish were done looting and destroying these ancient sites, Tiwanaku looked a bomb had hit it. Archaeologists attempted to reconstruct the Kalasasaya in the 1960s, but were unable to match the skill of the ancient builders who first erected it over 2,000 years ago.[331] Another notable feature at Tiwanaku was the use of metallurgy. The people mined copper from distant areas, and produced nickel and tin bronze from it, as well as unique copper-arsenic-zinc alloys not found in the Americas. They may have been the first to do this in the Americas.

They even had casts, or stone blocks with precisely-shaped sockets in which they poured molten metal. These cast bronze pieces were used as architectural cramps for the sophisticated limestone-conduit drainage systems built into the stone-block monuments. If it sounds technical and advanced, that's because it is!

They also worked metals like gold and silver using traditional metal-working tools and techniques. They had methods for gilding, welding, and even soldering. If soldering wasn't enough, there's even evidence that some of the gilding was electrochemical replacement gilding![332] Despite their mastery of the sciences, they didn't seek to "conquer nature" or negate its beauty. They built their structures to integrate with the natural features, like the sacred Illimani Mountain, where the ancestors were thought to live.

Tiwanaku (especially the Pumapunku complex and its surrounding temples) functioned as the spiritual and political center for Andean world, attracting pilgrims from far away to marvel in its beauty and partake in what Virginia Morell calls a "mind-altering and life-changing experience."[333] Studies of mummies from Tiwanaku reveal that the people used psychoactive drugs (like *ayahuasca*, made from a hallucinogenic plant) to heighten the experience, as did the people of Caral over 5,000 years before them (and as would many other pre-Columbian cultures, including the Incas). Modern-day Amazonian natives still use ayahuasca for shamanic rituals.

Also like the later Incas, Tiwanaku didn't rely on war and violence to expand. For the most part, they negotiated trade agreements (making other cultures dependent), spread their political influence, created colonies, and established state cults.[334] Religion also connected distant people to Tiwanaku, which was always seen as a spiritual center. Basically the same way ancient Egypt spread its power.

Consider all the details. Doesn't it seem like the Anu were here?

THE NAZCA LINES

The Nazca Lines are a group of designs engraved into the flatlands of the Nazca desert in southern Peru, spanning over 300 square miles. These designs are both abstract (lines, shapes, and spirals) and representational (monkey, spider, birds, flowers, etc.), with some designs several miles long. They were made between 900 BC and 600 AD, and are considered the most outstanding group of geoglyphs in the world.[*]

How did they make such geometrically precise lines and shapes (which are difficult, but not impossible, to see unless you're in the air or on a mountain top), and what do the figures mean?[†][336]

German mathematician Maria Reiche has studied the Nazca lines for decades. She describes them as a sophisticated astronomical observatory, created to mark risings and settings of the sun, moon and stars. Even if that's true, people will naturally wonder, "How did they ever see what they made? You can't see it from ground level!" This has led to wild speculation, most of it attempting to make the Nazca Lines out to be some sort of "UFO airport" with lines carved for landing strips.

But a faulty theory can't fill the gap in our understanding. The lines can't be landing strips because the ground they're carved into isn't packed solid enough to support a vehicle landing from the air. Yet, before you even get that far into your research, you should ask yourself, "If these intergalactic travelers were smart enough to travel across space and possibly time…why would they need visual aids to find their way back to their landing strip? You mean to tell me they got flux capacitors and warp drives but no GPS?" As we said earlier, "First it needs to make sense. Then I'll consider the facts."

---

[*] In the Appendix to this volume, we've included a guide to geoglyphs all over the world, including images carved into the ground in Australia that look just like some of the images from Nazca.

[†] It's not true that the lines can't be seen from the ground. They are visible from atop the surrounding foothills. The credit for the discovery of the lines goes to Peruvian archaeologist Toribio Mejia Xesspe, who spotted them when hiking through the foothills in 1927.

There's a theory that comes from the Peruvians themselves, who claim their shamans drank a liquid (probably ayahuasca) that took them on "soaring psychedelic journeys whose visions were later traced in lines on the ground."[337] Other accounts say the lines were walking paths for people taking mind-altering journeys of initiation.

But it's even possible that at least some of us did enjoy aerial views of these glyphs. As we suggested in our discussion of Nazca in "The Signs we Left Behind" in *The Science of Self, Volume One*:

> Even though they are only visible from the skies, they still point back to us! How? The evidence suggests they were constructed by humans who actually used hot air balloons (at least 1500 years ago!) to survey (and perhaps enjoy) their creations. (Yes, our history is THAT rich...*without* magic beings to help move the story along.)

Some of the glyphs and lines appear to line up with astronomical phenomena, but many of the lines cross over one another, like an old Etch-A-Sketch that still has the old lines showing even when you start a new design. Some archaeologists are puzzled by this "chaotic profusion." John Neal has proposed a theory I like:

> The whole desert of Nazca may be a testing ground and college of surveying. The conditions are ideal, and the apprentice surveyor would first have to interpret what was already there to its exact dimensions, then produce an accurate scale representation, perhaps on the square fathom plot beside the figure, and as a final test of his abilities, produce his own figure upon the desert floor, aligned to a calendrical date which he would have to calculate...One can imagine the compounded difficulties that would be encountered by a young surveyor, perhaps thrown in at the deep end by having to survey a degree of longitude in the mountains and jungles of Peru and Ecuador...
>
> Possibly, students would not have to make a special journey to Nazca in order to take a course in surveying, it may have been on an educational route. A doctorate in the ancient world may have entailed a complete circumnavigation of the globe by land and by sea, whereby the student would learn and apply the techniques of navigation, astronomy and surveying at all conceivable latitudes... Something along these lines may explain the sheer number of lines where the land has only ever supported a relatively low level of population; the bulk of the people would be there temporarily, as students, strictly for reasons of geography.[338]

This brings us back to the idea of ancient universities, where fieldwork was 80% of your grade. Perhaps the professors were the ones in the balloons, checking out their students' work.

NAZCA LINES IN THE AMAZON?

Earlier in this chapter, you read about the cultures of the Amazon.

Compare what you've just read about the first civilizations of the Andes and the first civilizations of the Amazon. Despite how different their environments were, what connections and similarities do you note? If you don't see that the cultures were once connected like two points on a long line, you'll be convinced when you find out there are Nazca Lines in the Amazon jungle.

The tragic deforestation of the Amazon has revealed that there are pictures carved into the earth there as well. And they're huge. Satellite images of deforested land (including spots you can find yourself using Google Earth) reveal hundreds of near-perfect geometric figures like circles, squares, and triangles, resembling the fantastic geometric carvings found in the famous Nazca lines of Peru to the west.[339] They're as much as six miles wide, with grooves up to 40 feet wide and 12 feet deep. If you've ever dug a hole of any size, you can imagine that digging a line like that is no joke.

What's REALLY deep is this: Do you think they carved these lines and designs across miles of densely wooded rainforest? Not likely. Studies have found that these designs must have been carved into the Amazon when it had much less forest.[340] And the Amazon Rainforest that we have now? WE planted it. Sha-King Ce'hum Allah explains:

> The Amazon rainforest isn't "natural," meaning that while the peoples of the Amazon were thought to be hunter-gatherers, much of the Amazon is actually deliberately planted and cultivated orchards – indigenous style, rather than European "mono-crop" style farming.

And the archaeological evidence supports his argument. When we look beyond the desert lines at Nazca and see similar lines carving out plots of settled land in the Amazon, it supports the theory that Nazca was an ancient surveying school. The Amazon 'geoglyph culture' was located at a crossroads between Andean and Amazonian cultures, and spans more than 150 miles, crossing both the floodplains and the highlands. With new evidence suggesting that Nazca became a desert after its people had cut down too many trees,[341] these people may have begun moving east in the Amazon, while they continued to practice surveying in the "sandbox" (or practice area) of the Nazca desert.

THE INCAS

Almost 3000 years later, the civilization of Norte Chico seems to have been "reborn" as the civilization of the Incas. Located in what is now Peru, the Incas had **a sophisticated and enormous empire.**

According to the so-called *Inca Chronicle*, written in 1615 by a native Andean, Felipe Guaman Poma de Ayala – the ancestors of the Incas were hunter-gatherers until a man named Manco Capac, "the Son of the Sun," came around 1200 AD and taught them stone masonry, agriculture, and salt mining.

They used sophisticated techniques, which are still not fully understood today, to construct stone walls and structures across several levels of mountainous land. They used a kind of sewer system to keep rainwater from eroding these structures. Many of these buildings were destroyed or hidden under plant growth when they were abandoned. One extraordinary site, Macchu Piccu, remains undisturbed because it sits at the top of one of these mountains. Macchu Piccu wasn't just a winter retreat for the emperor, it was **an observatory where Incan scientists could study the heavens above and the earth below.**

The Incas used the temperature differences between the top of the mountain and the bottom to simultaneously grow crops that needed different climates. The indigenous people there still use Incan waterways and *andenes* (tiered irrigation beds along the mountainsides). The Incas also used the science of stone masonry to build roads that covered much of western South America, spanning mountain ranges and crossing deep gorges. Like the ancient Egyptians, they were uniters, not dividers. They built over 15,000 miles of roads to bring together communities that spoke different languages. At its height, Inca rule extended to nearly a hundred linguistic or ethnic communities, comprising up to 14 million people. This would rival any European city of the time. But unlike in Europe, the Incan people prospered under this empire, which some historians call a "welfare state" because the empire took care of all of its citizens.

They also had road messengers stationed at different posts throughout the land, who would deliver messages across long

INCA STONEMASONRY

The images below come from Inca sites like Machu Picchu (the rulers' mountaintop retreat), Ollantaytambo (a fortified stronghold), Cuzco (the capital), and the Andenes of the Pisac Valley (where they farmed). Much of the best stonework was destroyed when the Spaniards tore them down, but some structures survived, either because they were too hard to reach (like Machu Picchu) or their bricks (some weighing up to 200 tons) were too massive to be removed!

distances via a relay system (like passing a baton). The "batons" they passed were quipus. These knotted cords conveyed messages in a universal mathematical language that allowed communities of different languages to communicate. This would be the first "digital" communication system in the Americas, long before white folks built the Internet. There is even evidence of advanced metalwork and successful brain surgery in Inca civilization.

What else? Highlights include:

❐ They were master architects. For example, they built the famed ceremonial complex of Machu Picchu at the top of a mountain.

❐ They knew the medicinal benefits of many local plants and used them regularly for a variety of purposes

❐ They had a powerful army, in which every male had to take part in at least one war

❐ They also practiced mummification and built pyramids

INCA STONEMASONRY

Like their predecessors at Tiwanaku, the Incas were incredible stonemasons. They built massive temples, monuments, and plazas, using stone-working techniques that are not fully understood today.

The Coricancha (originally named Inti Kancha ("Temple of the Sun") or Inti Wasi ("Sun House") was the most important temple in the Inca Empire. The walls and floors were once covered in sheets of solid gold, and its adjacent courtyard was filled with golden statues. Spanish reports say it opulence was "fabulous beyond belief."

Naturally, the Spanish went quickly from being astounded to enraged, seeking to destroy any evidence that the "savages" they were conquering were more civilized than them. In typical European fashion, they took to destroying whichever structures they could, and erecting their own buildings on top, with Peruvians and African slaves doing the labor. The Spanish colonists tore down as much of Coricancha as they could, and built the Church of Santo Domingo on top of its foundation. Construction took most of a century.

In 1950, a major earthquake nearly destroyed much of what the Spanish had erected throughout the city. The Church of Santo Domingo was nearly destroyed. Yet while the colonial-era buildings crumbled, the city's Inca architecture survived. In fact, the earthquake had only helped to reveal some of the Inca masonry hidden behind later European stonework, which was obviously quite shoddy in comparison.

Imagine that: the stone structures built by these "primitive" people were sturdier than those built by the "civilized" geniuses who were conquering them. The massive gap between the abilities of the Inca masons and the European masons led to a tradition of Incan descendants calling the Spanish InCAN'TS.

How did they turn boulders and mountainsides into stone blocks so perfectly cut that the blocks "locked" in place, firmly enough to withstand devastating earthquakes? Regarding the theory that the Incas cut and fit these massive stone blocks through a system of "trial and error," A. Hyatt Verrill writes:

> No sane man can believe that a twenty-ton stone was pecked here and there, dropped into position, hoisted out and trued and cut over and over again, until a perfect fit was obtained. Even if we can imagine such endless herculean labor being performed, it would have been impossible in many cases owing to the fact that the stones are locked or dovetailed together. Although some of the stones are fairly square or rectangular and with six faces, many are irregular in form, and some have as many as thirty-two angles. The only way in which such complex forms could have been fitted with such incredible accuracy was by cutting each block to extremely fine measurements, or by means of a template, a process which would indicate that these prehistoric people possessed a most thorough and advanced knowledge of engineering and the higher mathematics.[343]

So it's no surprise that even MODERN reconstruction efforts are unable to assemble stone walls that compare to the Inca's original work. What's especially deep is that the Incas weren't the even the best at this tradition.

Anywhere you look in the Andes, the largest, megalithic blocks and the finest stonework are always found at the lower levels of the buildings, walls, and towers. Massive blocks, positioned perfectly, cut to nearly machined precision, are found topped by stonework that still looks good, but just doesn't compare. This is because – despite how amazing the Incas were – there weren't the ones who introduced expert masonry to the Andes. They were carrying on a tradition they'd picked up from the predecessors. We're talking about the Anu people who introduced these traditions in the first civilizations of the Andes, thousands of years prior.

THE RISE AND REBIRTH OF TÚPAC AMARU

The Inca rulers were called the Sapa Inca. The first Sapa Inca was the semi-legendary Manco Capac. After him followed several others in a long succession of indigenous leaders. There is a painting in the

Larco Museum of Peru that depicts the Sapa Inca in their dark-skinned glory. It also shows when their reign ended.*

The last indigenous Peruvian king, Túpac Amaru, was executed by the Spanish in 1572. In the 18th century, a Peruvian mestizo claiming direct descent named himself Túpac Amaru II and led a massive rebellion composed of over 6,000 indigenous Andeans, mestizos, and enslaved Africans.

It began with Túpac capturing a Spanish governor† named Antonio de Arriaga. He gave Arriaga's African slave, Antonio Oblitas, the privilege of hanging him. Within days, Túpac's rebel alliance took over town after town, taking the head of every Spaniard they encountered. Yet, once in Cuzco, he was betrayed by loyalist Indians.

He was caught and sentenced to a cruel execution, where he was forced to bear witness to the execution of his African wife and most of his family. They tied his limbs to four horses, but found him too strong to be killed by quartering. Failing at this, on May 18, 1781, the Spanish beheaded him on the main plaza in Cuzco, in the same place his great-great-great-grandfather Túpac Amaru I had been beheaded.

Like the myth of Osiris, Túpac's body parts were scattered across the towns loyal to him, the houses demolished, their soil ruined with salt, his property confiscated, his relatives outcasted, and all documents relating to his descent were burnt. On the day of his execution, *Incan clothing and cultural traditions, and even self-identifying as "Inca" were outlawed.* The Spanish also instituted other measures to convert the indigenous and Afro-Peruvian population to Spanish culture.

Yet, Túpac's revolution was no failure. It was the first massive rebellion in the Spanish colonies, and it inspired thousands of people to fight back. After his death, revolts continued to sweep through southern Peru, Bolivia and Argentina, as multi-ethnic alliances of revolutionaries captured Spanish towns and beheaded whites.

Two years after Amaru's execution, Simon Bolivar was born in Venezuela. Bolivar would later lead Venezuela, Colombia, Panama, Ecuador, Bolivia, and Peru to independence from Spanish rule. And in the 1980s, Peruvians formed the Túpac Amaru Revolutionary Movement, a guerrilla movement dedicated to eliminating the

---

* This painting is also important because it depicts some of the last Moorish rulers of Spain, before the country fully transitioned into a white-dominated society.

† At this time, "governor" simply meant his job was to make the local Peruvians work for and pay their Spanish conquerors, who would send the money back to the monarchy in Spain.

remaining elements of neo-colonialism and establishing a socialist state that better reflect the people's original way of life. Afeni Shakur named her son, Tupac Amaru Shakur, after the same 18th century rebel leader. Ironically enough, one of Tupac's ambitions – before he was tragically killed – was to build a multiethnic "rebel alliance" throughout the hoods and barrios of North America.

REVIEW

There are many forms of genetic data that can be used to trace people back to their Black roots. For example, there are the human lymphocyte antigen (HLA) alleles that help determine what we're immune to. HLAs can tell us where a people have been (or who they've mixed with), because people acquire them after long periods of struggling against some sort of natural threat.

Scientists studying the indigenous people of the Americas have found a small group of HLAs which many of them have in common. But it's a different story at the cradles of American civilization. An extensive report compiled by James Guthrie reveals that populations who live near the sites of former Mesoamerican and Andean urban societies exhibit HLA alleles that came from Africa and Southeast Asia.*

Guthrie goes on to cite several waves of HLA "migration." At least four times in the past 10,000 years, South Asian and Afro-Asiatic HLAs have arrived along the coasts of Mexico and South America. These Anu migrations have been most concentrated at the former sites of the major civilization centers we've discussed in this chapter, and there's no mistaking the connection between these migrants and major developments in the areas they came to.[344] I think it's safe to say that there's now PLENTY of evidence that the earliest civilizations of the Americas were significantly influenced by Anu settlers from Asia and Africa. For more details on Guthrie's findings, see the Appendix.

---

* While European alleles could have been carried by Black settlers from early Europe, it's also possible that an ancient band of whites made it into the Americas after a steady campaign across Asia (between 4000 and 1200 BC) and the Pacific Islands. We'll explore these possibilities in Volume Four.

NORTH AMERICA

MESOAMERICANS & MOUNDBUILDERS

"Our purpose in life is to leave a legacy for our children and our children's children. For this reason, we must correct history that at present denies our humanity and self-respect." — Queen Mother Moore

In 1961, self-educated Black historian J.A. Rogers reported in *Africa's Gift to America* that America had a much longer Black history than most people would expect:

> Africa played a role, perhaps, the chief role in the earliest development of America – a period that antedates Columbus by many centuries, namely Aztec, Maya, and Inca civilizations. About 500 B.C. or earlier, Africans sailed over to America and continued to do so until the time of Columbus...C.C. Marquez says, 'The Negro type is seen in the most ancient Mexican sculpture...Negroes figure frequently in the most remote traditions.' Riva-Palacio, Mexican historian, says, 'It is indisputable that in very ancient times the Negro race occupied our territory (Mexico). The Mexicans recall a negro god, Ixtilton, which means 'black face.'[345]

Rogers' statement preceded the work of scholars like Floyd Hayes III and Ivan Van Sertima, who later wrote extensively on the Black presence in the pre-Columbian Americas, but he was not the first to make these claims.

In 1922, Leo Wiener authored a three-volume series titled *Africa and the Discovery of America*, covering mountains of evidence for this fact. Yet even before this, a statement issued by the 1854 National Emigration Convention of Colored People, headed by Martin Delany, said the following:

> Among the earliest and most numerous class who found their way to the new world, were those of the African race. And it has been ascertained to our minds beyond a doubt, that when the continent was discovered, there were found in the West Indies and Central America, tribes of the black race, fine looking people, having the usual characteristics of color and hair, identifying them as being originally of the African race.[346]

How much of this is true? How much of American culture is rooted in Black culture? Throughout this chapter and the one that follows, we'll address all of the evidence for these claims, and the story this body of evidence reveals.

"RACE MATTERS"

Once again, we have to be clear: We're not trying to "co-opt" the accomplishments of every culture in the world and "make them Black." I've seen people do this, and it doesn't help anyone. As I explained in "Why Race Matters" in Part One, doing so can alienate the people you are talking about (who have probably never thought of themselves as Black) and can lead to confrontations that don't need to occur if you handle the exchange of information properly. For starters, there is no single, homogenous, Black culture that looks one way or another. Black people are diverse. And we are talking about linguistic, genetic, physical, and cultural diversity.

But for most people, including many Black people in America and Africa, the idea of being "Black" is uncomfortable. And we're talking about people who are undeniably Black right here in our neighborhoods who feel that way! Stephen from *Django Unchained* is right around the corner!

There are many of us, so beaten down by centuries of oppression and miseducation, that we **hate the idea of being Black**. So imagine the rejection you'll experience upon telling a Chinese person they're Black. Or worse, that their entire culture was built by Blacks. In other words, they basically have nothing to claim as their own, and should be thanking you for building all their stuff back in the day. That's not gonna win you any allies.

You're gonna have a hard time convincing people who know their indigenous heritage that they're Black. For beginners, many Native American people believe their people originate in the Americas, and did not come from anywhere else...even when genetic evidence tells them they came from Africa. Similarly, many Chinese people are very proud of their national heritage, and would like to think of their people as originating in China...again, despite what the genetics say. Why? It's called "nationalism." People want to be proud of their communities. If you want to teach them or reach them, you can't begin by tearing that down. You've got to find common ground.

Then, you've got the brainwashing to deal with, because many of them have been taught to stay away from Black people ever since

THE AZTEC CODICES

The Aztec codices are books written by pre-Columbian and colonial-era Aztecs. They are our best records of Aztec thought and culture. The Aztecs learned bookmaking from the Mixtecs, who made codices like the one below. Here, we can see evidence of diversity among Mixtec people.

The Aztec codices dealt with divination, rituals, the gods and the universe. Most were burned by the Spaniards. All the surviving manuscripts show European influence. Colonial-era codices often feature Náhuatl or Spanish writing. Still, black-skinned people feature prominently in many codices.

KING NEZAHUALPILLI
(CODEX IXTLILXÓCHITL)

OTOMÍ WARRIOR
(CODEX MENDOZA)

But were these people the descendants of African visitors, as we find among the Olmecs and Mayans? By the time of the Aztecs, it appears that few Africans were making such a journey. Yet many of the Aztec priests, warriors, and elites were painting themselves black and allowing their hair to grow into locks, perhaps in reverence for the Black people of the legendary past.

A RANKING OF AZTEC WARRIORS
(CODEX BORGIA)

AZTEC DIGNITARY
(CODEX MENDOZA)

AZTEC PRIEST
WITH LOCKS

they were **the main ones helping the slaves get free back in the day.** Once Europeans saw that, they worked overtime to instigate animosity towards Black people in "Latino" communities. So you might have to conquer THAT too. For more on this, see "Those Foreigners" in the Appendix of Part One. For now, let's dig into the Black history of the Americas.

ANCIENT NORTH AMERICA

We really know as little about the people of ancient North America as we do about the people of ancient Central Africa. This isn't because either of them were "primitive savages" with nothing to show. It's because the ones who would tell what they saw were preceded by those who did little describing, but plenty of destroying.

In North America, the first anthropologists were preceded by explorers and missionaries who exterminated the people faster than any military campaign. People like Hernando de Soto conquered even in their absence, because they introduced diseases that killed millions. It's clear that at least some of this was intentional, as seen in later accounts of Europeans giving the Indians "smallpox blankets" as gifts. Scholars now suggest that 90% of the native population of the Americas was killed by European diseases.[347]

For example, When Pánfilo de Narváez came to Mexico in 1520, smallpox spread rapidly through the densely populated cities, killing over 150,000 in the capital city of Tenochtitlan alone (Tenochtitlan was the heart of the Aztec Empire, located in present-day Mexico City). It killed most of the Aztec army, the emperor, and 25% of the Aztec population. If not for this, Hernán Cortés could not have defeated the mighty Aztec empire in 1521. Around the same time, smallpox killed between 60% and 90% of the Inca population, with other waves of European disease weakening them further.

And the first Europeans may have shipwrecked in the Americas long before Columbus came. By the time they began moving in to make permanent homes for themselves, they found only the remains of the cultures that had once thrived in those areas. In many cases, these people originally had agricultural city states, but were reverting back to subsistence agriculture and hunting. When Spaniards introduced the horse, this sped up the process of Native Americans abandoning their original cultures. Meanwhile, they destroyed whatever they found, including monuments, city walls, and thousands of books. The missionaries went around encouraging Native Americans to reconsider their oral traditions in favor of "revised" traditions that leaned toward the white right. They also built "Indian schools," which were designed to systemically erase any traces of indigenous culture, language, scientific knowledge, or solidarity with other indigenous people. They fermented rivalries between neighboring nations, creating a disconnected array of indigenous people who were quickly losing touch with their past. It was a devastating, yet deliberate, process.

As a result, there are many gaps in our knowledge of the ancient Americas. Often the only traces we have of their once thriving civilizations are the mounds, moats, and buried city walls that were found along river valleys across the U.S. These remains suggest that many North American cities had populations greater than those in the ancient Near East. Around 4,000 years ago, new knowledge spread rapidly through North America, including ceramics, agriculture, and mound-building.[348]

The ancient civilizations of North America began actively "transforming their landscapes," by building complex compounds (out of the earth), cultivating plants, and domesticating a few animals. The first Europeans to visit the Lower Mississippi Valley reported groves of nut and fruit trees being managed as orchards, in addition to gardens and more expansive agricultural fields. Further away, prescribed burning (sometimes known as slash-and-burn agriculture) was used in the forest and prairie areas, which helped the growth of herbs and berry-producing plants, which were important for both food and medicine.[349] But whoever instituted these practices took care to incorporate cultural safeguards. In other words, taboos were designed to restrict the abuse of nature, so as not to upset its balance.* Had they seen what exploitation of one's natural resources does in other lands? If nothing else, this helps us understand why many of their oldest cities were built – often to monumental proportions – simply from soil and clay, rather than stone and wood.

But when anthropologists asked local Native Americans about who built these cities, they typically didn't know. In many cases, these ancestral people were the subject of myth. In some cases, they weren't ancestral at all, but a people of unknown origin who brought new ideas and technology.

In this chapter, we'll trace at least some of these important people back to their Black roots. But let's be clear. We don't want to take

---

* For more on this subject, see *The Science of Self, Volume One*.

anything away from the indigenous people of the Americas. For the way they resisted European domination alone, they should be saluted and seen as our brothers in struggle. Long before the white abolitionists, they were the first to harbor fugitive slaves and to fight side-by-side against the Spaniards and British. They married Africans, taught them their language, and absorbed them into their communities. It was like love at first sight.*

QUESTIONS TO CONSIDER

But what made them connect with Africans? Did they all look alike? Not by a long shot. There were certainly "traces" of those features among some Native people, but it definitely wasn't the norm. Something else inspired many Native American nations to ally with Africans at first contact. Perhaps it was the cultural similarities that we discussed in Part One. But did they have enough time to observe and make this judgment?

Or were Africans received with open arms because many of the 500 Nations recognized them from their past?

LEGENDS OF A BLACK PAST
THE POPOL VUH

The *Popol Vuh* has been described as "one of the rarest relics of aboriginal thought."[350] It has been subtitled *The Sacred Book of the Ancient Quiche Maya*,[351] but a literal translation of the title would be *The Book of the Community*, or *The Book of the People*. The *Popol Vuh* contains the popular traditions, mythology, religious beliefs, migrations, and development of the Indian tribes which populated the territory of the present Republic of Guatemala after the fall of the Maya Old Empire. The book itself is said to have existed "long ago; but its sight is [now] hidden from the searcher and the thinker."[352]

It is said to have been preserved by a long history of oral tradition. The Quiche say the *Popol Vuh* is indeed an old book which ancient kings and lords would draw upon for inspiration as well as prophecy and divination. It was first transcribed into Latin script in the Quiche language sometime between 1554 and 1558.

---

* Despite all the talk about Indians owning slaves, the only tribes who really did this were the "Five Civilized Tribes" of the American southeast, who were heavily influenced to adopt the ways and values of their white masters.

Numerous versions of the book exist now, each offering slight differences in wording and interpretation. The version I purchased in Mexico describes the first man being made from black clay. The author says this first man was imperfect, "however, the new creature had the gift of speech and sounded more harmonious than any music that had ever been heard before under the heavens."[353]

Though the gods would continue to make three more races of man before finally arriving at one with which they were satisfied (the second and third were violently destroyed), the first, Black race was allowed to live and given time to multiply and improve their kind. I have not found any mention of an original Black race in the other translations I have come across in the U.S.

Scholars have noted a line of cultural transmission from the Mayan people of the Mexico to the Indians of the American southwest. The *Popol Vuh*'s original Black race may have some relation to the Southwest Indian story of the Emergence, a story Runoko Rashidi says "is as important in the region as the Book of Genesis is to Christians." In this creation story, the First World is called the Black World.[354]

PROPHECIES OF A BLACK FUTURE

Lee Brown, a Salish Indian from British Columbia, Canada, had lived and studied among the Hopi for several years. In 1986, he gave a talk at the Continental Indigenous Council that should not be ignored. He begins with a commentary on the races of the Earth, expressing a strong solidarity with Black people:

> A medicine man from South Dakota put a beaded medicine wheel in the middle of the gathering. It had the four colors from the four directions. He asked the people, "Where is this from?" They said, "Probably Montana, or South Dakota, maybe Saskatchewan." He said, "This is from Kenya." It was beaded just like ours, with the same color... Always we were trying to live together. But instead of living together, you all know there was separation, there was segregation. They separated the races: they separated the Indians, and they separated the blacks.

What he says afterwards is especially significant:

> In 1776 when the United States Government printed the dollar, in one claw [of the eagle], if you've ever noticed, there is an olive branch in this claw. They said that represented peace. The Indian elders shared with me in South Dakota that to them that represents the enslavement of black people. In the prophecies of the Six Nations people they say there will be two great uprisings by black people to free themselves. We've seen one about 1964. There will be

a second, more violent one to come. I'll get back to what that means in a minute.

He continues:

> There was one more uprising coming for the black race of people and then they will be released and this is also going to have an effect on Native people, a good effect. There's a whole new set of prophecies from the Iroquois people about that and I won't have time to go into that this morning.

We can only imagine how much more there is to this story.

THE BLACK "STRANGERS" OF THE IROQUOIS

The Iroquois, also known as the *Haudenosaunee* or the "People of the Longhouse" (yes, they lived in longhouses, not teepees) are not one nation, but a league of several Native American nations who came together in the American northeast. They were also known as the "League of Peace and Power," comprising the Mohawk, Oneida, Onondaga, Cayuga and Seneca nations.

The Iroquois were an advanced agricultural confederacy, whose unique social structure influenced the formation of the American republic, and their "Great Law" inspired the U.S. Constitution. And this isn't a theory. The Senate passed a resolution stating this clearly in 1988.[355]

In fact, Benjamin Franklin himself is quoted as saying:

> It would be a very strange thing, if six nations of ignorant savages [the Iroquois] should be capable of forming a scheme for such an Union, and be able to execute it in such a manner, as that it has subsisted ages, and appears indissoluble; and yet that a like Union should be impracticable for ten or a dozen English colonies, to whom it is more necessary, and must be more advantageous; and who cannot be supposed to want an equal understanding of their interests.

In other words, Europeans saw this model of Pan-Indian unity as both the inspiration and blueprint by which to come together as one people sharing a common goal. Of course, as always, the goal was to destroy the people they got their ideas from.

But the Iroquois didn't claim to be originators. You see, the Iroquois give a lot of credit to "strangers" who came to them. It was a stranger who taught them the science of agriculture, leading to the myth of the three sisters (corn, beans, and squash).

The Iroquois weren't a Black people, by far. Ellsworth Huntington noted strong "Negroid" traits among them and the Algonquians, which he traced back to their origins,[356] but there's much more evidence that these Black traces were recent, stemming from the fruitful Black-Indian relations of the 1800s.

In fact, from the 1500s to the 1800s, Blacks and Indians throughout the eastern U.S. were so intimately close that many local Indian populations were half-Black by the time the census got to them. There are hundreds of examples, a few dozen recorded in the 1912 edition of the *Handbook of American Indians North of Mexico*.[357]

Getting back to the Iroquois, it's not unlikely that you can find evidence of Black ancestors among them. In fact, you may find more of a mix than you'd expect. Like the Olmecs, the Iroquois were a true melting pot, at least by North America's standards. They would actually capture people from other Indian nations and make them full members of the Iroquois nation, taking great care to naturalize them as full-fledged citizens. The Iroquois worked to incorporate conquered peoples and assimilate them as Iroquois, thus naturalizing them as full citizens of their adoptive nation. By 1668, two-thirds of the Oneida were Algonquians and Hurons who had been assimilated. The Onondaga had people from seven different nations, while the Seneca had eleven.[358]

So there's no telling WHO could have been absorbed into the Iroquois population. Could have been everybody and anybody, red, Black, and white alike. But when we look for clues as to who the famed "stranger" was, we're led in a very specific direction. Again, we're led back to black.

In other myths, the stranger reveals himself to have supernatural knowledge. In another, the stranger challenges the High God to a contest of power, involving who could move a mountain the farthest. The stranger is amazingly able to move a mountain, but is no match for the Creator, who moves it so close to the stranger that he disfigures his nose when he turns to see it.* This is said to be the origin of "false face" mask which the Iroquois' False Face Society

---

* In this myth, the Creator God, seeing the stranger's powers, doesn't want him to stay. But the stranger convinces him, on the premise that he would stick around to protect the people and heal them when they called on him. The stranger is sometimes called Grandfather, sometimes Chief.

FALSE FACES AND ALTER EGOS

JAGUAR FIGURINE
OLMEC MEXICO

HONGSHAN JADE "BEAST" MASK
NEOLITHIC CHINA

SHAMAN WITH TOTEM
SHANG DYNASTY CHINA

When historians find ancient artwork bearing "Negroid" traits, they claim they're really animal traits. For example, they say the Black features of the Olmec are really based on jaguars, because they had a jaguar cult. But look at the face on the top left. Jaguars don't have noses like that! The truth is, many of these "totemic" figures are based on a BLEND of a Black shaman and a totemic animal. You can see this in the bronze on the top right, where the shaman and totem are connected yet still separate.

In fact, many of the figures on totem poles (found among Indians of the Pacific Northwest) are not animals, but stylized versions of what looks a lot like Black people. The same Black faces are found on their masks. And these often grossly distorted faces aren't limited to the Pacific Northwest. The "twisted" Black faces found on Haida masks are also found in the masks of the Iroquois of the American Northeast.

"STONE GIANT"
IROQUOIS

FALSE FACE SOCIETY
IROQUOIS

LIGHT SKIN, BLACK MASKS?

SRI LANKA (COMPARE WITH PICTURE OF HAIDA SHAMANS)

FUNERARY MASK
TEOTIHUACAN

AZTEC GOD
IXTLILTON

SHAMAN'S MASK
NEOLITHIC CHINA

HAIDA MASK
NW CANADA

HAIDA SECRET
SOCIETY MASK
(NOTE SCARIFICATION)

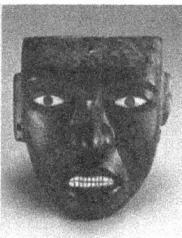

EGYPTIAN MASK
(GENGHIS KHAN'S
COLLECTION)

HAIDA MASK
CANADA

FESTAC MASK
NIGERIA

MEXICO

CAMEROON

CEREMONIAL MASKS, NEOLITHIC CHINA

Throughout the world, indigenous people use face masks for a variety of ceremonial uses. Typically, masks are worn by shamans, who personify the historical figure or "spirit" represented. No matter where you go in the world, these masks often resemble Black people. Sometimes, these features are distorted or exaggerated, creating a "grotesque" version that may not look fully human. But as the Aztec mask to the right suggests, these are still only stylized renditions of Black faces, sometimes merged with a totemic animal. Meanwhile, when several realistic masks have almost the exact same face, they may represent a well-known historical personality from the ancient past.

AZTEC (C. 1300 AD)

uses to honor the stranger.

If you look at ANY of these false face masks, you will see exactly who this stranger was. Might not be a pleasant depiction, but they were saying the stranger was Black. These masks are typically painted black, with the grotesque exaggeration of Black features that you can find in early European and Asian representations of legendary African people (not to mention in some indigenous art as well!). The eyes are large and bright, in either white or yellow (we find yellow eyes and the same grotesque exaggeration of features in depictions of the Hopi god Chaikwana).

On most masks you can find today, the hair is long and flaxen, made from black, red, or blonde horsehair. But before the introduction of horses by the Europeans, they used corn husks and buffalo hair. If you remember Bob Marley's song "Buffalo Soldier" then you know the texture of buffalo hair. Let's just say it's not like horsehair. In fact, among some Native American people, such as the Apache, the word for "Black man," *lizhena*, means "buffalo-black-haired."[359]

THE "OLD MAN" OF THE BLACKFOOT CONFEDERACY

Could a "stranger" have come to the Iroquois and introduced some of the cultural innovations associated with the Neolithic revolution of the Near East? If this is what happened, it would explain many of the traces of Anu DNA found among indigenous people in the U.S. And this influence extended deep into the Americas. In a Blackfoot myth describing their migration to Canada and the Great Plains, they say they came from Siberia:

> The first Indians were on the other side of the ocean, and Old Man decided to lead them to a better place. So he brought them over the ice to the far north.[360]

Among the Tsuu T'ina Nation of Canada, there is a myth recalling the same migration. Both myths note that somewhere in the Canada, possibly near Alberta, their ancestors were split into two groups. In the Tsuu T'ina version, they encountered something that frightened them and "those that ran toward the north became the Chipewyans, and we who ran toward the south are the Soteinna or Sarcee [an old name for the Tsuu T'ina]." In the Blackfoot version, the frozen ground split, forcing the people to separate.[361]

A Siberian origin story suggests that these people shared Mongoloid ancestry. Yet there is still strong evidence of Anu influence making a world of difference. Wissler and Duval continue the Blackfoot myth as follows:

Now Old Man led these people down to where the Blood Reserve now is, and told them that this would be a fine country for them, and that they would be very rich. He said, "I will get all the people here." All the people living there ate and lived like wild animals; but Old Man went among them and taught them all the arts of civilization. When he was through teaching them, he did not die, but went among the Sioux, where he remained for a time, but finally disappeared. He took his wife with him. He had no children.[362]

Who was the "Old Man"? Was he one of "escorts" proposed in Part One? Or was he simply an ancestral figure? Throughout Native American tradition, the "Old Man" or "stranger" is consistently someone who introduces many of the innovations associated with the Anu Cultural Complex. Rarely is he described as "one of the people." He is different. But who does he represent? It is my theory that he represents the Anu migrants who we know – based on genetic research – came among many of the indigenous people of the Americas long before Columbus. In an upcoming book titled *Black God*, we'll explore a few more connections between this "Old Man" and the Anu presence among the first Native Americans.

THE MOUNDBUILDERS
THE FIRST THING THEY SAW

After nearly 800 years of war,* Europeans finally defeated the Moors. This war – spanning from the year 711 to 1492 – was known as the *Reconquista* (meaning "re-conquest"). Spain and Portugal were soon filled with young men desperate for another chance at finding fame through the conquest of Black and brown people. As if by design, the same year the Moors were exiled, Columbus embarked on his fateful journey to the "New World" where Europeans could do just that.† It wasn't long before Spanish *conquistadors* (from *Reconquista*) had taken their campaign abroad, destroying the empires of the Andes, Mesoamerica, and the Mississippi Valley.

In 1527, a Spanish expedition led by Pánfilo de Narváez blazed a trail along the southern coast of what is now the United States. Well, they didn't exactly blaze a trail because millions of Native Americans already lived in the areas he passed, some with sprawling cities larger

---

* We'll discuss this war, and its deeper implications, in depth in Volume 5.

† It should be noted that Columbus was led by Moorish navigators, who knew the currents of the ocean well, suggesting that Africans were already familiar with sailing across the Atlantic.

than anything found in Europe at the time.

Not to mention that the Spaniards weren't leading the path, but being led by an African Moor they called Estevanico. This didn't fare too well, actually. They thought they'd be with other Spaniards, but found themselves far away from the nearest white people headquarters. So, rather than figure out how to live off the land as the "primitive" Indians did, they went totally savage. First, they were unable to figure out what to eat and nearly starved. So they ate their horses.

Then they hacked together some crude wooden rafts to sail the river but went almost naked, trying to plug holes in their rafts with their clothes. They couldn't sail these "primitive" rafts, so they ended up raftless too. Before long, they were naked, dirty, sick, and destitute.

It's like a case study in the inability of "modern" Europeans to do ANY of the stuff "primitive savages" do with ease. To make a long story short, they started dying off. Those who survived were in such sad shape that they eventually found themselves enslaved by the Indians! And not just once for a few days, but for a few years! They were passed around between various Indian nations, from the Hans to the Capoques, to the Karankawa, to the Coahuiltecans. Just despicable.

The Indians finally let their sorry behinds go. There were now only four survivors, one of them being Cabeza de Vaca, who wrote an extensive account of his experiences. After being passed around from nation to nation, de Vaca had witnessed their culture at a level deeper than most Europeans. And he developed a deep sense of respect and fondness for the indigenous people of the Americas. He sailed back to Europe in 1537. Unfortunately, his visit would have disastrous consequences for those he left behind.

In 1539, Hernando de Soto set out to explore the Lower Mississippi Valley, seeking gold and power. He'd just finished plundering the Incas in Peru, and had heard the reports of the gold and glory witnessed further north. De Vaca told him what he knew, but refused to return to join him. De Soto wanted to conquer and De Vaca wasn't with it.

De Soto took a path that would later become some of the southeast's most important highways. Along the way, he encountered dozens of distinct Indian nations and reported on the existence of large Indian cities. Like De Vaca, he probably wouldn't have made it through if it weren't for the Africans in his expedition, who often acted as "ambassadors" to the Indians. In fact, one report says a "queen" of the Yuchi people actually *ran away* with one of his slaves.

The De Soto expedition also hit rock bottom, wandering the American Southeast for four years, struggling against hostile reception, until eventually arriving in Mexico at a fraction of its original size. Yet, *somehow*, De Soto still **came, saw, and conquered.**

How? The Indians numbered in the millions, but they fared much worse than the members of the De Soto expedition, as the diseases introduced by the Spaniards devastated the populations and produced incredible social disruption. Some of these people had *already* begun dying off from the effects of their *last* Spanish visitors.

By the time Europeans returned a hundred years later, nearly all of the Mississippian groups had vanished, and vast stretches of their former territory were virtually uninhabited. Until recently, American historians thought the Spaniards' stories of densely populated, bustling Native American cities were all myth and exaggeration. **We now know that they weren't.**

POVERTY POINT, LOUISIANA

In West Parrish, Louisiana, there's a site called Poverty Point. It's one of America's most significant mound-structures, officially recognized as "the largest and most complex Late Archaic earthwork occupation and ceremonial site yet found in North America."[365] Its focal point is a set of concentric rings (made from the earth), radiating from the center of a river bank, spanning over 900 acres of land. The site dates back to around 1700 BC and was once a thriving center of civilization. Thousands lived here or nearby during its heyday.

What were the mounds for? Archaeologists have found evidence suggesting that Poverty Point could have been an astronomical circle, with wooden posts aligned with the solstices. Indian astronomers would have used these structures to plan their community's seasonal activities.

As the tradition evolved and became increasingly widespread, it moved north from the American southeast (where we find all the oldest mound sites). Many of these mounds were built to bury the dead, while others were platforms for astronomical observatories. Some mounds, known as effigy mounds, were made in the shapes or outlines of culturally significant animals. The most famous of these is Serpent Mound in southern Ohio, a giant 1,330-foot-long serpent, built around the same time as the famous earthworks of Cahokia.

CAHOKIA, ILLINOIS

Like at Poverty Point almost 3,000 years prior, there were wooden posts forming astronomical circles at the northern mound site of Cahokia in western Illinois, near East St. Louis. Built around 950 AD, Cahokia once had 120 man-made earthen mounds in a wide range of sizes, shapes, and functions. More than 300 years before Columbus came, Cahokia's population was **larger than any European city of the time**, and its population **would not be surpassed** by any U.S. city until the 1800s. Professors Susan McClintock and John Kincheloe have asked:

> In the 12th century this place was as large as London! It was the largest city in America until Philadelphia outgrew it in 1800! And it was thriving 800 years ago in the heartland of our country. At its center was Monk's Mound – towering as high as a 10-story building. So how come we've never heard about this?[366]

Um…I've got a guess as to why. It rhymes with light beeple.

WOODHENGE

There's a site at Cahokia called Woodhenge, where a circle of wooden posts was used to make astronomical observations, similar to what was found at Poverty Point in Louisiana. South of the mounds, there's a large field spanning over 50 acres. This area was once rough, hilly terrain, but it had been **expertly leveled and filled by the people of Cahokia** so they could use it as a public plaza. Can you imagine what it takes to turn *50 acres* into *flat, level land?*

MONKS MOUND

One of the most famous of Cahokia's mounds is known as Monks Mound. It's the largest known mound in the Americas, and at over 1,000 feet wide, is larger (at its base) than the Great Pyramid of Giza in Egypt. Not only did Monks Mound have a built-in drainage system created through a special mix of soils and clays inside the mound. What's especially deep is that – when they drilled 40 feet beneath the base of the mound, they found a layer of stone that shouldn't have been there. The drill pass through 32 feet of stone

RECONSTRUCTIONS OF CAHOKIA

Woodhenge

Cahokia Creek

IL

MO

Cahokia Creek

Borrow pit area where earth was extracted to build the mounds

Mound 72

Stockade

DISTANCE FROM MONKS MOUND TO MOUND 72 IS ABOUT A HALF-MILE (0.8 KILOMETERS)

1 or 2 pyramids: Less than 200 people
12 to 50 pyramids: 200 to low thousands
120 pyramids (Cahokia): 10,000 to 20,000

RECONSTRUCTION OF LOCAL MARKET

WOODHENGE

MONK'S MOUND

before **the bit broke off**, and the mystery of this limestone foundation remains unsolved.

Further excavation of Monks Mound found that it had been rebuilt several times, and was formerly built at a much steeper angle (about 40 degrees), and covered with a densely-packed layer of white clay that archaeologist think "would have presented a viewer with a dramatic image of a nearly white mound."[367] Reminds me of the white limestone casing on the Egyptian pyramids!

KOLOMOKI MOUNDS, GEORGIA

This too, was a tradition that came from the south. 500 years before Cahokia and Monks Mound, the moundbuilders of Georgia erected the Kolomoki Mounds around 400 AD. The largest mound was a flat-topped pyramid originally covered with a hard layer of white clay, and later by a solid layer of red clay. Between this platform mound and a cone-shaped burial mound, there was a large central plaza paved with red clay.

NEWARK EARTHWORKS, OHIO

The Newark Earthworks are the largest set of enclosed earthworks known in the world. The huge complex is divided into several distinct but connected sites including Octagon Mound State Memorial, The Great Circle Earthworks, and the Wright Earthworks.

The Octagon Mound is nearly perfectly preserved and is one of the best manicured mound sites you can visit. There is a near-perfect circular earthwork enclosing about 20 acres with earthen walls up to 14 feet high. **The Great Pyramid of Giza could fit in this circle.**

A narrow set of parallel walls connects the circle to an earth-walled octagon enclosing 50 acres of territory. Four Roman Coliseums could fit in this octagon! There's no way you could still think that Indians lived in tiny disconnected bands when the Spaniards came. There are 8 gaps in the walls of the octagon, but you can't see inside, because the line of sight at each of the gaps is blocked by a flat-topped pyramid inside the octagon.

THE FIRST AMERICAN HIGHWAYS

There were originally three walled roads exiting the octagon compound, with walls about three feet high and the paths inside almost 200 feet wide. Archaeologist Bradley Lepper, head of the Ohio Historical Society Museum in Columbus, discovered that one of these massive roads ran in a straight line for 56 miles, leaving the Newark Octagon and ending at a nearly identical circle and octagon at the Chillicothe site in High Banks, Ohio! This is **the equivalent of a ten-lane highway running from New York City to Bridgeport, Connecticut.**

There's more. In the mid-1980's, two professors found that the circle and octagon formations were used to track the moon's cyclic movements.ᐟ The moundbuilders had programmed in the same "lunar standstill" embedded in Stonehenge, as well as solar eclipses predicted well into the future.

Another of the Octagon Mound's walled roads connects to a geometric "maze" known as the Wright Earthworks, where a 20-acre square (containing a row of seven pyramid mounds) has another walled road leading to the Great Circle Earthworks.

The Great Circle Earthworks is a near-perfect circle enclosing 30 acres. Its outer wall is nine feet tall, and on the inside is a moat seven feet deep. Its size and basic layout is identical to England's Avebury site (minus the standing stones). The circle has one opening toward the northeast. The walls of earth are higher and wider at this opening, suggesting that it once held a defensive gateway. In the center of the Great Circle, there was a bird-shaped mound, its head facing the opening.

In 2006, British science writer Andrew Collins found that in 100 BC – two hours before sunrise at midsummer – the bird effigy mound aligned with the constellation Cygnus. Cygnus was known to both Native Americans and other indigenous cultures as a bird, reminding us that these settlements were almost always astronomically oriented.

What's interesting is that structures like those at Poverty Point and Cahokia weren't built by settled, agricultural societies, as you'd find with the monumental construction of the Near East and Europe. Instead, they were built by hunter-gatherer societies, often where people only occupied the sites on a seasonal basis (like at Caral, Nabta Playa, and many other pre-Neolithic sites).

For example, Watson Brake, a large circular complex of 11 platform mounds in Louisiana, was constructed beginning in 3400 BC and built up over 500 years. Poverty Point, which required over a million cubic meters of soil, was built up over a period of centuries or millennia, with additions made by successive generations. And there

---

ᐟ The moon goes through an 18.61 year cycle where the maximum and minimum moonrise and moonset is predictable. This could explain why the mounds were rebuilt so frequently, sometimes reported as intervals of 20 years.

MOUNDBUILDER CULTURES

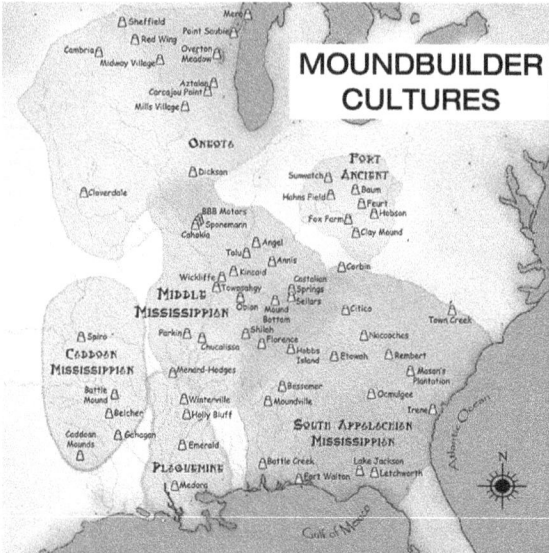

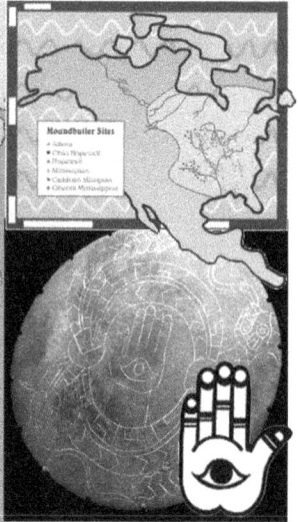

MISSISSIPPIAN HEAD EFFIGY POTS

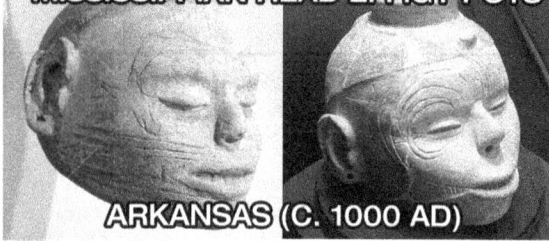

ARKANSAS (C. 1000 AD)

Note the facial structure, but also the scarification. These two pots (and others like it) clearly depict the same person. Who did this effigy pot represent? Why was he important? Where did he come from?

SERPENT'S MOUND, OHIO

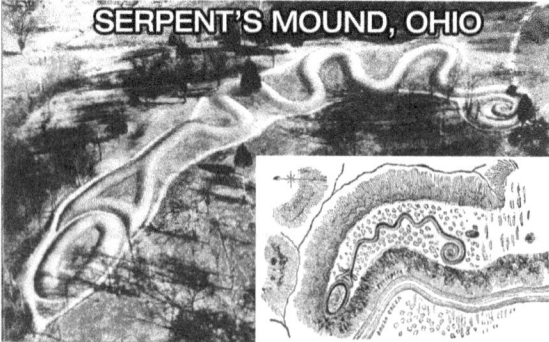

NEWARK EARTHWORKS

Why is the North African Eye of Fatima on a disc from an Alabama mound?

POVERTY POINT LOUISIANA

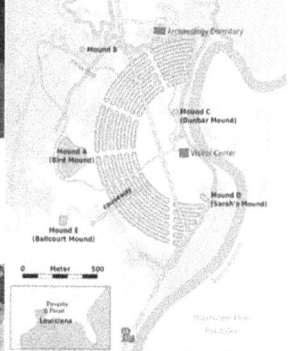

Why does a head effigy pot from the Wari culture of ancient Peru look so much like the pots found in Arkansas, over 3,000 miles away, and over 500 years later?

are even older mounds in Mesoamerica and South America.*

As Frank Joseph has written:

> Clearly, North America's so-called Indian Mounds were not crude
> poles of dirt heaped up by primitive savages. They were instead
> examples of applied geometry, materials handling, advance
> planning, design, an organized workforce and construction
> skills…public works engineers, astronomers and metalsmiths, the
> land's first farmers and potters.[368]

So how did a nomadic, non-agricultural people dedicate themselves
to this kind of labor? Better yet, why?

In the Nile Valley and the Near East, such complex construction
projects only emerged after the introduction of agriculture.
Archaeologists think a society must become sedentary and develop a
stratified hierarchy to organize large numbers of the peasant class in
collective labor. So what happened in the Lower Mississippi Valley?
Was there an outside influence involved?

WHERE DID THEY COME FROM?

There are enormous mounds in North America, Mesoamerica, the
Amazon, and the Andes (beginning around the same time that
similar structures were being built in Egypt and the Middle East). Yet
as independent researcher Alex Whitaker notes, similarities are not
enough to prove a direct link:

> The existence of pyramids in the Americas has often been
> suggested as a significant proof of contact between people from the
> 'Old' and 'New' worlds. However, this claim has been reasonably
> contended with the argument that the similarity in shape proves no
> such thing, and that such claims can only be validated by providing
> through substantiating proof, such as cultural, botanical and more
> recently, genetic research.[369]

This is an appropriate challenge. And there is now plenty of
evidence to suggest that the connection is real.

Could it have been an Anu people who introduced mound-building
to the Americas? This is supported by some of the history provided
by the Indians who were living in the area when Europeans came.

---

* People interested in the mounds of North America can consult *The Illustrated
Encyclopedia of Native American Mounds and Earthworks*, an authoritative guide to over
1000 Indian mounds and earthwork sites in America, including directions to all the
major sites with public access. A true encyclopedia, it contains over 500 photos,
maps, and recreations of what many of the sites looked like in their heyday. Yet,
even this massive book is not exhaustive in its scope. There are probably at least
100,000 mounds still in existence in North America alone. Every year dozens more
are discovered while hundreds more are destroyed.

DID YOU KNOW?
The people who brought the science of copper metallurgy to the Andes may have brought it to North America. Recent excavations have turned up a copper workshop at Cahokia's Mound 34, the only one of its kind.[371] We know that copper-working (in the Americas) began in the Andes, and later made its way to Mesoamerica. Did the metal-working people who built the mounds of South America bring their culture north? Or is it just a coincidence?

Local Creek Indians said they didn't know who built the mounds, but some of their ancestors could have been involved.

According to Gary Daniels of *Lost Worlds*, the construction of the Ocmulgee Mounds in Georgia may have signaled a migration of people bringing in a new phase of culture:

At this time newcomers arrived in the region and brought with them corn agriculture, a new style of pottery, new types of arrowheads and a more complex economic, religious and political system. It is thought that these were Muskogean speakers who later were called Creek Indians by Europeans. According to Creek Indian tradition, Ocmulgee Mounds was the site where they "first sat down" after their long migration from the west....One tribe of Creek Indians, the Cussitaw (Cusseta/Kasihta), have a migration legend which might relate to the settlement of Ocmulgee Mounds. It tells how they originated in a place much farther west, a place where the earth would occasionally open up and swallow their children (a possible reference to earthquakes). Part of their tribe decided to leave this place and began an eastward migration in order to find where the sun rose. On their journey they came to a mountain that thundered and had red smoke coming from its summit which they later discovered was actually fire (a possible reference to a volcano.) Here they decided to settle down after meeting people from three nations (Chickasaws, Atilamas, & Obikaws) who taught them about herbs and "many other things."[370]

DID THEY COME FROM THE SOUTH?

Daniels traces the moundbuilders of America back to Mexico, noting that Mexico is "the birthplace of corn agriculture, a defining characteristic of these newcomers," as well as tobacco cultivation and "cities consisting of flat-topped pyramid mounds arranged around open plazas which is the most noticeable feature of town planning at Ocmulgee." At some of the mound sites in Georgia, archaeologists have found pottery and other artifacts bearing strong similarities to sites in Mexico.

The possibilities of a southern origin are supported by oral tradition. Some of the migration myths associated with the Moundbuilder cultures of the southeastern U.S. suggest a Mesoamerican origin. Stephen Peet reports:

The Choctaws and other Muskogee tribes have a migration myth to the effect that they came from the west, issuing from a mountain of fire; but they tell also that they issued from a pyramid mound, the creator stamped upon the top of the mound and commanded them to come forth.[372]

John Denison Baldwin would agree with this theory. In 1871, he explained:

That appears to me the most reasonable suggestion which assumes that the Mound-Builders came originally from Mexico and Central America. It explains many facts connected with their remains. In the Great Valley their most populous settlements were at the south. Coming from Mexico and Central America, they would begin their settlements on the Gulf coast, and afterward advance gradually up the river to the Ohio Valley. It seems evident that they came by this route; and their remains show that their only connection with the coast was at the south. Their settlements did not reach the coast at any other point.[373]

Baldwin illustrates some of the connections that suggest this direct line of cultural transfer. Both the Moundbuilders of the Ohio Valley and the pyramid builders of Mesoamerica had small mounds (known as *teocallis*) as well as "large high mounds, with level summits, reached by great flights of steps." Baldwin describes the similarities:

Pyramidal platforms or foundations for important edifices appear in both regions, and are very much alike. In Central America important edifices were built of hewn stone, and can still be examined in their ruins. The Mound-Builders, like some of the ancient people of Mexico and Yucatan, used wood, sun-dried brick, or some other material that could not resist decay. There is evidence that they used timber for building purposes. In one of the mounds opened in the Ohio Valley two chambers were found with remains of the timber of which the walls were made, and with arched ceilings precisely like those in Central America, even to the overlapping stones. Chambers have been found in some of the Central American and Mexican mounds, but there hewn stones were used for the walls. In both regions the elevated and terraced foundations remain, and can be compared.[374]

Baldwin claims these low, wide mounds often served as the "terraced foundations for buildings, and if they were situated in Yucatan, Guatemala, and Southern Mexico, they would never be mistaken for any thing else." However, since the buildings on the Ohio Valley mounds were made of wood, they haven't survived to give us this impression.

Baldwin says, "This method of construction was brought to the Mississippi Valley from Mexico and Central America, the ancient inhabitants of that region and the Mound-Builders being the same people in race, and also in civilization, when it was brought here." Again we are led to ask, just who were the Moundbuilders? To find out, we need to trace them back to their origins.

IS THE SOUTH WHERE IT ALL STARTED?

A clue can be found in the fact that not all of these mounds were made from soil. At the Sapelo Island Shell Ring Complex off the coast of Georgia, there are large mounds made almost entirely from different types of seashells, including oysters, clams, and conch.[375] They are ring-shaped with a flat plaza in the center, and date back to 2170 BC. In Florida, similar sites like the Horr's Island Mounds and Guana River Shell Rings are even older.

This suggests that the people who introduced shell mounds to Florida could have sailed from the Gulf of Mexico. This explains why Georgia's Hitchiti-Creek have migration legends that suggest they came by boat. Their earliest settlements in the U.S. coincide with the appearance of corn (which came from Mexico), and their language has words that suggest Mayan origins.

But mound sites in Mexico get older as we move towards the west coast, not the east coast. And they show up in western Mexico around the same time they show up in the Norte Chico civilization of Peru. In other words, there was an influx of new culture hitting the western shores of the Americas.

So it makes perfect sense that oldest mounds in the Americas are found off the Pacific coast of Chiapas, Mexico. There, a 240-foot-wide mound is made almost entirely from clam shells. The mound has been dated back to at least 3024 BC, with carbon dating suggesting that it could date back to 3700 BC or earlier, and that additional layers were added every 20 or 30 years until around 2575 BC. The shell mound is made of several platforms, capped with what archaeologists call "a cement-like material made from burned shell and sand."[376] Now that REALLY sounds like what the pyramid builders of the Nile Valley would do if they were on an island that lacked a stone quarry.

DID THEY COME FROM ASIA?

Most of this evidence suggests the Moundbuilders could have come from East Asia. And it makes sense, considering that most of the "pyramids" of ancient China are not stone structures, but pyramid-shaped burial mounds. These were built by the Black builders of ancient China, who may have brought their culture further east.

When you look at the effigy sculptures produced by Mississippian people, there are signs pointing back to ancient East Asia. And there is at least some skeletal evidence that the builders of these ancient monuments were Black people from Asia. In 1907, remains described as "Australoid" were reported in a burial mound in Douglass County, Nebraska.[377]

They could have sailed from east Asia, landing first at sites along the Pacific Coast of Central and South America (such as Mexico and Peru), where we find some of the earliest mounds in the Americas. They could have then moved north, sailing to the southern tip of Florida before spreading throughout the Lower Mississippi Valley, eventually giving birth to the Mississippian culture which ultimately carried their ideas as far north as Ohio and Illinois.

When you look at the effigy sculptures produced by Mississippian people, there are signs pointing back to ancient East Asia. And there is at least some skeletal evidence that the builders of these ancient monuments were Black people from Asia. In 1907, remains described as "Australoid" were reported in a burial mound in Douglass County, Nebraska.[378]

DID THEY COME FROM AFRICA?

Moundbuilding could have also come with the migrations that traveled across the Atlantic. The practice of mound-building is also found in West Africa, a fact noted by Leo Weiner in *Africa and the Discovery of America*. According to Graham Connah's *African Civilizations: An Archaeological Perspective*, there are at least 822 such mounds throughout West Africa, especially in Cameroon, Chad, Nigeria, and the Niger Delta.*

Like the mounds in the Mississippi Valley, most of these mounds were the sites of urban settlements, and were enclosed with walls of stone or earth, banks or ditches, wooden fencing, or densely planted trees.†

Just west of Niger, Mali has few settlement mounds but plenty of burial mounds. There are actually hundreds of burial mounds, or tumuli, throughout West Africa, stretching from the Sahara to the Atlantic coast of Senegal.[379]

---

* It should be noted that Van Sertima theorized that the Mande people did not live on the coast, but would have access to the Atlantic Ocean (and its carrying currents) simply by sailing down the Niger River.

† There was little need for these defenses in the most ancient periods, but fortifications eventually became widespread – even in West Africa – for reasons we'll explain in Volume Four of this series.

<table>
<tr><td>

DID YOU KNOW?

In *America B.C.*, Professor Barry Fell says a massive wave of North African colonists sailed to North America. Fell says that, in both North Africa and Western Europe, these Berbers buried their dead in stone tombs which were then enclosed in large earthen mounds, a tradition they continued across the Atlantic in North America, where many mound-builder tombs have the same layout. Fell details dozens of other connections, including linguistic and cultural ties across the Atlantic. But before you think Barry Fell was a hero, please know that Fell made these Berbers out to be WHITE. He even claimed "Blonde Tuaregs" were responsible at one point. The lesson here is to always be careful about an author's agenda when you consider his evidence. Still, Fell unintentionally provides us a strong body of evidence for a BLACK North African presence in the Americas.

</td><td>

The Saloum Delta is a river delta in Senegal at the mouth of the Saloum River, where it flows into the Atlantic Ocean. There, you can still find dozens of well-preserved tumuli, or burial mounds, as well as shell mounds like those found in Florida on the other side of the Atlantic.[380] Further east, reliefs depict the huts of the people of ancient Punt resembling the Toquls of the modern Sudanese, built on mounds reached by ladders.

In the 1905 text *Aboriginal Religions in America*, Stephen Peet discusses the history and significance of American mounds, connecting them to the pyramids of Egypt and the Near East. In both regions, pyramidal structures were preceded by burial mounds. Anu people also introduced burial mounds to ancient Europe.

In many of these places, a small group of Anu migrants was able to mobilize a large community of people (often a non-agricultural people) to produce

</td></tr>
</table>

these massive monuments. Considering that so many of these mounds (as well as other structures made from stone) were burial sites, it's possible that Anu "teachers" introduced new advances in agriculture, astronomy, urbanization, and social structure – all developments that occur wherever we find these monuments – and the indigenous populations honored them with elaborate burials. These burial sites, fittingly, became astronomical observatories that made full use of the innovations their owners introduced.

Thus it makes sense that – in the tradition of the Lacandón Indians of western Mexico (who descend from the Maya) – it was "unthinkable" to harvest anywhere such mounds existed, as these mounds were believed to be the dwelling place of the Wayantekob, or the "Wandering Gods."[381]

Were the Moundbuilders the "wandering gods"? We certainly know where they wandered *to* (the American southeast, followed by the Ohio Valley), but where exactly did they wander *from*?

Ultimately, the migration of the moundbuilders could have come across the Pacific or the Atlantic. We don't know if the ancient mound-building civilization of the Amazon is older than the one in Peru, so either route is possible. One thing is for sure: Wherever they came from, they brought with them the full Anu Cultural Complex.

They also brought their genetic markers with them. Genetic research has revealed Anu HLAs⁺ in many of the Indian populations native to Moundbuilder sites. Some of these genetic markers could have come from Asia, but others could have come from Africa. Again, things aren't entirely clear, and future research is needed.

Perhaps it's possible that the ancestors of the Moundbuilders were a composite culture, born from the meeting of two Anu populations from either side of the globe. To investigate this possibility, we must investigate the place they came from before they traveled north into the Mississippi Valley. That place is known to historians of the ancient world as Mesoamerica.

MESOAMERICA

Most people know that North America is made up of Canada, the United States, and Mexico. But wait. There's also Central America, the strip of land connecting North America and South America. When archaeologists and historians talk about the ancient world, they call Central America (including Southern Mexico) *Mesoamerica*. It simply means "Middle America."

One of the most well-known cultures from this region was that of the Aztecs. It was the Aztec Empire who the Spanish conquered when they came to Mexico in the early 1500s. The Aztecs had been a mighty empire, but they certainly weren't the first civilization in the area. In fact, they were one of the last.

THE ZAPOTECS, MIXTECS, TOLTECS, AND AZTECS

In the valley of Oaxaca, Mexico, the Zapotec culture took form around 900 BC. The Mixtec culture conquered the Zapotecs. By the early 1400's the Mixtecs were a colony of the mighty Aztec empire. These two cultures continue their existence today in the State of Oaxaca, which is inhabited by nearly two million of their descendants. Further north, the Toltecs reigned from 950 to 1300 AD. The Toltecs went to war with the Mayas and eventually defeated

---

⁺ For an explanation of what we mean by Anu HLAs, see "Unexpected Genes in the Americas" in the Appendix.

AMERICAN PYRAMIDS

In addition to the dozens of other pyramids featured throughout this book, there are literally hundreds of pyramids in the Americas. In North America, these structures are mostly made from earth and clay. In Central and South America, there are stone pyramids built on top of older temples and burial mounds. Here are just a few of the popular ones. Can you figure out where they're found?

TEOTIHUACAN

Whether through accident or design, it is a fact that the 'Pyramid of the Sun' at Teotihuacan has the same base dimensions (but half the height) of the Grea pyramid at Giza, making it the third largest pyramid in the world.

Within and below the Pyramid of the Sun (above) and the Pyramid of the Moon (middle row), archaeologists found hundreds of ancient artifacts from the cultures who contributed to their stage-by-stage construction (below).

DAYS AT THE MUSEUM

A collection of artifacts from my trips to the National Museum of Anthropology in Mexico and the National Museum of History in Costa Rica. Such visits are an exceptional way to personally discover the missing pieces of our story.

them, creating a cross-Toltec-Mayan religion and society.

The Aztec civilization reigned supreme in Mexico from 1345-1521 AD. They borrowed heavily from their Olmec, Toltec, and Mayan predecessors to develop a complex linguistic, religious, artistic, architectural and military heritage. The Aztecs were still thriving when the Spaniards arrived in 1519. Within two years, this mighty empire came to a sudden and tragic end.

How? Despite their massive military, the Aztecs were no match for sick Europeans. I mean that literally. Sick Europeans, meaning the diseases introduced by the Spaniards effectively destroyed the Aztecs. When Hernando Cortez came to Mexico in 1519, he almost immediately attempted to take control, demanding tribute and the construction of Roman Catholic shrines to replace the Aztec gods. The Aztecs weren't having it. The Aztec army quickly overwhelmed his troops, killing many and causing the rest to retreat.

But the Aztecs contracted smallpox from the Spanish soldiers, and the rest is history. By 1520, 25% of the Aztec population had died, and the military was in shambles. The emperor was dead and the chain of command was gone. By 1521, it was almost **easy for a small Spanish army to take full control of what was once a sprawling empire**.

THE MAYAS

Long before the Aztecs or Toltecs, the civilization of the Mayas reigned supreme. From 2000 BC to about 900 AD, the Mayan Empire shifted centers several times, but for much of this time, it was headquartered in what is now Guatemala. Mayan influence extended far beyond this area, however, reaching from the Sierra Madre Mountains in the west to the Caribbean shores in the east. Mayan influence spanned the Honduras, Belize, Guatemala, El Salvador, and Mexico.

The Mayas did quite a lot, in case you didn't know. Some of their accomplishments include:

- [ ] They had a highly sophisticated calendar and knowledge of astronomy
- [ ] They also had a system of hieroglyphic writing. In fact, they had one of the only known fully developed written languages of the pre-Columbian Americas
- [ ] They had ball courts and extravagant sporting ceremonies
- [ ] They built great, lavish palaces, temples, and pyramids
- [ ] They had huge plazas where people would buy, sell and trade goods
- [ ] Their system of mathematics had positional notation and the use of the zero
- [ ] The Mayan site of Kaminaljuyu has been described as one of the greatest of all archaeological sites in the "New World"

The Mayas built some of the most amazing urban centers in the pre-Columbian Americas. They are world-renowned for their accomplishments in mathematics, astronomy, architecture, and their "nearly unparalleled" calendar system.

From the Pre-Classic period (c. 2000 BC – 250 AD) to the Classic period (c. 250–900 AD), they built hundreds of massive temples and stone monuments, often integrating the natural features of the environment in their layout. They cultivated maize, beans, and squash, as well as other important "Latin American" foods.

They also developed a pictographic script (like hieroglyphics) which dates back to about 300 BC,[382] and which may have been derived from the script introduced by the Olmecs. Over the next several centuries, they developed their language and body of literature to heights unmatched anywhere else in the Americas. When the Spaniards arrived, they promptly began burning thousands of Mayan books. As linguist Michael D. Coe notes:

> [O]ur knowledge of ancient Maya thought must represent only a tiny fraction of the whole picture, for of the thousands of books in which the full extent of their learning and ritual was recorded, only four have survived to modern times…[383]

The Spanish didn't just burn books. They destroyed monuments and killed native historians. They were determined to destroy any traces of the greatness that once was. They also killed off millions of indigenous Mesoamericans, many of them direct descendants of the original Mayas.

But contrary to popular myth, the Mayas did not truly "disappear" or go extinct. Countless people fled the old sites of the Mayan Empire, choosing to live in the jungles rather than submit to Spanish rule, or extinction. One such people are the Lacandón Indians, who now inhabit the forests of the upper Usumacinta River.

The Lacandón are descendents of Yucatán Maya who fled the Spanish. They are shorter and darker-complexioned than other native people in the area, and often have curly hair, low noses, and long heads, suggesting they are more closely related to an aboriginal Black population than their neighbors. Scholars have connected them to the Australoid people of the Pacific and the Veddoid people of India.

In 1975, geneticist Dr. Alfonso de Garay identified the gene for malaria-resistance (which also produces sickle cells), among the Lacandón. Researchers have expressed intrigue with how a people who have not been known to mix with outsiders in post-Columbian times could possess a 10,000 year old gene "usually found only in the blood of Black people."[384] It's no wonder that Lacandónes called themselves Hach-Winick, or "Real People."[385]

The evidence available to us (both genetic and artistic) suggests that the original Mayas were not a light-skinned people. **But were they Black?** You mean ALL Black? Before we dig into that question, let's first be clear that most of the indigenous people who built Mayan civilization looked very different from most African people. In their artwork, they tend to depict themselves with broad, hooked noses, straight hair, and reddish to dark brown skin.

There are plenty of Mayan descendants still living in Mexico today who have many of these features, minus the dark skin. A few, like the Lacandón, may even have dark skin. Still, you might get jumped trying to say ALL the Mayas were people who sailed over from West Africa. Or people might just laugh and shake their heads.

Now, if you're able to connect the dots, you can ultimately trace Mayan features back to the diversity found among the Original people of Africa, but there's a lot of Native American history along the way. The point is, the majority of the Mayan people weren't recent arrivals from West Africa.

Still, you can see examples of the cultural continuity we talked about among Native Americans, who preserve many of the traditions and tendencies of indigenous African culture going back to the Paleolithic era.

For example, the role of the shaman (sometimes called medicine men) in Africa, Asia, and the Americas is pivotal. It's like they all have the same guidebook. In fact, African shamans may be the prototype of the tradition, giving even recent African shamans an "all access pass" to VIP status anywhere in the world where shamanism is practiced.

This may explain why the brown-skinned Mayas preferred a Black-skinned priesthood. In fact, the jet-black, long-haired Mayan men depicted in our Heritage Playing Cards are priests! Not only can this be seen in early Mayan and European paintings of the Mayan priests, there's hard evidence in the archaeological record as well. Frederick Peterson, in his 1959 work *Ancient Mexico*, remarked:

> We can trace the slow progress of man in Mexico without noting any definite Old World influence during this period (1000-650 BC), except possibly a strong Negroid substratum connected with the Magicians.[387]

The "Magicians" may have been West Africans who traveled to Mexico or a class of Black people who could only marry among themselves, effectively preserving the African phenotype over untold generations. This reverence for Black people may have something to do with why many Native Americans, including the Mayas, respected enslaved Africans (who they said had "Great Medicine" in their bodies),* revered Black gods that represented the principles of healing and good fortune, and told fanciful legends of the DBP. In his 1921 *Africa and the Discovery of America*, Leo Wiener writes:

> In the first volume I show that Negroes had a far greater influence upon American civilization than has heretofore been suspected. In

---

* Old accounts of Native American culture say "Great Medicine" means God.

THE MAYAN BONAMPAK MURALS

Similar characters also appear on Mayan vases as gods, warriors, and traders. In later years, some Mayans paint themselves Black to meet with African traders. This practice continues even after such visits become rare.

the second volume I shall chiefly study the African fetishism, which even with the elaborate books on the subject, is woefully misunderstood, and I shall show by documentary evidence to what extraordinary extent the Indian medicine-man owes his evolution to the African medicine-man.

Later, when the influx of Black people decreased, many Mesoamerican priests began painting themselves Black to continue this tradition, which continues today. But it didn't begin with black body paint. It began with black skin. Although Fred Peterson later denied his claims about a Black presence in Mexico, there's now plenty of evidence to prove it. We'll start with the art.

THE BONAMPAK MURALS

Inside a small temple in Chiapas, Mexico, you'll find the Bonampak murals, one the most important examples of Mayan artwork. Unlike the art found at many other sites, these images are full-color frescoes, exquisitely detailed, and exceptionally well-preserved, despite being over 1300 years old.

Yale University's Mary Miller conducted an extensive study of the Bonampak murals. She wrote:

> Perhaps no single artifact from the ancient New World offers as complex a view of Prehispanic society as do the Bonampak paintings. No other work features so many Maya engaged in the life of the court and rendered in such great detail, making the Bonampak murals an unparalleled resource for understanding ancient society.[389]

There's a good chance that – even if you've learned about the Maya – you've never seen the Bonampak murals. In the full-color insert to this book, you'll understand why. Not only are most of the Maya painted a rich chocolate-brown complexion (darker than most of us would expect), but many of their features resemble those of African people, while others are more characteristically Native American.

Some of the characters look especially African, with even darker skin and "snub noses." Many of the artifacts, apparel, and gestures in the panoramas resemble those of ancient Egypt, while others look like carryovers from West Africa. There are even individuals wearing what looks to be dreadlocks!

THE XULTUN MURAL

In May of 2012, archaeologists found an even older Mayan fresco over 200 miles south of Chiapas, in Xultun, Guatemala. The mural – dated back to 800 AD – depicts a scribe, captioned "Younger Brother Obsidian" recording for another man, captioned "Older

Brother Obsidian." Archaeologists say the site is important because it presents the oldest Mayan calendar found to date.

Unlike the last Mayan calendar they found, this one goes well past 2012, effectively deading any talk of a "Mayan Endtime Prophecy." This calendar actually goes 7,000 years into the future. I think this is interesting, but I always knew the Mayan end-of-the-world myth was invented by a few unscrupulous authors selling fear and myth, while modern Mayas shook their heads in disgust at how their prophecies had been perversely twisted.

Knowing this, what I found more interesting was something that most reports on the find left OUT. Photos from the site showed the two Obsidian brothers, but they weren't too well-preserved. You could see the dark reddish-brown skin of the scribe, but his features were hard to make out. I found an artist's reconstruction of the scribe, and it looked good...until I realized the artist had replaced the nose from the mural with a more "classic" Mayan nose. So I went in and traced the outline of the nose and lips myself, revealing what the artists and photographers had concealed (intentionally or unintentionally): that these brothers kinda looked African.

And then I found out more. The photographers were intentionally leaving out three figures seated behind the scribe! Why? Because they REALLY looked African. In fact, they're painted nearly jet black, and are wearing what archaeologist William Saturno calls "headdresses of a sort never before seen in Maya art." When you see the picture of these headdresses, it's obvious what they look like. The crowns of Egyptian pharaohs.

Could these Black men – hidden from most media reports on the site – be remnants of a Nubian expedition that landed in Central America? Are these "three wise men" from the East? Or did they descend from the Olmec? And – considering that the scribe is making calculations for the Mayan calendar – what exactly is the role of these seated, crowned, observers?

And there's yet another hidden figure, this one hidden by the artists themselves! "Older Brother Obsidian," who may be a king, has more of the classic Native American features, and is a shade of lighter brown, looking like many Mayas today. But behind him, a dark-skinned male is seated, mostly concealed by the throne. It looks like a scene from the Wizard of Oz, with the man in the back manipulating the arms of the figure in the front. If that weren't enough, a rod above this part of the mural was once used to hang a curtain, which could conceal or reveal the dark-skinned man behind the throne.

What does all of this mean? What does it prove? And what more lays hidden? According to Saturno, although the Xultun site was first discovered in 1915, less than 0.1 percent of it has been explored.[390]

BLACK GODS OF THE AMERICAS

[AN EXCERPT FROM BLACK GOD, AN UPCOMING RELEASE]

Many of the gods of the Native Americans were Black, a convention that appears to be more than artistic. Runoko Rashidi notes:

[S]cientists have found a host of cultural parallels between ancient Africans and native Americans, including architectural patterns and religious practices. As for the latter, some native American communities worshipped black gods of great antiquity, such as Ekchuah, Quetzalcoatl, Yalahau, Nahualpilli and Ixtliltic, long before the first African slave arrived in the New World.

These gods were worshipped far and wide. For example, Ekchuah was the sixth most commonly depicted deity in the Mayan codices, portrayed at least forty times. He is painted Black with thick lips. **His name means "Black Star"** (*ek* means "star" and *chuah* means "black" in Yucatan Maya).

Floyd Hayes III reports that among many of the Indians of Guatemala, "the black Christ is referred to in private as Ekchuah," who Harold Lawrence describes as "black and woolly-haired" and "unmistakably Negro." Lawrence adds:

An examination of ancient Indian religions yields additional information of the condition of early Africans in the Americas. Several Indian nations, such as the Mayans, Aztecs, and Incas, worshipped black gods along with their other deities, and the Mayan religion particularly exemplifies the high esteem in which the negroes were held.[391]

Kokopelli is a well-known fertility god and hunter among the Hopi and Zuni people of the America southwest. As the spirit of fertility, he is seen as responsible for introducing corn (agriculture) to various peoples across the Americas. Kokopelli was first found in Anasazi rock carvings, but he also appears in Mississippian artifacts.

Throughout South America, he is known as Ekoko. He is believed to descend from the Mayan Ekchuah. Kokopelli is identified with the southwestern Tewa people's god *Nepokwa'i*, a great hunter who is described as "a big black man."[394]

WHERE DID THESE BLACK GODS COME FROM?

And how did a group of people who don't look African end up with gods who do? As always, they were once real people.

Leo Wiener provides a detailed account of the Black gods of Mexico in the third volume of his *Africa and the Discovery of America*, adding Mayan gods L and M, and high god Xaman Ek to the list.[395] Wiener traces these gods back to Black merchants trading prized goods like cacao, feathers, and animal skins, which they imported from afar.

In his *Yucatan Before and After the Conquest*, Diego de Landa says "Ekchuah is the recognized god of the merchants, the *beyom*, or 'traveling man.' At first, Ekchuah was a god of warriors, but became a beneficial god for merchants.

The same story is told about the Black God M.* These traditions appear to tell the story of the Africans who arrived in the Americas, first establishing themselves as formidable warriors, then as master traders, and perhaps finally as cultural leaders.

THE OLMECS

The most prominent evidence of pre-Columbian reverence for Black people can be found among the Olmecs. It was the Olmecs who authored the blueprint and laid the foundation for all the Mesoamerican civilizations that followed. The Olmec heartland is recognized as one of the two "cradles of civilization" in the Americas (the other being the Andes).[396] Still, much remains unknown (or misunderstood) about these important people.

Coming to power around 1200 BC, the Olmecs produced Mexico's first established civilization, born along the eastern coastal states of present-day Veracruz and Tabasco, along the Gulf Coast of Mexico. The Olmec civilization established the cultural blueprint that all succeeding indigenous civilizations would follow in Mexico. These

---

* In an upcoming work titled *Black God*, we'll discuss Bishamon and Daikoku, two of the Black gods of Japan who share nearly the same story as that of Ekchuah. There are also stories of Black warrior/merchant gods in Europe and India, suggesting that ancient African traders traveled far and wide, establishing reputations of mythical proportions.

THE OLMECS

THE 17 COLOSSAL OLMEC HEADS

Many do not know that there are 17 Olmec heads (so far). Here we present them all. There's no mistaking that they were predominantly Black people.

Colossal Head No. 1
San Lorenzo

Colossal Head No. 2
San Lorenzo

Colossal Head No. 3
San Lorenzo

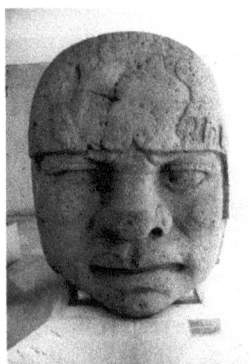

Colossal Head No. 5
San Lorenzo

Colossal Head No. 6
San Lorenzo

Colossal Head No. 7
San Lorenzo

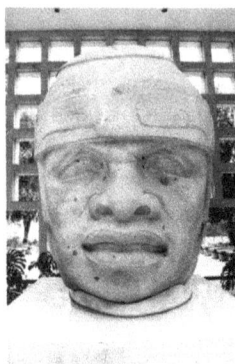

Colossal Head No. 8
San Lorenzo

Colossal Head No. 9
San Lorenzo

Colossal Head No. 10
San Lorenzo

Monument 1
La Venta

Monument 2
La Venta

Monument 3
La Venta

Monument 4
La Venta

Monument A
Tres Zapotes

Monument Q
Tres Zapotes

Monument No. 1
Rancho La Cobata

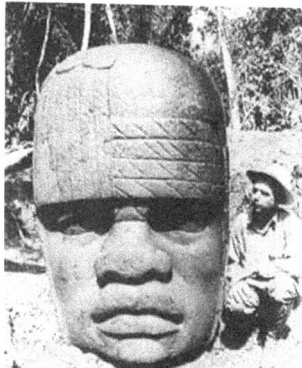

Colossal Head No. 4
San Lorenzo

Most of the heads clearly resemble living Black populations in the Sudan (Nubia) or the Niger Delta area.

These heads represent a group of elites. Where did they come from? What did they do to become so highly revered? Where else did they go?

cultures – including the Mayas, Toltecs, Mixtecs, Zapotecs, Aztecs, and others – borrowed heavily from the Olmec's religious, architectural and artistic traditions. They're noted for many accomplishments:

- ❐ Despite the absence of a local supply of stone, they built massive buildings.
- ❐ They created an advanced calendar including the concept of zero.
- ❐ The built the first known pyramids in Mesoamerica.
- ❐ They introduced the earliest written script in the Americas.
- ❐ They pioneered agriculture, cultivating the staple crops that later Indians would call "the Three Sisters" (maize, beans, and squash).
- ❐ Their well-planned cities also had aqueducts and drainage systems.
- ❐ They were highly skilled in pottery and metallurgy

They're probably best known for the colossal stone heads they sculpted from massive boulders found outside the city. Some are over six feet tall and weigh over forty tons. So far, seventeen have been found.

These seventeen heads represented elite members of their society. The "amazingly Negroid" features of their faces have disrupted the archaeological community for decades. After all, why would these presumably Native American people quarry, carve, and erect these massive heads, often after dragging a forty ton stone several miles to its intended display site, only to represent what looks like a group of Africans?

During the Early Formative Period (beginning 1500 BC), sedentary villages in the Gulf Coast of Mexico begin increasing their agricultural productivity (cultivating maize, beans, and squash), ultimately giving rise to permanent villages. Somehow, the founders of the Olmec culture went into high gear around 1200 BC, and they quickly surpassed all their neighboring cultures. From then until about 400 BC, Olmec political centers at San Lorenzo, La Venta, and Tres Zapotes grew to epic proportions.

They were run by a theocratic elite, with an economy that supported thousands of artisans and farmers. The built monumental structures, such as huge platforms 3,000 feet long and 1,000 feet wide, reaching heights of 150 feet, as well as pyramids, altars, tombs, and elaborate drainage systems and aqueducts carved from stone blocks.[397]

At La Venta, the Olmecs built what is regarded as one of the earliest pyramids in Mesoamerica – a step pyramid 100 feet high, containing an estimated 130,000 cubic yards of earth fill. As Ivan Van Sertima notes, "When pyramids appear in America in the Olmec culture they are oriented astronomically."

The Olmecs were soon so powerful and influential that other Mesoamerican cultures became "colonies" of the Olmec, adopting their culture in a process Mary Pye calls "Olmecization." This lasted for a couple centuries, but after 800 BC, Olmec stylistic influence over the region went into decline. By 300 BC, the Olmec culture basically disappeared. This is when the Mayas and other Mesoamerican cultures (like the Zapotecs) emerged.[398] That much we know for sure. The rest is the subject of ongoing debate.

For starters…nobody can seem to agree on who the Olmecs actually were, or where they came from. Most historians say there's no precedent to their culture. Olmec expert Michael Coe has observed that "the Olmec style of art and **Olmec engineering ability suddenly appeared full-fledged from about 1200 BC.**"[399]

WHERE DID THEY COME FROM?

"We do not know where the Olmec homeland lay," said Michael Coe. "Wherever it was, they already knew how to move and carve huge basalt boulders." Coe was talking about the colossal stone heads found throughout the Olmec centers.

Let's make an important distinction. None of the evidence suggests that ALL of the people living in Olmec society looked like those colossal stone heads. But Alexander von Wutheneau makes an important statement when he says:

> The Negroid element is the exception, but is well proven by the large Olmec stone monuments as well as the terracotta items and therefore cannot be excluded from pre-Columbian history of the Americas. *Furthermore, it is precisely the Negroid representations which often indicate personalities of high position, who can unhesitatingly be compared to the outstanding Negroes who served as models for great works of art in Egypt and in Nigeria.*[400]

All the evidence suggests that Olmec civilization was a composite society, with an ancestral population coming from the indigenous people of the Tabasco area (who had already established a solid culture in the area), and infusions of influential foreigners who quickly rose to positions of prominence, propelling the Olmec civilization in directions previously unseen in Central America.

WHO WERE THESE FOREIGNERS?

It's possible that some of the Olmec people came from East Asia by boat. Professor Mike Xu, Paul Shao and a number of other Asian scholars see a connection between the Shang Dynasty of China and the Olmecs. The art of the Olmecs certainly suggests an East Asian presence. You can't look at Olmec art and not see it.

Also intriguing is the ancient practice of head deformation among the Olmecs (as well as the ancient Peruvians and Mayas), which was also practiced among the people of ancient China.[401] As we explain elsewhere, this practice has its roots in Africa, with the goal being to look the most "strongly African" (i.e. long-headed).

While the China-America connection is interesting, there's a much clearer trans-oceanic connection that scholars tend to ignore. Veracruz is much closer to West Africa than it is to China. And the colossal heads look *very African*. It seems natural to think that they were Africans.

Scholars like Patrick Huyghe say that the headgear on the Olmec heads resemble the helmets worn by Nubians and Egyptians of that era. There is evidence that the Egyptians, or another group of North Africans, could have arrived in the Americas before Columbus, or that the Olmec elites could have come from deeper within Africa.

Ivan Van Sertima, Leo Wiener, Floyd Hayes III, and Clyde Ahmad Winters have cited evidence going back to the Mande people of West Africa,* as well as evidence pointing to ancient Nubia. If nothing else, we can say that the African contribution to Olmec civilization belonged to the Anu language family. The Nubians, Egyptians, North Africans, and even the Mande could be considered Anu populations.

LOOKS AREN'T EVERYTHING. WHERE'S THE EVIDENCE?

The problem with getting mainstream scholars to accept any of these theories has been the lack of evidence from human remains. After all, what better way to tell who was who back then?

---

* The Mande don't live on the coasts, but they would only have to sail down the Niger River, from where they'd be carried across the Atlantic by the ocean currents.

WHERE DID THE OLMEC COME FROM?

The Olmec Empire was not entirely indigenous. The colossal heads suggest that at least some of the elites were Africans who could have easily sailed over thanks to the the ocean currents (see below).

But countless Olmec sculptures also have East Asian features. It would be just as ridiculous to deny the obvious East Asian presence as it would be to deny the African presence.

Yet note that many of the East Asian faces in Olmec art are not "purely Mongoloid." They tend to have Black features as well. Could some of them be the Black people of ancient China?

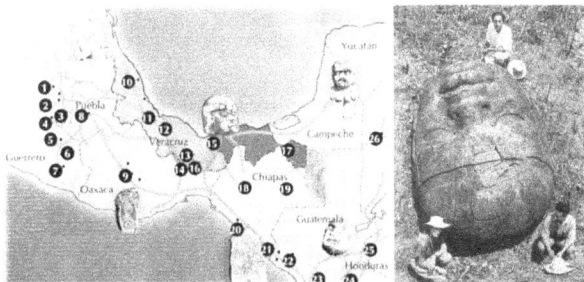

Olmec sites or sites with Olmec influence
1. Tlatilco
2. Cuicuilco
3. Chalcatzingo
4. Texpa
5. Teopantecuanitlan
6. Olinalá
7. Oxtotitlán
8. Las Bocas
9. Monte Albán
10. El Viejón
11. La Mojarra
12. Tres Zapotes
13. San Lorenzo
14. Las Limas
15. La Venta
16. El Manatí
17. Balancán
18. Chiapa de Corzo
19. Xoc
20. Pijijiapan
21. Izapa
22. Abaj Takalik
23. Monte Alto
24. Chalchuapa
25. Copán
26. Cuello

EAST ASIAN OLMEC FACES

AFRICA/AMERICA OCEAN CURRENTS

UNITED STATES

☐ CHIAPAS
▨ VERACRUZ
■ TABASCO

Olmec Heartland

Pacific Ocean

0   300 Kilometers
0   300 Miles

→ Mokaya Heartland ★ GUATEMALA

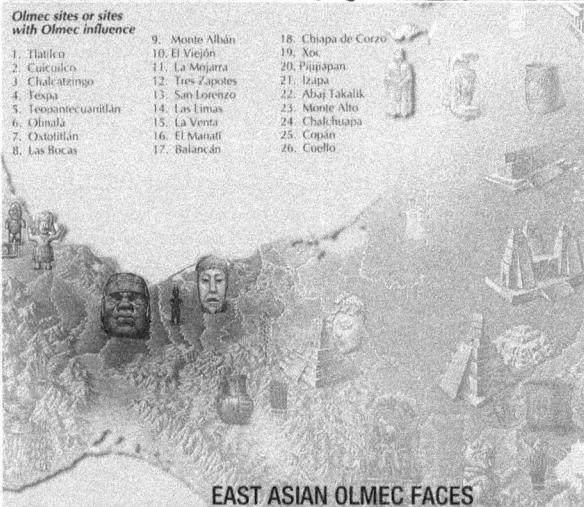

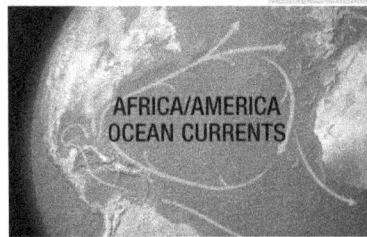

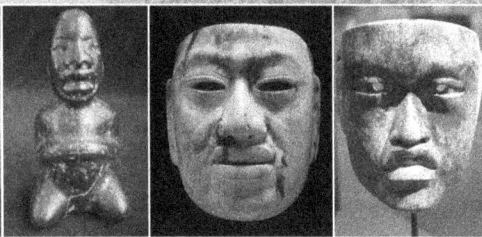

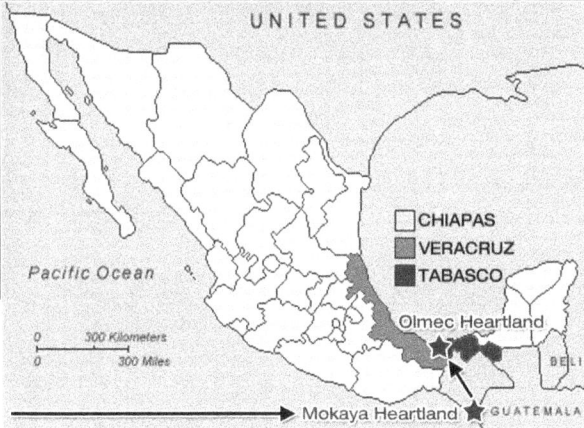

This brings us back to the Mokaya's East Asian Blacks and their role in founding Olmec civilization.

That's where Polish craniologist Andrzej Wiercinski, head of the Department of Anthropology at Warsaw University, came in. Wiercinski found skeletal evidence for Africans among the Olmec. He reported that 13.5% of the crania from the pre-Classic Olmec cemetery at Tlatilco were of the African type, as were 4.5% of the Classic-era remains at Cerro de las Mesas.[403] This tells us that the Black presence was strongest in the formative years of the Olmec empire, and declined over time, most likely through absorption into the increasingly Mongoloid population.

But did all of the Black Olmecs come from Africa? A recent reevaluation of Wiercinski's findings (factoring in types that describe Black people who don't fit the typical Bantu profile) raises the estimates of a Black population to 26.9% and 9.1% respectively. At least some of these people could have come from Southeast Asia.

These findings are supported by a recent study of dental traits from early Olmec and Baja remains. Many of their teeth did not have the expected Mongoloid trait of "sinodonty" but instead resembled the dental traits of Australians and Southeast Asians.[404] In fact, Mike Xu believes the "Negro" features of the massive Olmec heads was connected to early Shang art, suggesting an African presence may have come from China.

Other scholars, noting the similarity between "Negroid" Samoans and the Olmec heads, have suggested the Black elites of ancient Mexico came from Asia by way of the Pacific Islands. As we noted earlier, wherever the Olmec homeland originally was, "they already knew how to move and carve huge basalt boulders." Where do we find evidence of ancient people moving and carving massive stone heads? In the Pacific Islands.

THEY CAME BEFORE THE OLMECS

There's no reason to doubt that there were other cross-oceanic Black migrations before and after the expedition that brought the Olmec elites to Mexico. The Mokaya culture was settled on the Pacific coast of Mexico near Chiapas, and was permanently settled as early as 2000 BC. The Mokaya were one of Mesoamerica's earliest sedentary villagers. The earliest reported phase of their culture is the Barra phase (1900-1700 BC), when both agriculture and ceramics were introduced.

Between the Barra Phase (1900-1700 BC) and the Ocos Phase (1250-1150 BC), the Mokaya transitioned to agriculture, built Mesoamerica's first palace/plaza architectural complex, its first ball court, and established the first settlements on raised mounds.[405] This is the period when there is strong evidence of a Black presence among the Mokaya, peaking around 1700-1500 BC.

As Clyde Ahmad Winters notes:

> The figurines of the Ocos are the most significant evidence for Blacks living in the area during this period. The female figurine from Aquiles Serdan is clearly that of an African woman.

Indeed, the figurines of the Mokaya clearly represent Black people as well as Mongoloid people. But these weren't influences from the Olmecs. It's true that the Mokaya were under the influence of the Olmecs by the time of the Cherla Phase (1100-1000 BC). But the Black presence is much older than that. There are at least 500 years between the earliest evidence for a Black presence at Mokaya and the emergence of a Black elite among the Olmec. In other words, the first Black people of Mokaya could have become some of the first Black people of the Olmecs.

R.A. Diehl, author of *The Olmecs*, has noted:

> The identity of these first Olmecs remain a mystery. Some scholars believe they were Mokaya migrants from the Pacific coast of Chiapas who brought improved maize strains and incipient social stratification with them. Others propose that Olmec culture evolved among local indigenous populations without significant external stimulus. I prefer the latter position, but freely admit that we lack sufficient information on the period before 1500 B.C. to resolve the issue.[406]

However, most Mesoamerican scholars don't see any local predecessor to the Olmec culture, not even among the Mokaya.[407] Yet there are obvious lines of cultural transmission connecting the Black presence on the Gulf Coast of Mexico to the Black presence on the Pacific Coast, which predated the Olmecs. And the Pacific Coast is the same region where the first moundbuilders landed, before they sailed northeast into Florida, later establishing Moundbuilder cultures across the United States. (See "The Moundbuilders").

In fact, the earliest Mokaya constructions are shell mounds along the Pacific Coast. It's very likely that the ancestors of the Mokaya are the ones who built the earliest shell mounds in the Americas on an island off the Pacific coast of Chiapas. All of this suggests they came from the Pacific, and that they continued carrying this culture east.[408]

For example, the earliest Mokaya ceramics copied the styles of fancy gourd vessels. This is another indicator they came from the Pacific, where African gourds were carried across a long stretch of islands

MOKAYA

Veracruz

Veracruz

Guerrero

There are plenty of sculptures with Africoid features throughout ancient Mexico, not limited to the colossal basalt heads of the Olmec empire, such as those seen on the right (black backgrounds).

Some of these sculptures are found in Olmec territory (both before and after the reign of the Olmec), but we can also find representations of Black people along Mexico's western coasts. The examples on the left (white backgrounds) come from the Soconusco Region of Chiapas, where the Mokaya crafted the first known representations of Black people in Mesoamerica.

The fact that many of these faces and figurines predated Olmec influence suggests that the Black people of the Mokaya culture may have come from the Pacific Islands and later carried their culture into the Gulf, where the Olmec civilization formed.

Also, note the representations of DBP on Mokaya pendants.

DBP?

Central Plateau of Mexico

Did you note the "Venus" features of the two female figurines?

before showing up in Western Mexico and the Andes. The Mokaya were processing and consuming liquid chocolate out of these vessels as early as 1900 BC. Soon after, liquid chocolate shows up among pre-Olmec people in the Gulf Coast area (c. 1750 BC). Chocolate quickly spreads from the Olmec heartland throughout all of Mesoamerica. The cultivation of maize (corn) takes the same journey.[409]

A QUICK HISTORY OF CORN

Genetically modified foods are a serious problem, for reasons we discuss in depth in *The Hood Health Handbook*. There's no GMO crop more widespread than corn. But guess what? We were the first to genetically modify corn…over 10,000 years ago.

Over the course of thousands of years, American indigenous peoples domesticated, bred and cultivated a large array of plant species. These species now make up more than half of all crops in cultivation worldwide. One of the foremost of these crops was maize, which we know as corn. ("Corn" is just a name Europeans use for any cereal grain.) Maize was first domesticated from the small seeds of a short bushy plant named teosinte, beginning on the Pacific coast of Mexico between 7,500 and 12,000 years ago.

This date matches perfectly with the time when the first Black seafarers landed there. They would have brought the techniques they used to domesticate millet and rice along the coasts of East Asia around the same time. Millet, an African grain also grown by the Black people of ancient India, is a more nutritious grain than rice, preceded the domestication of rice in China.[410]

Around 3000 BC, another migration of people arrived along the western shores of the Americas. At this time, maize cultivation became even more advanced, and spread widely and rapidly, reaching the Andes by 2500 BC, and the indigenous people of the American southwest by 2100 BC.[411] Around this time, the Mokaya people of the Pacific Coast of Mexico may have introduced it to the Olmec heartland, where it quickly became the staple crop of the Olmec, with some gods clearly being associated with maize production. In fact, the maize fields are where the Olmec farmers placed their colossal stone heads, suggesting that the people represented by these heads may have had something to do with the cultivation of maize.

REVIEW

If the ancestors of the Mokaya started out on the Pacific Coast near Chiapas and later sailed to Florida, it's very likely they passed through the Olmec heartland. Could this region have been a cultural crossroads, where Black people from East Asia met traders from Africa, coming together to produce the dynamic and cosmopolitan Olmec civilization? If so, it wouldn't be the first time this happened. And there's evidence for this theory in the linguistic data. As James Guthrie notes:

> Veteran linguistic scholars such as Key (1999), Foster (1999), and Stubbs (1998) note elements common to Afro-Asiatic and Austronesian languages in certain Mexican and South American Indian languages long before post-1492 contact.[412]

For example, Mary LeCron Foster, one of the few scholars with knowledge of both Afro-Asiatic and Mesoamerican languages, has noted an ancient Afro-Asiatic component in the Mixe-Zoquean and Quechua languages of the Olmecs and Mayas. Foster also notes Austronesian elements in these languages, supporting my theory that these civilizations were the byproduct of the combined efforts of Black people from East Asia and Africa.[413]

This theory addresses the gaps left by theories that sought a single-origin for Olmec civilization. These theories don't work, because there's no single culture that could have fathered – or mothered – the Olmecs on its own. **It took two.**

And this was the way of the world, everywhere we find advanced urban civilizations. Original people came together, solving each others problems, teaching each other what they knew, and working together to structure a society that could support a rapidly-growing population.* Wherever we find an ancient civilization being sparked into "rapid growth," we find some trace of the Anu coming among a long-established indigenous population. Among the Olmecs, they appear to have had two distinct Anu populations come together in the Central American heartland that gave birth to many of North America's most well-known ancient cultures.

---

* Pre-urban populations of mixed origins would grow rapidly because of improved agricultural techniques providing a steady supply of food, but also (and perhaps more importantly) because of a more abundant supply of partners among people who adhere to the tradition of exogamous marriages (only marrying people outside of your clan). Many of these societies were polygamous, which also increased birthrates.

BLACK AND YELLOW?

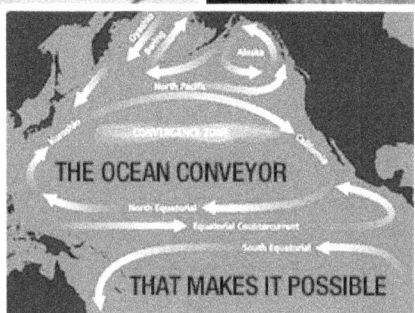

THE OCEAN CONVEYOR

THAT MAKES IT POSSIBLE

Squatting Jade Figurine
Representing the Yi,
A Black Sailing Culture in Eastern China

Squatting Jade Figurine
Olmec Culture
(c. 900-500 BC)

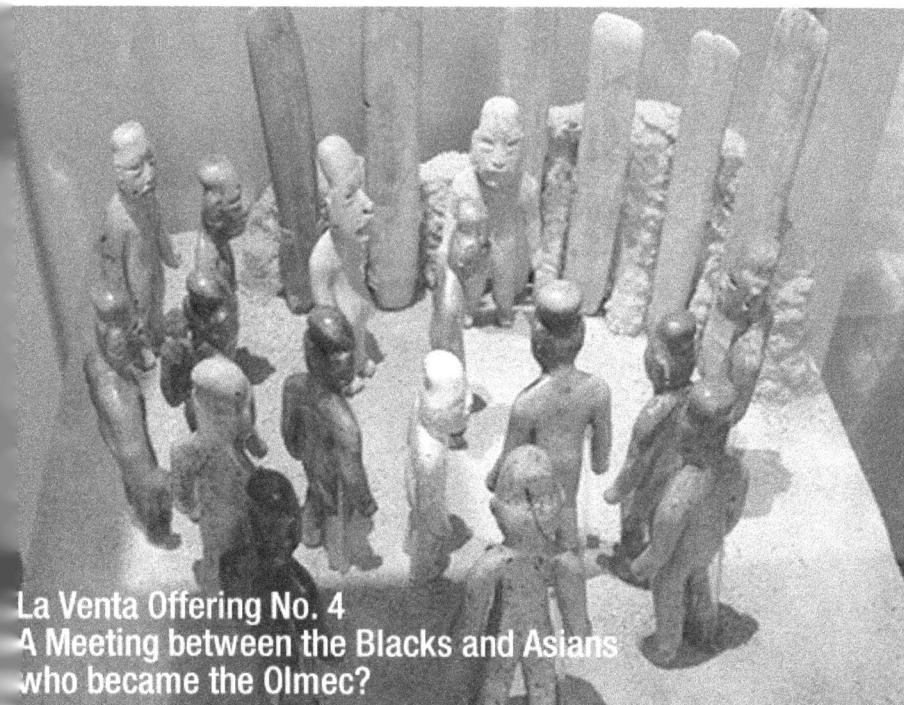

La Venta Offering No. 4
A Meeting between the Blacks and Asians
who became the Olmec?

THE MEETING

When I first formulated this theory, it made a great deal of sense and explained a lot of otherwise unanswered questions about the Olmecs and other communities influenced by the Anu. I was content with including it in the book because the evidence seemed solid. Then, I went to Mexico and found the "smoking gun."

Seated in a private room in the back of the National Anthropology Museum's library, I was given a book on the Olmecs that I would not be allowed to take out of that room. One of the pictures stood out to me. It was an arrangement of stone figurines appearing to have some sort of meeting, surrounded by stone pillars erected in a semi-circular formation. It's known to archaeologists as "La Venta Offering No. 4." You'll find a full-color image of it in this book.

At first, I assumed someone had dug up all these items and arranged them creatively for a museum display. Not so. It appears that this ancient "meeting" was modelled and buried, just as it looks now, below the surface of a temple courtyard about 3,000 years ago. At some point after the initial burial, the site was opened again through the courtyard floor (clearly, someone knew exactly where it was located) and dug up, but just to the level of the figurines' heads. Afterwards, the arrangement was reburied. It was an inspection. After the inspection, this "time capsule" wasn't checked again until modern archaeologists found it.

Why am I calling it a time capsule? To this date, no one has discussed why this "meeting" could have been so significant. When you see the picture, it should become clear: This was a meeting between two communities, one very dark-skinned and the other having a more yellowish complexion. This meeting represents the inception of Olmec civilization, when Black people and Mongoloid people came together to pioneer one of the Western Hemisphere's most important cultures. So why bury it and inspect it to make sure it was still intact? Perhaps they wanted us to find it. And by us, I mean *us*.

REVIEW

Clearly, the Olmecs and the Mayans had strong Black influences. But don't think the Olmecs were *all* Black or that it was *only* Black folks who built Mayan civilization. (Unless, by "Black," you simply mean "people of color.")

In other words, saying that ALL of these people "Africoid" is an oversimplification of a complex history that simply deserves more respect and consideration. As Ivan Van Sertima – who wrote THE authoritative text on the subject – says in *They Came Before Columbus*, Black people from Nubia (or the Mande region of West Africa) may have been highly influential in the Olmec heartland, but these cultural leaders didn't make up the majority of the Olmec citizenship.

The Mayans, too, had strong relationships with Black people, but were not a predominantly "Africoid" population. We should still consider them "Original People," but we make sure to explain that **most of the world's ancient civilizations were produced by indigenous people forming constructive alliances with Black people who came to work with them.**

These indigenous people were themselves descended from Black people long ago, so this coalition was simply a way of them "getting back to their roots." And we have an incredible opportunity to reproduce this process today and, again, change the world.

MODERN EUROPE

Atlantic Ocean

North Sea

Mediterranean Sea

Black Sea

Caspian Sea

JAN MAYEN

ICELAND

FAROE ISLANDS

ISLE OF MAN

IRELAND

UNITED KINGDOM

GUERNSEY

JERSEY

GIBRALTAR

PORTUGAL

SPAIN

ANDORRA

MONACO

VATICAN CITY

FRANCE

BELGIUM

NETHERLANDS

DENMARK

GERMANY

SWITZERLAND

SLOVENIA

ITALY

SAN MARINO

CROATIA

AUSTRIA

HUNGARY

SLOVAKIA

POLAND

ROMANIA

BULGARIA

ALBANIA

GREECE

MACEDONIA

TURKEY

MALTA

NORWAY

SWEDEN

FINLAND

ESTONIA

LATVIA

RUSSIA

BELARUS

UKRAINE

MOLDOVA

GEORGIA

ARMENIA

AZER.

AZERBAIJAN

5° 0° 5° 15° 25° 35° 45° 40° 50° 60° 70°

1. LITHUANIA
2. LUXEMBOURG
3. LIECHTENSTEIN
4. CZECH REPUBLIC
5. BOSNIA & HERZEGOVINA
6. SERBIA
7. MONTENEGRO
8. KOSOVO

EUROPE

RIGHT BEFORE WHITE FOLKS

"It is the race with the oval or long heads and dark hair which have led forth the human race from barbarism... The whole history of our [European] civilization must be considered the history of the Mediterranean race." – Historian Angelo Mosso

In Europe, there is an obvious gap between the end of the Paleolithic and the beginning of the Neolithic. It's as if cultural development went into standby mode for a minute. More than a minute, actually. More like ten thousand years.

In other words, after the Aurignacian period, when the first Black humans in Europe conquered the Neanderthals and spread their culture and technology far and wide across the continent, Europe went into a technological and cultural standstill.* We know that climate changes really hit the people hard around this time, so that explains some of the gap, but when the Neolithic period begins in Europe, it's like a tsunami of culture sweeping through.

Sir Arthur Evans traced the cultural "Renaissance" of both periods back to Africa. As Evans explains:

> The nascent flame of primeval culture was thus already kindled in that older world and, so far as our present knowledge goes, it was in the southwestern part of our continent on either side of the Pyrenees that it shone its brightest. After the great strides in human progress already made at that remote epoch, it is hard, indeed, to understand what it was that still delayed the rise of European civilization in its higher shape. Yet it had to wait for its fulfillment through many millennia. The gathering shadows thickened and the darkness of a long night fell not on that favored region alone, but throughout the wide area where Reindeer man had ranged. Still the question rises—as yet imperfectly answered—were there no relay runners to pass on elsewhere the lighted torch?[414]

---

* Some historians have proposed that the Azilian culture occupied that gap, but others describe Azilian as "an impoverished survival of the Aurignacian."

In other words, why didn't Europe continue to pass on the flame of civilization that it had sparked so well in the Aurignacian period (the Reindeer Age)? The answer lies in the fact that Europe is quite literally the poor part of the planet Earth, and was never a good place to call home. Because of its hostile climate and resource-poor land, Europe was known – since at least the time of Homo erectus – to be a pretty bad place to live, especially compared to the tropical climes of Africa, southern Arabia, India, and Australia (before desertification). So why did we ever go there?

Because that's where all the Neanderthals were. We needed to eliminate them in order to get beyond the Nubian Complex in Arabia. So long as there were Neanderthals in the area, our settlements outside Africa would be attacked *mercilessly*. We went into Europe, and over 10,000 years of culture and combat, eliminated one of the biggest threats to our survival – **all while establishing the sense of community and culture that would help us survive other challenges.**

Once that was done, there was less reason to expand into Europe with new developments. For the next 10,000 years, our settlements continued to spread into more environmentally favorable regions, with the only significant exception being the population that traveled the northern land route into the Americas.

So what (or who) brought the Neolithic to Europe? And why? We know that Neolithic techniques were responses to environmental and societal conditions but we also know that these techniques diffused* VERY quickly throughout the Near East and then into Europe, in a much more rapid succession than we find in other spots in the world where similar methods emerged. **Who introduced them?**

Well, now that we've dismantled the idea that the first Europeans (40,000 years ago) were white cultural innovators, let's also dismantle the notion that the Neolithic phase of European civilization (4,000 years ago) was white-owned as well. In fact, this phase of modernization was ushered in by the Black Anu people who had just pioneered modern civilization in Africa and Asia.

Beginning around 11,000 years ago, Black Anu farmers from the Middle East traveled into Europe, where they introduced the same Neolithic cultures they birth in the Near East. These people may have come directly from the Natufian homeland in Palestine.[415] Between 9,000 and 2,000 BC, at least three waves of Anu people introduced agriculture, animal domestication, metallurgy, writing, architecture, and medicine to the people of Europe.

And they were just as Black as the Aurignacian folks. Rene Verneau connected the features of both prehistoric and modern races to survivals or reappearances of the Grimaldi types, meaning these later people had Black or "Negroid" features as well. Verneau wrote:

In Brittany, as well as in Switzerland and in the north of Italy, there lived in the Polished Stone period, in the Bronze Age and during the early Iron Age, a certain number of individuals who differed in certain characters from their contemporaries', in particular in the dolichocephalic [long-headed] character of their skull, in possessing a prognathism that was sometimes extreme, and a large grooved nose. This is a matter of partial atavism which in certain cases, as in the Neolithic Breton skull from Conguel, may attain to complete atavism. Two Neolithic individuals from Chamblandes in Switzerland are Negroid not only as regards their skulls but also in the proportions of their limbs. Several Ligurian and Lombard tombs of the Metal Ages have also yielded evidences of a Negroid element.[416]

Boule and Vallois agreed, noting that Verneau's findings were just the *tip of the iceberg* regarding the Black presence in prehistoric Europe:

Since the publication of Verneau's memoir, discoveries of other Negroid skeletons in Neolithic levels in Illyria and the Balkans have been announced. The prehistoric statues, dating from the Copper Age, from Sultan Selo in Bulgaria are also thought to portray Negroids. In 1928 Rene Bailly found in one of the caverns of Moniat, near Dinant in Belgium, a human skeleton of whose age it is difficult to be certain, but which seems definitely prehistoric. It is remarkable for its Negroid characters, which give it a resemblance to the skeletons from both Grimaldi and Asselar [from West Africa].

It is not only in prehistoric times that the Grimaldi race seems to have made its influence felt. Verneau has been able to see, now in modern skulls and now in living subjects, in the Italian areas of Piedmont, Lombardy, Emilia, Tuscany, and the Rhone Valley, numerous characters of the old fossil race.[417]

H.J. Fleure makes a similar observation in his 1945 study "The Distribution of Types of Skin Color":

In a few places in Sweden, Britain, and France people have been noticed who show characteristics of the skull and face that remind one of late-Paleolithic man: these people are usually darker, in hair and eyes, than their neighbors; sometimes they even have swarthy skins. Although this fact may not have great weight in argument, it does hint that there has been depigmentation in this region. The many stories of golden hair and blue eyes suggest that sexual selection may have helped the change.[418]

It appears that the Black Asiatic migration into Europe was eventually absorbed by the white Europeans who came to dominate all of Europe after 4,000 BC. The genetic evidence suggests that the first white settlers in Europe were accompanied by Anu "escorts."

The Anu people did not proliferate in Europe as the Europeans did. The Europeans quickly left multiple descendants by mating with the indigenous populations of Europe, quickly spreading in number and expanse. Eventually the Anus nearly disappeared as a separate people, leaving only small traces of their presence in the mtDNA of modern Europe.

However, they did also leave behind a strong presence culturally, introducing the farming and animal breeding techniques that swept through Europe even after their founders were gone, as well as massive monuments marking their ancient presence, known today as megaliths. All of these traditions had originated in the Afro-Asiatic homeland in Africa.

THE MEDITERRANEAN RACE?

When we talk about ancient Europe, we have to begin in the Mediterranean Sea. This is the area where all the first Neolithic cultures of Europe are found. Between 10,000 and 2500 BC, remarkable civilizations emerged on the islands of Crete, Cyprus, Malta, Sardinia, and many of the smaller islands that dot the Mediterranean Sea and its neighbor, the Aegean Sea. Along the shores, civilizations thrived in Anatolia and pre-Hellenic Greece.

The people who built these civilizations were said to have been Europeans of the Mediterranean Race. These people were said to be brown-skinned, curly-haired, full-lipped, broad-nosed…white people?

It was this branch of the great white race that built all of the earliest European civilizations, most of which predated the birth of Greece and Rome by thousands of years.

Italian anthropologist Guissepi Sergi first popularized the idea of a Mediterranean race towards the beginning of the 20th century. He provided mountains of evidence that a cultural community of people situated near the Mediterranean Sea were the ones who authored much of Europe's earliest history. Yet historians used this framework to argue that these were simply a sun-tanned group of white people, and praises of the Mediterranean race of Europe were printed side-by-side with claims that Blacks have contributed nothing to world civilization.

European historians of the early 20th century credited this legendary race with much of the development characteristic of the Neolithic, Copper and Bronze Ages of Europe, North Africa and the Near East.

The people the term "Mediterranean" describes are said to be of lean build, long-headed, dark-haired, dark-eyed, and dark-complexioned (this part was always omitted or described some other way).[419] Their hair was coarse, wavy, or curly, and their features were like those we find in many East African people today. Yet this "euphemistic term for Negro," as Diop has labeled it,[420] somehow referred to a third division of the European race, adopted at a time when European scholars realized the traits of the Alpine and Nordic races didn't describe the folks who actually established most of Europe's ancient civilizations.

But it's not as if everyone didn't know better. After all, if white folks were the first torchbearers and civilization-builders, why then didn't a slew of civilizations emerge along The Black Sea or the Caspian Sea which border the Caucasus Mountains? Simple. The Mediterranean Sea is the stretch of water that connects Southern Europe to North Africa. In 1901, Sergi argued this point exactly, beginning with a critique of the theory that the "Mediterranean Race" was simply a branch of whites turned brown. Instead, Sergi said:

...In opposition to the theory of a migration from the north of Europe to the west and then to Africa, I am, on the contrary, convinced that a migration of the African racial element took place in primitive times from the south towards the north. The types of Cro-Magnon, L'Homme-Mort, and other French and Belgian localities, bear witness to the presence of an African stock in the same region in which we find the dolmens and other megalithic monuments erroneously attributed to the Celts.

In other words, not only did the Mediterranean Race come from Africa, but these Africans were the ones who brought civilization to ALL of Europe, even its northernmost extremes. Sergi continued:

It is the cranial and facial forms that lead us to accept the consanguinity of the African Hamites, of red-brown and black colour, with the Mediterranean peoples; the same characters reveal the consanguinity of the primitive inhabitants of Europe, and of their remains in various regions and among' various peoples, with the populations of the Mediterranean, and hence also with the Hamites of Africa.

For some time past I have reached the conclusion that the so-called Reihengraber type of the Germans and the Viking type of the Scandinavians, being identical in character with the Mediterranean and Hamitic types, had the same African origin; the populations with these cranial and facial forms in the north of Europe are, as I have shown, of African origin, separate branches of the same trunk.[421]

Naturally, this roused a storm of criticism from academic circles in both Europe and the United States.[422] Sergi had it rough. But soon, others were forced to agree.

Angelo Mosso would later admit, "It is the race with the oval or long heads and dark hair which have led forth the human race from barbarism." He added, "The whole history of our [European] civilization must be considered the history of the Mediterranean race."[423]

Note that Mosso could identify long heads and dark hair, but made no mention of complexion. Yet Mosso also said that during the Neolithic, not just Southern Europe, but "**the whole of Africa, Egypt and Arabia are also inhabited by the Mediterranean race**."[424] The whole of Africa? Well, what is he saying, then, about the Mediterranean race? They're BLACK!

THE DARK RACES OF EUROPE?

British anthropologist Alfred Cort Haddon made distinctions between the "dark" races of Europe. In addition to the Mediterranean race, Haddon identified the presence of a "Eurafrican or white race." These "white" people had following features:

> Hair dark; rather **dark skin**, florid complexion; moderately tall stature, average about [66 inches], very **long, dolichocephalic head**, hypsicephalic, **receding forehead**, prominent glabella and supra-orbital ridges; cheek-bones somewhat broad, often slightly **prognathous; nose often broad**; eyes dark. Two variants may be noted:
>
> (1) with wavy hair, large measurements, and strong physique;
>
> (2) with rather close curly hair, prognathism, and smaller measurements; this type with almost Negroid characters may be connected with the Grimaldi type. [425]

Haddon says these Eurafricans could be found in the ancient remains of Europe and the Near East, but also among the living populations of Algeria, Somaliland, north Abyssinia, and Egypt, as well as numerous specific regions across Europe.[426] From his description, they sound like the **Australoid and Africoid** descendants of the Aurignacian communities that cleared the Neanderthals out of prehistoric Europe. As we noted in Part One, some of their descendants survived into relatively recent times.

Haddon also refers to "Hamitic" races in the same regions.

According to Haddon's definition, the Hamite has "hair which is dark brown or black, curly, sometimes wavy; skin reddish-brown, sometimes brown-black," medium height (5'5" or shorter), and a slender build. He says the men are muscular or well-defined, and the women have large hips and breasts. Like the Mediterranean and Eurafrican "races" these people are also long-headed and have many of the features of modern East African people.[427]

In *The Mediterranean Race*, Sergi maintained the following conclusions:

> (1) The primitive populations of Europe, after Homo Neanderthalensis, originated in Africa; these constituted the entire population of Neolithic times.
>
> (2) The basin of the Mediterranean was the chief centre of movement whence the African migrations reached the centre and the north of Europe.
>
> (3) From the great African stock were formed three varieties, in accordance with differing telluric and geographic conditions: one peculiarly African, remaining in the continent where it originated; another, the Mediterranean, which occupied the basin of that sea; and a third, the Nordic, which reached the north of Europe. These three varieties are the three great branches of one species, which I call Eurafrican, because it occupied, and still occupies, a large portion of the two continents of Africa and Europe.

Despite how many lines these ethnologists attempted to draw, the bottom lines is that if any of these "mysterious races" were to drive down highway I-95 today, they would be pulled over for Driving While Black.

THE NILOTIC NEOLITHIC

In Signs and Symbols of Primordial Man, Albert Churchward describes how Australoid people gradually displaced their predecessors, as did the ancestors of the Bantu people as they expanded westwards from Sudan:

> The Ainus, Australian and New Guinea aborigines descended from the Nilotic negroes, have still many of the forms, rites, and ceremonies of the early Totemic age....They drove out and exterminated the first primitive people, as we find the Ainu and Australians did in Japan and Australia, and as the Neolithic did the Paleolithic here in these islands and Europe generally. This probably took a very long time, as all would not be at first exterminated.

In saying "as the Neolithic did the Paleolithic here," Churchward is saying the same process occurred when the Anu introduced the Neolithic Age to Europe. In every case, the displacement of the older Black population was not a quick genocide but a slow, yet significant, process of displacement, replacement, and absorption.

Who is the Original Woman?

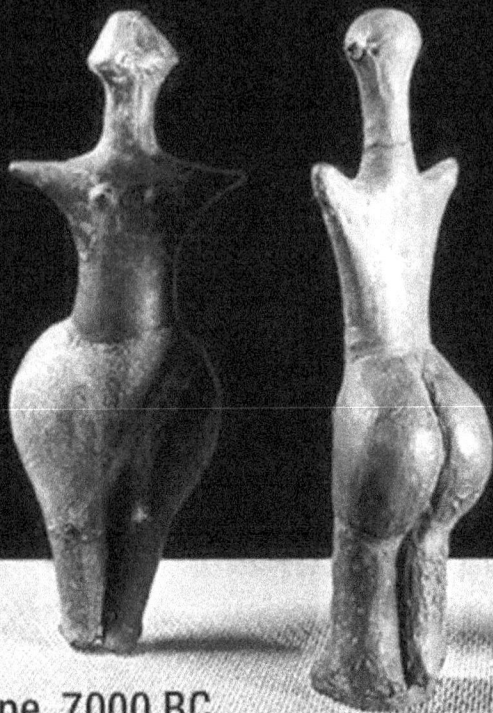

Europe, 7000 BC

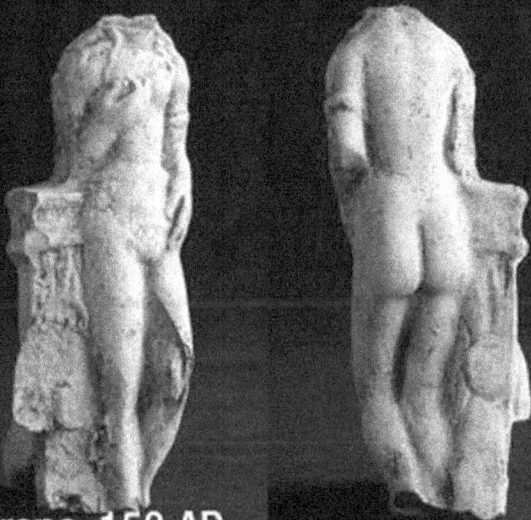

Europe, 150 AD

WhenTheWorldWasBlack.com

Churchward suggests that these Anu people settled in the same regions that were settled long before by the Original Black people of Europe (circa 45,000-20,000 years ago):

> The types of Cro-Magnon and Homme-Mort, and others in French and Belgian localities, as well as the oldest remains in these Islands, bear witness to the presence of an African stock in the same region in which we find the dolmens and other megalithic monuments erroneously attributed to the Celts. All these were widely extended over the world and had the same primitive funeral customs, shaped skulls, long forearms, etc., until they were modified by men and stronger influences, and only in Egypt can we find the centre from which these originated and migrated. The remains found at Harland Bay, Cornwall and Naqada are typical.[428]

Churchward gives this "megalithic race" much credit for their cultural innovations:

> When their culture was greatly advanced, they cultivated the soil, bred animals, understood the art of spinning, weaving, of pottery making, also working in copper, tin and gold, and had the knowledge of the Stellar Mythos. In some parts of Europe, at least, the gap between the Paleolithic and Neolithic is so abrupt and striking that it is only by assuming an entire or nearly entire disappearance of the former, and a subsequent re-peopling by the latter, who came up from Egypt and the Nile valleys, that one can understand the past, because, while primitive man was still struggling for existence with the mammoth and other animals, a relatively advanced degree of culture had already been developed in the Nile valleys; and this exodus spread all over the world.[429]

These Anu, according to Churchward, replaced the totemism and shamanism of their predecessors with a "stellar mythos" they soon spread all over the world. We'll explore the theological transitions that Churchward is alluding to in Volume Three.

THE MELANOCHROI

According to 19th century ethnologist Thomas Huxley, the Melanochroi (literally meaning "black-colored," but translated as "dark whites") were the indigenous peoples of Southern Europe, the Middle East, Southwest Asia, and North Africa. He included in this category some of the British, Gauls, Spanish, Italians, Greeks, Syrians, Arabs, and Persians, as well as the Celts, Iberians, Etruscans, Romans, Pelasgians, Berbers, Saharans, North Africans, and Semites.

He described them as having coarse, wavy, or straight black hair, long heads, and dark eyes. Some were said to be darker-complexioned than others. In other words, these were the people that other scholars of this time called "Hamites," "Eurafricans," the

"Mediterranean Race," and so on.

Meanwhile, the Xanthochroi (or "fair/blonde whites") were essentially the white people of the world, from the people of central and northern Europe to the Aryans of India. He described them as having fair skin, yellow or red hair, blue or grey eyes, and long or broad heads. Huxley's concept was influential in the development of the theory of the Nordic race, which would become a cornerstone in the concept of race purity espoused by white supremacists.

THE BROWN RACE?

Some historians only spoke of a single "brown race." Grafton Elliot Smith finds remains of this same 'brown race'...

> ...among the ancient Neolithic inhabitants of the British Isles, France, on both shores of the Mediterranean, the proto-Libyans, ancient and modern Egyptians, Nubians, Beja, Danakil, Hadendoa, Abyssinians, Galla, Somali, throughout the Arabian peninsula, on the coasts of the Persian Gulf, Mesopotamia, Syria, the coastal regions of Asia Minor, Anau in Turkestan, and among the early Indonesians.[430]

Some of these settlers may have sailed directly from North Africa. Genetic data confirms that others crossed into Spain from northwest Africa. Yet a large part, possibly the largest, came from the Near East. In *The Negro in the New World*, Sir Harry Hamilton Johnston writes:

> Quite probably the very ancient negro invasion of Mediterranean Europe (of which the skeletons of the Alpes Maritimes are vestiges) came from Syria and Asia Minor on its way to Central and Western Europe.[431]

These people didn't simply settle in the region. They introduced all of the major developments that led from the Neolithic to the Bronze Age. Essentially, they took Europe out of the Stone Age. Angelo Mosso was not exaggerating when he gave these people credit for "the whole history" of European civilization.

It was the so-called Mediterranean people, who we call the Anu, who founded ancient Crete, which gave birth to the Minoan civilization, which then spawned Mycenaean civilization, which then fathered ancient Greece, the legendary "granddaddy" of European civilization. Of course, while later Europeans gave all credit to Greece and Rome, the Greeks and Romans themselves looked to ancient Egypt and the Anu people as the true fathers of civilization. No, Greece, you are not the father.

FINALLY, THE AFRICANS OF EUROPE!

According to Johnston, the Anu of Europe could be traced back to Northeast Africa:

> This negroid type would seem (judging from skulls and skeletal remains) to have penetrated north-westwards as far as Brittany, and quite possibly to Britain and Ireland. Eastwards it is traceable to Switzerland and Italy, coming down through the neolithic to the historical period and fusing with the northern races. In modern times and at the present day it is obvious that there is an old Nigritic element in the population of North Africa, Spain, France, Ireland and West Britain, Italy, Sardinia, Sicily, and the countries bordering the Eastern Mediterranean, not entirely to be accounted for by the historical slave trade. Yet the ancient negroid elements in these European populations seem to possess slightly more affinity with the Asiatic negroes or with those of North Eastern Africa than with the typical African negroes or Bushmen of today.[432]

In 1904, W.E.B. Du Bois published a paper summarizing Sergi's arguments in the following way:

> 1. That the primitive populations of Europe originated in Africa.
>
> 2. The basin of the Mediterranean was the chief center of the movement whence the African migration reached central and northern Europe.
>
> 3. From this great Eurafrican stock came:
>
> (a) The present inhabitants of northern Africa.
>
> (b) The Mediterranean race.
>
> (c) The Nordic or Teutonic race.
>
> 4. These three varieties of one stock were not "Aryan," nor of Asiatic origin.
>
> 5. The primitive civilization of Europe is Afro-Mediterranean, becoming eventually Afro-European.
>
> 6. Greek and Roman civilization were not Aryan but Mediterranean.[433]

Were these claims far-fetched? Could the Greeks and Romans have once been Black? The answer is not so simple. Let's dig in.

THE BLACK FOUNDATIONS OF ANCIENT GREECE

As early as the 1800s, historians were aware that the ancient Greeks had been preceded on the mainland by non-white populations like the Pelasgians. For example, John Denison Baldwin wrote:

> The Greek race – settled around the Aegean Sea, in Asia Minor, Thrace, Macedonia, Thessaly, Epirus, and throughout the Grecian peninsula – consisted of a group of tribes or families as closely related in origin and language, probably, as the Scandinavian group

in Northwestern Europe. They inherited the culture of their predecessors, the Phoenicians, or Cushites, and the Pelasgians, who, in more ancient times, established the oracle of Dodona, made Thrace eminent as a seat of civilization and science, established enlightened communities in Asia Minor, and carried their civilizing influence into the Grecian peninsula itself.[434]

Modern research has confirmed these theories, showing that the Pelasgians were Anu people. These Anu people were the same ones who founded the first settled communities in Greece, and who built the first Greek pyramids.

THE PYRAMIDS OF GREECE

There are at least 16 pyramid-like buildings, or their remains, scattered throughout Greece. Early Greek historians like Pausanias documented encountering many more such structures in his travels, but none of these structures remain fully intact today to test how closely they resembled the pyramids of Egypt. There are two surviving pyramid-like structures still available to study, one at Hellenikon and the other at Ligourion.

With these two pyramid's base stones remaining, we can tell that Greek pyramids existed, but were a much simpler construction than those found in Egypt. An innovative dating method dated the Helleniko pyramid to 2730 BC (with an error factor of plus or minus 720 years). It also dated the Ligourio pyramid to 2260 BC (plus or minus 714 years). With those ages, it's clear they were built by Blacks, who were the first inhabitants of Greece.

THE END OF BLACK RULE

The Anu settlers of pre-Hellenic Greece also introduced the scripts that gave birth to the Greek alphabet (which ultimately gave birth to our English alphabet). They built pyramids there and introduced many of the foundational elements of Neolithic culture.

But these pre-Hellenic people were nearly annihilated when a horde of white invaders swept into the Greek mainland. They survived long enough to pass on some of their culture, and perhaps a few fragments of their community survived on the margins of Greek civilization. But Greek civilization was essentially the white European "copy" of the older Black civilizations in the immediate area.

The Minoan civilization of ancient Crete gave way to the Mycenaean civilization that later developed into ancient Greece (which, in turn, bestowed its legacy to Rome and then the Roman Christian Empire as a whole). But, as readers of Martin Bernal's *Black Athena* and

George G.M. James' *Stolen Legacy* know quite well, ancient Greece would not be world-renowned for its intellectual, philosophical, and scientific "accomplishments" if it were not for its debt to Egypt. Truly, if Minoan Crete was Greece's mother, Egypt was its daddy.

This is why the ancient Greeks spoke so highly of the ancient Egyptians. Yet they spoke even more highly of the Ethiopians. They revered them both, sometimes even deifying them, but with the Ethiopians (that is, the Black people living just south of Egypt), they considered these people the "utmost" of humanity. They gave the Ethiopians credit for not only producing the civilizations of ancient India, Arabia, Palestine, and Egypt. It's thus no surprise that Godfrey Higgins believed that all of the Greek gods originally represented Black people.

Of course, you'll have a hard time convincing a fan of European history how deep this reverence and cultural borrowing really goes. Renowned linguist and historian Christopher Ehret has said:

> If you make *any* connection between Africa and what the Greeks were doing, our Western upbringing can come back to surface in a way people don't realize is taking place. They don't realize it because they feel they have eliminated racism from their thinking. They're sure that Africans, given different circumstances, would have been just as advanced as everyone else. They don't realize that, actually, Africans *were* just as advanced.

"Just as" advanced? I'd have to go a step further than Ehret and say they were **quite certainly more advanced**. The ancient Egyptians would have agreed. In 360 BC, Greek philosopher Plato wrote *Timaeus*, where he details his friend Solon's visit to Egypt. I wish I had space to quote all of it, but here's how the story begins:

> In the Egyptian Delta, at the head of which the river Nile divides, there is a certain district which is called the district of Sais...To this city came Solon, and was received there with great honour; he asked the priests who were most skilful in such matters, about antiquity, and made the discovery that neither he nor any other Hellene knew anything worth mentioning about the times of old.

Poor little Tink Tink. But he tries his best:

> On one occasion, wishing to draw them on to speak of antiquity, he began to tell about the most ancient things in our part of the world- about Phoroneus, who is called "the first man," and about Niobe; and after the Deluge, of the survival of Deucalion and Pyrrha; and he traced the genealogy of their descendants, and reckoning up the dates, tried to compute how many years ago the events of which he was speaking happened.

The Egyptians were not impressed. Solon literally gets "sonned" by an Egyptian priest:

> Thereupon one of the priests, who was of a very great age, said: O Solon, Solon, you Hellenes are never anything but children, and there is not an old man among you. Solon in return asked him what he meant. I mean to say, he replied, that in mind you are all young; there is no old opinion handed down among you by ancient tradition, nor any science which is hoary with age.

Buurrrn. In other words, "Shut your mouth when grown folks are talking. Your "first man" was a latecomer. You white folks are just babies on this planet." The priest continues:

> The fact is, that wherever the extremity of winter frost or of summer does not prevent, mankind exist, sometimes in greater, sometimes in lesser numbers. And whatever happened either in your country or in ours, or in any other region of which we are informed – if there were any actions noble or great or in any other way remarkable, they have all been written down by us of old, and are preserved in our temples.

Just think about that. This isn't Supreme Understanding saying this. This is an Egyptian priest saying this more than 2300 years ago. He's verifying much of what I'm saying about the Anu and their knowledge of "every square inch" of this world. The priest then continues to hammer Solon about his people's lack of history:

> Whereas just when you and other nations are beginning to be provided with letters and the other requisites of civilized life, after the usual interval, the stream from heaven, like a pestilence, comes pouring down, and leaves only those of you who are destitute of letters and education; and so you have to begin all over again like children, and know nothing of what happened in ancient times, either among us or among yourselves.

> As for those genealogies of yours which you just now recounted to us, Solon, they are no better than the tales of children. In the first place you remember a single deluge only, but there were many previous ones; in the next place, you do not know that there formerly dwelt in your land the fairest and noblest race of men which ever lived, and that you and your whole city are descended from a small seed or remnant of them which survived. And this was unknown to you, because, for many generations, the survivors of that destruction died, leaving no written word.

> For there was a time, Solon, before the great deluge of all, when the city which now is Athens was first in war and in every way the best governed of all cities, is said to have performed the noblest deeds and to have had the fairest constitution of any of which tradition tells, under the face of heaven.[435]

The priest is talking about the time when Greece was first settled by Anu people. He says this happened about 9,000 years ago, which

THE MINOANS

The Minoan civilization of ancient Crete was one of the precursors to ancient Greece. Historians have either ignored them or attempted to whitewash them.

For example, the famous "Minoan Boxers" fresco (above left) appears to be painted in light flesh tones but most of this is part of the reconstruction. If you look closely, the original fragments of the fresco are darker. A better image is found in the fisherman (above center) or the Egyptian murals recording Minoan trade visits (above right). Of course, by 1600 BC, all Minoans were not Black (as seen in a fresco of one of their boats), but Blacks were clearly the founders of this civilization, as well as many others throughout the Mediterranean Sea.

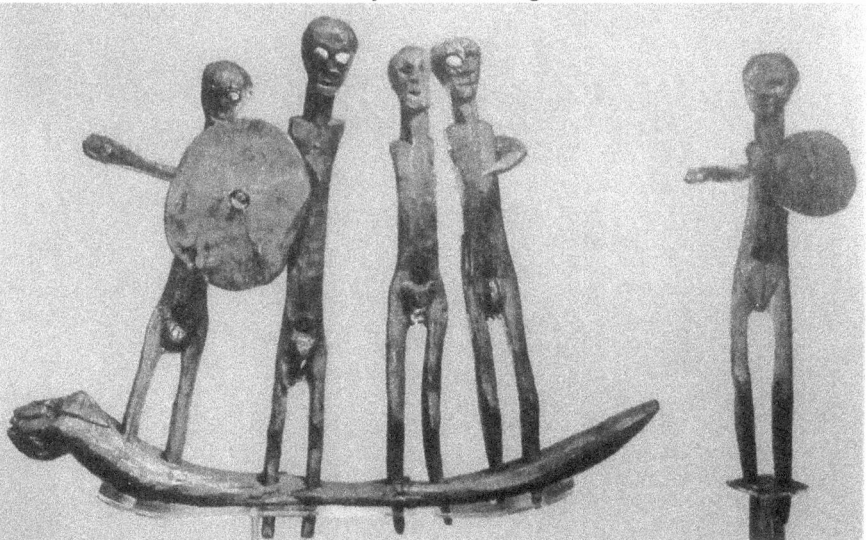

These seafaring Black traders also went around the coast of Spain and as far north as the waters allowed. Above, a set of dark wooden figurines with inlaid eyes was found in a Bronze Age site in Holderness, England. They look just like ancient rock carvings of seafarers in Scandinavia. There is no mistaking who the earliest culture-bearers and traders of ancient Europe were.

DON'T BE FOOLED

Sometimes, a figurine can fool you. Many ancient statues were crafted from white clay but were then painted with ochre and other pigments. The clay survives; the pigment often doesn't. As a result, seeing a mostly white figurine with a straight nose, we can easily assume that it represented a white person.

This is why it's important to keep in mind how physically diverse the Black populations of the world are. Take, for example, this beautiful figurine of a Minoan bull-leaper, made around 1600 BC. By this time, neither Crete (nor the rest of the Mediterranean world) were 100% Black. But this figurine does not represent a white person. The elites who performed the bull-leaping ceremony were Black. We know this because we have a fresco to prove it.

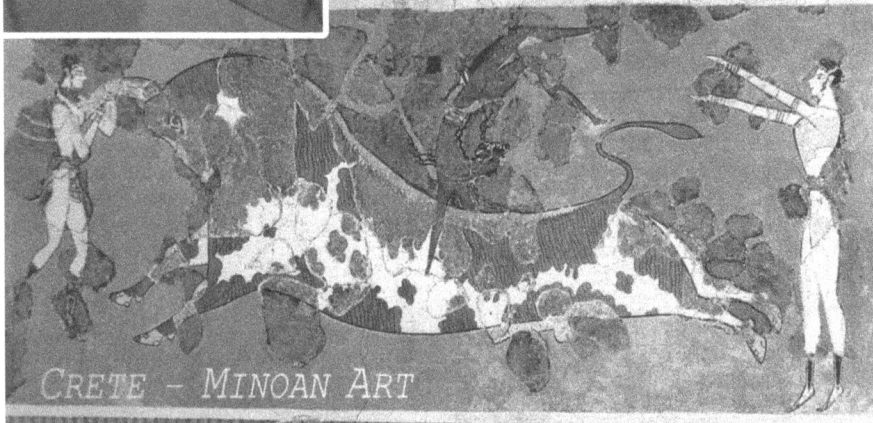

CRETE – MINOAN ART

So, when we see a statue or figurine that looks like this Minoan statue to the left, we should keep in mind that, unless we have evidence to the contrary, the person it represented most likely looked like the man in this Minoan fresco to the right. It's also important to keep in mind that such paintings can also be reconstructed in a biased way.

PHOTO 1   PHOTO 2

After all, when only fragments remain (see sketch), artists can recreate the missing or obscured elements however they choose. Often, they will use lighter flesh tones or distort the hair texture or shape of a character's nose or lips. You can see an example of this in our correction of the Mayan scribe from Xultun, Guatemala elsewhere in this book. The way an image is photographed and printed can also play a significant role in our final impression.

roughly corresponds with the archaeological evidence for when the first farming populations settled in Greece.

These Anu people may have been the Pelasgians. The historian Ephorus, building on fragments of older accounts from Hesiod, says the aboriginal Pelasgians lived a "military way of life," by which they colonized Crete, Epirus, Thessaly, and throughout the Mediterranean and Aegean Seas. As a result, Herodotus said, their name occurs throughout this area in a variety of forms (e.g., "Pelasgia").

In 1897, a Black man named Wesley John Gaines said:

> The Pelasgic empire was at its meridian as early as 2500 B.C. This people came from the islands of the Ægian, and more remotely from Asia Minor [Anatolia]. They were originally a branch of the sun-burnt Hamitic stock, that laid the basis of civilization in Canaan and Mesopotamia, destined later to be Semitized. Rome itself was Pelasgian to 428 B.C.

What happened to the Pelasgians and other Anu people in the area?

> But in Greece and Italy the Hamitic stock was displaced by Aryan, as in Asia it had been by Semitic. The Hellenes were the Aryans first to be brought into contact with these sun-burnt Hamites, who, let it be remembered, though classed as whites, were probably as strongly Negritic as are the Afro-Americans.

> These Hellenes were savages or barbarians. But Aryan strength and energy were thus brought into contact with Hamitic culture. Then occurred that great struggle of centuries for social equality between the blond Aryan and the Pelasgian, the dark child of the soil. Had it not been for that mixture of dark blood in the Greek composition, that race of poets, artists, and philosophers would never have existed.[436]

THE MINOANS

We've talked about the people who were in Greece before white people took over, but – if those people were either wiped out or absorbed – their former presence doesn't necessarily address the question of how Greek civilization rose to such intellectual and scientific heights.

Contrary to popular belief, ancient Greek civilization did not simply spring forth, fully-grown, like Minerva from the forehead of Zeus. As Greece itself was forebear to Rome, so too was the Mycenaean civilization of 1400-1200 BC to Greece. Mycenaean civilization, in turn, had expanded out of late developments in yet another, earlier civilization, a vital precursor to Mycenae, Greece, and all those European civilizations which would at some point owe their cultural heritage to the imagined starting point of ancient Greece.

This civilization took shape on the island of Crete in the Aegean Sea. It began during the Neolithic Age, but only emerged as a veritable force in the ancient history of the Near East with its entrance into the Early Bronze Age in approximately the 3rd millennium BC. The name applied to the Bronze Age culture of the island by its foremost excavator, Arthur Evans, was "Minoan" after its legendary King Minos and his Palace at Knossos, from where we get our myths of the Minotaur and the Labyrinth.

The origin of the earliest Cretans has been in dispute since the era in which the ancient Greek historians had their say. In the earliest phases, these people were Black. This was common knowledge among the ancient Greeks, who placed the Pelasgians at the earliest point of Cretan history.[437]

DID THEY COME FROM NORTH AFRICA?

"Pelasgian" simply refers to the indigenous population of Crete, that is, those spawned from the eponymous ancestor Pelasgus. Of this "Divine Pelasgus" himself, 6th century poet Asius described him as brought forth "from black earth, to be of mortal race."[439] Anu lineages E1b1b, J2, and R1b are common among early Cretan remains, and most of their skulls are long-headed, often resembling the measurements of modern Somalians or pre-Dynastic Egyptians.

In *The Sea-Kings of Crete*, James Baikie writes:

> It is possible enough that both the Nilotic and the Minoan civilization sprang from a common stock, and that the Neolithic Cretans and the Neolithic Egyptians were alike members of the same widespread Mediterranean race.[440]

Yet most sources suggest that the bulk of these sea populations came from Anatolia. Some elements of the population could have come from mainland Greece, while others most likely came from North Africa. According to John G. Jackson, some of the Minoans "dwelt in the grasslands of North Africa before that area dried up and became a great desert. As the Saharan sands encroached on their homeland, they took to the sea, and in Crete and neighboring islands set up a maritime culture."

H.R. Hall, in his 1923 *Rhind Lectures*, argued that we could trace at least some of the ancient Cretans back to North Africa. Hall added:

> The physical resemblance of the Minoan Cretans to one of the dominant Egyptian types is evident from the Egyptian representations of them. In feature, expression and figure they resembled each other more than either resembled either the Semites or the Anatolians.[441]

Thus the most important question becomes, "Where did the science of Minoan civilization come from?" Sir Arthur Evans, faced with the question of how Crete could, in a few generations, "outstrip its Aegean neighbors, and become the high early civilization we call Minoan," answered:

> That the main impulse came from the Egyptian side can no longer be doubted...this impulse was already making itself felt in Crete in the Age that preceded the First Dynasty.[442]

Donald Mackenzie, author of *Crete and Pre-Hellenic Europe*, noted:

> As the great bulk of its historic population were of Mediterranean type, it would appear that North Africa was the source of the high civilization obtained at Knossos during the Late Neolithic Period. The religion of the Cretan agriculturalists resembled in essential details that of the Egyptians.[443]

H.R. Hall said:

> While the majority of the original Neolithic inhabitants of Crete probably came from Anatolia...another element may well have come in oared boats from the opposite African coast, bringing with them...the seeds of civilization that, transplanted to the different conditions of Crete, developed, when touched by the magic wand of copper...into the great Minoan culture.[444]

There are many other islands in the Mediterranean that deserve attention. For example, there is Malta, an important Neolithic site where Anu people built some of the world's oldest temples. And just south of Anatolia, the massive island of Cyprus was home to a thriving Black culture over 10,000 years ago.

The Anu people who first settled Cyprus actually imported animals to produce wild populations of game for future generations of hunters![445] They also cultivated crops, rerouted water channels, built wells, domesticated animals and conducted other "breeding experiments."[446] In other words, they "made" the ecology of Cyprus.

Think that's heavy? That's not even the half of it. But that particular story is one that we'll tell in full in Volume Four of this series. For now, we're going to follow the sailboats along the coast of Europe.

BLACKS IN SPAIN BEFORE THE MOORS
SETTLEMENT OF THE IBERIAN PENINSULA

Heading west from Italy, across the Mediterranean Sea, our next major stop would be in Iberia, also known as the Iberian Peninsula. This is the name given to the westernmost stretch of Europe where we find the modern nations of Spain and Portugal. Here, the earliest Black settlers introduced their African genetic lineages from the Maghreb **thousands of years before the Moors.**

Others may have come into Spain via the land route from the Near East, while another contingent could have come by way of Italy. What we know for sure is that Anu people built dolmens, stone circles, and other megalithic monuments (their trademark) throughout Spain and Portugal, as a testament to their presence.

Did they displace the original settlers who still lived in these areas thousands of years after the conquest of the Neanderthals, or were they absorbed? Studies of prehistoric Iberian genetics can help us find out. However they came to be, there is now a people in Spain who may represent one of their surviving "remnants." They are known as the Basque.

The Basque speak a language that is unrelated to any of the other European languages in the area. There is even genetic evidence linking the Basque and Niger-Congo speakers.[447] The Basque are also culturally and politically isolated from their neighbors. So much so that they have even resorted to terrorism to stake their independence!

However, the Basque don't look too different from many of the other tan-skinned people in Spain, so they're not typically labeled as terrorists. In other words, they pass the brown paper bag test. Yet if you were to ask the wrong Basque "Are you white?" you might get punched.

And the Basque aren't alone. There are actually many other ethnic groups who preserve traces of an older Black presence in Europe. These people are often recorded as being darker-complexioned than their neighbors, with dark (often curly) hair and dark eyes. But they are not descendants of the Moors or another more recent influx of Black people, because all of their languages are pre-Indo-European, meaning these people were around before white people spread throughout Europe (c. 4,000-1500 BC). Examples include:

❑ Basques, Tartessians and Iberians (Western Europe)
❑ Picts (Britain)
❑ Lapps (Scandinavia)
❑ Ligures (Britain)
❑ Rhaetians (Alpine Region)
❑ Elymians and Sicani (Sicily)
❑ Eteocretans (Crete)
❑ Eteocypriots (Cyprus)
❑ Etruscans and Camunni (Italy)
❑ Pelasgians and Lemnians (Greece and the Aegean)

Many of these people have not survived into the present day. At least one of these groups, the Lapps, may descend from a wave of Mongoloid settlers. Most others descend from the Anu people who were migrating through Europe between 10,000 and 2,000 BC, while others may descend from even older Black populations of hunter-gatherers who had been settled in those regions since the earliest times (of occupation by humans).

Most of these people were displaced, absorbed, or annihilated by the later arriving Indo-Europeans. This is why Indo-European myths typically feature a "clash of the gods" where the primordial creations, described as dark dwarfs, giants, or demons (who represent the Original people), are conquered by the "fair gods," who are meant to represent the whites who authored the myth.*

By the time these myths come become widespread, the Original people of the region are either gone, or have been pushed to the fringes of their old homeland. They survive mostly in myths, with a few genetic or linguistic survivals in the new population.

This has happened throughout Europe, but there's a very clear and well-recorded history of such a transition in the history of the British Isles. David MacRitchie covers evidence of this history in great depth in his works *Ancient and Modern Britons, Testimony of Tradition,* and *Fians, Fairies and Picts.*

Not only does MacRitchie attest to an ancient Black presence in ancient Britain and neighboring areas, he says these Black people

---

* For more on this, see *Black God.* Check www.TheScienceOfSelf.com for updates.

only disappeared within recent centuries. Since then, they survive in faint genetic traces and in mythical legends of pixies, fairies, trolls, leprechauns, and giants. For example, the Picts were a dark-skinned people living in ancient Scotland. Their name, Picts, means "painted people" and provides the basis for later legends of magic "pixies."[448]

But these people were concrete enough for archaeologist Harold Peake to declare their time of arrival:

> Now the Egyptians and the other peoples of North Africa are considered by all anthropologists as typical members of the Mediterranean race…who reached Spain about 7000 BC, and formed the bulk of the population of the British Isles about 5000 BC.[449]

And they were Black enough for Grafton Elliot Smith to say this in his 1911 work *The Ancient Egyptians*:

> So striking is the family likeness between the early Neolithic peoples of the British Isles and the Mediterranean and the bulk of the population, both ancient and modern of Egypt and East Africa, that a description of the bones of an Early Briton of that remote epoch might apply in all essential details to an inhabitant of Somaliland.[450]

In other words, Black people came here and built all this stuff. Of all the legendary exploits of ancient Europeans, one of the most well-known is the construction of Stonehenge. Here, too, we are led to details of an all-important Black people.

THE BLACK BUILDERS OF STONEHENGE

In addition to creating images on rock surfaces, our ancestors created images and formations from rocks themselves. This is where we find some of the clearest evidence that we saw ourselves as "makers" of the Earth. While many have disappeared due to erosion, vandalism, or plant overgrowth, there are still enough examples for us to know this, too, was a worldwide phenomenon. While some designs were created with stones the size of shopping carts, many other arrangements were made from stones weighing over 100 tons each.

Now, how (and why) would prehistoric people move twelve 200,000 pound stones into a formation that they couldn't even live in? What was that about? These stone formations are called megaliths and they served a multitude of purposes – some you'd never even imagine.

And a quick disclaimer: There's nothing primitive about making things out of stone. For those who have ever worked in construction, you know that stonemasonry is one of the most expensive and highly-sought-after trades in the industry. People know that building with stone takes incredible skill and considerable labor. Long before we made mud bricks and mortar, our ancestors were the world's first masons, hewing monuments from stone.

The Original People didn't attempt to reorient the natural landscape by erecting massive stone buildings and monuments, but they knew the fundamentals (like quarrying, cutting, and drilling).

Despite the fact that the "Stone Age" dates back to the first stone tools almost two million years ago, it was the Anu people who really turned the world to stone within the last 10,000 years. They travelled the globe, erecting dolmens, menhirs, obelisks, stone circles, and temples. Any place you find massive stones in places they shouldn't be, Anu people were there.

When stone wasn't readily available, or when the "right" stone wasn't available, they built similar structures out of earth and wood, as their ancestors had done thousands of years before them. After all, those pyramids and stone pillars were preceded by mounds and wooden pillars.

In many cases, however, Anu people wouldn't settle on organic materials. They desired permanence, and stone clearly outlasts wood and soil. But that often required long journeys to distant quarries, followed by the unimaginable labor of transporting a 50-ton granite block over 200 miles of hills and rivers. Wait, not just one 50-ton block, but 50 of them!

The crazy part is that there are many cases where our ancestors skipped over local supplies of stone to get stones from areas much further away. Examples include:

❏ Giza, Egypt: 50+ ton Granite stones transported from Aswan, over 300 miles away.
❏ Carnac, England: 300+ ton menhirs transported over 25 miles.
❏ Stonehenge, England: Over 80 Bluestones moved over 250 miles,

with part of the journey crossing a large stretch of water, despite comparable stones being found nearby.

- ❏ Ollantaytambo, Peru: 50+ ton Porphyry stones transported 7 miles over mountains and valleys.
- ❏ Teotihuacán, Mexico: 90-square-foot sheets of Mica transported over possibly 1000 miles

Why move these massive blocks over such large distances…when you don't have to? This tells us that either the location or the stone itself was considered to have special properties. In other words, our ancestors really had some science in mind when they put these things together. We can find evidence for this in one of the few recorded accounts of ancient megalith construction: the story of Stonehenge.

WHO BUILT STONEHENGE AND WHY?

Stonehenge is the best known example of an ancient stone formation. Most of us have never heard of megalithic circles anywhere else in the world. Why? Stonehenge gets the most acclaim primarily because it's in Europe. It's something white people can point to and say, "Even if we admit that you guys were building pyramids 5,000 years ago, look at what WE did around the same time. We were lifting massive stones and doing astronomical calculations too."

And Stonehenge wasn't just some isolated monument. In fact, recent LiDAR laser surveying has revealed that the monument was actually part of an ancient complex of over 30 monuments, including wooden versions of the Stonehenge monument that were so large they would have required the clearing of an entire forest, according to Irish archaeologist Joe Fenwick.

Archaeologist Mike Pearson found a massive circle of ditches and earthen banks enclosed concentric rings of huge timber posts, and a paved road leading to the Avon River, which acted as an off-ramp to a river freeway that probably carried thousands of people back and forth to the monument complex. They call it Woodhenge.

Nearby there were houses with hearths and wooden furniture, including cupboards and beds.[451] Bear in mind this site dates back to over 4,300 years ago! Away from the village, they found more buildings that may have been home to chiefs or priests who lived separately from the rest of the people.

The evidence suggests, Pearson said, that "Stonehenge was just one-half of a larger complex." He got that part right, but when asked what was all this actually *for*, he gave the lame answer we've all heard before about monuments like this: "The village was probably built as

MEGALITHS

Dolmens are enormous stone slabs resting horizontally on upright stones.

Some dolmens are covered by a mound of earth, also known as a tumulus.

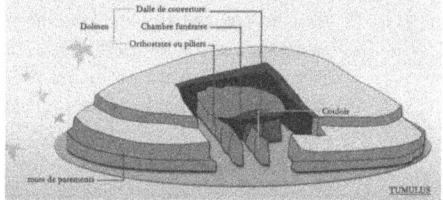

A menhir is a huge stone standing upright like a pillar. (An obelisk is how the Egyptians did their menhirs, carved to be smooth and precisely shaped.)

There are many other megalithic formations. Sometimes a dolmen is surrounded by a group of menhirs, known as a cromlech. There are also stone circles of menhirs, or upright stones with lintels (stones on top), such as Stonehenge. A menhir is sometimes accompanied by a Mên-an-Tol, or a massive round stone with a hole in it. These represent the masculine and feminine principles, respectively. There also many underground burial structures, like the long barrow (a long underground chamber built from stones and covered with a mound) and cairn (a massive mound of stones). Megalithic techniques were also incorporated into other forms of architecture, such as the design of fortifications, temples, and other important sites.

We are left with two questions: (1) How did anyone transport and erect such enormous stones? (2) Who were the people who accomplished these feats?

a religious center, presumably for people who worshiped the sun." This is total nonsense. If you're interested in why, or the true science behind these monuments, check out "The Science of Stone Monuments" in the Appendix.

This all seems like a pretty exceptional accomplishment for ancient Europeans. But Stonehenge – like the other megalithic circles everywhere else – wasn't built by Europeans. We built it.

STONES IMPORTED FROM AFRICA?

According to Thomas Moore's 1835 *The History of Ireland*:

> One of the old English traditions respecting Stonehenge is that the stones were transported thither from Ireland, having been brought to the latter country by giants, from the extremities of Africa; and in the time of Giraldus Cambrensis there was still to be seen, as he tells, on the plain of Kildare [in Ireland], an immense monument of stones, corresponding exactly in appearance and construction with that of Stonehenge.[452]

The 12th century writer, Geoffrey of Monmouth, says in his work *History of the Kings of Britain* that giants from Africa built a stone circle in Ireland that was later transported to England under the direction of the famed "magician" Merlin. Merlin – who historically may have himself been a Black man, or (as a legend) an avatar (symbol) of various Black personages – tells King Aurelius that if he wants to grace a burial site with "a work that shall endure for ever," he must send for the stones of the "Dance of Giants," an ancient stone circle situated on a mountain in Ireland. The story continues:

> At these words of Merlin, Aurelius burst out laughing, and quoth he: 'But how may this be, that stones of such bigness and in a country so far away may be brought hither, as if Britain were lacking in stones enow [enough] for the job?'
>
> Whereunto Merlin made answer: 'Laugh not so lightly, King, for not lightly are these words spoken. For in these stones is a mystery, and a healing virtue against many ailments. Giants of old did carry them from the furthest ends of Africa and did set them up in Ireland what time they did inhabit therein. And unto this end they did it, that they might make them baths therein whensoever they ailed of any malady, for they did wash the stones and pour forth the water into the baths, whereby they that were sick were made whole. Moreover, they did mix confections of herbs with the water, whereby they that were wounded had healing, for not a stone is there that lacketh in virtue of [healing].'
>
> When the Britons heard these things, they bethought them that it were well to send for the stones, and to harry the Irish folk by force of arms if they should be minded to withhold them. At last they made choice of Uther Pendragon, the King's brother, with fifteen

thousand men, to attend to this business. [453]

This story reveals several things. First, it confirms the theory that the stones used in megalithic construction weren't simply "rocks." Our ancestors certainly understood geology (See "The Science of Stone Monuments" in the Appendix), so they knew the physical properties of these stones as well as their aesthetic values, but it appears they also saw various types of stone, especially igneous stone, as having deeper properties.

The story also tells us that it took the ability to mobilize a massive labor force to put these things together. That means there had to be a social structure in place – one where large numbers of skilled and unskilled laborers would come together to work at the bequest of an elite ruling class. Kurt Mendelssohn described these labors as *collective efforts by communities* to construct "symbols of greatness."

At first, the purpose of building fantastically large structures (such as the earliest stone circles) may have been to unite the people in establishing monuments of their society's greatness. Later monuments (such as the pyramids of Egypt) also united the people through a common purpose, while at the same time reinforcing the social hierarchy of the ruling class. [454]

According to Godfrey Higgins, Albert Churchward, and David MacRitchie, **the people who built Stonehenge were Black.** In *Ancient and Modern Britons*, MacRitchie writes:

> [T]here are several reasons for believing that the unidentified builders of our stone-circles, cairns, and dolmens, were dark-skinned people; and the races with which they have most similarity are Professor Huxley's Australioids and Negritos. [455]

Higgins, on the other hand, said that Stonehenge was built by a group of Blacks from India who appeared in Europe as the Celts:

> In my Essay on *The Celtic Druids*, I have shewn, that a great nation called the Celtae, of whom the Druids were the priests, spread themselves almost over the whole earth, and are to be traced in their rude gigantic monuments from India to the extremity of Britain. Who these can have been but the early individuals of the black nation of whom we have been treating I know not, and in this opinion I am not singular. The learned Maurice says, "Cushites, i.e. Celts, built the great temples in India and Britain, and excavated the caves of the former." And the learned mathematician, Ruben Burrow, has no hesitation in pronouncing Stonehenge to be a temple of the black, curly-headed Buddha. [456]

Albert Churchward traced these Blacks back to Egypt:

> They were undoubtedly descendants of the ancient Egyptian priests,

who came over and landed in Ireland and the West of England, and who brought with them their religious doctrines and taught and practised them here. The Tuatha-de-Dananns, who came to Ireland, were of the same race and spoke the same language as the Firbolgs and the Formarians, possessed ships, knew the art of navigation, had a compass or magnetic needle, worked in metals, had a large army, thoroughly organised, and a body of surgeons; had a "Bardic or Druid class of priests." These "Druids" brought all their learning with them, believed and practised the Eschatology of the Solar doctrines, and all came out of Egypt.[457]

Many early 19th century scholars proposed that Stonehenge and many other stone monuments across Europe were built by the Druids, until it was found that the Druids simply *performed their rituals* near these ancient sites. As Alexander Winchell reported in 1878:

> The "dolmens" were for centuries regarded as the stone altars of the ancient Druids; but we now know that they were as mysterious to the Druids, two thousand years ago, as to ourselves.[458]

Whatever additional connections they drew, these three (white) historians were all saying Stonehenge was the work of Black people, over 100 years ago, and **it wasn't popular then either**. Since then, few people have followed their trail and said anything similar. So Stonehenge – for most people – is still thought of as a European accomplishment.

But now these authors are finally getting some support. Linguists say a study of Irish and other Celtic languages has produced evidence that when the Celts invaded Ireland and Britain there were already Afro-Asiatic speakers there. Celtic languages – Irish, Scots Gaelic and Welsh – still have grammatical traits found in Afro-Asiatic tongues that are otherwise unrelated, according to research published in the May 2000 issue of *Science*:

> The only other non-linguistic evidence that could point towards this connection is in blood type, but it is not definitive. Irish and British people have different proportions of blood types to most Europeans. Where there are comparable proportions is in the Atlas mountains in Northern Africa, home of the Berber people.

Berber is a branch of the Afro-Asiatic language group. It's been widely known for some time that when the Celts invaded Ireland there were people already there. But now we know those first people – the builders of Stonehenge, who appear to have inhabited the area since at least 7,000 BC – were Black.

And this is the case for just about ANY megalith or monument in Europe that predates 1,500 BC – the time when we first start seeing evidence that white Europeans were producing anything similar (although, even then, they were only replicas of our creations).

To be fair, whites may have been constructing war chariots around 2,000 BC (based on Egyptian models), but they certainly weren't producing anything resembling a monument for quite some time. The only problem with "proving" that all these other European constructions were the handiwork of Blacks is that nobody is in a rush to do that kind of research.

So for now, we are limited to the accounts of people like Higgins and MacRitchie, and the occasional piece of linguistic or genetic evidence that makes it through the filter. We'll get deeper into THAT story in Volume Four.

REVIEW

Like the megalithic builders who erected massive stone monuments throughout Europe's coastal areas, the builders of Stonehenge were Black and their culture was Anu. We can determine this by correlating the linguistic evidence, the genetic evidence, historical accounts and folk legends, and the similarity of their buildings and practices to those associated with Anu people elsewhere in the ancient world.

In *Adamites and Pre-Adamites*, Alexander Winchell describes an ancient race of men he calls "Stone Folk." He says the Iberians, who came from "Atlantis and the northwest part of Africa," went into Spain "at a period earlier than the settlement of the Egyptians in the northeast of Africa." He says the "Stone Folk" – who other writers called the "megalithic race" and who we simply call the Anu – were spread across Spain, Italy and the British islands over 6000 years ago, and could ultimately be traced back to "the tropical or sub-tropical regions of Africa and Asia." Winchell continues:

> That some uniform race of men populated the Orient from India to Great Britain, in remote prehistoric times, is evinced by the similarity of the monuments left behind in all the intervening countries. I refer especially to tumuli and huge stone structures of a certain style…The megaliths or huge roughly hewn blocks of stone, arranged in rude structures, abound in nearly all the countries of Europe.[459]

When Anu seafarers rounded the coasts of Europe after Iberia, one of their next stops would be the shores of the British Isles. The British Isles are a group of islands off the northwest coast of continental Europe that includes Great Britain (a large island split into England, Scotland, and Wales), Ireland, and over six thousand smaller isles. Just northwest of Great Britain, we find similar evidence placing the Anu people in Ireland. This is where we find the history of the so-called Black Irish.

THE BLACK IRISH

The Celtic music of Ireland is different from other traditional European music. How different? So different it sounds almost *African.* After British musician Simon Emmerson came to Senegal to work for a local artist, he explained, "The music of ancestral West Africa seemed to resonate [with] a very deep strata of the British Isles. Hearing and recording this music, I heard melodies and rhythms that were familiar."

Emmerson took the recordings back to England and played them for a traditional Celtic musician Davy Spillane. "He said a lot of Irish musicians have always felt deeply connected with African music and West African music…there is this theory that the aboriginal Irish, the Fir Bolg, were very dark skinned and could well have come from Africa." Emmerson went on to assemble a group known as the Afro Celts, made up of an African harpist, a Celtic harpist, an African drummer, and a Celtic drummer.[460]

This story leaves us with a question: Who were the aboriginal people of Ireland? One thing's for sure: They weren't white.

BEFORE THE WHITE IRISH

It is a widely-accepted belief that the Irish (along with the Scottish and Welsh) can be traced back to the Celts, who migrated from central Europe around 500 BC. The *Keltoi* (Celts) were a diverse group, but the Irish trace themselves back to a specific group of Celts known as the Gaels. The Gaels were known to the Romans as a tribe of Germanic "barbarians" with *cold blue eyes and hair like flames.*

But the people of Ireland are not ALL pale-skinned with light eyes and red hair. There is a distinct group of people in Ireland who tend to have darker complexions, black or brown hair, and dark brown eyes. These people live predominantly on the western side of the island, have a different genetic signature, and are known to others as the "Black Irish."

Who are the Black Irish, and where do they come from? The "Black Irish" ultimately descend from several waves of Black people who came into Europe over the past 50,000 years. Within the past 2,000 years, Europe has seen the spread of Moors (who occupied much more than just Spain) as well as African envoys of the ancient

Roman Empire. But Ireland was settled by Black people long before either of these people came.

And unlike Scotland, England, and many other areas in Europe, Ireland was never colonized by the Romans. As a result, Ireland remained relatively isolated until the English conquests of the Middle Ages. Gaels and other white populations settled there, but these invasions were late into Ireland's 10,000 year long history of human habitation. Some isolated parts of Ireland (particularly the western seaboard) have been relatively untouched by outside genetic influence since hunter-gatherer times.

Recent genetic research has confirmed that the early inhabitants of Ireland were not directly descended from the *Keltoi* of central Europe. Instead, the closest genetic relatives of the Irish are to be found among the Basque people of Spain. The Basques are one of the few surviving pre-Indo-European people in Europe today, and they are distinct from their neighbors in Spain – genetically, linguistically, culturally, and visibly so. Studies have connected some of the people of Britain – especially the Scottish – to the Basques as well, suggesting they come from the same ancient roots.

And this isn't new. In 1882, English historian Charles Elton noted, "the dark population in parts of the British Islands and the Basques of the Pyrenees are descended from a common stock."[461] In fact, as early as the first century AD, Roman historian Tacitus had come to similar conclusions:

> Who were the original inhabitants of Britain, and whether they sprang from the soil or came from abroad is unknown, as is usually the case with barbarians. Their physical characteristics are various, and from this conclusions may be drawn. The red hair and large limbs of the Caledonians point clearly to a German origin. The dark complexion of the Silures, their usually curly hair, and the fact that Spain is the opposite shore to them, are evidence that Iberians of a former date crossed over and occupied those parts. [462]

In other words, the Black people of the British Isles arrived from Spain. Historians called these people the Silurians. Other translations of Tacitus' account (quoted above) have him describing the Silurians of Spain as "swarthy with hair mostly in tight curls."[463] Elton notes that white emigrants into the British Isles...

> ...were forced into contact with the people of a more primitive age, dark slight-limbed Silurians, and the dusky tribes who were called the children of the night. Some, according to their fortune in the wars, were driven by the new invaders into the western woods and deserts; others were able to hold their own until in course of time the two races became fused and intermixed. [464]

But the Silurians weren't the people with whom it all began. It goes back much further.

WHERE DID THESE DARK PEOPLE COME FROM?

"Every one who is black, loquacious, lying, tale-telling or of low and groveling mind, is of the Firbolg descent," while *"every one who is fair haired, of large size, fond of music and horse riding, and practices the art of magic, is of Tuatha De Danann."* – Book of Mac Firbis, circa 1650

Ireland has several well-documented historical traditions of the populations that preceded white people. Traditional accounts like the 11th century *Lebor Gabála Érenn* (or *Book of Invasions)* refer to a number of ancient groups in Ireland, such as the Fomorians, the Nemedians, the Fir Bolg, the Tuatha Dé Danann, and the Milesians.

We should begin with the most recent invasion to settle Ireland. The *Book of Invasions* says the Milesians (who represent the Gaelic Celts) first "overflowed Scythia" (near the Caucasus) and invaded Egypt. They trace their ancestry to a Scythian present at the fall of the Tower of Babel, and Scota, a daughter of an Egyptian pharaoh (from whom they got the name Scots). Presumably these two are symbolic of their racial origins.

The *Book of Invasions* says two branches of their descendants left Egypt and Scythia, which researcher Greg Noonan connects to Egyptians fleeing the Hyksos conquest, and a pursuing fleet of Hyksos.[465] After they "advanced past Africa," they settled the shores of the Mediterranean, later settling in Spain, before ultimately coming to Ireland.

Long before the Milesians sailed in from Spain, several other waves of people had come to Ireland. According to the *Book of Invasions*, most of these people came from the Caucasus. There are two exceptions:

First, there are the *Fir Bolg*. They are often described as "dark" and having pygmy traits, meaning they could have been a migration of DBP people, or a DBP survival of Europe's first settlers. This is why Elton notes:

> [N]o Spanish origin is attributed to the Feru-Bolg, or Fir-Bolgs, who are identified in many other traditions with "the old stock," the short and swarthy people of the western and south-western parts of Ireland.[466]

The Fir Bolg fought fiercely against the white Celts who attempted to remove them from Ireland, and may have become mythologized as leprechauns and other small semi-divine beings.

Second, there are the *Fomorians*, a "semi-divine" race who introduced the Neolithic Age to Ireland. Some accounts say they came between 4000 and 2500 BC, while others say they were "beings who preceded the gods, similar to the Greek Titans." The Fomorians could represent the Anu migration into Ireland.

WHO WERE THE FOMORIANS?

Many scholars have attempted to figure out who the Fomorians were by deciphering what the name "Fomorian" derives from. Unlike the other names, its origins are unclear. It may derive from *muir* (or "sea"), suggesting that they came by boat, with some etymologies pointing directly to the shores of Africa. Others say it comes from *mahr* (or "phantom," as in "night-mare"), connecting the name to later myths of "evil" Black people (known popularly as "children of darkness") in early Europe.

Still others connect it to *mór* or *már* (meaning "great").* Whatever their name meant, we have evidence they (as well as the Fir Bolg) were Black, unlike the hordes of invaders who followed them, because there are dozens of accounts that describe them as such.

For example, a medieval Irish tale entitled *The Training of Cú Chulainn*, speaks of a Fomorian woman, "shapely, dear and beautiful, the most distinguished damsel of the world's women," who cries to the Gaelic warrior Cú Chulainn about a group of Fomorians coming to exact tribute from her. When asked who is coming, she answers: "Three sons of Alatrom of the Fomorians, and Dub, Mell and Dubros are their names." It's notable that both *dub* and *mel* literally mean dark or black, but the description that follows is even more explicit:

> Not long had they been at those talks when they saw the well-manned, full-great vessel approaching them over the furious waves of the sea. And when the damsel's people saw the ship coming, they all fled from her, and not a single person remained in her company save only Cú Chulainn. And thus was that vessel: a single warrior, dark, gloomy, devilish, on the stern of that good ship, and he was laughing roughly...[467]

---

* Could any of these words have a connection the Greek mauros (meaning "dark")? It's possible, as mauros manifested itself in several derived names in later history, including the semi-divine *mauri* of the Basque, the *mouros encantados* of Portugal, the Mauri people of North Africa, and (much later) the Islamic Moors who ruled over much of Europe. To be sure, a full linguistic análisis needs to be done.

There's more. Several other accounts, many even older than *The Training of Cú Chulainn*, describe the Fomorians as a "dark" race. Recent investigators have noted parallels between accounts of the Fomorians and cultural practices known in Ancient Egypt.[468]

I'M NOT MAKING THIS UP!

Now, I know, sometimes you might read pieces like this and say to yourself, "Okay Supreme, I think you're stretching now." But I promise I don't stretch. I'll tell you if I'm speculating or theorizing. And when it comes to the racial identity of the first people in Ireland, I feel pretty comfortable making my claims.

If you don't believe me, read what renowned ethnologist James Mooney had to say in 1888:

> The Irish, like every other historic nation, are a mixed race, and the native annals, which unquestionably go back to a remote antiquity, recount several invasions or colonizations of the island long before the Christian era. The aborigines of the country, or, more correctly speaking, the earliest colonists, were known as Fomorians, which, however, was not their true name, but that imposed by their conquerors. They are said to have come originally from Africa. Then we have accounts of colonies which made no permanent impression until the landing of the Firbolgs, supposed to have taken place about seven hundred years before Christ. The Firbolgs conquered the country, established a regular form of government and drove the aborigines before them until the remnant took refuge on the islands which skirt the western coast, where they earned the name of Formorians or Pirates by their forays upon the settlements of the invaders upon the mainland. About one hundred and seventy years later another people, the Tuatha de Dananns, landed upon the eastern coast and demanded a portion of the island.

The *Tuatha de Danann* were a later wave of white invaders, often described as having blonde hair and blue eyes, and being more culturally advanced than their barbaric predecessors. However, the Fir Bolg and the Fomorians **were not interested in giving up Ireland**. Mooney continues:

> This demand being refused, the invaders advanced rapidly into the interior while the Firbolgs retired before them until the latter, having apparently been joined by the Fomorians, concentrated all their forces on the plain of Moytura on the southern border of the County Mayo. Here about five hundred and thirty years before Christ, took place the most celebrated battle in the ancient annals of Ireland, the struggle lasting four days and resulting in the total defeat of the Firbolgs and the death of their king. The magnitude of the conflict is attested by the number of sepulchral mounds and monumental pillar stones extending for miles and giving to the plain

the appearance of one vast cemetery, as it is in fact the grave of the Firbolg nation. The survivors were allowed to remain in the western province of Connaught and the adjacent islands, where the remnant of the Fomorians still existed. Here they were joined by their kindred from all parts of the island, while the conquerors took possession of the other portions of the country. [469]

This would explain why only the western fringes of Ireland appear to preserve the traces of this original Black presence:

> The blond race is most numerous east of the Shannon, the portion occupied by the Tuatha De Dananns, while the darker race is found chiefly along the west coast, to which the old Fomorians and Firbolgs retired when their power was broken. [470]

Mooney concludes:

> At all events we have evidence of the former existence in Ireland of a pre-Keltic dark race, physically and intellectually different from the conquering race, and there is good ground for the opinion that either the Firbolgs or the Fomorians were a part of that ancient people who preceded the Kelts in western Europe, and who, under the various names of Silures, Iberians and perhaps Ligurians, have left traces of their former presence in Britain, France, Spain and Italy, but whose limits have been contracted by centuries of conquest and absorption, until their modern descendants, the Basques, are now confined to the valleys of the Pyrenees. [471]

We can reasonably assume that these same groups of settlers also settled in nearby areas where we don't have similar historical records.

Thus, the same Black populations could have contributed to the ancestral pool of early Irish, Scottish, Welsh, British, and Scandinavian people. And the same invaders would have annihilated or expelled the original Black people of ancient Britain, Ireland, Scotland, Spain, and Scandinavia, leaving only traces behind. [472]

THE SILURIANS OF SPAIN

Earlier we quoted a few historians who traced the Black people of Ireland back to a people known as the Silures, or Silurians. Who were the Silurians? The Silurians were considered "one of the bravest of the ancient British nations, and defended their country and their liberty against the Romans, with the most heroic fortitude." [473]

In his *Memoirs of the Celts of Gauls,* Joseph Ritson says the Silurians came from Spain:

DID YOU KNOW?
Ever seen a movie called Black Knight? Turns out Martin Lawrence might have been onto something. According to some sources, the famed King Arthur was in fact a king of the Black Silures. And his Knights of the Round Table?
At least one of them, Sir Morien was a Black knight. Runoko Rashidi says, "It is noted that Morien was as "black as pitch; that was the fashion of his land-- Moors are black as burnt brands." Ultimately, and ironically, Morien came to personify all of the finest virtues of the knights of medieval Europe."
King Arthur's trusted Merlin, too, was associated with the Silures, and has been described as a Black man. Sir Morien, like Merlin, was connected to the legend of Stonehenge's erection. In *A Book of the Beginnings*, Gerald Massey adds, "Morion is said to have been the architect of Stonehenge...Now, as a negro is still known as a Morien in English, may not this indicate that Morien belonged to the Black race, the Kushite builders?"

The swarthy complexion of the Silures, and their hair, which is generally curled, with their situation opposite to the coast of Spain, furnished ground to believe, that the ancient Iberians had arrived from thence, and taken possession of the territory.[474]

"Silures" may have been a name applied to the Basque-speaking people of Spain, one of the Iberian populations who were not related, genetically or linguistically, to the white people who later came to dominate the region.

In David MacRitchie's phenomenal *Ancient and Modern Britons*, he provides extensive evidence of Black people who predated the white presence in Europe. Of the Silurians he writes:

For the black people, as we know, ante-date the Danish branch of that stock by many centuries, how many, no one can tell. Professor Huxley, speaking on this subject, says "that probably in the time of Caesar, and certainly in that of Tacitus, there existed in these islands two distinct types of population: the one of tall stature, with fair skin, yellow hair, and blue eyes; the other of short stature, with dark skin [as dark as an Ethiopian's, says Pliny; as dark as a "Moor's," says Claudian], dark hair, and black eyes. We further learn that this dark population, represented by the Silures, bore considerable physical resemblance to the people of Aquitania and Iberia; while the fair population of parts of South-East Britain – the present counties of Kent and Hants – resembled the Belga; who inhabited the North-East of France and the country now called Belgium. These Belgae, again, were closely akin in physical characters to the tall fair people who dwelt on the east bank of the Rhine, and were called Germani. These two distinct ethnological elements (continues Mr. Huxley) probably coexisted in these islands when the country was discovered by the Romans; and the subsequent invasions to which Britain has been subjected have not introduced any new stock, but have merely affected one or other of the pre-existing elements." Accepting this conclusion, then, as, in the main, correct, we have before us undeniable evidence – historical and ethnological – of the immemorial presence of the blacks in this country.[475]

It appears that Spain was simply one of many stopping points for an ancient Anu migration across and around Europe. These people didn't walk land routes so much as they sailed Europe's waterways.

As a result, their oldest and most densely populated settlements aren't found in Europe's interior, but along the coasts. This is why we find so many traces of Anu people in Italy, Spain, Ireland, Scotland, England, Wales, and Scandinavia – all coastal areas – while many of the "white barbarians" of ancient Europe (who later became its dominant population) expanded across its interior. Elton explains:

> Whether or not the Fir-Bolgs of Irish tradition can be connected with the pre-Celtic tribes, it is clear that in many parts of Ireland there are remnants of a short and black-haired stock, whose tribal names are in many cases taken from words for the Darkness and the Mist, and whose physical appearance is quite different from that of the tall light Celts. The same thing has been observed in the Scottish Highlands, and in the Western Isles, where the people have a "strange foreign look," and are "dark-skinned, dark-haired, dark-eyed, and small in stature." And it is a matter of familiar knowledge, that in many parts of England and Wales the people are also short and swarthy, with black hair and eyes, and with heads of a long and narrow shape.
>
> Some class together in the same way all the short peoples with black hair and eyes, whether paleskinned or ruddy in complexion, calling them Iberians on account of their supposed affinity with the dark races remaining in the south of Europe. All the tall, roundheaded and broad-headed men are described together as comprising "the van of the Aryan army," with whom became intermingled tall dark and red-haired men from Scandinavia, and fair people of Low-German descent. All the short and dark races, whether long-headed or roundskulled, are treated as descendants of a primitive non-Aryan stock, including "the broad-headed dark Welsh man and the broad-headed dark Frenchman," and connected by blood not only with the modern Basque, but with the ancient and little-known Ligurian and Etruscan races.[476]

You didn't even read all that, did you? C'mon now! You could be missing something awesome. Go back and read it. I'll wait.

Got it? Didn't I tell you? So, Elton concludes that these dark populations are not recent arrivals but survivals from the original people of Neolithic Europe:

> These facts render it extremely probable that some part of the Neolithic population has survived until the present time, with a constant improvement no doubt from its crossing and intermixture with the many other races who have successively passed into Britain. And this gives a particular interest to everything which can be

definitely ascertained about the special characteristics of the "Silurians."[477]

As we know, the Black people who introduced the Neolithic to Europe were the Anu. The Anu, as we know, dispersed from Northeast Africa. J.A. Rogers believed they came from the Nile Valley.[478] In 1897, in *The Negro and the White Man*, Wesley John Gaines argued that the ancient Iberians came from North Africa.[479]

Gaines cites the work of Dr. Alexander Winchell, the author of *Pre-Adamites*. Winchell says the dark-skinned Iberians came from North Africa before the rise of ancient Egypt, and "overran the Spanish peninsula, founded cities, built a navy, carried on commerce, extended their empire over Italy, as Sicanes, when Rome was founded, long before the sack of Troy."[480]

Winchell adds that they "extended their conquests" as far as the British Islands. These Iberians, he says, were then "dispossessed by immigrations, first, of Hamitic Pelasgians, and, afterward, of Aryan Illyrians and Ligurians." In other words, they were displaced by the first white Europeans. "In our times, all that remains of them is the little nation of Basques in the north of Spain and the south of France," he concludes.

THEN WHAT HAPPENED?

"The Irish are the blacks of Europe, so say it loud, I'm Black and I'm proud."
— The Commitments (1991 film about the city of Dublin)

Perhaps this "Black history" explains why the Irish (and to a lesser extent the Scottish and Welsh) were once so hated by the rest of Europe. Same with the Basques in Spain.

So how and when did things change? Let's look at the history of the Irish. In a nutshell, *the Irish became white.* That is, they transcended their historical identification with the dark-skinned people of ancient Europe by *identifying with whiteness.* **It wasn't an instant change, however.** They were once the most hated people in Northern Europe, later despised by the British, and, after that, made to suffer some of *the same wretched conditions as Blacks in America once they emigrated here.* In fact, the Irish were considered "no better than Negroes." In 1741, a riot broke out in New York, where investigators discovered a conspiracy between Irish, African, and Native American men and women. Some Irish conspirators were overheard swearing they'd kill as many "white people" as possible.[481] As late as 1848, soldiers from St. Patrick's Battalion fought on the side of Mexico in the War of 1848. You would think that Black-Irish solidarity could have taken off, but that's not the way things tend to work.

After centuries of white conquest, the people of Ireland – even those considered "Black Irish" were white enough to join the rest of the white world in whiteness. It sounds silly, but it's so serious. In fact, this is a subject explored by several historians and cultural anthropologists – the story of how the Irish became white.

Long story short, it started with the white invasions that displaced most of the original population, but it reached its climax when poor Irish people in America decided to become white at the expense of poor Black people. As a Black journalist explains in an 1860 edition of *The Liberator*:

> Fifteen or twenty years ago, a Catholic priest in Philadelphia said to the Irish people in that city, "You are all poor, and chiefly laborers, the blacks are poor laborers; many of the native whites are laborers; now, if you wish to succeed, you must do everything that they do, no matter how degrading, and do it for less than they can afford to do it for." The Irish adopted this plan; they lived on less than the Americans could live upon, and worked for less, and the result is, that nearly all the menial employments are monopolized by the Irish, who now get as good prices as anybody. There were other avenues open to American white men, and though they have suffered much, the chief support of the Irish has come from the places from which we have been crowded.[482]

The most important such transition came when the Irish were compelled to join the police force, a job once seen as "low-class" yet – for obvious reasons – unavailable to Blacks in America. In this role, the Irish became the new oppressors, and Blacks became their victims. Irish people became "part of the clique" when they actively began terrorizing anyone who was not white. Racism spread far and wide throughout Irish communities – who quickly adopted an "Us vs. Them" attitude towards Black and brown people.

SCOTLAND
WHERE ELSE DID THE ANU PEOPLE GO?

Remember the movie *Highlander*? You know, "There can only be one"? Well, the original Highlanders of Scotland were Black. Charles Elton reports:

> The Highland people bear a strong resemblance to the Welsh, the South-western English, the Western and South-western Irish." Campbell, [in his] West Highland Tales…speaks of the short, dark natives of Barra…[483]

These people were known to the Romans as Picts. The Romans used this term because Pict means "painted or tattooed" (as in pictures).

David MacRitchie called them "Moors" (meaning they were Black),[484] and he wasn't the only one. According to the 1828 *Annals of Caledonian, Picts, and Scots*, "The Highlanders are generally diminutive, with brown complexions, and almost always with black curled hair and dark eyes."[485] The Picts ruled Scotland for more than 500 years.*

As far north as Scandinavia, these Black people settled and introduced their way of life. This is why John Denison Baldwin said the influence of the Cushite race could be felt as far north as Norway and why Professor Rolleston noted a "dark" population still living in Britain, Germany, Belgium, Scandinavia, and coastal France. Rolleston said that some "are of the exceptionally dark type which is attributed to a survival of the pre-historic population."

WHO WERE THE CELTS?

You see, all "Celtic" people were not white. The Romans called any unconconquered or un-Romanized people *Keltoi*, or Celts, which simply means "stranger." This is why there were "white Celts" (like the Gaels) and "Black Celts" (like the people who introduced the Bronze Age to the British Isles). White Celts typically came across the mainland (from the Caucasus via Germany), while Black Celts appear to have sailed a coastal route, circumnavigating Europe from the Mediterranean.

In 1905, Charles Squire described "two distinct human stocks in the British Islands at the time of the Roman Conquest," adding that "there is no evidence of any others." Squire writes:

> The earliest of these two races would seem to have inhabited our islands from the most ancient times, and may, for our purpose, be described as aboriginal. It was the people that built the "long barrows"; and which is variously called by ethnologists the Iberian, Mediterranean, Berber, Basque, Silurian, or Euskarian race.
>
> In physique it was short, swarthy, dark-haired, dark-eyed, and long-skulled; its language belonged to the class called "Hamitic", the surviving types of which are found among the Gallas, Abyssinians, Berbers, and other North African tribes; and it seems to have come originally from some part either of Eastern, Northern, or Central Africa.
>
> Spreading thence, it was probably the first people to inhabit the

---

* Some traditions say the Romans left because they simply didn't want Ireland or because it was too cold. Instead, indigenous Black populations, like the Picts, Fir Bolg, and Fomorians, prevented the Roman conquest of Ireland. The Romans were so afraid of the Picts they built massive walls to protect themselves, such as Hadrian's Wall, built across Northern England around 120 AD. The Romans left around 400 AD without taking Ireland.

Valley of the Nile, and it sent offshoots into Syria and Asia Minor. The earliest Hellenes found it in Greece under the name of "Pelasgoi"; the earliest Latins in Italy, as the "Etruscans"; and the Hebrews in Palestine, as the "Hittites".

It spread northward through Europe as far as the Baltic, and westward, along the Atlas chain, to Spain, France, and our own islands. In many countries it reached a comparatively high level of civilization, but in Britain its development must have been early checked.

We can discern it as an agricultural rather than a pastoral people, still in the Stone Age, dwelling in totemistic tribes on hills whose summits it fortified elaborately, and whose slopes it cultivated on what is called the "terrace system", and having a primitive culture which ethnologists think to have much resembled that of the present hill-tribes of Southern India.

It held our islands till the coming of the Celts, who fought with the aborigines, dispossessed them of the more fertile parts, subjugated them, even amalgamated with them, but certainly never extirpated them. In the time of the Romans they were still practically independent in South Wales.

In Ireland they were long unconquered, and are found as allies rather than serfs of the Gaels, ruling their own provinces, and preserving their own customs and religion. Nor, in spite of all the successive invasions of Great Britain and Ireland, are they yet extinct, or so merged as to have lost their type, which is still the predominant one in many parts of the west both of Britain and Ireland, and is believed by some ethnologists to be generally upon the increase all over England.

The second of the two races was the exact opposite to the first. It was the tall, fair, light-haired, blue- or gray-eyed, broad-headed people called, popularly, the "Celts", who belonged in speech to the "Aryan" family, their language finding its affinities in Latin, Greek, Teutonic, Slavic, the Zend of Ancient Persia, and the Sanscrit of Ancient India. Its original home was probably somewhere in Central

Europe, along the course of the upper Danube, or in the region of the Alps. The "round barrows" in which it buried its dead, or deposited their burnt ashes, differ in shape from the "long barrows" of the earlier race.[488]

In other words, Black folks came first, around the same time they were civilizing the rest of the world. White folks came next. The Romans called them all strangers, or Celts.

But nobody's heard of Black Celts. I've asked Irish people and they don't know either. So here are some more quotes from credible sources with no reason to lie on behalf of an ancient Black empire.

In 1875, the Gaelic Society of Inverness reported the presence of "Black Celts" as far west as Canada (where many Scottish Highlanders had emigrated), specifically noting their "dark African faces."[489] In 1884, Thomas Huxley included among his racial classification of "Melanochroi" (or "dark whites") the "Iberians, 'black Celts' of Europe, and the dark-complexioned white peoples of the shores of the Mediterranean, Western Asia, and Persia."[490]

Could this be why the Pictish and Celtic languages appear to have Afro-Asiatic roots? Linguistic evidence becomes especially helpful in identifying Anu influence wherever later Europeans wiped out any physical traces of their predecessors. For example, the Black Celts – who spoke Afro-Asiatic languages – authored the culture of the white Celts – who ended up speaking Indo-European languages with strong Afro-Asiatic influences.[491]

Digging deeper, Roger Blench notes that Afro-Asiatic (not just Semitic) seems to have some very early loan words into Caucasian, suggesting that the Afro-Asiatic people maintained an influential presence along the Caucasian steppes, influencing its inhabitants, who would later develop the family of languages we today know as Indo-European.[492] As much as I'd like to tell more of this story, it deserves a book of its own. So this will have to be one of the stories we'll revisit in future volumes.

A QUICK NOTE ON PYRAMIDS IN NORTHERN EUROPE

You won't find many pyramids, or their remains, in the rest of Europe, but there were once earthen mounds that covered tombs (and which may have been modeled after pyramids). The most common type of megalithic construction in Europe is the portal tomb, commonly known as a dolmen. However, many local names exist, such as *anta* in Portugal, *stazzone* in Sardinia, *hunebed* in the Netherlands, *Hünengrab* in Germany, *dysse* in Denmark, and *cromlech* in Wales. It is assumed that most portal tombs were originally covered by earthen mounds. And like Stonehenge, the evidence suggests these other megaliths were built by Black builders.

QUESTIONS TO CONSIDER

Do the Afro-Asiatic roots of Celtic languages have anything to do with the early Celtic crosses found in Ireland, inscribed with the *Bismillah* ("In the Name of Allah," the opening words of the Koran) in Kufic Arabic? Essayist Hakim Bey (who happens to be a white guy born Peter Lamborn Wilson) says:

> The Celtic Church, before its destruction by the Roman hierarchy, maintained a close connection with the desert hermit-monks of Egypt. Is it possible this connection persisted past the 7th/8th centuries, & that the role of the monks was taken up by Moslems? by Sufis? in contact with a still-surviving underground Celtic Church, now become completely heretical, & willing to syncretize Islamic esotericism with its own Nature-oriented & poetic Faith?

> Such a syncresis was certainly performed centuries later by the Templars & the Assassins (Nizari Ismailis). When the Temple was suppressed by Rome & its leaders burned at the stake, Ireland provided refuge for many incognito Templars. According to The Temple & The Lodge, these Templars later reorganized as a rogue Irish branch of Freemasonry, which (in the early 18th century) would resist amalgamation with the London Grand Lodge. The Islamic connection with masonry is quite clear, both in the Templar & the Rosicrucian traditions, but Irish masonry may have inherited an even earlier Islamic link – memorialized in those enigmatic crosses![493]

If Bey is onto something, couldn't we stretch his timeline back even further to include the Celts' first interaction with Anu people as the initiation of this recurring connection? Effectively, the Moors – perhaps even after the Cushites – were the final phase of this cycle.

BLACKS IN RUSSIA?

There was once an ancient civilization in the state of Georgia, known for its Black people. No, I mean the other Georgia. The one in southeastern Europe, right between the Caucasus Mountains and the coast of the Black Sea. In Southern Russia.

You wouldn't think there were ever any Black people there, right? Wrong. There, the state of Georgia (and Russia as a whole) owes much of its heritage to an important ancient kingdom known as Colchis. "It would seem natural," local historian Cyril Toumanoff says, "to seek the beginnings of Georgian social history in Colchis, the earliest Georgian formation."

WHO WERE THE COLCHIANS?

Around the 13th century BC, the Kingdom of Colchis was formally established after several centuries of consolidation between bands of people. These people had lived in the area since, as local poet Vladimir Ankvab notes, "time immemorial." The Colchians became known for their agriculture, their metallurgy, their linens, and their thriving trade networks. **The Colchians were Black people.**

When 5th century historian Herodotus described them in Book II, Chapter 104 of his *Histories,* he observed:

> [It] is undoubtedly a fact that the Colchians are of Egyptian descent. I noticed this myself before I heard anyone else mention it…My own idea on the subject was based first on the fact that they have black skins and woolly hair.

Around the same time, the Greek poet Pindar described Jason and the Argonauts having fought "dark skinned" Colchians. As late as 400 AD, Church fathers St. Jerome and Sophronius referred to Colchis as the "second Ethiopia" because of its Black population.[494]

BUT WHERE DID THESE BLACK PEOPLE COME FROM?

Herodotus said that "the Colchians, the Egyptians and the Ethiopians are the only races which from ancient times have practiced circumcision," a custom which he claims the Colchians inherited from remnants of the army of Pharaoh Sesostris. These people were said to have been left behind after Sesostris led a Black army northward through Syria and Turkey all the way to Colchis through the southern Balkans to Greece, returning home the same way.

On the other hand, the Caucasian myths known as the *Nart Sagas* – which date back several thousand years – say that a band of "black-skinned horsemen" equipped with bows and arrows escorted the ancestors of those who would settle the Caucasus Mountains and make a permanent residence there.[495] The legends say most of these Black warrior returned home, but some remained. One *Nart Saga* says they settled in a town named Adzyubzha.[496]

In Volume Four, we'll explore these stories in depth. What's certain is that the ancestors of the Colchians **were not recent Black immigrants.** They were certainly not "deposited" there by the slave trade, as white scholars often assert about Black people found in places they aren't expected to be found – like southern Russia.

Indeed, the area once known as Colchis was originally settled by a consolidation of small bands of people. These Black people have been associated with some of the non-Indo-European cultures and languages that surrounded the Caucasus 6,000 years ago. Today, the

BLACKS IN THE CAUCASUS?

Who were the Colchians? Why were these Black people settled near the hostile mountains of the Caucasus? How long had they been there? Where did they come from? And what became of their descendants in Abkhazia?

BLACK ABKHAZIAN, CIRCA 1870

COLCHIAN STATUETTE C. 250 BC

COLCHIAN COINS

CIRCA 1920

CIRCA 1930

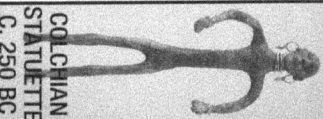

PRESENT DAY

BLACK ABKHAZIAN FAMILY CIRCA 1914

WWW.WHENTHEWORLDWASBLACK.COM

area once known as Colchis is known as Abkhazia. And Black people are STILL living there.

"The fact of the existence of Negroes in Russia should be known to every one and become an object of scientific study," the Russian magazine *Argus* wrote in its March 6, 1913 issue. P. Kovalevsky, a Russian scientist, added:

> Besides the Abkhazians, Abkhazia is inhabited by other peoples as well. But what is most surprising and even strange for Russia, is that a whole village is inhabited exclusively by Negroes.[497]

Indeed, in 1912, a Russian naturalist by the name of V.P. Vradii identified a small colony of Black people on the southwestern coast of Georgia. In 1927, the Russian writer Maxim Gorky, together with the Abkhazian writer Samson Chanba, visited the village of Adzyubzha and found elderly Black people still living there.

Many of these people have been fully assimilated or absorbed into the white populations that surround them, but their presence is well-recorded. Yet since P.T. English published one of the most concise studies of the ancient Black history of Georgia in 1959,[498] things have become difficult for the Abkhazians. Anthropologists Kesha Fikes and Alaina Lemon report:

> Anecdotal evidence indicates that state agents in the Caucasus may have tried to **erase African communities by deporting and dispersing them**... Khanga (1992) argues that when African Americans learned about and tried to connect with these communities, state officials **made such meetings difficult**. What could be read as an effort to silence (and as discussed above, disperse and dilute) the black Abkhazian can be observed against the accounts of Africans and African Americans who voluntarily relocated to the Soviet Union.[499]

And thus...this history could have been entirely "erased," along with the descendants of the people who made this history, were it not for those of us who preserve our history and make sure that the lies don't one day eclipse the truth.

THE END OF BLACK EUROPE

What happened to the Black people of ancient Europe? What do you think? They were killed off, but not right away. It literally took thousands of years. Between 3,500 and 500 BC, massive hordes of Caucasians swept through all of Europe, effectively eliminating many of the old populations who stood in their way. But some went into hiding, while others put up a fierce resistance. Some remained "elite" even after their kin in other nations were brutally cut down. This was especially the case in areas where Blacks had settled in large numbers, like Spain and the British Isles.

For example, archaeologists recently unearthed the grave of an African woman in Yorkshire, England. Named the "Ivory Bangle Lady," her stone coffin dates back to the 4th century, a time historians have assumed that "African immigrants in Roman Britain were of low status, male and likely to have been slaves."[500] Instead, the Ivory Bangle Lady was an "elite," buried with a wealth of valuable items, including a bone placard that reads "Hail, sister, may you live in God."[501] You *know* that had to come from Black folks.

What happened to people like her? From the collapse of the Western Roman Empire in the 5th century until the beginning of the Renaissance (around the 14th century), the Black people of Europe endured a slow genocide. It is no coincidence that the gradual persecution, demonization, and eventual elimination of the aboriginal Black people of Europe went hand-in-hand with the campaign to suppress and expel the Moors who had conquered Europe. In fact, the despised Moorish occupation may have prompted Europeans to target all Black people, whether Moorish or indigenous.

Even after the Moors were forced out of Europe in 1492, small pockets of Black people – some Moorish, some Anu, some Aboriginal – remained in Europe. These people became the targets of a widespread publicity campaign that sought to associate Blackness with evil. In fact – as we'll explore in Volume Five – the hunting of "witches" in Europe from about 1480 to 1750 was based on the elimination of Black women and those who continued to preserve the traditions of Black Europeans. We were the "Black magic" they hunted and killed off.

Of course, wars are never fought on only one field. There were certainly incidents where Europe's Blacks were killed *en masse* or hunted down individually, but much of their disappearance is due to the process of amalgamation or race-mixing. British scholar David MacRitchie has provided us extensive documentation of this ancient Black presence in his works. In Volume Two of *Ancient and Modern Britons*, he presents his take on Europe's early race wars:

> In most of the examples cited, of whatever nature, the two great types [Black and white] appear as enemies; which was their natural attitude. And a great number of the legendary instances preserve the memory of this mutual enmity.

Natural enmity huh? That's deep. MacRitchie continues, describing a time when Blacks ruled over whites:

> The black "giants" of the Welsh, and other tales, are "hateful " and "horrid." The Welsh Black Oppressor, and the Black Knight of Lancashire are fierce tyrants, the cruel foes of all white people. At a later date, when the whites were gaining the ascendancy, and the blacks were cut up into straggling bands, or lurking, like the Black Morrow of Galloway, in solitary dens and forest-shades, out of which they issued by night, intent on murder and rapine, even at this stage of their history, the blacks were the dreaded enemies of the whites.
>
> Indeed, it is of this epoch that the popular imagination has most retained the impression. The days of the "black oppression" are so remote that their memory only lives in half-forgotten legends. Not so the time when the black castles were owned by another race, and their former masters were skulking among woods and caves.

In other words, these Black rulers eventually found themselves broken up and outcasted. The stories of the times that followed are the ones that have survived best in popular myths and legends of dark demons, trolls, and boogeymen:

> So vivid was the fear of them, and so lasting its impression, that children of the nineteenth century, peering into dark recesses, timorously, or peasant girls, seeing suddenly their own image, reflected by the candle from the dark window-pane, shiver all over with apprehension at the vision of the dreaded "black man" – a mere imaginary bugbear to them, but a real terror to those from whom they inherited the feeling.
>
> But this state of things could not last for ever. No two races – however antagonistic – could inhabit the same territory for countless generations, without amalgamating. Such a thing is an impossibility. Whether in an authorised fashion or not, a mixed race eventually comes into being. And this is what we see in our own history. Long ages ago, and in spite of a gradually dwindling party of "Irreconcilables," the two great sections may be seen uniting here and there.

MacRitchie explains that this "amalgamation" of enemies eventually produced large numbers of Europeans who looked white but had a Black ancestor, a situation that was common in the U.S. when he wrote:

> But, just as our hypothetical octoroon family on the other side of the Atlantic might forever after continue to intermarry only with their white kindred, so might our British octoroons have done likewise: with the result, in either case, that the far-down posterity of the negro, or Moor, would be so " white " that no ethnologist could detect the presence of any other blood. And yet, in both cases, the male descendants would bear the surname first given to

DID YOU KNOW?
David MacRitchie writes:
"But the traces of our black ancestry are visibly existent in a hundred surnames. Some of these denote complexion, others do so, but indirectly. The first class includes a great many. There are the clans Ruari and Dougal (spelt Dubgaill, or "black strangers," in their own genealogy), there are all the varieties of Dubh (black), such as Duff, Dow, Macduff, and others, there are Donns, Carrs, and Dargs, with their equivalent Dunns, Browns, Greys, and Blacks. All these are colour names, showing a black or tawny ancestor. So also is the name of Dubh-glas, or Douglas, literally Black Swarthy; and that of Murray, with its kindred forms of More, Moore, etc..."

their remote authors, a surname signifying "the black man."[502]

This multi-faceted war against Europe's Black roots was not limited to the British Isles. Such genocidal campaigns went on throughout all of Europe – and extended well beyond its borders, if you consider what all of the earliest expeditions out of freshly-liberated Spain and Portugal accomplished in the Americas, Asia, Africa, and Oceania. Centuries later, few Blacks survived in Europe, with the exception of oppressed minority groups.

"The Jews had brought the Negroes into the Rhineland with the clear aim of ruining the hated white race by the necessarily-resulting bastardization." – Adolf Hitler, Mein Kampf

Thus it's no surprise that Adolf Hitler, before beginning his campaign against the Jews (who, even among the Ashkenazi Jews, carry a significant amount of African DNA), sterilized and tortured thousands of Black Germans.[503] Ironically enough, Hitler himself had the same African DNA he sought to eliminate![504]

BLACK GENES IN EUROPE

Despite centuries of mixture, much of the above is confirmed by genetics. For example, the African Haplogroup L is rare in Europe, with the exception of Spain and Portugal (frequencies as high as 22%) and some regions of Italy. But among these rare lineages, what we find is interesting. According to a 2012 study, about 65% of these African lineages came within the last 2000 years (particularly during the Moorish conquest, but also during Roman rule and much later because of the slave trade), but about 35% of these African lineages form the basis of prehistoric European bloodlines, going back at least 11,000 years ago![505]

And long before the Moors, African lineages from the E1b1b1b Y-DNA subclade entered Europe from Northwest Africa via Spain.[506] African lineages also show up in Eastern Europe, particularly around the Caucasus, beginning around 6500 years ago. These were the Anu people we describe as "guard" communities in Volume Four.

THE FALL OF CIVILIZATION

WHAT HAPPENS AFTER THE RISE?

"A great civilization is not conquered from without until it has destroyed itself from within." – Historian Will Durant

What have you learned so far? What do these stories reveal to us about ourselves? Let's review the meaning of civilization, and what we can pull from the past to apply to the present and future.

THE PROBLEM OF CIVILIZATION

Earlier in this book, we discussed several misconceptions about the history of civilization. We've covered problems with chronology (when things are said to have begun), sloppy methodology, and, of course, the racism that denied or distorted the Black role in founding the world's civilizations.

WAS IT ALL PROGRESS?

There's another problem with the way they tell the story of "the rise of civilization." We're led to assume that developments like agriculture and metallurgy constituted "discovery" and "progress" for humans. In other words, we "found something new and became better because of it." Not so.

As we discussed earlier, the mainstream view is that human society is "civilized" once it is urbanized, beginning with the transition from natural subsistence (i.e., small, mobile communities thriving on a hunter-gathering culture) to urban societies (large, sedentary communities sustained by plant and animal domestication). This is supposed to be a story of progress and social evolution.

That is, like a Black child diagnosed with ADHD, we aren't "civilized" until we learn how to sit down (settle) and do our work (agriculture). FN: Seriously though, social scientists have actually compared children diagnosed with ADHD and hunter-gatherer populations, even suggesting some sort of "genetic link." But that's another story, perhaps one appropriate for *How to Hustle and Win, Part Three.*

THEY'RE STILL SAYING WE WERE SAVAGES

This model implies that the Western world (white people) are the bearers of modern civilization and the rest of world (indigenous people of color) lack civilization until they encounter white people. They perpetuate this myth by skipping over any discussions of ancient civilizations that were predominantly Black or brown, and by only promoting images of indigenous people living like what they'd consider "savages." As a result, we grow up thinking that our ancestors were in bad shape, looking damn near homeless in the jungle, fighting with tigers and kangaroos. You'd think they never had clothes, never had values, never had anything really.

In reality, many of these "primitive" people FLED into the forests when outsiders came to take over. That is, those who refused to be a part of the "modern" civilization of India instead CHOSE to become outcasts and refugees, rather than become part of a system where Black meant evil and would remain at the bottom of the social order.

Those who remained, they suffered too. Grafton Elliot Smith, after studying among the "primitive" people of the Earth, concluded, "It is important to recognize that instead of bringing enlightenment and appeasement, civilization is responsible for most cruelties and barbarities."[507] Western civilization wasn't the best thing to happen to indigenous people. It was one of the worst. Not only were our cultures, philosophies, and value systems corrupted, the rates of depression, interpersonal violence, disease, intertribal warfare, alcoholism, malnutrition – the list goes on forever – all went skyhigh within a few years of receiving this "gift" of Western civilization. I couldn't believe my ears when I learned that some communities of Australian Aborigines are now dealing a growing crack-cocaine problem.

BUT WHO STARTED IT?

But modern civilization wasn't engineered by white people. Western civilization may be, as Mark Twain once said, "a shoddy, poor thing and full of cruelties, vanities, arrogances, meannesses and hypocrisies," but it's not the first civilization. Civilization begins with Black people, long before it all went downhill.

When asked why he called cultural communities in Africa (like the Nilo-Saharans) "civilizations," Christopher Ehret responded:

This question comes down to the problem of what the word "civilization" really means. Unfortunately, the idea that comes most often to people's minds is to contrast "civilization" to "disorder." So it becomes a value judgment about behavior. Because being civilized is a good thing, we tend to credit ourselves with being civilized. This is unexamined baggage.

The word, of course, goes back to the Latin *civis*, and the idea of living in a town. So, again, we often think of a civilization as consisting of people who were urban, with more art, more culture, and more of the things we associate with towns and cities. So you can say, okay, let's say "civilizations" have towns and cities. This is the tack that Graham Connah takes in his book, *African Civilizations*. That book is very informative, because it reminds people of just how old urban life is in Africa. It develops long, long before European colonialism.

He's right. So in this book, we've examined the historical phase when our ancestors began building cities and urban complexes. We now return to the question of whether this has been an "advance."

It makes sense that large, dense populations will require agriculture to provide adequate food supplies, which will also lead to city planning, governmental regulation, stratification of society, boundary demarcation, legal codification and a number of other civic features that all relate to the questions of "Who is in charge here?" and "Who owns what?" But in those instances where we transitioned to agriculture as a response to the scarcity of natural food sources, is that progress?

No. These technologies aren't the earmarks of civilization itself. You don't have to domesticate plants and animals to be civilized. As John Iliffe notes in *Africans: The History of a Continent*:

> The origins of African food production are therefore contentious and there is often a wide gap between the linguistic evidence, which generally suggests early origins for agriculture and pastoralism, and archaeological research, which usually gives later dates. Nor is it even clear why people should have begun to produce food at all. The idea that food production originated in the Near East and spread through Africa where it was eagerly adopted by starving hunter-gatherers is untenable. Studies of modern forager-hunters suggest that many can obtain more nutrients with less effort and more freedom than most herdsman or agriculturalists. Skeletal evidence from the Nilotic Sudan suggests that one consequence of food-production there was malnutrition. Another was probably disease, for many infectious diseases, such as tuberculosis, were probably contracted from domestic animals, while the clearing of land for agriculture encouraged malaria and the larger populations of food-producing societies sustained diseases which could not have

survived among scattered forager-hunters. Given Africa's abundant wild produce, the drudgery of food-production can have been tolerable to prehistoric people only if it offered marked advantage over their previous lifestyle as a result of major change in their circumstances.[508]

In other words, our ancestors only applied these techniques where needed. Sometimes, approaches are abandoned after it's learned that they don't work well in the long run.

GREEN TECHNOLOGY - 10,000 YEARS AGO

This explains why innovations sometimes "pop up" along the archaeological record, often with huge "gaps" in between. It's also why some technologies – particularly those with low environmental impacts – were maintained for hundreds of thousands of years (like the use of stone tools or foraging), despite the availability of more modern practices (which often had more environmental impact). In other words, most of human history has been about people living a "natural way of life."

But some of those practices won't work as well with a growing, diverse population, so they needed to update their culture. This is where things like urbanization came in. There's nothing wrong with ceasing to migrate/relocate and settling down to build a home (it had to happen at some point), but that doesn't mean the group who settled was "better" than those who chose not to.

As we may all know by now, urbanization has serious impacts on the environment. Even the most ancient settlements affected the weather, creating stronger summer storms through "heat islands" pumping hot air into the lower atmosphere, with each new road and building providing dark surfaces to soak up midday heat.

As cities grow, this may cause more flooding and greater storms. Coastal areas and desert areas alike are affected. To counteract this, our ancestors planted more trees, used light colored materials for the surfaces of building materials, built more underground dwellings, and created fractally organized city plans that more evenly distributed heat and energy.[509]

These are solutions modern society is having a hard time implementing today (even though we are in an environmental crisis), yet these methods were in use throughout our ancient civilizations! You'll see countless examples of "green technology" in this book, but you'll also see examples where excessive construction led to the downfall of a society.

It seems the best way is to simply "live off the land" (or use temporary, organic materials like thatched "beehive" huts) and to split up large populations when groups get too large for the local ecosystem…which is what we were doing 100,000 years ago.

THE BOTTOM LINE

Bottom line, the traditional view of history is wrong. Not only have we being doing "just fine" before we transitioned to the cultural patterns we normally associate with "modern civilization," but we've also been doing things that resemble modern civilization far longer than most people think as well. An easy way to look at all this is to say that – when our circumstances called for it – we've built advanced "urban" societies, and when our circumstances allowed for a more naturalistic approach, we went in THAT direction instead (up to as recently as the modern day).

Are we saying that nothing actually "develops" and that all the technology we've ever used has ALWAYS been available? Not necessarily. New circumstances require responses that may not have been required before. At least not in that particular form. You see, there's nothing new under the sun.

So there's never a "new" technology in the sense of something that was never seen or conceived before in ANY form or fashion. There are more "reinventions" than there are "inventions," and more old ideas used in novel ways than new ideas that never existed before.

But there's no NEED for a sewage system in a hunter-gather society. You don't need that until you have a settled urban society like the kind you find in Harappan India. But we ALWAYS had the IDEA of controlling waste. In hunter-gather societies, we distributed our own waste in areas we were leaving behind, so that it would fertilize the land for future plant growth, perhaps when we or another group returned to that area. Same idea, different applications.

All this goes back to the fundamental, timeless set of principles that underlie all human activity (and all life and matter in general): a set of natural laws we call Supreme Mathematics. Other societies have called these laws by other names. Some have standardized them, some haven't. But everyone, from the ancient Egyptians to the Moors of Spain to Taoists in China, have recognized a set of principles that undergird the structure of all we see and do.

These principles explain why we can see the same pattern of activity in cultures that are separated by thousands of years. For example: the principle of food consumption, energy production, and waste elimination. It occurs both in the human body and in EVERY human society, as we've seen above. If you look at a society with only 40 members foraging and moving nomadically, and then again at that same place on the earth when there are now 40,000 citizens in a massive urban complex, you will of course see that the urban society has introduced new laws, new social structure, new architecture, new technology, new industries, and new economic practices…but none of these "new" practices are "discoveries" so much as they are modern applications of timeless principles in new contexts. So the only thing NEW is the context. That is, there is no "new," there's only the NOW.

In our view, you don't need cities to be considered "civilized." "Civilization" is something we carry in the mind, and many of our people living in the "jungles" are more "civil" than we are. After you review the contributions of the Anu people – who introduced the world to "modern" civilization over 10,000 years ago, make sure you revisit Part One of this volume. There, you'll see that the Original People – who lived a "natural way of life" involving few material possessions – possessed the fundamentals of all these sciences over 100,000 years ago. It's all been a cycle. Not a rise and fall as much as a cycle of rebirth.

Every 25,000 years, a branch of the Original People (such as the founders of the Nubian Complex, the founders of the Aurignacian culture, the founders of the Anu culture) radiate from their seat at the Root of Civilization and change the world. About 15,000 years ago, the founders of the Anu Culture Complex introduced the world to "modern civilization."

THE ANU CULTURAL COMPLEX

Anu people were responsible for spreading…

- ❏ stonemasonry and the erection of stone monuments
- ❏ the trade of semi-precious stones (particularly jade and obsidian)
- ❏ the loom and many textile techniques (especially the production of cottons and linens)
- ❏ metallurgy (copper, bronze, and later iron)
- ❏ metalworking in precious metals
- ❏ the domestication of hundreds of plants
- ❏ the domestication of dozens of animals (e.g. horse, cow, sheep, goat, donkey, pig, chicken, etc.)
- ❏ imported crops like millet, dates, and cotton
- ❏ the potters wheel and many ceramic traditions

- ❏ the first social caste systems
- ❏ leadership structures and governments
- ❏ written language and numerals

All of these traditions were introduced to the world and then "re-introduced" in an improved form by a later wave of Anu people. For example, the loom and potter's wheel were constantly improved and diffused to other civilizations from the Near East to Japan, over a period of roughly several thousand years.[510]

All of these innovations diffused from somewhere in the root area of the Anu Complex. Most of them first appeared in the area between and 10,000 and 13,000 years ago, the same time the Natufians emerged in the Near East. For example, obsidian was a prized commodity among Natufians who used it to create jewelry and razor sharp knives with wooden handles. Obsidian was traded locally by at least 10,000 BC. By 9000 BC, there's evidence of obsidian trade throughout the Mediterranean.

Around this time, jade also appears as trade object in the area. It's not long before obsidian and jade show up in East Asia, then along the west coasts of the Americas, as well as in the Amazon (where it begins at a site on the east coast that faces the ocean current coming in from West Africa). Jade and obsidian rapidly become the most sought-after stones in Mesoamerica. In fact, control of the obsidian trade is what allowed the ancient city of Teotihuacan to rise to power.

So, yes, these innovations all seem to radiate from the Near East area. But that may not have been where they BEGAN. Sometimes their seeds are found in East Africa, and at other times the seeds are found among Original People in distant parts of the globe. For example, African people carried gourds as natural containers everywhere they went. And they're easy to find in the wild across Africa and southern Asia.

But over 10,000 years ago, the people of Japan found a need to domesticate gourds, perhaps to ensure a more steady supply of a resource that was becoming scarce locally. This was the same area where our ancestors crafted the first ceramic vessels. And what were these pots for? To serve the same purpose as a hollowed-out gourd. In other words, there must have been a need not fully met by what nature supplied – and new techniques were used to meet those needs.[511]

Looking at things this way, it puts the many "advances" of Europe and the Near East in a different light. Was Africa naturally abundant in all the things our ancestors needed, while the resource-poor regions further north required a greater focus on innovation?

In the end, even when such an "innovation" is first found somewhere outside of the Root, the earliest, most organic, form of this practice was most likely "rooted" in Africa. This is the theme we explore in *Black People Invented Everything*.

It's the same with the Anu languages, especially the family known specifically as Afro-Asiatic, where there's been tons of research done. Linguists trace many of the later Afro-Asiatic languages, especially the Semitic ones, to a center of diffusion somewhere in the Near East, but the oldest branches point us back to a true origin somewhere in northeast Africa. Again, the seeds go back to the root of civilization.

CULTURAL CHANGE AND HISTORICAL RENEWAL

The oldest ceramics can be found at Jōmon sites over 10,000 years old in Japan.* But Anu people picked up these seeds, further modified these techniques, and – from the root of civilization – re-released this knowledge in a 2.0 version. Of course, not everyone they met adopted the 2.0 version, but many did. And this is the way it was with every wave of Anu migration and every cultural innovation they released and re-released.

This is why we can find the oldest *whatever* over 5,000 miles from the Anu root of civilization, yet it was Anu people who served this knowledge to the world after they'd refined it for mass distribution. It's no different than what Microsoft or Google does with software packages. And quite literally, it's all technology.

Thus, with all the cultural changes they introduced, Anu people were simply "renewing" the history of the Original People who laid the foundation for them over 100,000 years prior. In fact – as we'll explore in Volume Three – it appears that these cyclical patterns of history repeat in set cycles – the most prominent being a 25,000 year cycle that coincides with the precession of the Earth's axis and climate changes (such as global Ice Ages).

THE WAY THINGS WORK

Cultures and civilizations emerge and develop according to the same mathematically structured process as every other natural system.

---

* For more on the early innovations that spread across the ancient world, the Past Worlds Atlas of Archaeology is an excellent resource, packed with full-color images, maps, and straightforward explanations, without too much emphasis on white folks.

Refer back to *The Science of Self, Volume One* for details on how this process played into the formation of the physical universe, the origin of life, and the evolution of man himself. These same mathematical laws were present in man's formation of city life.

This process (1) began with the foundation of the first man, who then (2) diverged, spread, and attempted whatever was in its capacity, and then (3) came to realizations about what worked and what didn't. This led to (4) humans developing institutions, cultures, and traditions based on what was effective, as well as social groups that engaged in the same patterns of behavior. Many of these bands of people (5) grew considerably in size and industry due to their consolidation and shared culture, and developed into (6) egalitarian societies with an equal distribution of labor, ownership, prestige, and responsibility. However, this eventually gave way to (7) the rise of leadership and privilege, with some individuals esteemed over others, and therefore possessing more property, knowledge, and/or rank in the society. When this occurs, it leads to (8) a natural process of accumulation and loss, progress and problems, advance and sacrifice, power and poverty. In essence, the rise must come with a fall. This is all part of the natural order though, and even massive extinctions of entire population groups can sometimes be the necessary consequence of the trajectory of this course. That is the nature of how all processes are brought to (9) completion, so that another cycle can begin.

QUESTIONS TO CONSIDER

But how would a cultural community that only dates back about 15,000 years have any idea how to reproduce historical patterns that preceded them by 100,000 years or more? I'll tell you my theory.

You see, most of the changes we associate with Anu people were not the work of ALL Anu people. It's not like we were the Borg, capable of developing highly scientific blueprints as a hive-mind sharing many bodies. Nah, most Anu people were just people. But among the Anu people there emerged a very special group of individuals. These individuals, constituting maybe 5% of the Anu-speaking population, were responsible for all of the cultural changes associated with the Anu Cultural Complex.

And it's not as if there was some infinite supply of Anu people to settle the globe. Nor were they multiplying exponentially. There just a limited amount of these individuals who did all the work, at least in terms of the scientific expertise, cultural influence, esoteric knowledge, and political leadership. And just 5% is all it took. That's all that was required for the world to change. (Well, we did it once – actually more than once – why not do it again?)

WHO WERE THE 5%?

Perhaps they were the "Original People." In Part One, we focused on the movements of the Original People, who settled the entire planet and pioneered the foundational human cultures that gave birth to all of the world's people today. It's good to know who these first Black populations were, but it's too easy to get caught up in how long ago these people did what they did. Despite the fact that so many still survive today (although significantly marginalized), people don't think of these Original People as the ones who brought modern civilization to the world. Instead, they are seen as "archaic" populations. They might have been primary, as in first, but they're also made to seem quite primitive. So they're sometimes described as "relic" populations, as in "leftovers" from the original colonization of the world.

Seeing them this way requires us to ignore two things:

❑ First, they never stopped teaching people how to live. They simply weren't able to do so out in the open because their communities were always under threat of extinction.

❑ Second, the same "Root" that produced the Original People continued bearing fruit long after they left the Root.

How do we know about the connects between the Anu and the Original People who settled the Earth 100,000 years before them? This is where genetics can shed some light.

ANU GENETICS

There are two primary genetic lineages associated with the expansion of the Anu population throughout the Near East, Africa, and Europe. By association with these two ancestral lineages, there are several other DNA lineages that had some part in Anu population movements.

E1B1B

E1b1b is straight up East African. The first E lineage established itself in Africa about 50,000 years ago, and expanded westwards, ultimately becoming the dominant lineage throughout all of Africa. One major branch became concentrated in West Africa, where the oldest E people lived side-by-side with later lineages of E. About 22,000 years ago in East Africa, E1b1b1 emerged. After suffering through the climate changes of the Nile Valley at this time, branches of E1b1b1 migrated to the Middle East around 13,000 years ago. This marks the Mushabians' migration into the Levant.[512] One branch of this lineage, the E1b1b1a2 subclade, has been identified among the Natufian remains, and has been associated with the spread of farming into Europe at the time of the Neolithic transition.[513]

R1B

R1b is about 18,000 years old. Somewhere in the Near East, they'd split away from the rest of the R people who were making a westward migration across Asia after Toba. One branch (identified by genetic marker V88) continued west into Africa, where it now retains a strong presence among Afro-Asiatic speakers in Chad and Cameroon (near where the Bantu expansion began). Another branch (identified by genetic marker P297) settled in Anatolia and later expanded into Europe, becoming part of the earliest wave of Anu migrants, and a major player in the events we'll discuss in Volume Four of this series.[*]

About 15,000 years ago, Haplogroup E1b1b and Haplogroup R1b converged near the root of civilization. These two branches would play significant roles in the spread of the Afro-Asiatic language family in Africa, Asia, and Europe. E1b1b is a descendant of the DE clade associated with Africoid survivors of Toba, while R1b is a descendant of the CF clade associated with Australoid survivors of Toba (particularly those who fought the Neanderthals), suggesting that the people associated with the Anu languages were indeed descendants of these ancestral people coming together.[†]

---

[*] There are other DNA lineages that can be associated with Anu people, but they're all connected to E1b1b1 or R1b. For example, haplogroups J and T can be associated with the expansion of Semitic and Cushitic-speaking people across Arabia and Northeast Africa, as well as with the older waves of Afro-Asiatic-speaking farmers who first introduced the Neolithic to Europe. Yet in either of these movements, they were accompanying R1b. One associated lineage, Haplogroup X, is an anomaly for reasons we discuss elsewhere in this book. Other associated haplogroups expanded in other directions.

[†] Of course, by the time Anu emerged as a language family around 15,000 years ago, these older populations had been around quite a long time and had spawned multiple lineages and offshoots throughout the world. Thus, the Anu people were by no means their only descendants. They are simply the ones associated with the Anu Cultural Complex.

THE ORIGINAL PEOPLE

Yet, in the same area as the Anu homeland, many of the indigenous people of the Nile Valley, particularly in Sudan and Ethiopia, still possess the same genetic lineage as the Original People. To this day, the people of Haplotype A live in the same communities that produced the Mushabians, the Cushites/Nubians, the Egyptians, the Moors, and any other population we've discussed as the "brains" of the Anu populations throughout the ages.

Studies suggest that some of Anu-speaking people were closely related to the Original People of the planet. According to John Illife's *Africans: The History of a Continent*:

> Genetic analysis suggests that the ancestors of the San peoples of southern Africa became relatively isolated from other human populations at an early date. Skeletal evidence from burials likewise convinces some archaeologists that ancestral San were long the sole human populations south of the Zambezi. Their closest relatives, according to genetic evidence, were probably the slightly built Afro-Mediterranean peoples who inhabited north-eastern Africa and parts of the north.[514]

In other words, some of the closest relatives to the oldest people of Africa are found among the Anu-speaking people of northeast Africa. Makes sense, as some of the oldest genetic lineages in Africa can be found here. Genetic data suggests that even the Khoisan did not originally live in the south, but originally come from this area, along with the ancestors of DBP people like the Ba Aka and Ba Twa.[515]

Perhaps we can explain the connection between Anu populations and the people of ancestral Haplogroup A and B by identifying the presence of A and B lineages among Anu expansions. And what we'll find is that, wherever Anu people went – no matter what the genetics of the bulk of their population – there are also traces of a very small percentage of people carrying much older lineages like L (mtDNA) and A or B (Y-DNA).

QUESTIONS TO CONSIDER

If this is what happened, what exactly was happening? Were the Original People maintaining a strict and direct line of inherited tradition – one that kept their lineage stable for over 100,000 years while the rest of the world became fractured and fragmented?

Were the keepers of this tradition also the keepers of some sort of esoteric knowledge? Did these people "manufacture" social change throughout the world, by introducing this deep knowledge to the world by means of Anu populations?

Were they also doing the very same thing 50,000 years ago when a similar pattern of population movement conquered the Neanderthals in Europe and the Near East (where remains suggest a small but decisive presence of Original People flanked by large numbers of Aurignacian people from all over Africa and Asia)?

If so, it's as if the Original People kept using "shells" to go everywhere and make everything happen. Rather, if we consider that these Original People had ancestors themselves, going all the way back to a time before man and a time before life itself, isn't it more like the KNOWLEDGE kept using shells or vehicles?

Questions like this are ontological in nature and can't be answered conclusively. But we can amass a body of evidence that suggests if we're on the right track. After you've finished this book, reread *The Science of Self, Volume One*, and you'll see what the body of evidence says to us.

As I noted in *Rap, Race and Revolution*:

> Elders and shamans in West Africa have said that, as the slave trade progressed, the "very best" of their people were sent to intentionally be captured by the slave traders. Their intention was that these people would produce a lineage of greatness that would one day emerge to redeem its right place in the world.[516]

The same tradition was recorded by Universal Shamgaudd, who said Allah (the founder of the Five Percenters) told him that the Five Percent were not descendants of the Tribe of Shabazz, but the Tribe of Jabbaar, a people who predated the lineages of everyone else in the area. This tribe, Shamgaudd said, boarded the slave ships on their own will, mixed in among other West and Central Africans who Fard Muhammad said were members of the Tribe of Shabazz.

THE FALL?

We've proposed that history is not a story of linear progression, but one of cycles. Like a Fibonacci spiral, these cycles are made to change. That is, it's not like the movie *Groundhog Day*, where the same exact things happen again and again. It's more like *The Butterfly Effect* or *Cloud Atlas*, where the next cycle is heavily influenced by what happened in the last cycle.

If we look back at ourselves 100,000 years ago, our ancestors settled the planet, bringing with them a "natural way of life" that proved especially prosperous in areas that were rich with resources. Prosperity, in those days, wasn't about material possessions, but the size and stability of one's family. Thus, across the world, fertile strips of land were home to growing populations who developed their own unique traditions. By about 30,000 years ago, our ancestors continued to live relatively peaceful lives, only occasionally having to utilize practices like mining and plant cultivation to get the resources that weren't easily available otherwise.

By 20,000 years ago, we were quickly outgrowing our ability to move around and gather needed resources without difficulty. There were too many of us. Conflicts brewed, and many of us had lost our "old culture" after thousands of years of separation from the Root of Civilization. Around 16,000 years ago, at least one such conflict resulted in a mass migration away from the densely populated regions of southern Asia.

Meanwhile, something different was brewing at the Root of Civilization. About 20,000 years ago, at least two distinct genetic populations actually converged – coming together instead of diverging as other populations were doing at the time. In doing so, they brought together the knowledge of East Africa's Nilotic people and the experiences (or "wisdom") of a migration had recently traveled across Asia.

Then, about 15,000 years ago, this consolidated community traveled north, first settling in the Levant (where, upon coming together with a local population, they became the Natufians), then India (where they did the same), then China (ditto), Japan, Australia, the Pacific Islands, all the way into the Americas.

Everywhere they went, they introduced revolutionary innovations and initiated major cultural transitions. Wherever they went, we can find their signatures in the artwork, mythology, theology, technology, traditions, and monuments of the world's ancient civilizations.

The most important thing to keep in mind is that change does not imply progress. For example, small villages do tend to become large towns, and then those large towns become urban cities, which sometimes become massive states containing multiples cities and towns. But this has more to do with increases in population and decreases in available resources (which create new needs), than with "new" discoveries."

Life didn't become "better" because of metallurgy or agriculture…those two technologies were simply responses to a changing set of circumstances. Yet once they took root and became popular approaches to solving those problems, they would forever change the face of civilization.

And the Anu People who introduced these changes didn't just come once. Repeatedly, new influxes of migrants made their way into local communities (across the world), introducing new solutions to changing problems.

After all, the world was increasingly becoming a difficult place to live. Many of the changes we associate with modern civilization were accompanied by significant problems. Hunter-gatherer communities that grew large (which was a good thing) faced difficulty feeding all their people through traditional methods (which was bad).

Thus, we "enhanced" our existing practices of plant management, and transitioned communities into early agriculture and animal domestication. People now had plenty of food (which was good), but these practices led to increased malnutrition, disease, and corruption (which was bad).

WHY CORRUPTION?

Anytime a community has a surplus of a needed resource, they're likely to find these resources controlled by some sort of de facto leadership. In any species, a small percentage of the population becomes "exploiters," who attempt to get more out of the society than what they put in.* Next thing you know, you've got corruption in high places. The Original People (that is, the people who settled the globe 100,000 years ago and who survive now as the world's DBP) wouldn't tolerate such personalities, but the urban complexes of the ancient world needed management, so these issues became commonplace.

For example, we didn't always "own" things. We shared resources. Most DBP don't hoard possessions like we do. If they have two shirts, they give one away. The idea of property ownership came with the advent of animal domestication (gotta know whose cattle those

---

* For more on this, refer back to *The Science of Self, Volume One.*

WHEN THE WORLD WAS BLACK

> **DID YOU KNOW?**
>
> There are very few instances of prehistoric warfare before the advent of agriculture (which allows a community to support a standing military).
>
> One exception, known as Cemetery 117, is a 14,000-year-old site near the Egypt-Sudan border where 59 skeletons are buried together, many with arrowpoints or spearheads in them. This site is associated with a time when this particularly area went through an ecological crisis and people were struggling to survive.[517]
>
> These may have been the conditions that originally prompted the first Anu people to leave, perhaps to prevent or circumvent similar problems elsewhere in the world.

are!). But this led to disparities in ownership (also discouraged among the Original People, but to be expected in a sedentary urban population). This quickly led to theft, property disputes, and an increasing divide between the well-off and the not-so-well-off.

By 7,000 years ago, things had gotten bad. Not only had all the issues above become worse with time, the rapid desertification of North Africa and the Near East pushed many people to the brink of desperation. Until this time, there's very little evidence of human-vs.-human warfare.

By 6,000 years ago, the conditions in the Near East were ten times worse than they had been at Cemetery 117. This is the period that Steve Taylor describes in *The Fall: The Evidence for a Golden Age, 6,000 Years of Insanity, and the Dawning of a New Era.* Taylor writes:

> From around 4000 BCE onwards a new spirit of suffering and turmoil enters human history. It is now – and only now – that a "horrifying sense of sin" becomes manifest in human affairs. At this point, it seems, a completely new type of human being comes into existence, with a completely different way of relating to the world and to other human beings. In Riane Eisler's words, now comes "the great change – a change so great, indeed, that nothing in all we know of human cultural evolution is comparable in magnitude."
>
> It wasn't completely out of the blue. There had been warning signs for the past 1,000 years or so – occasional outbreaks of social violence around the Middle East and Anatolia, linked to temporary episodes of drought and aridity.[518]

Even with all of the Anu People's repeated "updates," civilization was destined for collapse. Throughout this book, you've seen hints of how and when it happened.

THE REBIRTH

What will it take to fix it? We've seen hints of that as well. When we look at the history of our ancestors, we can clearly identify several phases of cultural solidarity:

❑ When the Original People came together (after separating) to outperform and eventually outlast other hominids. (200+ kya)

- When the Original people came together (after separating) to exit Africa. (c. 130 kya)
- When the Original people came together (after separating) to conquer the Neanderthals and expand their cultural complex across Europe and Northern Asia. (c. 50 kya)
- When the Original people came together (after separating) to become the Anu People who "re-civilized" the world. (c. 20kya)

So here we are, 20,000 years after the ancestors of Anu People first began coming together. Since then, we are again divided. We are again at odds with each other. We are again unaware of each other's struggles and accomplishments.

And we again have the opportunity to get to know each other, to help devise solutions for each other's problems, and to come together in solidarity to overcome the latest threat to our survival. In order to do so, we'll need the background knowledge provided in this book, but also an understanding of what the Original People of the world all have in common, as well as a complete and thorough understanding of how the latest threat against us came to be and why it has nearly succeeded.

Our goal, as always, is not simply to tell the story of the past, but to draw lessons from it. In order to regain what we've lost, we have to know exactly what we lost, how we built it in the first place, and – perhaps most importantly – how exactly we lost it. In Volume Four, we'll explore this story in depth.

FIJI

Appendix

ALL THE STUFF THAT DIDN'T FIT

Thought we covered everything? Nah, there's always more! In all of our books, we do our best to fill the Appendix with resources that might be useful throughout the course of your reading, or additional essays and reference materials to consult when you're not reading the text in a linear order. So here's all the stuff that didn't fit anywhere else in Part Two!

THE SCIENCE OF STONE MONUMENTS

Whether we're talking about mounds, megaliths, or Mesoamerican pyramids, Anu people seem to have done something very different from their ancestors. Whereas the Original People typically went among more recent arrivals of settlers and instructed them on how to become a farming community, or some other needed knowledge, with almost no recognition for their contribution – Anu people, on the other hand, expected proper credit and "all praise due". Thus those menhirs, dolmens, earthworks, and stone pyramids were always attributed to somebody. They were built by many, but credited to a select few.

Kurt Mendelssohn described these labors as collective efforts by communities to construct "symbols of greatness." At first, the purpose of building fantastically large structures (such as the earliest stone circles) may have been to unite the people in establishing monuments of their society's greatness. Later monuments (such as the pyramids of Egypt) also united the people through a common purpose, while at the same time reinforcing the social hierarchy of the ruling class.[519]

But it's not as if Anu people came expecting tribute, having done nothing to deserve it. They certainly deserved it. When the Younger Dryas began making life harder for people living hunter-gatherer lifestyles, the competition for resources became a problem. The advent of agriculture presented a solution. And people went around teaching it. DBP people had always possessed this knowledge, so they occasionally talk recent arrivals how to farm – even when the DBP didn't farm themselves. But DBP people didn't seek to create social orders, or establish any sort of hierarchy of government. They only want to persist as a community. They became revered (unintentionally) but what they really wanted was to be able to reproduce and maintain their claim on the lands they occupied. Instead, they often became the subject of fanciful myth and amazing art, while – as a human community – they were driven to near extinction.

When Anu people emerged between 20 to 15,000 years ago, they quickly began spreading the knowledge of agriculture. Yet Anu people may have either consciously decided NOT to go the way of the DBP, or they simply saw a need to establish a different kind of social order wherever they went. Whatever their motives, they made themselves cultural leaders, rulers, priest-kings, and god-kings. Perhaps it wasn't even their idea but the idea of the indigenous populations they came to. After all, unlike the DBP, they weren't the "old heads," they were the "new kids." And the new kids were treated like gods, while the old heads may have been added to the pantheon for nostalgia's sake.

But what did the Anu people introduce to receive so much acclaim and status? Essentially, they introduced an entire cultural complex, effectively changing the "whole way of life" for most of the people they influence. Think about it: From foraging to farming, from everybody can do anything to specialization of social roles, from stone tools to metal-working, from hunting to animal domestication, from animism to a God-King incarnate, from community meetings to government arbitration, from no ownership to property rights, from oral tradition to written records, from barter and trade to an international market economy, from calabash gourds to an entire ceramic industry. All of these are sweeping changes. They're not necessarily "improvements," but they're definitely sweeping changes that can change an individual's whole way of life.

THE SCIENCE BEHIND THE STONES

According to archaeologist Mike Pearson, the evidence suggests that "Stonehenge was just one-half of a larger complex." He got that part right, but when asked what was all this actually *for*, he gave the lame answer we've all heard before about monuments like this: "The village was probably built as a religious center, presumably for people who worshiped the sun."

So you mean to tell me that these people – who were smart enough to build a massive astronomical calendar out of wood and stone – were still somehow primitive enough to think the Sun had to be *worshipped?*

As we've discussed before, we didn't *worship* the Sun. We measured it, tracked it, and created myths and monuments to record those observations for future generations. And evidence suggests that the Stonehenge complex didn't have year-round inhabitants, and was probably a summer or winter event center, just like the megalithic circle in Nabta Playa, which we'll discuss in a minute.

In fact, the nearby Woodhenge arrangement was aligned with winter solstice sunrise, while the giant stone monument at Stonehenge frames the winter solstice sunset. When the farming was done, we came together at the retreat, buried our dead, held a ceremony, and made plans for the next harvest (thanks to the calendar and other resources on site). But think of it like a convention more than a funeral, because the evidence doesn't suggest we saw death in sad, morbid terms like we do now. In fact, there's evidence we kicked it pretty hard at Stonehenge. Like Nabta Playa, debris of broken pots, jars and animal bones was everywhere, suggesting large feasting and wild parties.[520]

It makes perfect sense that the builders were Black. How else could you explain the similarity of form and function between Stonehenge and Nabta Playa any of three dozen other sites that looked and worked the same way. And these circles did more than calculate the cycles of the heavens and earth. Some scholars say these sites were purposely built along specific lines on the Earth's electromagnetic grid, providing Original people with increased access to the Earth's energy. Perhaps they were like the world's first free Wi-Fi hotspots?

Some have theorized that the original wooden "casing" around Stonehenge and the mud walls built around European dolmens are clues that the earliest megalithic constructions were actually well-built structures for habitation. Basically, the standing stones were the corner stones or support pillars and the original walls and roofing may have been made of some organic material that hasn't survived. It's quite possible, since the earliest dwellings in Paleolithic Europe were constructions of stone, mud, wood, and animal skins.

Another theory has proposed that the very earliest megaliths were single standing pillars that represented the male counterpart to the female principle represented by the Venus figurines of the same period. That is, these stone phallic symbols, known as menhirs when they are erected (ahem) to stand alone, were precursors to Ancient

Egypt's obelisks. It is possible these massive stone pillars were recycled to form later constructions like Stonehenge. We'll explain this in a minute.

One megalithic site in southern Portugal revealed that there were many reasons behind the stones they used:

As different rocks had different appearances and physical characteristics it is suggested that they were chosen according to a pre-conceived design. In addition, the locations of the sites of origin of the different material represents main celestial directions from the megaliths. This makes it likely that the monuments also represent certain symbolic values associated with the landscape and certain cosmologies.[521]

In other words, some stones were chosen according to a pre-conceived "look" but the source location was also critical. The points of origin for these stones in these graves corresponded to the main astronomical paths from the megaliths. According to Philine Kalb, "This makes it likely that the monuments also represent certain symbolic values associated with the landscape and certain cosmologies."[522]

Archaeologist Gabriel Cooney calls such sites "a transported landscape in which structural elements were extracted, carried and re-assembled to link together physically places that had been distant."[523] Fittingly, stones transported over long distances to build megaliths have been described as "pieces of places."[524] Thus, it is no surprise that the legend of Stonehenge's construction traces its stones (and its builders) back to Africa.

Sergi traced the megaliths back to the "brown" Mediterranean race of East Africa:

As regards megalithic and sepulchral monuments in general, of various forms, after studying their construction and diffusion throughout the Mediterranean, on the North African coast, including Egypt, and in various parts of Europe, I am convinced

---

* Anu people erected Menhirs (phallic pillars) and Menatols (hole in a rock, representing the female and used in rebirthing ceremonies), across Africa, the Near East, Arabia, India, the Pacific Islands, and Europe (particularly at its coasts).

that they owe their origin to a stock which I have called Mediterranean, but which is of African origin. The term "Mediterranean," as I use it, has not the extension given to it by French anthropologists, and by those who follow Miller's classification. I understand by it all those primitive peoples who have occupied the basin of the Mediterranean, and have such fundamental physical characters in common as to enable us to assign to them a single place of origin, which must be in east Africa and to the north of the Equator.[525]

With this in consideration, it's also no surprise that – in the absence of the Anu people who originally led the assembly of these "sacred" monuments – local populations scrambled to reassemble new monuments from the pieces of old ones.

MEGALITH RECYCLING

When archaeologist C.T. Le Roux was doing restoration work on a capstone at a tomb of Gavrinis, located on an island off the Brittany coast, he discovered the rock fit perfectly with the capstone of the Table des Marchands, another famous megalithic monument two and a half away. This was impressive enough, since the piece at Gavrinis weighed about 20 tons and had to be transported across several waterways. But Le Roux soon found a third piece used as a capstone on another monument nearby. Together, the three capstones originally formed a much older, much more massive stele 46 feet high and 12 feet wide. The total stele would've weighed about 100 tons!

Nature writer Paul Bahn proposed that this stele once stood near an even larger stele called Grand Menhir Brise or "er-Grah," which is also broken into pieces. Bahn argued that the period of megalithic tomb building, began about 5,000 years ago but was preceded by a period when larger, decorated stelae were erected. These stelae were later pulled down and broken up for use in constructing tombs.

It's possible that the Anu people who brought agriculture to Europe had originally introduced the stelae, and that their monuments (or scientific instruments?) were torn down by later people, either in homage, to entomb the Anu torch-bearers, or in sacrilege.[526] Or, yet another possibility: They were struggling to reproduce Anu culture – given its "divine" qualities – using whatever these people had left behind.

This is why the 12th century writer, Geoffrey of Monmouth, says in his work *History of the Kings of Britain* that tall men from Africa built a stone circle in Ireland that was later transported to England under the direction of the famed "magician" Merlin.

According to legend, when Merlin explains to the king why it is necessary to transport these stones, he says:

> Laugh not so lightly, King, for not lightly are these words spoken. For in these stones is a mystery, and a healing virtue against many ailments. Giants of old did carry them from the furthest ends of Africa and did set them up in Ireland what time they did inhabit therein. And unto this end they did it, that they might make them baths therein whensoever they ailed of any malady, for they did wash the stones and pour forth the water into the baths, whereby they that were sick were made whole. Moreover, they did mix confections of herbs with the water, whereby they that were wounded had healing, for not a stone is there that lacketh in virtue of [healing].[527]

WAVES OF BUILDERS

What we do know is that the megaliths were not built all at once but by waves of builders. While dating stone structures is always a difficult task, evidence from France, Scandinavia, and Iberia suggests that currently accepted patterns of dates suggest that were was an "event-like tempo to the construction of megalithic monuments, with large numbers being built within relatively short periods of time." That is, there were likely waves of builders moving though Europe, during whose stay megalith construction took off.[528]

In 2010, *USA Today* reported on findings that suggested these megaliths were tombs for the people who introduced their construction:

> Rather than a single "megalithic" culture stretching across Europe, the outburst of mound tombs likely represents an idea reaching local cultures, he suggests, which then "stopped and started" across the centuries. "One big implication is the realization that the people buried in this fashion represent only a small fraction of the people who were alive then," Scarre says. "Until the Roman era, thoughtful burial of the dead may have been a rare thing in this part of Europe."[529]

MEGALITHS OUTSIDE EUROPE

Where did these builders come from? Well, we know that circular stone formations like those in Europe are found on remote hilltops and valleys throughout Saudi Arabia. The rings are 15 to 300 feet in diameter and are surrounded by stone walls a foot or two tall. Some of the rings have "tails" that stretch out for hundreds of meters.[530]

South Arabia may be a step in the right direction, but let's look a little further and follow the Afro-Asiatic people to where they come from. This first brings us to North Africa, where some of the earliest megalithic sites can be found. According to T.E. Peet's *Rough Stone Monuments and their Builders*:

> North Africa is a great stronghold of the megalithic civilization, indeed it is thought by some that it is the area in which megalithic building originated. Morocco, Tunis, Algeria, and Tripoli all abound in dolmens and other monuments. Even in the Nile Valley they occur, for what looks like a dolmen surrounded by a circle was discovered by de Morgan in the desert near Edfu, and Wilson and Felkin describe a number of simple dolmens which exist near Ladò in the Sudan.[531]

In the early 80s, archaeologists made several discoveries of megalithic structures in the central Sahara as well. These included V-shaped monuments, spiral and geometric-line carvings, cup-and-ring markings like those prevalent in northern Europe, and "axle-type" monuments (which consist of a central hub with two straight projecting arms) like those found in Malta and other Near Eastern sites.[532]

This brings us to the site we mentioned earlier, Nabta Playa. Nabta Playa is situated in the Western Desert of Egypt, near the Sahara, and was built by people who – as we've noted earlier – were undeniably Black.

To the west, the Mzora stone ring of Morocco is situated about 27 kilometers from the ruins of an ancient city known as Lixus. Plutarch, in the first century AD, may have referred to Mzora in his *Life of Sertorius* as the tomb of the giant Antaeus who was killed by Hercules. Mzora originally had 175 stones in a circular formation, the tallest of which was over 15 feet tall. It's not a perfect circle, but elliptical like the shape of the Earth (and the Nabta Playa circle).

We can tell Mzora was built by the same culture that built the European megaliths because it's constructed using the same Pythagorean right-angled triangle used in over 30 British stone ellipses, including the Sands of Forvie and Daviot Rings.

And according to James Watt Mavor, at least seven of the Mzora stones mark sunrises and sunsets of the winter and summer solstices and the equinoxes. The trail doesn't stop there. If we look further south, we're less likely to find massive stone industries because of the dense tropical environment. Yet what we find might still surprise us. As Elizabeth Isichei reports in *A History of African Societies to 1870*:

> In some parts of Africa megaliths survive which are somewhat reminiscent of Stonehenge. Hundreds of them are to be found in the borderland between Cameroon and Central African Republic.

They are thought to be memorials, but contain no human remains, and were made by cultivators during the first millennium BCE. That they had the energy and resources to cut, transport and erect stones so large that they posed a danger to modern excavators shows the strength the religious or other beliefs which inspired them. It also reflects a culture which could afford this type of extravagance.[533]

These include the Wassu stone circles of Gambia and the Bouar megaliths of the Central African Republic. The Bouar megaliths are over 7,400 years old. The *UNESCO General History of Africa* notes:

> We cannot be certain where the Bouar megaliths should be placed in the Neolithic period but the culture which erected them can at least be said to be contemporary with the Neolithic.[534]

In other words, the culture who built these monuments was probably the same culture who erected megaliths during the Neolithic transition everywhere else.

Because stone formations won't survive well in tropical soil, especially without the protection afforded to European historical sites, we have no idea how much more has been lost to time, the elements, and foreign vandalism. Even Stonehenge is a fractured shell of what it once was, thanks to later Europeans hacking away pieces of the stones as desired.[535]

But the existence of such ancient megalithic circles throughout Africa is clear evidence that they are another common feature of Anu civilization throughout the Neolithic world, and were built by the same people. As we look to the east, there are megaliths in Ethiopia that link with similar sites in Arabia. This could be the pathway by which megalith-building reached southern India.

Ancient stone circles have even been found in Hokkaido, Japan. There's even one in the Amazon![536] J. Macmillan Brown describes "a megalithic track through Southern Europe and Asia" that reaches well into the Pacific Islands:

> The great stones are scattered sparsely along the countries on the northern shore of the Mediterranean and the Black Sea, through Syria, Armenia and Irania, along the Persian Gulf, through Northern India, over the Khasi and Naga Hills into Burmah, thence along the Malay Peninsula into Sumatra and Java.[537]

It's a good thing we know who laid this ancient path. Otherwise I can imagine that we'd be quite confused.

COON'S CONFUSION

Carleton Coon, in his 1933 work *The Races of Europe*, appears to have suffered from this sort of confusion. He says that a long-headed race of Mediterranean people came into Europe, teaching the "Neolithic manner of living" which "differs radically from that of Palaeolithic and Mesolithic man, since it involves the production of food by agriculture and animal husbandry." These people, Coon says, came from the Near East and demonstrated a "control over nature."

Some of them sailed into Europe via the Danube River, others migrated along fertile stretches of land, and still others sailed the coasts. Coon attempts to say these people were white, but it just doesn't make sense. First, he says there was a "short-statured" group of Mediterraneans that fit the DBP profile. Coon continues, making things difficult for himself:

> The other half of the Neolithic Mediterranean race is noted for tall stature and a more extremely dolichocephalic [long-headed] skull form. This variety was found in East Africa; it was also common in early Mesopotamia and Iran, while the Egyptians belonged more nearly to the smaller Mediterranean variety. This tall, longer-headed half of the race is longer faced, narrower nosed, and less delicate in bony structure than the other. It also seems to fall closer to such possible prototypes as Galley Hill and Combe Capelle from the Palaeolithic.

> This tall branch is again sub-divided. One sub-branch, with moderate vault and face heights, travelled, in all likelihood, by sea from the eastern Mediterranean to Gibraltar, around Spain, and up to western France, Britain, and Scandinavia. In the last two countries, and especially in the British Isles, it contributed an important element to the population. It is not easy to find the prototype of this Megalithic group; some of the Mesopotamians seem to have been very close to it metrically, and some East Africans as well; we shall later find evidence of it on the shores of the Black Sea. For the moment we can only postulate that it came from some as yet unidentified part of southwestern Asia, southeastern Europe, or northeastern Africa.

Yet, somehow, these people were white? Seriously?

QUESTIONS TO CONSIDER

Some of these megaliths defy explanation. For example, the obelisk at Luxor (in Egypt) weighs more than 400 tons. How did we quarry and transport THAT? And how about the polished black granite walls of the King's Chamber in the Great Pyramid and the hollowed-out sarcophagus of chocolate-colored granite in the same room? These granites are much harder than limestone and even harder than the copper saws and drills that the Egyptian stoneworkers had at their disposal. So, how did they work their granite?

In 1999, Denys Stocks tested the effectiveness of copper tools on

Egyptian granite. In one test, workmen successfully used a large copper saw to cut a slot 1 inch deep and 3 feet long. But it took 14 hours![538] According to C. Dunn in *The Giza Pyramid*, drill marks on the sides of the sarcophagus in the King's Chamber imply that Egyptian drills worked about 500 times faster than possible with the toughest modern drills!

Also, how did they fit their blocks together so well? As we noted in our chapter on the Andes, there is considerable evidence for "prefabrication" according to a pre-designed template. But how do you giant rocks to a template? We're not saying it required spaceman laser beams or anything, because all the evidence points directly back to man, but what did these men know?

If you research the kind of science they used simply to level the land for the pyramids, it's amazing what they could do with some wood, some water, and a whole lot of mathematics. The monuments in the Americas are no different. I can only imagine how the Black builders of ancient Peru were able to transport a massive stone "sheet" all the way from the beach, up and down miles of hills and valleys, only to ultimately put it underneath a structure so that no one could see it!

For more on megaliths, you can visit Wikipedia and check out the following topics: menhirs, megalith, tumulus, standing stone, list of megalithic sites, and dolmen.

THE ANU LANGUAGE

Throughout the ancient world, Anu people came and introduced a common culture, but left behind different languages. Many of these languages can be connected to the Afro-Asiatic language family, but not all. Why?

When different branches of Anu people went to different parts of the world, they brought variants of this ancestral language that had changed significantly over the course of their travels. When linguists can identify connections between language families, they can trace them back to a common origin, a proto-language that spawned Afro-Asiatic as well several other closely related language families. Linguists call this ancestral language family Nostratic, but we prefer to call it Anu.

In *Black Athena*, Martin Bernal argues that Nostratic dispersed from Africa,[539] while S.O.Y. Keita proposes that Afro-Asiatic and Nostratic emerged as sibling language groups in Northeast Africa.[540] Other linguists, even those who don't accept the Nostratic theory, will admit that there was some early connection between Afro-Asiatic, Elamite, and Dravidian, which is essentially the baseline for the Nostratic theory.[541]

Christopher Ehret dates the origins of proto-Afro-Asiatic to around 15,000 years ago in Northeast Africa, right before the Mushabians carried this language into the Near East.[542] Recent studies suggest that Afro-Asiatic itself may be about 11,000 years old, but its Anu root is 15,000 years old.[543]

WHAT ABOUT WRITTEN LANGUAGE?

In a book titled *African Origins*, we show how many of the world's written languages derive from Original People. While the people of the world have spoken different languages for as long as there have been different communities on the planet, written language is a relatively recent invention. Throughout Africa, the Near East, India, Europe, and a few other places, we can trace back the written scripts to Anu people and their descendants. Depending on where you connect the dots, they all kind of look alike at some point or in some way.

Beyond this part of the world, in China, Japan, and Mesoamerica, the writing looks quite different. Yet, even in these areas, there is evidence that Anu migrants significantly influenced the emergence of pictographic writing that evolved to be quite different from the scripts of the Near East and Europe. Of course, the earliest written marks are much older than any Anu language that we know of. Perhaps the first written marks predate the emergence of both Anu and Mongoloid people, and each community carried their own version of this ancestral script wherever they went, resulting in a very different evolution of written language in the places they went.

It certainly looks like this is the case for the Anu side of things. At Wadi Mataha, a site in Jordan that marks the transition from Kebaran to Natufian, there's evidence suggesting the 'emerging territoriality' of Natufian communities. Ofer Bar-Yosef and Anna Belfer-Cohen suggest that the marking of objects isn't simply the origin of written language as we know it.[544] Instead, they propose that these simple marks reflect a "cognitive, stylistic or symbolic grammar common to all late Pleistocene hunter-gatherers rather than a system of symbols for the storage or projection of information restricted solely to the Natufian world." In other words, there was a written language of symbols that Anu people could use and understand across the Near East (and possibly beyond) long before the advent of Egyptian hieroglyphics or Sumerian cuneiform.

This language must have been symbolic, but was it made up of representational pictures, or simply lines and dots that only our enlightened ancestors could decode? As we discuss in the Appendix to this series, we had lines and dots before anything else, but we were also carving pictographs or rocks and cave walls more than 40,000 years ago. So who knows? I'm leaning towards the idea that the first written language was a binary code. Perhaps, some time during my life time, somebody will develop a software program to process all the lines and dots in some prehistoric rock-carving, and the end result will produce a sentence we can understand. If they can decode DNA, I'm sure they can make sense out of the marks found on the walls of Daraki-Chattan Cave in India or on the Lebombo Bone of Southern Africa.

UNEXPECTED GENES IN EARLY AMERICA

Most Native Americans descend from a small number of DNA lineages. Over 90% of the indigenous people of the Americas fall into the A, B, C, and D mtDNA haplogroups. A, C and D also occur in Siberian peoples, suggesting that these people took the land route into the Americas. But the B lineage isn't found anywhere near this route, although it is found elsewhere in southern Asia, suggesting that this group took the sea route into the Americas.[545]

That's difficult enough for most historians, who want to deny anything beyond a single migration by land. But then there's another mysterious piece to this puzzle: Haplogroup X. It's not found in Northeast Asia OR Southeast Asia OR the Pacific Islands. It's found in Europe, the Near East, and Africa.

Haplogroup X is not common throughout the Americas, but it's heavy in some Native people of the Northeast, like the Algonquians, the Ojibwa, the Sioux, the Navajo, as well as some people in Brazil. The only other place on earth where X is still found at these levels is among the Druze of northern Israel and Lebanon. The Druze may have been a "genetic refugium" where much older ancestral populations – like the Egyptians and other Anu-speaking people – developed a long-standing community.[546]

The X lineage originated by splitting off from the N lineage somewhere near the root of civilization (in Northeast Africa or the Near East) around 30,000 years ago. X split into two main branches about 20,000 years ago. One branch of X (X1) remained at the root, and is now found throughout North Africa, East Africa and the

Near East. X2, on the other hand, traveled far and wide. It is found in North Africa, Europe, the Near East, Central Asia, and North America

According to Nicholas Wade, X reached India before it "participated in two migrations" beginning around 16,000 years ago. One went west into Europe, while another "joined the expansion" into Central Asia and Siberia.[547]

At least one of these branches arrived in northeastern North America 12,000 years ago. Since X is only 1200 years old in the northwest (Washington State), it suggests that X traveled across the Atlantic Ocean, from Europe into North America. Because X is originally associated with Anu (Near Eastern and African) populations, it's possibly that Haplogroup X represents an "escort" population that accompanied the Mongoloid migrations into the Americas. (See Part Two) This could also explain why Solutrean technology "disappears" from Europe right before it pops up in North America.[548]

THE SHAWNEE MIGRATION MYTH

The Shawnee people of the Eastern U.S. are one of the several Native American Nations to describe their migration in myth, but they are unique because they say they came from the east. Like other Algonquin creation myths, they say their ancestors originated in a different world – an island balanced on the back of a giant turtle – and traveled to this one. But the Shawnee provide a few more details than fellow Algonquians like the Ojibwas:

> When the first people were on the island, they could see nothing but water, which they did not know how to cross. They prayed for aid and were miraculously transported across the water. The Shawnees are the only Alonguin tribe whose creation story includes the passage of their ancestors over the sea, and for many years they held an annual sacrifice in thanks of the safe arrival of their ancestors to this country.[549]

Could the Shawnee – who are the southernmost people of an extensive Algonquin group of nations spread across northeastern Canada and the U.S. – be describing their journey across the Atlantic Ocean? And what kind of "miracle" brought them over?

THE NA-DENE LANGUAGE FAMILY

According to Joseph Greenberg's controversial classification of the languages of Native North America, Na-Dené (including Tlingit, Eyak and Athabaskan, and possibly Haida). Merritt Ruhlen claims the Na-Dene migration occurred 6,000 to 8,000 years ago, placing it around five thousand years after the previous migration into the Americas by the people who introduced the Amerind languages. Ruhlen says the Na-Dené speakers may have arrived in boats, initially settling near the Pacific Northwestern coast of Canada.

Who were these people? The Na-Dene languages may have been spoken by an Anu community that seems to have trailed the first exodus from Siberia/Central Asia into the Americas. They too, departed from this region, but also appear to have utilized water routes to get to the Americas.

These Black people quite likely became the cultural icons who are honored in the artwork, mythology, and rituals of Na-Dene speakers. This is the cultural evidence that the people who introduced the Na-Dene languages (not necessarily the people who speak them now) were a Black people. Na-Dene speakers include the Tlingit, Eyak, Athabaskan, and Haida communities. The Haida's linguistic links are not as clear because the original Haida population (and thus its original language) didn't descend from the same base population as the bulk of Tlingit, Eyak and Athabaskan people. You see, the majority of these people descend from the same base population that left Central Asia about 14,000 years ago. They only speak Na-Dene languages because of the Na-Dene migration. The Black people who introduced the Na-Dene languages were highly influential in those communities.

We have more linguistic traces of this migration than genetic traces. In other words, cultural diffusion more than demic diffusion. In other words, a few Black people spread their ideas far and wide, but didn't have a bunch of children.

"If you want to lay your stake on immortality, have children and/or teach." – The Science of Self, Vol. One

The linguistic evidence suggests that Na-Dene was first spoken by a branch of Black people who migrated into Central Asia or Siberia .

You see, Na-Dene is related to Yeniseian, a language family from Siberia, as well as the development of the Sino-Tibetan family of East Asia. That makes sense if you associate Na-Dene with people who began in Central Asia. But Na-Dene also related to several other language families that occur in unexpected places. As part of the larger Dené–Caucasian language family, the people who introduced Na-Dene are related linguistically (and culturally) to:

❑ the people who introduced Basque (and other Vasconic languages, such as Iberian) to Spain,

❑ the people who introduced the North Caucasian languages, which we will associate with Anu military communities in Volume Four,

❒ as well as possible connections with the speakers of Tyrsenian, a language family of pre-Hellenic people living in Greece and the Aegean (including some connections with the Minoans) before Greek took over.

There are even some links to the languages of the Sumerians.[550] Linguist Morris Swadesh has argued that, in addition to the above, there are many other language families that are closely connected to this community. Swadesh says these include Uralic, Altaic, Japanese, Eskimo-Aleut, Dravidian, and Austronesian. This constitutes further linguistic support for the Anu community and their ancient scope of influence. The Na-Dene languages may be evidence of one of the American arms of this influence.

And there is some genetic evidence for Anu people in this unlikely end of the Americas. For example, the Na Dené languages are associated with Native Americans who carry the Anu Haplogroup X.[551] There are also smaller clues, like two genetic markers from the Rhesus System, Cde(r') and cdE(ry), which are common among the Na-Dene and neighboring populations, but not elsewhere in America. These markers are found among the Basques and several populations in Asia, Arabia, and Africa. According to James Guthrie:

> Cde(r'), characteristic of South India, reaches high frequencies among the Chamula, Tarascans, and certain Mayans, with lower frequencies among the Seminoles and various Chibchans. In populations for whom we have HLA data, Cde was noted among the Aymarans, Quechuans, Nahua, Trio, and Navajo. CdE(ry) has a similar distribution, being prominent in the Otomí sample, with lower levels among Tarascans, certain Mayans, the Chamula, and the Central Amerind composite. It is more characteristic of Arabia than of India, and apparently is not present in South America.

Guthrie suggests that these genes reached South and Central America through a trans-Pacific migration from East Asia (or India via Southeast Asia). In other words, these genetic markers, found among Na-Dene speakers in the Americas and among related linguistic communities in Europe and Asia, may be indicators of ancient Anu migrations.

But the Na-Dene languages dispersed from Siberia long after Anu people would have arrived there, which suggests these people may have developed a new cultural complex, significantly different from the traditional Anu Cultural Complex associated with populations that remained closer to tropical environments. The pre-existing culture and climate of Central Asia could have been what gave rise to the shamanic culture spread by Na-Dene speakers in the Americas.

WORLD FREQUENCIES (%) OF AFRO-ASIATIC HLAS

ive America groups/composites underlined)

A*32		A*30	
Samoa	36.4	Samoa	26.0
Tuareg	15.8	San	23.5
Honshu	12.0	Central Bantu	21.3
Mapuche	9.0	Sardinia	16.3
Sardinia	8.3	Ba Aka	12.6
Punjab	6.8	Ibo	10.7
Oyampí	6.6	Basque	8.9
C Amerind	6.5	Navajo	8.5
Khoisan	6.5	Saudi Arabia	6.6

RLD FREQUENCIES (%) OF "SOUTHERN ASIAN" HLAS
ve American groups/composites underlined)

	A*10		B*13		B*22	
28.9	Australia	30.6	Australia	20.9	Melanesia	32.3
28.7	Fiji	17.0	New Guinea	18.5	Polynesia	29.6
28.5	Ainu	16.9	Uzbekistan	11.8	New Guinea	26.8
26.7	Uzbekistan	15.9	China	11.1	Australia	25.0
22.8	Pakistan	15.7	Thailand	9.8	NW Eskimo	12.2
22.6	Khoi	14.7	Melanesia	9.1	Micronesia	8.8
20.2	New Guinea	14.5	Samoan outliers	7.6	Korea	7.6
19.7	Melanesia	14.4	Lebanon	7.4	Japan	7.5
19.0	Philippines	13.0	Bali	7.1	Tibet	7.5
16.1	Polynesia	13.0	Russia	5.9	North China	7.2

OTHER GENETIC MARKERS

There are several mysterious DNA strains among Native American populations, all pointing to Black ancestry. For example, the Cherokee have some mysterious pre-Columbian DNA in their gene pool.

The Cherokee are genetically diverse* and their lineages suggest that they may, at least in part, have migrated to the American Southeast from Mesoamerica. They are also genetically very close to the Nahua people of the American southwest, which could mean they first passed through the Southwest. But Cherokees also have Haplogroup U, which has been matched to the Middle East, and Cherokee levels of haplogroup T (26.9%) are close to those in Egypt (25%), one of the only lands where T remains a major lineage, three times greater than the levels found in Europe.[552]

What does this mean? Where did the Cherokee ORIGINALLY come from? This is where the study of HLAs has been especially enlightening. Both the Cherokee and Eastern Mayas have Afro-Asiatic and southern Asian HLAs. One HLA, known as A*33, came from the Near East via Southeast Asia and is the most important "non-Indian" allele in the Cherokee, Eastern Maya, Quechan, and Aymaran populations.

Other genetic studies have found that the Cherokee were closely related to Hokan speakers of the American southwest, especially the Diegueño of California, in a cluster connecting the Cherokee, Diegueño, Maricopa, Nahua, Pima, Papago, and Zuni people. Barry Fell, author of *America B.C.* believed the ancient Hohokam people of the American southwest came from the Middle East and North Africa, where they had perfected adobe construction and canal irrigation of crops. Fell pointed to the parallels between Pima and Papago and Berber languages. This could explain why Padre Francisco Garcés saw "dark" people at Zuni in 1775, said by a native informant to have been "the original inhabitants."[553]

It's reasonable to think that some of these people could have been Anu. The Uto-Aztecan language family is found almost entirely in the Western United States and Mexico and includes Ute, Hopi, Nahuatl, and Shoshone. In fact, the name "Arizona" is a Uto-Aztecan word, meaning "little spring" in the Tohono O'odham

---

* Unfortunately the genetic data on other people who were historical neighbors of the Cherokee is quite limited, and doesn't allow us to form a detail portrait of how similar, or different, these people were to the Cherokee.

language. Linguist Bryan Stubbs has identified a strong Afroasiatic influence in Uto-Aztecan languages,[554] while Key has suggested a proto-Indo-European/proto-Afro-Asiatic root to Uto-Aztecan (as well as other American language families).[555]

In other words, Uto-Aztecan founders were speakers of the Anu language family. This corroborates the genetic data, in which the Afro-Asiatic HLA B*21 reaches frequencies of about 10% in samples of Uto-Aztecan speakers. Neighboring communities have similar levels of influence. Other scholars have noted Afro-Asiatic elements in the Nahuatl language.[556] This could explain why Plains Indians – who used sign language to communicate with whites who didn't speak their language – **would use the sign for "Black man"** when they spoke about the Ute.[557]

In an extensive review of the available literature, James Guthrie cites several scholars who see South America and Mesoamerica as "endpoints in a process that carried elements of Mesopotamian and Near-Eastern culture throughout the Pacific." He notes two main routes: one by way of India and Southeast Asia, and another through China, and cites dozens of studies that present lists of cultural traits that were likely transmitted along these routes. In both cases, these were Anu people carrying the Anu Cultural Complex from the root of civilization across southern Asia and the Pacific.

Guthrie establishes that indigenous people living near former urban centers in the Americas tend to have genes that are most common in the Near East, India, Africa, Northwest Europe, or Southeast Asia (including Pacific Oceania). Guthrie is clear that these genetic markers must be pre-Columbian:

> The apparently foreign HLA alleles are usually less characteristic of Spain, Portugal, or West Africa [places associated with post-Columbian contact] than of places alleged to have had earlier contact, such as Pacific Oceania, North Africa, or Southwest Asia, and in many instances other "marker" genes of modern European and West African populations are absent.

Guthrie refers to these HLAs as the "non-Indian" or atypical alleles. After careful consideration of all the HLAs Guthrie identifies, we are comfortable saying that all of these HLAs identify Black people.

This is because these genetic markers fall into only three categories: Afro-Asiatic, Southern Asian, and European. The Anu family, which we discussed earlier, includes both the Afro-Asiatic and Southern Asian (e.g. Dravidian) populations. That both these groups are Black should be obvious to readers of this book. But all of the HLAs identified as European can also be traced back to regions where Afro-Asiatic people settled in early Europe.*

In fact, they are the most noted areas of Afro-Asiatic settlement. These are the places discussed by Higgins, MacRitchie and several others who postulate that the ancestors of the Druids, the first Celts, and the ancient Britons were Black. These are also the places identified in this book as bearing early evidence of an ancient Black Anu presence. In other words, all of these "Non-Indian" HLAs point to Black people.

The following are Guthrie's Non-Indian HLA Alleles, in order of their occurrence.

Allele	%	Designation	Allele	%	Designation
B*21	10.4	Afro-Asiatic	A*33	9.6	Southern Asian
B*7	9.1	European*	A*30	8.0	Afro-Asiatic
A*32	7.9	Afro-Asiatic	B*14	7.0	Afro-Asiatic
B*12	6.9	European	A*1	6.5	Afro-Asiatic
B*22	6.4	Southern Asian	A*11	5.4	Southern Asian
A*3	4.7	European	B*8	4.5	European
A*10	4.0	Southern Asian	B*17	2.6	Afro-Asiatic
B*13	2.4	Southern Asian	A*29	2.0	Afro-Asiatic
B*18	1.9	Afro-Asiatic	B*37	0.6	Afro-Asiatic

SUMMARY FINDINGS

The following are Guthrie's summary findings:

❐ Approximately ten of the 29 HLA varieties tabulated by Cavalli-Sforza, Menozzi, and Piazza almost certainly were present in founding American populations, but they indicate predominantly southern Asian rather than northern Asian origins for the American

---

* HLAs associated with Europeans often derive from Black migrant populations. For example, Guthrie notes the connection between B*7 in Northwest Europe and North Africa, where the Tuareg and Algerian Flitta traveled the ancient amber and gold routes. A proto- form of the Tuareg's Tifinagh alphabet is found in Scandinavia, Italy, and eastern Canada, but Guthrie thinks the European variant came before the African variant, suggesting that gene flow went from Europe into North Africa. Because of the work of scholars on the Black presence in ancient Europe, we know that the African presence in northwestern Europe predated the Tuareg traders, suggesting that earlier Black populations introduced both proto-Tifinagh and B*7.

population base.

❐ As many as 18 of the HLA alleles that occur in the Western Hemisphere may have been introduced at various times after early colonization. However, these constitute only 6-7% of the total, varying from zero in some isolated South American tribes to 24% in the Nahua sample. They are concentrated in areas once occupied by urban societies and are also characteristic of certain parts of the Eastern Hemisphere that are claimed to have been in early contact with America.

❐ Three "non-Indian" alleles (B*21, A*33, B*7) are most important, each contributing about 10% of the atypical HLA total. Their presence seems to reflect an early Near Eastern influence on the American west coast (A*33), European input to eastern Eskimos (B*7), and an Afro-Asiatic influence in southwestern North America (B*21). These interpretations are supported by findings of atypical genes from other systems, especially immunoglobin, transferrin, Kell, and Rhesus.

❐ Ninety percent of American B*21 is clustered in speakers of Uto-Aztecan languages and contiguous Navajo. The Papago frequency is one of the highest in the world, comparable to the frequencies of B*21 among the North African Tuaregs and Berbers.

❐ Ninety percent of American B*21 is clustered in speakers of Uto-Aztecan languages and contiguous Navajo. The Papago frequency is one of the highest in the world, comparable to the frequencies of B*21 among the North African Tuaregs and Berbers.

❐ The distribution of A*33 seems associated with transmission of traits from the Near East through Southeast Asia and is the most important "non-Indian" allele in the Cherokee, Eastern Maya, Quechuan, and Aymaran populations.

❐ A North African or Iberian contact with the Atacama and Mapuche is indicated by the distributions of B*14 and A*1. The Atacama of northern Argentina have the highest recorded frequency of B*14, similar to the B*14 frequencies of the Berber, Iraqi, Iberian, and Irish samples. The Mapuche have the fourth highest world level of B*14 and, together with the Atacama, possess 70% of reported American B*14. These two also have the highest American levels of A*1, a characteristic of North Africans and Southwest Asians but now highest among the Irish. The Atacama also have the African FY*0 allele of the Duffy blood group, known otherwise in only one other American sample (Cayapó of Brazil).

❏ On the North American continent, HLAs characteristic of Afro-Asiatic populations are cluster in the Papago, Pima, Navajo, Cherokee, and composite Central Amerind samples. Voyages to the Gulf of California (B*21), Caribbean region, and Atlantic coasts of South America (A*30 and A*32) seem likely. The Central Amerind composite sample of 18 tribes is unique in having "non-Indian" HLAs only from the Afro-Asiatic set (B*21, A*30, and A*32).

❏ Alleles A*30 and A*32 appear near the mouths of the Amazon (Oyampí, Trio, Parakana), the Plata-Paraná (Guaraní), and the Orinoco (Warao), suggesting exploration of rivers by expeditions from the Mediterranean. The Oyampí, Parakana, and Guaraní are Tupians. The distribution of the apparently Mediterranean or Indian A*32 seems to connect Tupians with the Mapuche via river traffic. The A*30 pattern suggests Greek or Arabian influence on America and also on parts of Africa.

❏ Southern Asian HLAs seem to have come in several episodes: B*22 to western Eskimos and the other four (A*10, A*11, A*33, B*13) to the west coasts of Mexico and South America at various times, supporting claims of early Oceanic or Indonesian inputs to Ecuador and Peru, and later Oceanic, Indian, and Chinese influences on Nahua, Mayan, and Araucanian societies. Genes from systems other than HLA also indicate influence from India, Indonesia, or Arabia on the Aymaran, Quechuan, and Mayan populations as well as on various Mexican and South Andean groups for which we lack HLA data.

❏ Proposals that Indonesians reached Brazil by way of Madagascar and South Africa seem supported by the distributions of A*11, B*13, and genes from other systems found in samples from the Caingáng and Trio of the Brazilian coast. The Andean Aymara-speakers seem to have the greatest concentration of anomalous genes that might have an Indonesian source. These traits could have come by river traffic from the east or directly across the Pacific.

❏ European alleles A*3, B*7, B*8, and B*12 seem associated with migrations across Asia that continued on to the western Eskimos, Nahua, Quechua, and Araucano. All but A*3 are also important in Japan. B*7 seems also to have come from Northwest Europe to eastern Canada, where the other European HLAs are nearly absent. Both HLA and immunoglobin distributions reflect partially separate genetic heritages of the eastern and western Eskimos. The dominant atypical HLA alleles are the southern Asian B*22 in the west and the European B*7 in the east. The western Eskimos have the Asian immunoglobin type fa;b, whereas the eastern Eskimos have the European type f;b.

❑ HLA B*7, now concentrated in extreme northwestern Europe, displays unexpectedly high frequencies both in eastern Canada and in parts of North Africa where the Amber trade is thought to have introduced a Scandinavian influence. Similar rock carvings in all three places appear to confirm some degree of intercontinental commerce at about 700 BC.

❑ Distributions of "American" HLAs A*28 and A*31 suggest genetic backflow from Brazil to Africa. Both are characteristic of eastern South America, where highest world frequencies occur, but anomalously high levels appear sporadically in Africa (especially Tigre, Tuareg, Mande). More complete sampling in Africa is needed to assure that this is not a sampling artifact.

A WORKING TIMELINE OF AMERICAN MIGRATIONS

Guthrie readily accepts the ambiguities regarding genetic data, particularly as one goes further back in time. He suggests that the earliest colonization of the Americas could date back to 40,000 years ago or more, but notes that details for such early periods "are controversial and are steadily being revised." He supports the idea of "serial migrations" following the initial colonization period, culminating in a migration from Africa, via the Atlantic, between 8,000 and 6,000 BC. After this point, the Anu HLAs of Guthrie's report come to increasing significance.

The following are his notes on the evidence for migrations after this period:

> Most literature on early voyages to America is about evidence for later incursions. These seem to form clusters, probably reflecting episodes of favorable climate and economic cycles that periodically generated societies with a combination of maritime prowess and commercial aggressiveness or the need to expand into new lands. The Americas seem to have been "discovered" repeatedly and exploited to whatever degree was possible at the time. Clusters of activity listed below reflect the findings that seem best supported or most frequently advocated:

7500-3500 BC:

❑ Expansion from China through the Philippines to Indonesia and certain Pacific Islands, conveying Austronesian languages, reaching Peru and Ecuador by 3500 BC.

❑ Expansion from Japan beginning about 6000 BC, southward to certain Pacific Islands and eastward to Ecuador by 3500 BC.

❑ Oceanic trade network in place by 4000 BC, connecting Borneo, Southeast Asia, and islands of the western Pacific; in a position to reach South America.

2500-2000 BC:

☐ Trade routes developed to link Mesopotamia, Baluchistan, Afghanistan, the Indus Valley, the Arabian coast, central Asia, Indonesia, and parts of Southeast Asia. These overlapped with the Oceanic routes, allowing traits from India and the Near East to be transmitted in modified form to Southeast Asia and America.

☐ Trans-Atlantic voyages by "Pan-Atlantic" populations, both from Scandinavia to North America and from Iberia and Africa to the Caribbean region and eastern South America, extending up rivers as far as Ecuador and Peru.

☐ Increased navigation of the Caribbean, extending to the Gulf Coast and Mississippi River.

1600-1200 BC:

☐ Accelerated voyaging from India and Southwest Asia to Indonesia, Peru, and Mexico.

☐ Chinese voyages to western America.

☐ Trans-Atlantic voyages from North Africa and the Aegean region, with significant impact on the Andean societies and in northeastern North America.

800-500 BC:

☐ Indian influences on Korea, Japan, Indonesia, Colombia, Peru, and Mexico.

☐ Japanese and Chinese voyages to Mesoamerica and Northwest South America.

☐ Siberians and Chinese along coasts from Alaska to California and Mexico.

☐ Indonesians and Africans from East Africa around Africa to South America.

☐ Further voyages to American east coasts and rivers by various groups (Phoenician, Greek, Cycladic, Berber) based in North Africa.

200 BC-100 AD:

☐ Renewed trans-Atlantic excursions of multicultural populations from Iberia and North Africa, introducing apparent Greek, Berber, Celtic, Punic, Sephardic Jewish, and Roman elements. Activity may have resulted in part from the Punic wars.

400-1000 AD:

☐ Increased connections between Ecuador and Mesoamerica.

☐ Peak of interactions of Mexico with Indianized Indochina as well as with India.

☐ Backflow from the Caribbean to West Africa, about AD 500.

☐ Tupi expansion up the Amazon and Paraná River systems, circa AD 500.

- Arabian expeditions to America via both Oceans, about AD 900.
- Norse voyages to North America by AD 1000.
- More trans-Atlantic expeditions bringing Mediterranean and Aegean influences.

Much of this evidence is discussed in the extensive annotated bibliography compiled by John Sorenson and Martin Raish, titled *Pre-Columbian Contact with the Americas across the Oceans.*[559]

RECOMMENDED READING

Despite the fact that we always cite numerous texts throughout our books, readers often ask us for a list of "recommended books" to continue their studies. I suggest they look at the texts we've cited, and if they're interested in reading more, to pick up that text at a library (or start browsing its content on Amazon or Google Books) before making a purchase. Still, I understand some people want a specific list of recommendations. So, for this book in particular, here's what I'd recommend you read to get a better understanding.

First, start with some popular texts written for mainstream audiences. These books are written by white authors, but they provide great overviews of the subjects we're covering. They include:

- Before the Dawn by Nicholas Wade
- Guns, Germs, and Steel by Jared Diamond
- The Real Eve by Stephen Oppenheimer
- The Fall by Steve Taylor
- The Past Worlds Atlas of Archaeology by Chris Scarre (editor)

Once you've done that, you need to get the Black perspective on these subjects. White authors, even those with the best intentions, tend to gloss over some facts or misinterpret others. A Black author's insight is needed, preferably one who was exceptionally knowledgeable in his field. These include the following, which I've listed roughly in order of reading difficulty:

- World's Great Men of Color by J.A. Rogers
- Ethiopia and the Origin of Civilization by John G. Jackson

- Introduction to African Civilizations by John G. Jackson
- Ages of Gold and Silver by John G. Jackson
- The Wonderful Ethiopians of the Ancient Cushite Empire by Drusilla Dunjee Houston
- Echoes of the Old Darkland by Charles Finch
- Star of Deep Beginnings by Charles Finch
- African Presence in Early Asia by Runoko Rashidi
- African Presence in Early Europe by Ivan Van Sertima
- African Presence in Ancient America by Ivan Van Sertima
- Egypt: Child of Africa by Ivan Van Sertima
- They Came Before Columbus by Ivan Van Sertima
- African People in World History by John Henrik Clarke
- Precolonial Black Africa by Cheikh Anta Diop
- African Origin of Civilization by Cheikh Anta Diop
- Civilization or Barbarism by Cheikh Anta Diop
- Black Man of the Nile and His Family by Yosef ben-Jochannan
- Africa: Mother of Western Civilizations by Yosef ben-Jochannan
- The Destruction of Black Civilization by Chancellor Williams

Most of these books were written over twenty years ago, so there are many topics that need to be updated to reflect what we have learned in that period, but that work is the responsibility of today's authors. It is my hope that this book helps empower a new generation of Black and brown scholars who seek to investigate all of the issues that remain unresolved and to propose new ways of thinking that move us from a glorious past to a glorious future.

As historian Dr. John Henrik Clarke has said:

> History is a clock that people use to tell their political and cultural time of day. It is also a compass that people use to find themselves on the map of human geography. The role of history is to tell a people what they have been, and where they have been, what they are and where they are. The most important role that history plays is that it has the function of telling a people where they still must go and what they still must be.

And again, there are plenty of resources named in the text and in the endnotes that follow. If I don't mention a title, either I haven't heard of it yet, or I have…but I just can't recommend it. For example, one very popular book on "untold Black history" seemed like a great resource until I attempted to verify its sources. Out of the ten quotes I checked, seven were not found in the sources cited. Now, I might get one or two wrong (out of a hundred!) but a 70% margin of error is a little too high for me to recommend. Another book, which came highly recommended by some of my Facebook friends, was so full

DID YOU KNOW?

Avatar wasn't the only film to base itself on indigenous culture (relocated to outer space). George Lucas used real North African towns across Tunisia and Morocco for scenes of Tattooine, the desert home planet of Luke Skywalker, first in 1977 and then again in 1999 and 2002. Tunisia was used in every *Star Wars* movie, except Episode V. Tattooine, by the way, is a real Tunisian town. The rebel base, 'the Massassi Outpost on the fourth moon of Yavin', seen toward the end of Episode IV, is the giant Mayan temple complex at Tikal, Guatemala.

of unsupported theories that I became frustrated with the fact that people were promoting this book without having any way to evaluate how much of it was true. In fact, much of the book's thesis was based on Mormon myths that were discredited decades ago. And so on and so on. There's a lot of silliness masquerading as science out there. I'm okay with getting a few things wrong here and there, so I've designed this book as "open source" history, open for revision and renewal. I don't want to be the "last word" on any of these subjects, so it's my hope that some of you continue this work. But PLEASE continue it the right way.

RECOMMENDED VIEWING

There are a few decent documentaries on the history of our ancestors, but none (that I know of) have covered all the content you'll find in this book. Still, you can find bits and pieces of the story if you know where to look. For example, Spencer Wells' *Journey of Mankind* has some good coverage on early human history (even though it gets a few things wrong in the process). National Geographic's *Birth of Civilization* is decent as well. Through CGI, recreations and expert interviews, this documentary is what they call "an epic account of 80,000 years in mankind's history, from man's emergence on the planet through his continued quest to dominate the world." Missing a lot of the story, but not terrible either.

NatGeo's *America Before Columbus* is also decent. This documentary embarks on an expedition into the "mysterious world" of ancient American history, exploring the rise of fall of several pre-Columbian civilizations in the Americas. The producers say:

> History books traditionally depict the pre-Columbus Americas as a pristine wilderness where small native villages lived in harmony with nature. But scientific evidence tells us that America wasn't exactly a "New World," but a very old one whose inhabitants had built a vast infrastructure of cities, orchards, canals, and causeways. But after Columbus set foot in the Americas, an endless wave of explorers, conquistadors, and settlers arrived, and with each of their ships came a Noah's Ark of plants, animals—and disease. In the first 100

years of contact, entire civilizations were wiped out and the landscape was changed forever.

Sounds pretty honest, huh? There's even a kinda-sketchy/kinda-good one called *Secret Civilizations*. There are a few others on Netflix. Whatever you do, however, don't waste your time watching *Ancient Aliens* or anything similar. There's an entire website debunking that boatload of BS, fittingly named www.ancientaliensdebunked.com. Those guys don't even TRY to tell the truth, and have made *The History Channel* the laughing stock of nonfiction television.

ANTHROPOMETRY OF THE BLACK MAN

All Black people don't look alike. Facial features vary. Head shapes vary. Hair textures vary. All of these things have been use to split the world's people into separate races. Thomas Huxley, in his 1865 work *On the Methods and Results of Ethnology*, classified the world into two macro-races: the Ulotrichi (meaning "woolly hair") and the Leiotrichi (meaning "straight hair"). Yes, his criteria was *hair texture*.

Huxley said the Ulotrichi race was comprised of Africans, the Andaman Islanders, and other Asian Negritos. In other words, the Ulotrichi was everyone who looked distinctly African, with woolly hair.

The Leiotrichi was a more diverse group, containing the Australian Aborigines, the Amphinesians (today's Pacific Islanders), Native Americans, Mongolians and other East Asians, the indigenous people of the Arctic (like the Inuit), the Melanochroi, and the Xanthochroi. In other words, these were all the "other" people, who must have been related because they shared straight (or almost straight) hair.

But does this make sense? Are some Black-skinned people not truly "Black" because they have straight hair? What about nose shape? Does that decide things? If not, then what?

In "Who and What is Black?" we do a lot of "deconstructing" of racial stereotypes, explaining how the features we associate with West African people and their descendants are not the ONLY features of Black people throughout the Diaspora, but really just one subset of a massive "superset" that includes almost 90% of the physical diversity found on the planet.

When we realize that there's no such thing as a "Black nose" or "Black hair," we ask ourselves what makes a people Black? And we conclude that color, culture, and consciousness are the most

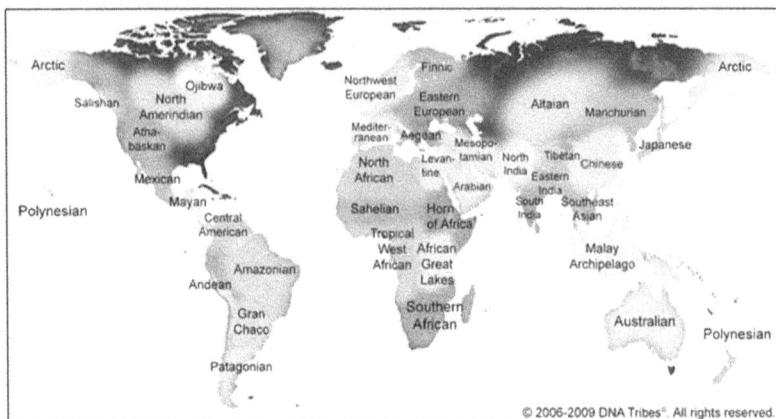

These are the cultural areas of the modern world.

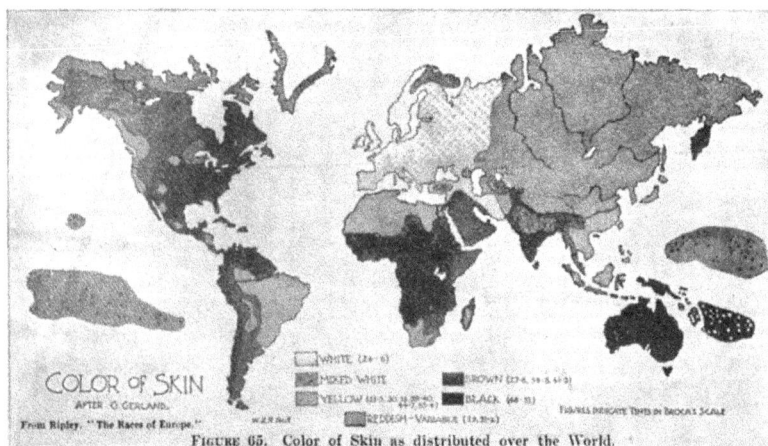

COLOR OF SKIN
AFTER O. GERLAND.
From Ripley. "The Races of Europe."

WHITE (24 - 6)
MIXED WHITE
YELLOW (23-0, 30, 38-39-40, 44-47, 55-57)
BROWN (27-6, 54-5, 61-3)
BLACK (66-91)
REDDISH - VARIABLE (18.39-6)
FIGURES INDICATE TIMES IN BROCA'S SCALE

FIGURE 65. Color of Skin as distributed over the World.

Note the areas identified with very dark skin in 1899.

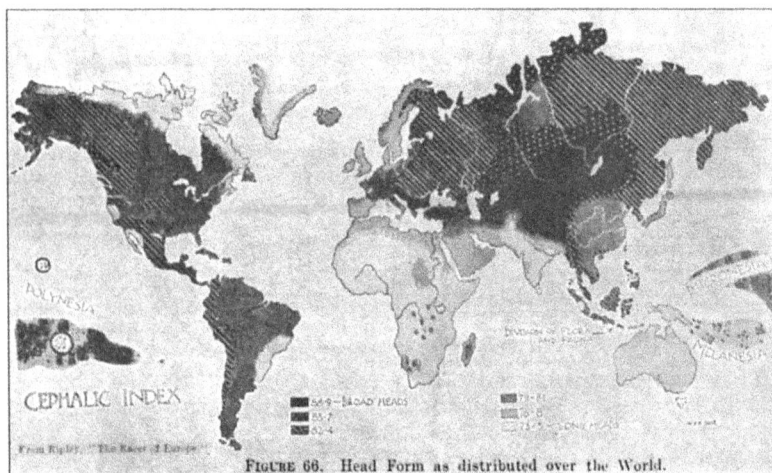

POLYNESIA

CEPHALIC INDEX
From Ripley. "The Races of Europe."

54-9 — BROAD HEADS
85-7
82-4
79 - 81
76-8
73-5 — LONG HEADS

MELANESIA

FIGURE 66. Head Form as distributed over the World.

Note the areas identified with long-headed people.

important factors. Those are especially relevant when we look at people today, but when we're looking at ancient skulls and human remains, there's gotta be something physical to help us assert that a group of people were Black. Otherwise, human remains will (and have been) claimed by white people anywhere ancient civilizations were being built. If we know their DNA, it's a bit easier because there are only a specific batch of DNA lineages (or haplogroups) that can be identified with mostly white people. But if all we have is some fossilized bones, we need to consult the science of anthropometry.

Anthropometry is the study of the measurements of the human body. Anthropologists used anthropometry heavily in the 19th century to start classifying groups of people into different categories. For example, different groups of people have different body proportions, a fact we noted in *The Science of Self, Volume One*, in regards to the proportions of Leonardo da Vinci's "Vitruvian Man."[561]

Regarding limb proportions, we know that people who come from tropical regions tend to have what's known as a "**tropical body plan**" where, for example, forearms and other extremities are longer. This is a sign that these people came from hot climates and were naturally dark-skinned. These proportions can be used to establish everything from the Blackness of the first Europeans to the Blackness of Da Vinci's "Vitruvian Man." For example, studies have proven that, although many of the ancient Egyptians had coarse hair and straight noses, they had an undeniably African body plan.[562]

One of the most prominent measurements of the human body is the length of the skull. Throughout this book, many of our sources refer to these skull types: *dolichocephalic* (long-headed) and *brachycephalic* (broad-headed or round-headed).*

For at least the past 15,000 years, Black and brown people throughout the world have been almost exclusively long-headed. White people† are more characteristically broad-headed. Italian physiologist Angelo Mosso imagined a line extending from the Alps to the Himalayas, separating the dolichocephalic, who live below the line, and the brachycephalic, who live above it.[563] In other words,

---

* There's also mesocephalic, which typically refers to "mixed" people, but can also describe "intermediate" types between the two categories.

† Asians are also often round-headed, which may derive from white ancestry or much older roots, as many DBP people are broad-headed instead of long-headed.

everyone in southern Asia, southern Europe, Australia, and Africa was related.

In his "two-race" classification system, Thomas Huxley also noted that most woolly-haired people were long-headed. Yet there were exceptions:

> It is curious to observe that almost all the woolly-haired people are also long-headed; while among the straight-haired nations broad heads preponderate, and only two stocks, the Esquimaux [Eskimo] and the Australians, are exclusively long-headed.[564]

Broad-headedness is common among more recent populations of European or Asian descent. But broad-headedness wasn't unknown in the ancient past. This trait was found among the Black Cro-Magnon remains of Europe, and can still be found in some of the oldest surviving populations of Black people today. As Huxley noted:

> [T]he diminutive Mincopies of the Andaman Islands lie midway between the Negro and Negrito races, and, as Mr. Busk has pointed out, occasionally present the rare combination of brachycephaly, or short-headedness, with woolly hair.[565]

This tells us, again, that Original people present the superset of all possible physical types and thus may present ANY of the phenotypical possibilities found in later populations. Some populations, like East Asians for example, simply descend from a group of Original People where a specific subset of those traits occur and are bred out (intentionally or unintentionally) to become widespread over several generations of genetic drift. This is how we end up with members of the different "races" having a common set of physical traits.

Still, most of the remains associated with the Anu People were certainly long-headed. And everyone knows white people aren't long-headed. Despite any old populations of Original People that don't have this trait, we know that most Black people – and their descendants – have been long-headed over the past 15,000 years.

WHAT DID THEY DO WITH THIS KNOWLEDGE?

European fascination with anthropometry went hand-in-hand with phrenology, a bogus "science" they fabricated to assign personality traits (especially deviance and criminality) to people based on the shape of their head. You can just imagine what long-headedness (a Black trait) must have signified. Phrenology has been thoroughly disproven, but similar ideas have been proposed in recent years using genetic markers, such as the alleged "**warrior gene**" that makes

Maori men more prone to deviance and criminality.

Other studies have recently claimed a link between melanin and aggression. Such studies have focused on darkly colored animals and report that "as predicted, darker wild vertebrates are more aggressive, sexually active and resistant to stress than lighter individuals."[566] *Sound familiar?*

If that wasn't clear enough, some scientists have gone even further, and attempted to demonstrate these same results in human populations. A July 2012 study concludes that:

> [D]arker pigmented people average higher levels of aggression and sexual activity (and also lower IQ)...[which explains] the covariation found between human (and non-human) pigmentation and variables such as birth rate, infant mortality, longevity, rate of HIV/AIDS, and violent crime.[567]

This ain't some stuff they came up with in the 1800s either! This is a study from 2012!

No wonder so many of us are still questioning Western science! But, as we explained in *The Science of Self, Volume One*, such cases aren't evidence for why the scientific method is "wrong." They're simply reminders that scientists can manipulate data, and have been doing so since the origins of Western science. And this is why we need MORE Black scientists, not more people who shun science altogether.

It is our hope that this volume of our *Science of Self* series has pushed even more young men and women into the sciences, particularly (based on the focus of this particular book) in fields like history, archaeology, genetics, anthropology, and linguistics.

THE NEW SCHOOL OF BLACK STUDIES

> "The writing of history reflects the interest, predilections and even prejudices of a given generation. This means that at the present time there is an urgent need to re-examine our past in terms of our present outlook. I think knowing one's history leads one to act in a more enlightened fashion, I can not imagine how knowing one's history would not urge one to be an activist." – John Hope Franklin

Ever since Europeans began using ideological arguments to justify their conquest and exploitation of Original People, people have emerged to attack and dismantle these false premises.

This happened in ancient times (which we'll discuss in Volume Four), but has also happened in recent American history. First, the abolitionists (both Black and white) of the 18th and 19th centuries were able to demonstrate that the Bible didn't condemn Black people to perpetual inferiority. Instead, some Black abolitionists, writers, and preachers (like Henry McNeal Turner, Richard Allen, and David Walker)[568] began demonstrating that the authors of the Bible *revered* Black people.

So those who were in power found new arguments. Self-taught Black historian J.A. Rogers noted this in *Sex and Race, Volume 3*:

> The fight both for and against slavery in the United States was waged first along scriptural lines...With the superseding of religion by science the battle of inequality shifted from a scriptural wording to a scientific one. Now it was no longer what "God had said" but what color, hair, and skull showed...In other words, the pro-slavery faction and the antislavery one had entered the stage in new costumes. Underneath were the same bodies.

This is just one example of how science can be misused to satisfy a political agenda. This trick has been recycled in recent years. Scholars (both Black and white) soon began demonstrating that all those "negative" physical traits associated with Black people actually revealed them to be not just the first humans, but the foundational people of all the world's civilizations. Black scholars began digging deeper into this evidence, soon uncovering that Black skin was not a curse nor a defect, but something great. This prompted another revision.

Now the arguments revolve around genetics. Genetics have been misused to argue that Blacks are more violent, more criminal, and less intelligent. Genetics have been misused to conceal the ethnicity of the people who built the world's civilizations by enshrouding them in a mysterious language of mitochondrial DNA and SNP markers. And now it is our turn to do it all over again, to use genetics to show the world the same things we showed them the last time they tried to lie on us.

But it's going to take more than a working knowledge of genetics. There are new challenges to the African-origin theories every day. They keep trying to produce ANY evidence they think will bolster their case. If they prove that people A built civilization, and then later realize that people A is African, then civilization must have actually come from people B. When they prove that people B were also African, civilization must have come from people C. And they'll use all 26 letters on you! And they'll never admit that their intention isn't to unearth the real history, only to take the credit away from Black people somehow.

"A people's status in the world is easily measured by the emphasis that they put on their history and culture. Strong people emphasize their history and culture all of the time. Weak people do not." – Runoko Rashidi

Such battles are ongoing. And they can all be fought and won, but it will take a new generation of scholars. What skills must these new scholars possess? There are many:

- ☐ You've gotta know genetics, and I mean DNA, and I mean the subclades, their SNPs and everything else that comes with it, like HLAs, or the antibodies that distinguish some populations from others.

- ☐ You've gotta know anthropometry, meaning the indexes that tell the limb lengths and other dimensions of the body, which are pretty consistent among related populations. Knowing these bones means you also need to know dental traits and who they indicate.

- ☐ You've gotta know linguistics, and I don't mean you can find two words and show how they sound alike. I mean REAL linguistics where you can identify the root words from the phonemes and then identify analogues in related languages, all while establishing the historical points of contact where these words would have been exchanged from one culture to another. It's simply not enough to show that Tibetans say *yak* and Hondurans say *yuk*.

- ☐ You gotta know anthropology, and I don't mean you watched two ritual dances from different cultures and now you think they're the same people. You've got to know the world's cultures so well that you can accurately connect 100 dots at once.

- ☐ You've gotta know archaeology, and I don't mean you can guess that the pyramids of Egypt are over ten thousand years old because two authors have said so. I mean you actually GET how the science of archaeology really works. And I don't mean simply knowing the methodology and dating methods, or knowing the archaeological artifacts produced by different cultures, or even being able to identify a culture (and the time period) from an artifact. I also mean knowing how to critique the claims of the biased or outright fraudulent archaeologists. Like the kind of people who say Giza is ten thousand years old.

In fact, with every science above, you have to know the INs of that field as wells as the OUTs. That is, know how it works, and also know how exactly it DOESN'T work so you can't be fooled by inaccurate or deceptive claims. Also, so you can critique others appropriately, rather than simply screaming, "You're lying!"

These are the concerns I've attempted to address in this work. It is my hope that the multidisciplinary approach I've employed is both well-received and well-understood. I've incorporated just about every form of data imaginable – from skull measurements to linguistic data – to connect the dots between the world's prehistoric cultures and ancient civilizations – and the Black people who established them.

Ironically, much of this evidence is now considered outdated. For over a century, European scholars used it – first, to connect the dots between Black people everywhere, then to show that they were all inferior to the people who came after them. Then, Black scholars began citing the same papers, while subtracting the inferiority nonsense. That's the moment it became outdated.

Nowadays, you'll have a hard time finding a modern book mentioning "Negroid" features among ancient remains. Even cultural connections tend to be ignored in favor of genetic data. So this book may be the last of its kind. We've covered nearly all of the old data, and the case it makes is clear. Now it's time to continue the arguments with new data, which we've also covered, but with many new questions now unanswered.

Who will continue the work? How will they do it? How many of us will become accredited archaeologists, geneticists, historians, forensic artists, and anthropologists? To do so seriously, are you prepared to enter those white institutions and learn what they know (and what they don't) better than them?

In *The Destruction of Black Civilization*, Chancellor Williams challenges us to shed our fears of "the white man's science" by jumping into "enemy territory":

> This is why I urge those students who intend to accept the great challenge of basic research in this discipline [Black studies] to go into "enemy territory," linger there, study and critically analyze their lectures and their "scholarly" writings, for they are some of the most rewarding sources for African history, precisely because in shrewdly attempting to delete, disguise, or belittle the role of Blacks in world history, they often reveal the opposite of what was intended...
>
> In particular, we should seek out those works with the special mission to "prove" the superiority of "whites" by "proving the inferiority of Blacks – all in language so subtle and scientific, that to the uncritical mind their "truths" seem self-evident. But it is also noteworthy that while the most hostile racist writers usually prove the very opposite of what they intended, their works inevitably contain useful factual data that must be accepted. Indeed, it is doubtful whether anyone, even a devil, could write a book completely devoid of truth.[569]

AFTERWORD

WHAT THEY TOOK

When Europeans came to the lands of Original People, they didn't just take our land. They plundered our artifacts, books, and sacred items. Whatever they couldn't carry away, they attempted to destroy. They burned the books that contained our ancient knowledge, and defaced the statues and figurines that looked unmistakably Black. Anytime you see an ancient status with a missing nose, its nose probably looked like a Black nose. Some statues even have their lips broken off.

The rest, they took. This is why so many of our most important items will never be seen by the general public. They are either housed in museums that we've never heard of, or – better yet – stored in the museum's basement but not on display. You know who's got a ton of our stuff? London? Yes, but I mean more than them. Paris? Yes, but even more than them. Done guessing? The Vatican! They have literally TONS of our stuff. Most of it, you'll never see. Some of it we only know about because European authors mentioned these artifacts a hundred years ago or more, like the Papal Chair that has the Islamic Shahadah inscribed on it. Yup, deep like that. And let's not forget all the private collectors.

White folks have more of our stuff in their living rooms than we do in our imagination. This isn't rhetoric either. This is a well-known fact among anyone in the scientific community. And if you don't believe me, why don't you check out one of the auctions that sells these things on a regular basis. You don't even have to leave your house, because many of these auctions are online now, like www.liveauctioneers.com or www.christies.com

The reason you won't find many of the images in this book anywhere else is because I found those artifacts at auction sites like these. In fact, you can even find some of our stuff on eBay now. One of the ancient Moche pots (depicting a Black woman) which I included in this book was sold on eBay for only $55!

If that upsets you, we probably shouldn't even begin to discuss how they took our land. Needless to say, there are very few places on the

Earth today that can be rightly considered "free." Some places, like Palestine and the Sudan are under significant attack as we speak. It is no coincidence that these were the epicenters of the Black cultural movements that shaped the world as we know it, and have remained "genetic refugiums" for our ancestral communities. Yes, much of the Middle East – despite how many of its people look today – harbors some of the oldest African lineages on the planet outside Africa. Other places, like the Andaman Islands, stand to suffer the same fate as Tasmania (south of Australia), Baja del Sur (California) and Tierra del Fuego (in South America), and the Saisiyat region of Taiwan where the Original People have been exterminated.

SO WHAT DID THEY TAKE?

They took our things, they took our lands, they took our people, they took our women, they took our lives…but above all they took our minds. They took our knowledge of ourselves and our ability to see what all they had taken. And I mean this quite literally, because they burned all of our books, killed all of our historians and elders, and introduced new myths and cultural traditions to the point where its hard to tell which stories came from the missionaries and which ones came from us. And they did this everywhere. In fact, they did the same everything everywhere. Let's review:

First, the explorers came. Sometimes it was a suicide mission, but the diseases the explorers introduced helped weaken the people, sometimes killing thousands in a few years.

Then the traders came, bringing cheap goods that we thought would make our lives easier (things like iron pots and glass beads, right before they brought the rum and guns). As people died from disease, it was important to spend less time making beads and clay pots. At first, they traded for food products and commodities like palm oil, but that was just to get in the door.

Because they often "adopted" a local outcast and brought him back to Europe so that he could (a) report to the Europeans on all the local affairs and (b) report to the local people about how great the Europeans were living, he served as a bridge between the two communities. So, essentially, it began with "traders" and "traitors."

Meanwhile, the missionaries came. The missionaries didn't have anything interesting to offer on their own, but they represented the belief system of the traders who seemed prosperous, especially if the "traitor" regaled people with his stories of witnessing European luxury. Ironically, the Europeans were hardly living in luxury in the

1500s, but – to an outcast – anything "other" than his own way of life looked good.

Once the missionaries had the minds of the people, the soldiers came. Sometimes the soldiers came early, just to "help" the missionaries secure the minds of the people with a little bit of coercion. Before long, we had the Bibles and they had the land…and everything else they wanted. Sometimes, we didn't even get the damn Bibles. Talk about a bad trade.

The worst part is that, in taking our minds, they encouraged us to be blind to what they took. It wasn't just the religion they gave us. It was a comprehensive ideology for life. We were taught that we, too, could become prosperous if we worked the system. Instead, the system has worked us. In the process, we have lost almost everything. Fortunately, there are two things that cannot be destroyed.

One, the Black seed of life that – even after 200,000 years of hardships and mass extinctions – survives in us, the Original People.

Two, the Black mind that – even after thousands of years (because they didn't start in the 1500s) of brainwashing and culture-twisting – we still retain so much of the primordial cultural elements that make us Original People. Our color, culture, and consciousness are muddled in the mix, but these colors don't run. If they brainwashed us, there's no bleach strong enough to change our colors for good, so all we have to do is wash our minds clean of everything they gave us. In doing so, we'll be set to take back everything that's been lost. But it begins by reclaiming our minds and our cultures. This is the curriculum we've designed into Volume Three of this series.

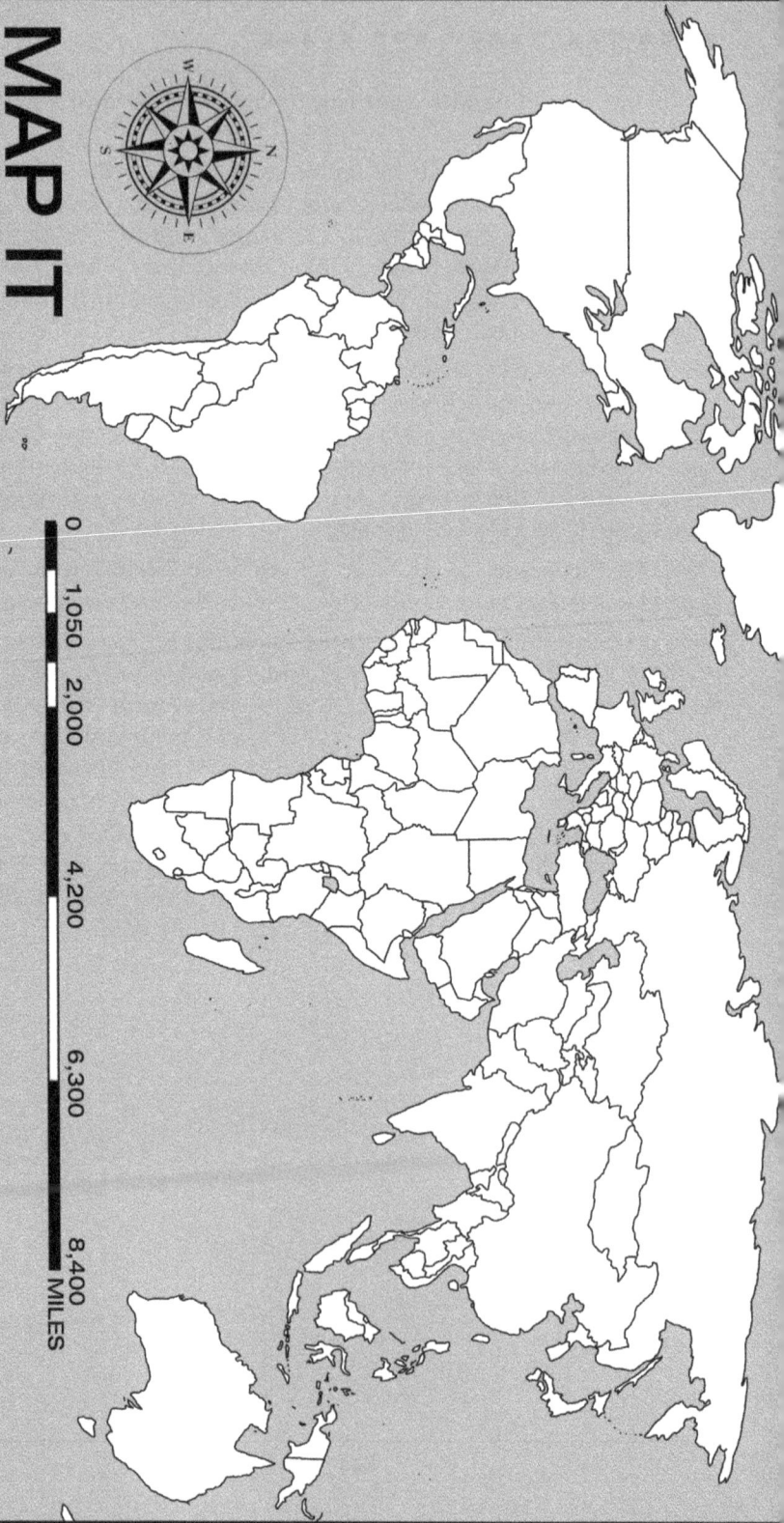

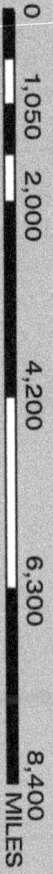

MAP IT
YOURSELF

USE THIS BLANK MAP TO HELP VISUALIZE MIGRATIONS, DISTANCES, CULTURES, CIVILIZATIONS, LANGUAGES,
DISCOVERIES, MODERN NATIONS, RIVERS, MOUNTAINS, DESERTS, TROPICAL REGIONS, ETHNIC GROUPS, ETC.

0   1,050   2,000   4,200   6,300   8,400
MILES

ENDNOTES

SOURCES CITED

As you know, my citations aren't always perfect, but I use a style that conveys the necessary information while conserving much-needed space. After all, who reads the endnotes? Well, you should! You can find other books and articles worth reading, as well as additional details we couldn't include in the body of the text.

1 Solheim, W.G. (1972) An earlier agricultural revolution. Scientific American 226: 34-41
2 Godfrey Higgins. (1833). Anacalypsis An Attempt To Draw Aside The Veil Of The Saitic Isis. Two Horizons Press (In Production).
3 William Henry Ferris. (1911, republished 2012). The African Abroad: The Black Man's Evolution in Western Civilization. Vol. 1 and 2. Two Horizons Press.
4 John Denison Baldwin. (1869). Pre-historic nations: or, Inquiries concerning some of the great peoples and civilizations of antiquity, and their probable relation to a still older civilization of the Ethiopians or Cushites of Arabia. Harper and Brothers. p.17.
5 John Denison Baldwin. (1869). p.19.
6 Henry Welsford. (1845). On the origin and ramifications of the English language: Preceded by an inquiry into the primitive seats, early migrations, and final settlements of the principal European nations. Longman. p. 42.
7 John Denison Baldwin. (1869). p. 55.
8 John Block Friedman. (1981). The Monstrous Races in Medieval Art and Thought. Harvard University Press. p. 35.
9 Andrew Lancaster. (2009). Y Haplogroups, Archaeological Cultures and Language Families. Journal of Genetic Genealogy, 5(1), 35-65.
10 William Flinders Petrie. (1939). The Making of Egypt. p. 68.
11 Edouard Naville. (1908). Annual Report of the Board of Regents of the Smithsonian Institution, June 30 1907. Government Printing Office.
12 John Denison Baldwin. (1869). p. 97.
13 Kroeber, Alfred L. (Jan-Mar 1940). "Stimulus diffusion." American Anthropologist 42(1), p. 1–20.
14 Gérald Gaillard. (2004). The Routledge Dictionary of Anthropologists, p. 48.
15 Bruce G. Trigger. (1998). Sociocultural Evolution: Calculation and Contingency, p. 101.
16 Wesley John Gaines. (1897). The Negro and the White Man. A.M.E. Publishing House.
17 Quoted in Wesley John Gaines. (1897).
18 Constantin-François Volney. (1801). Travels in Syria and Egypt, during the years 1783, 1784, & 1785, Volume 1. Will Morrison. Often wrongly attributed to his other book, Ruins of Empire, by later writers who must not have checked their primary sources.
19 Van Sertima, Ivan. ed. Egypt: Child of Africa. Transaction Publishers, 1995. p. 78
20 Constantin Francois de Volney. 1890. The Ruins, or, Meditation on the Revolutions of Empires: And the Law of Nature. Twentieth Century Publishing Co. Originally published in 1791. p. iii-iv
21 For more on the Black gods of the Americas, see Black God, a forthcoming work from Supreme Design Publishing, to be released in the Summer of 2013.
22 Gerald Massey, (1881). A Book of the Beginnings. Vol. 1. Williams and Norgate, p. 4

23 Hamilton, Paul L. African Peoples' Contributions to World Civilizations: Shattering the Myths, Volume 1. R.A. Renaissance Publications, 1995. p. 84

24 S.O.Y. Keita and A.J. Boyce, (1996). "The Geographical Origins and Population Relationships of Early Ancient Egyptians", in Egypt in Africa, Theodore Celenko (ed), Indiana University Press. p. 20-33 "Analysis of crania is the traditional approach to assessing ancient population origins, relationships, and diversity. In studies based on anatomical traits and measurements of crania, similarities have been found between Nile Valley crania from 30,000, 20,000 and 12,000 years ago and various African remains from more recent times. Studies of crania from southern predynastic Egypt, from the formative period (4000-3100 B.C.), show them usually to be more similar to the crania of ancient Nubians, Kushites, Saharans, or modern groups from the Horn of Africa than to those of dynastic northern Egyptians or ancient or modern southern Europeans."

25 W.E.B. Du Bois. (1915). The Negro.

26 S.O.Y. Keita, (1993). "Studies and Comments on Ancient Egyptian Biological Relationships," History in Africa 20, p. 134.

27 E Massoulard. (1949). Historie et protohistorie d'Egypte. Institut d'Ethnologie. p. 402.

28 Frank Yurco. (1996).

29 Nancy C. Lovell, (1999). "Egyptians, physical anthropology of," In Kathryn A. Bard and Steven Blake Shubert (Eds.), Encyclopedia of the Archaeology of Ancient Egypt. Routledge. p. 328-332.

30 Edward Wilmot Blyden. (1873). From West Africa to Palestine, T.J. Sawyer. p. 114.

31 W.E.B. Du Bois. (1915).

32 Brunton, Caton-Thompson. (1928). The Badarian Civilization and Predynastic Remains Near Badari; William Flinders Petrie, (1920). Prehistoric Egypt.

33 S.O.Y. Keita, (Nov. 2005). Early Nile Valley Farmers, From El-Badari, Aboriginals or "European" Agro-Nostratic Immigrants? Craniometric Affinities Considered With Other Data, Journal of Black Studies, Vol. 36 No. 2, p. 191-208. http://wysinger.homestead.com/badari.pdf

34 Alan Gardiner. (1966). Egypt of the Pharaohs. p. 392.

35 Walter, P., et al. (1999). "Making Make-Up in Ancient Egypt," Nature, 397:483.

36 Bard, Kathryn A. (1994). The Egyptian Predynastic: A Review of the Evidence. Journal of Field Archaeology 21(3):265-288.

37 Constantin Francois de Volney. (1890).

38 Constantin Francois de Volney. (1890). p. iii-iv

39 Constantin Francois de Volney. (1890). p. iii-iv

40 Flora Louisa Shaw. (1905). A tropical dependency: An outline of the ancient history of the western Soudan with an account of the modern settlement of northern Nigeria. J. Nisbet & Co. p. 17-18.

41 E.A. Wallis Budge. (1928). History of Ethiopia, Vol. I., Preface.

42 E.A. Wallis Budge. (1928). p. 2.

43 Richard Pankhurst. (2001). "Ethiopia's Image in World Literature." www.meskot.com/Ethiopia_RP.htm

44 Drusillla Dunjee Houston. (1926)

45 William Flinders Petrie, (1939).

46 Tracy L. Prowse, Nancy C. Lovell, (Oct 1996). Concordance of cranial and dental morphological traits and evidence for endogamy in ancient Egypt. American Journal of Physical Anthropology, Vol. 101, Issue 2, p. 237-246.

47 Brunton, Caton-Thompson. (1928). p. 41-42.

48 Myra Wysinger, Ed. "Ancient Africa's Black Kingdoms." http://wysinger.homestead.com/ancientafrica.html

49 www.carnegiemnh.org/exhibitions/egypt/guide.htm

50 Keita, S. O. Y. (Apr 1995). "A brief review of studies and comments on ancient Egyptian biological relationships," Journal International Journal of Anthropology, Vol. 10, Nos. 2-3, p. 107-123

51 Stephen Savage, (Jun 2001). "Some Recent Trends in the Archaeology of Predynastic

Egypt," Journal of Archaeological Research, Volume 9, Number 2, p. 101-155.

52 William M. Flinders Petrie. (1939).

53 Breasted, John Henry. (1907). Ancient Records of Egypt: Historical Documents from the Earliest Times to the Persian Conquest, collected, edited, and translated, with Commentary, vol.II, p. 658

54 White, Jon Manchip. (1970). Ancient Egypt: Its Culture and History. Dover Publications, p. 141. "It may be noted that the ancient Egyptians themselves appear to have been convinced that their place of origin was African rather than Asian. They made continued reference to the land of Punt as their homeland."

55 William M. Flinders Petrie. (1939). Petrie states that the Land of Punt was "sacred to the Egyptians as the source of their race."

56 E.A. Wallis Budge. (1914). Short History of the Egyptian People. Budge says "Egyptian tradition of the Dynastic Period held that the aboriginal home of the Egyptians was Punt…"

57 Pankhurst, Richard (2001). The Ethiopians: A History. In Ancient Egypt: Its Culture and History, John Manchip White adds: "It may be noted that the ancient Egyptians themselves appear to have been convinced that their place of origin was African rather than Asian. They made continued reference to the land of Punt as their homeland. Also see White, Jon Manchip. (1970). Ancient Egypt: Its Culture and History. Dover Publications, p. 141.

58 The researchers consulted Egyptian records describing baboons imported from Punt, then chemically analyzed hair samples from baboon remains in Egypt to identify their place of origin. http://heritage-key.com/blogs/owenjarus/baboon-mummy-tests-reveal-ethiopia-and-eritrea-ancient-egyptians-land-punt

59 Judith Weingarten. (Apr 25 2010). "Eti, the Eritrean Queen of Punt?" Zenobia: Empress of the East. Available at http://judithweingarten.blogspot.com

60 Myra Wysinger. "Prehistory of Africa and the Badarian Culture." http://wysinger.homestead.com/badarians.html

61 Christopher Ehret. (1996). "Ancient Egyptian as an African Language, Egypt as an African Culture," in Egypt in Africa, Theodore Celenko (ed), Indiana University Press, p. 25-27

62 Christopher Ehret, (1996).

63 Christopher Ehret, (1996). p. 25-27

64 Rappoport, S. (1904). "The Waterways of Egypt," History of Egypt, Volume 12. The Grolier Society. p. 248-257.

65 Wendorf, Fred, and Schild, Romuald, (1998), "Nabta Playa and its role in Northeastern African Prehistory" Journal of Anthropological Archaeology 17:97-123.

66 Brophy, T.G. and Rosen, P.A. (2005). Satellite Imagery Measures of the Astronomically Aligned Megaliths at Nabta Playa, Mediterranean Archaeology and Archaeometry 5(1), 15 - 24

67 Brophy, Thomas G. (2002). The Origin Map: Discovery of a Prehistoric, Megalithic, Astrophysical Map and Sculpture of the Universe, p. 104

68 Ricaut and Walekens (2008) 'Cranial Discrete traits…' Human Biology, 80:5, p. 535-564

69 Thomas G. Brophy and Paul A. Rosen. (2005).

70 Hanotte O, et al. (2002) African pastoralism: Genetic imprints of origins and migrations. Science 296:336–339.

71 Wim Van Binsbergen (Ed.). (2011) Black Athena Comes of Age. LIT Verlag Munster.; Takács, Gábor. (1999). Etymological Dictionary of Egyptian, Vol. I: A Phonological Introduction. Brill.

72 Frank Yurco, (1996).

73 Olivia Vlahos. (1967). African Beginnings. Fawcett Premier.

74 Nile Valley Study Group. (2003-2009). Peopling of the Nile Valley. www.africanamericanculturalcenterpalmcoast.org/historyafrican/nilevalleypeopling.htm

75 John Gledhill, Barbara Bender, Mogens Trolle Larsen, (Eds.). (1998). State and Society: The Emergence and Development of Social Hierarchy and political centralization. Taylor

and Francis Group. p. 192-214.

76 Diop, Cheikh Anta. (1974). The African Origin of Civilization: Myth or Reality. Trans. Mercer Cook. L. Hill.

77 Nile Valley Study Group. (2003-2009).

78 Robert July, (1975). Pre-Colonial Africa: An Economical and Social History. Scribner, p. 60-61.

79 Hanotte O, et al. (2002).

80 Wendorf F, Schild R. (1998). Nabta Playa and its role in northeastern African prehistory. J Anthropol Archaeol 17:97–123.

81 J. Peters. (1993). Mesolithic Fishing along the Central Sudanese Nile and the Lower Atbara, Sahara 4: 33-40.

82 Rossella Lorenzi . (Jun 2011). "Dig for Pharoah's Boat Begins." http://news.discovery.com/history/buried-pharaonic-boat-110623.html

83 D. Usai, S. Salvatori. (Dec 2007). The oldest representation of a Nile boat. Antiquity 81(314).

84 D. Usai, S. Salvatori. (Dec 2007).

85 Olivia Fleming. (Oct 2012). "Meet the 14th Century African king who was richest man in the world of all time." www.dailymail.co.uk/news/article-2218025/Meet-14th-Century-African-king-richest-man-world-time-adjusted-inflation.html

86 "Africa's oldest ceramic unearthed in Mali." (Sep 2009). American Ceramic Society Bulletin. Vol. 88 Issue 8, p. 4.

87 John Iliffe. (2007). p. 10

88 Flora Louisa Shaw. (1905). p. 15.

89 Amadou Hampâté Bâ. (Aug-Sep 1979). "Tongues that span the centuries: The faithful guardians of Africa's oral tradition." The UNESCO Courier. UNESCO.

90 Clammer, Paul (2005). Bradt Travel Guide, Sudan. Bradt Travel Guides, p. 159,160,

91 Fellner, R.O. (1995).

92 John Croft. (2005). "The Search For The Afroasiatic Urheimat: Linking Archaeology To The Linguistics." Unpublished research paper.

93 Ehret C. (1983) in Population Movement and Culture Contact in the Southern Sudan, eds Mack J, Robertshaw P (British Institute in Eastern Africa, Nairobi), p. 19–48.

94 Ehret C. (1983).

95 Ehret, C. (1984). Historical/linguistic evidence for early African food production. In J.D. Clark & S.A. Brandt (Eds.) From Hunters to Farmers: The Causes and Consequences of Food Production in Africa (p. 26-35). University of California Press.

96 Blench, R. (1995). Recent developments in African language classification and their implications for prehistory. In T. Shaw, P. Sinclair, B. Andah, & A. Okpoko (Eds.) The Archaeology of Africa (p. 126-138). London: Routledge., p. 128-129; Ehret, C. (1984); Murdock, G.P. (1959). Africa: Its Peoples and Their Culture History. New York: McGraw-Hill, p. 44, 64-68

97 G. Mokhtar. (1990). UNESCO General History of Africa, Vol. II (Ancient Africa). Cambridge University Press.

98 Murdock, G.P. (1959).

99 Greenberg J.H. (1972). Linguistic evidence regarding Bantu origins. Journal of African History 13:189–216; Phillipson D. (1975). The chronology of the Iron Age in Bantu Africa. Journal of African History 16:321–342; Berniell-Lee G, et al. (2009). Genetic and demographic implications of the Bantu expansion: Insights from human paternal lineages. Mol Biol Evol 26:1581–1589.

100 Ehret C. (2001) Re-envisioning a central problem of early African history. Int J Afr Hist Stud 34:5–41.

101 The extent to which the spread of the Bantu languages was associated with the migration of populations vs. a diffusion of language and technology among populations is still the subject of debate.

102 Tishkoff SA, et al. (2009). The genetic structure and history of Africans and African Americans. Science 324:1035–1044.

103 Lim L. (1992) A Site-Oriented Approach to Rock Art: A Study from Usandawe, Central Tanzania. PhD thesis. Brown University.

104 Cavalli-Sforza LL, Menozzi P. (1994). History and Geography of Human Genes. Princeton University Press.

105 Newman J. (1997) The Peopling of Africa. Yale University Press.

106 Ehret C, ed (2006) The Nilo-Saharan Background of Chadic. Ohio State University.

107 National Geographic News. (May 2001). "Ancient Fertile Crescent Almost Gone, Satellite Images Show." http://news.nationalgeographic.com/news/2001/05/0518_crescent.html

108 Laura B. Scheinfeldta, Sameer Soib, and Sarah A. Tishkoff. (2012). Working toward a synthesis of archaeological, linguistic, and genetic data for inferring African population history. Proceedings of the National Academy of Sciences.

109 H.G. Wells. (1919). Outline of History. p. 175.

110 "Bones of Cannibals: A Palestine Riddle." (Aug 4 1932). New York Times, p. 21

111 Drake, J.G. St. Clair. (1987). Black Folk Here and There: An Essay in History and Anthropology. Volume 1. Center for Afro-American Studies, UCLA.

112 Trenton W. Holliday. (2000). "Evolution at the Crossroads: Modern Human Emergence in Western Asia, American Anthropologist, 102(1) p. 62

113 Angel, J.L. (1972). Biological Relations of Egyptians and Eastern Mediterranean Populations during pre-dynastic and Dynastic Times. Journal of Human Evolution, p. 307-313.

114 C. Loring Brace, et. al. (2006). The Questionable Contribution of the Neolithic and the Bronze Age to European Craniofacial Form. Proceedings of the National Academy of Sciences. PNAS 103: 242-247.

115 F. X. Ricaut, M. Waelkens. (2008). Cranial Discrete Traits in a Byzantine Population and Eastern Mediterranean Population Movements. Human Biology. 80:5, p. 535-564.

116 Bar-Yosef, O. (1987). "Pleistocene connexions between Africa and Southwest Asia: an archaeological perspective". African Archaeological Review 5(1): 29-38.

117 Bar-Yosef O (1987).

118 R. J. Wenke. (1999). Patterns in Prehistory (Fourth Edition): Chapter 7, The Origins of Agriculture. Oxford. p. 291.

119 R.O. Fellner. (1995). Cultural Change and the Epipalaeolithic of Palestine. p. 122.

120 Ofer Bar-Yosef. (1998). The Natufian Culture in the Levant, Threshold to the Origins of Agriculture. Evolutionary Anthropology. p. 167.

121 Bar-Yosef, O. (1987).

122 S.O.Y. Keita; A. J. Boyce. (2005). Genetics, Egypt, and History: Interpreting Geographical Patterns of Y Chromosome Variation. History in Africa, 32, p. 221-246.

123 Christopher Ehret. (1979). "On the antiquity of agriculture in Ethiopia," Journal of African History 20, p.161.

124 J.D. Clark. (1977). "The origins of domestication in Ethiopia," Fifth Panafrican Congress of Prehistory and Quaternary Studies, Nairobi.

125 Barker, G. (2002). Transitions to farming and pastoralism in North Africa. In Bellwood P, Renfrew C (Eds.), Examining the Farming/Language Dispersal Hypothesis, 151–161.

126 John Croft. (2005). "The Search For The Afroasiatic Urheimat: Linking Archaeology To The Linguistics." Unpublished research paper.

127 Giuseppe Sergi. (1901). The Mediterranean Race: A study of the origin of European peoples.

128 Dana Reynolds-Marniche. (1994). "The Myth of the Mediterranean Race," in Ivan Van Sertima (Ed.), Egypt: Child of Africa. Transaction Books. p. 120-121.

129 Jason A. Ur, Philip Karsgaard, Joan Oates, (Aug 2007). "Early Urban Development in the Near East" Science 31, Vol. 317. No. 5842, p. 1188, DOI: 10.1126/science.1138728

130 Rick Gore. (Oct 2004). Who Were the Phoenicians? National Geographic. http://ngm.nationalgeographic.com/features/world/asia/lebanon/phoenicians-text/1

131 Rick Gore. (2004).

132 William Henry Ferris. (2012). In other chapters of his two-volume series, Ferris

explores the Black presence in other ancient civilizations.

133 W.E.B. Du Bois. (1915). The Negro.

134 John G Jackson. (1985). Ethiopia and the Origin of Civilization. Black Classic Press.

135 W.J. Perry. (1937). The Growth of Civilization. Penguin Books. p. 60-61.

136 H.R. Hall, (1916). The Ancient History of the Near East. Methuen & Co. Ltd, p. 173-174

137 John Denison Baldwin. (1869). p. 18.

138 John Marshall. (1996). Mohenjo-Daro and the Indus Civilization: Being an official account of Archaeological Excavations at Mohenjo-Daro carried out by the Government of India between the years 1922 and 1927, Asian Educational Services.

139 Iorwerth Eiddon S. Edwards, (1970), The Cambridge Ancient History, Vol. I, Part I. p. 358. The Cambridge Ancient History notes, "Keith's interesting conclusions – that the skulls of the ancient Sumerians were relatively narrow, that they were dolichocephalic, a large-headed, large-brained people, approaching or exceeding in these respects the longer-headed races of Europe, and that the men's noses were long and wide – is applicable to some of the 'Ubaid dead of the latter half of the third and the beginning of the second millennium B.C.

140 Buxton and Rice. (1931). Excavations at Kish.

141 Buxton and Rice, "Report," 69. Cited by Wesley Muhammad. (2012). www.blackarabia.blogspot.com

142 Penniman, T.K. "A Note on the Inhabitants of Kish." Excavations at Kish, 1923-33 Vol 4. p. 65-72. Penniman wrote: "First there is the Eurafrican…In ancient times, this type is found in Mesopotamia and Egypt and may be compared with the Combe Capelle skull. It is possibly identical with men who lived in the high desert west of the Nile in paleolithic times…"

143 W. Hallo, W. Simpson (1971). The Ancient Near East. Harcourt, Brace. p. 28.

144 William L. Langer. (1972). An Encyclopedia of World History. Houghton Mifflin.

145 This is just a group of mounds where remains from the Elamite city Kabnak were found. Things such as ceramics, tiles and vases with mythological motifs, tools and remains of powder along with text references the use of makeup.

146 Found in the legendary "Burnt City" in Sistan-Baluchistan province, southeastern Iran.

147 George Rawlinson. (1885). The Seven Great Monarchies Of The Ancient Eastern World.

148 Potts, Daniel T. (1999). The Archaeology of Elam: Formation and Transformation of an Ancient Iranian State, Cambridge University Press.

149 Potts, Daniel T. (1999).

150 Henry Field. (Dec 15 1939). "Contributions to the Anthropology of Iran. Field Museum of Natural History Anthropological Series, Volume 29, Number 2.

151 Henry Field. (1939).

152 Henry Field. (1939); Brinton, Daniel G. (1895). The protohistoric ethnography of Western Asia. PAPS, vol. 34, pp. 1-32.

153 Henry Field. (1939); Brinton, Daniel G. (1895).

154 Sir Harry Hamilton Johnston. (1910). The Negro in the New World. p. 27

155 Josiah Conder. (1825). The Modern Traveller. Oliver and Boyd.

156 Henry Field. (1939); Dieulafoy, Marcel Auguste. (1893). L'Acropole de Suse, d'apres les fouilles ex'cutees en 1884-6, sous les auspices du Mus& du Louvre; Morgan, Jacques de. (1892). Rapport de M. J. de Morgan sur sa mission en Perse et dans le Louristan.

157 Houssay, Frederic. (1887). Les peuples actuels de la Perse. Bulletin de la Societe d'Anthropologie de Lyon, vol. 6, pp. 101-148. Lyons.

158 Sykes, Ella C. (1921). A History of Persia. 2nd ed, vol. 1, p. 50-53

159 Henry Field. (1939).

160 McAlpin, David W. (1981). Proto Elamo Dravidian: The Evidence and Its Implications, American Philosophy Society.

161 George Starostin, "On the Genetic Affiliation of the Elamite Language," http://starling.rinet.ru/Texts/elam.pdf

162 Hahn, W.J. (2002). A Molecular Phylogenetic Study of the Palmae (Arecaceae) Based on atpB, rbcL, and 18S nrDNA Sequences. Systematic Botany 51(1): 92-112.
163 W.H. Barrifield. (1993). "Date Palm Products." FAO Agricultural Services Bulletin No. 101. Food and Agriculture Organization of the United Nations. www.fao.org/docrep/t0681E/t0681e02.htm
164 W.H. Barrifield. (1993
165 Arif Gamal. (2005). "Deconstructing Nubia." www.thenubian.net/decnubia.php
166 W.H. Barrifield. (1993).
167 Ian Hodder. (Jun 2006). "This Old House: At Çatalhöyük, a Neolithic site in Turkey, families packed their mud-brick houses close together and traipsed over roofs to climb into their rooms from above". Natural History Magazine.
168 "Town Plan from Catal Hyük (6200 B.C.)." www.henry-davis.com/MAPS/Ancient%20Web%20Pages/100B.html
169 Balter, Michael. (2004). The Goddess and the Bull: Çatalhöyük: An Archaeological Journey to the Dawn of Civilization. Free Press
170 Tangri, D.; Cameron, D. W.; Zias, J. (Jan 1 1994). A reconsideration of "Races" and their impact on the origins of the Chalcolithic in the Levant using available anthropological and archaeological data. Human Evolution (1994) 9: 53-61.
171 James E. Brunson. (1995). "Unexpected Faces in Early Asia." In Runoko Rashidi and Ivan Van Sertima (Eds.). African Presence in Early Asia. Transaction Publishers.
172 Drusilla Dunjee Houston, Peggy Brooks-Bertram. (2009). Wonderful Ethiopians of the Ancient Cushite Empire: Origin of the Civilization from the Cushites, SUNY Press. It should be noted that Houston, according to those who knew her work, was arguing (like Chancellor Williams) that the original Aryans were Black! The problem with the term "Aryan" is that it was an adopted term. So the whites who eventually named themselves Aryans took it from an already established term that was in use among Original people. So you have Black groups and white groups that were utilizing the same terms. That's why you have to use additional information to determine the makeup of the people during certain eras. It's the same with words like European, Eurasian, Mediterranean, Semitic, and even Caucasian!
173 John Baldwin. (1869). Pre-historic Bations or Inquiries Concerning Some of the Great peoples and Civilizations of Antiquity. Harpers.
174 Charles Hardwick. (1872). Traditions, Superstitions and Folklore. Ireland and Company.
175 Henry Field. (1902). Arabs of Central Iraq; Their History, Ethnology and Physical Characters, Anthropology Memoirs Volume 4.
176 G. Elliot Smith. (1923). The Ancient Egyptians and the Origins of Civilization. p. 54
177 Iraq Petroleum Company. (1948). Handbook of the territories which form the theatre of operations of the Iraq Petroleum Company, Limited, and its associated companies. The Iraq Petroleum Company.
178 Ibn Mugawir as cited in Jean Retso. (2003). The Arabs in Antiquity, p. 231, note 52.
179 John Denison Baldwin. (1869). p. 57-61.
180 Semino O, et al. (2004) Origin, diffusion, and differentiation of Y-chromosome haplogroups E and J: Inferences on the neolithization of Europe and later migratory events in the Mediterranean area. Am J Hum Genet 74:1023–1034.
181 Drusilla Dunjee Houston. (1926).
182 Alessandra Avanzini. (1997). Profumi d'Arabia: atti del Convegno. p. 285
183 Michael D. Petraglia, (2009), The Evolution of Human Populations in Arabia: Paleoenvironmental Prehistory. p. 264.
184 Anati, Emmanuel. (1968). Rock-Art in Central Arabia, I: The 'Oval-Headed' People of Arabia. Oriental Institute.
185 Klaus Schmidt, (2000). Göbekli Tepe and the rock art of the Near East, TÜBA-AR 3.
186 Grafton Elliot Smith. (1909). "The People of Egypt," The Cairo Scientific Journal 3: p. 51-63. Quoted in Wesley Muhammad. (2012). Egyptian Sacred Science and Islam: A Reappraisal.

187 Grafton Elliot Smith, (1923). p. 101-102. Quoted in Wesley Muhammad. (2012).
188 Dana Reynolds, (1992). "The African Heritage & Ethnohistory of the Moors," in Ivan van Sertima. (Ed.) Golden Age of the Moor. Transaction Publishers, p. 100, 105-106.
189 F. Lenormant. (1869). Manual of Ancient History, Book VIII.
190 Cheikh Anta Diop. (1974). p. 124.
191 Francis Rawdon Chesney. (1850). The Expedition for the Survey of the Rivers Euphrates and Tigris. Longman, Brown, Green, and Longmans. p. 47.
192 F. Lenormant. (1869). Quoted in Cheikh Anta Diop. (1974). p. 124.
193 Cheikh Anta Diop. (1974). p. 124.
194 Frank Yurco. (1996). "An Egyptological Review." In MR. Lefkowitz and GM Rogers, Black Athena Revisited. The University of North Carolina Press, p. 62-100.
195 Eugen Georg. (1931). The Adventure of Mankind. p. 121–122.
196 Augustus Caesar. (Originally written 14 CE). Res Gestae Divi Augusti, or The Deeds of the Divine Augustus. Trans. Thomas Bushnell. Available at http://en.wikisource.org/wiki/Res_Gestae_Divi_Augusti
197 Lothrop Stoddard. (1920). The Rising Tide of Color Against White World-Supremacy. Scribner and Sons.
198 Vidya Prakash Tyagi. (2009). p. 2
199 John Marshall. (1996). Mohenjo-Daro and the Indus Civilization: being an official account of Archaeological Excavations at Mohenjo-Daro carried out by the Government of India between the years 1922 and 1927, Asian Educational Services.
200 Christoph von Fürer-Haimendorf. (1982). Tribes of India: The Struggle for Survival. University Of California Press.
201 John Marshall. (1996).
202 Thomas Huxley. (1870). Huxley wrote: "[A]lthough the Egyptian has been much modified by civilization and probably by admixture, he still retains the dark skin, the black, silky, wavy hair, the long skull, the fleshy lips, and broadish alæ of the nose which we know distinguished his remote ancestors, and which cause both him and them to approach the Australian and the "Dasyu" [of India] more nearly than they do any other form of mankind."
203 Taylor, Thomas Griffith. (1937). Environment, race, and migration; fundamentals of human distribution. The University of Chicago Press, p. 189.
204 Sjoberg, Andre. (1971). "Who are the Dravidians." Symposium on Dravidian Civilization. Pemberton Press. p. 13
205 Omar Khan. (Ed.) (1996-2008). "The Ancient Indus Civilization." www.harappa.com/har/indus-saraswati.html
206 Quoted in Supreme Understanding and Robert Bailey. (2012). 365 Days of Real Black History Calendar. Supreme Design Publishing.
207 Drusilla Dunjee Houston. (1926).
208 Josiah Conder. (1825). The Modern Traveller. Oliver and Boyd. Conder adds that this race of pioneers and culture-bearers somehow became a "subject race" wherever they were found.
209 Drusilla Dunjee Houston. (1926).
210 Drusilla Dunjee Houston. (1926); Also see Francis Rawdon Chesney. (1845). The expedition for the survey of the rivers Euphrates and Tigris.
211 John Denison Baldwin. (1869). p. 65.
212 Diodorus Sicilus, Book I. 11, 12. Quoted in John Watson M'Crindle. (1901). Ancient India as described in classical literature. A. Constable and Co., Ltd.
213 Taylor, Thomas Griffith. (1937), p. 189. He continues: "These skulls are of considerable interest in connexion with the affinities of the Lower Melanesian negro with the African negro; for not many links are known in the wide extent separating the two groups."
214 Drusilla Dunjee Houston. (1926).
215 John Block Friedman. (1981). p. 18
216 Majid Husan. (2008). Geography of India. Tata McGraw-Hill.

217 Thomas Huxley. (1870). "On the Geographical Distribution of the Chief Modifications of Mankind."

218 Coppa, A. et al. (2006). Early Neolithic tradition of dentistry: Flint tips were surprisingly effective for drilling tooth enamel in a prehistoric population. Nature, 440.

219 Tom Housden, (2002). "Lost City could Rewrite History, BBC News. news.bbc.co.uk/hi/english/world/south_asia/newsid_1768000/1768109.stm

220 Quoted in Drusilla Dunjee Houston. (1926).

221 Taylor, Thomas Griffith. (1937), p. 189, 210-211

222 John Denison Baldwin. (1869). p. 54.

223 Christoph von Fürer-Haimendorf. (1982). He writes: "Although modern technology would make it easy to record the Pardhans' recitations on tape, so far no one has taken any steps in that direction, and the sacred oral literature of the Gonds may well disappear without leaving much trace."

224 See C.R. Bijoy. (Feb 2003). "A History of Discrimination, Conflict, and Resistance." www.pucl.org/Topics/Dalit-tribal/2003/adivasi.htm

225 See "Outcasts" and other essays in Supreme Understanding. (2009). Rap, Race, and Revolution: Solutions for Our Struggle. Supreme Design Publishing.

226 Meskill, John T. (Ed.) (1973). An Introduction to Chinese Civilization. Heath and Company, p. 4.

227 Bishop, Carl Whiting. (Sep 1934). "The Beginnings of North and South in China." Pacific Affairs, Vol. 7, Issue 3. p. 300.

228 Cheikh Anta Diop. (1989).

229 Roberts, J.A.G. (1996) p. 5.

230 Goodrich, L. Carrington. (1959). A Short History of the Chinese People, 3rd ed. Harper & Row. p. 5.

231 Eberhard, Wolfram. (1982). China's Minorities: Yesterday and Today. Wadsworth Publishing Co. p. 12-13. Quoted in Brunson, James E. (1995). "African Presence in Ancient China." In Rashidi, Runoko and Ivan Van Sertima. Eds. African Presence in Early Asia. Transaction Press, p. 233.

232 Brunson, James E. (1995). p. 233.

233 Liu, Li. The Chinese Neolithic: Trajectories to Early States.

234 Zhang, J., Xinghua Xiao, and Yun Kuen Lee. (2004). The early development of music. Analysis of the Jiahu bone flutes. Antiquity 78(302): 769-779.

235 Again, other accounts report differing dates, as is common with the Xia and the Shang dynasties. The Bamboo Annals says of the Shang that they rose to power over the Xia in 1523 B.C.

236 Li Chi. (1973). The Beginnings of Chinese Civilization. Univ of California Press. p. 15.

237 Eberhard, Wolfram. (1969). p. 17, 40.

238 Li Chi. (1973). p. 16-17.

239 Li Chi. (1973). p. 17.

240 Bishop, C.W. (1934) p. 299.

241 Eberhard, Wolfram, (1969). A History of China. University of California Press, p. 16.

242 Zhimin, An. (Dec. 1998) "Archaeological Research on Neolithic China." Current Anthropology. Vol. 29, No. 5. p. 754-8.

243 Bagley, Robert. (1999). "Shang Archaeology." Cambridge History of Ancient China. Cambridge University Press, p. 131. The Shang chariot exhibits a number of parallels with both Egyptian and West Asian models. p. 206-7.

244 Li Chi. (1973) p. 29-30.

245 Goodrich, L. Carrington. (1959). p. 4. The diffusion of this practice may prove quite intriguing if further researched, as the custom of exchanging cowry shells as currency is also a quite ubiquitous African custom.

246 Creel, Herrlee G. (1970) p. 201; Needham, Joseph. (1954) p. 85-86. Needham proposed alternately that they may have come from the east, specifically the Pacific Coast south of the Yangtze estuary. The Shang use of cowry shells for exchange is undoubtedly the origin of the fact that so many words with the general significance of "value" are based

on the character "Pei," which originally meant cowry shell. Also, the intimate relations between the Shang and the Eastern Yi is elucidated by the Zhou's capture, from the Eastern Yi, of an inventory of several elephant tusks, cowry shells, and a great quantity of southern bronze.

247 James Guthrie. (2001).

248 "Few Tourists Will Gaze on Pyramid Nest in China." (Mar 31 1947). Rocky Mountain News.

249 Chang, Kwang-Chih. (1999) "China on the Eve of the Historical Period." Cambridge History of Ancient China. p. 69.

250 Lihui Yang, Deming An, Jessica Anderson Turner. (2008). Handbook of Chinese Mythology. Oxford University Press. p. 84.

251 Keightley, David. (1999). p. 282-3.

252 Te-K'un, Cheng. (1960). Shang Civilization, Vol. III. W. Heffer and Sons, Ltd. p. 214.

253 Liang Shih-Chiu. (ed.) (1973). "Entry 7248: Li." A New Practical Chinese-English Dictionary. The Far East Book Company, Ltd., p. 1271.

254 Liang Shih-Chiu. (1973). "Entry 7250: Hei." p. 1271. Hei-zhong is written in the Wade-Giles system hei-chung.

255 Liang Shih-Chiu. (1973). p. 1272-3.

256 Liang Shih-Chiu. (1973). "Entry 7252: Ch'ien." p. 1272. In Wade-Giles, Qian is written Ch'ien.

257 Te-K'un, Cheng. (1960). p. 81. Linguists have identified Austroasiatic loanwords in Chinese that demonstrate the "strong likelihood of an Austroasiatic presence in south China in pre-imperial times."

258 Manansula, Paul Kekai. "Austric in India." International Journal of Dravidian Linguistics, Vol. XXVIII, No. 1.

259 Manansula, Paul Kekai. "Austric Origin of the Sumerian Language." Language Form, Vol. 22, No. 1-2. (Jan.-Dec. 1996).

260 Manansula, Paul Kekai. "Austric in India."

261 Nicholas Wade, (May 4 2011). "Finding on Dialects Casts New Light on the Origins of the Japanese People," NY Times.

262 Olsen, Sari; Miller-Antonio (1992). "The Palaeolithic in Southern China". Asian Perspectives 31 (2): 129–160.

263 Chang, K.C. (1989). translated by W. Tsao, ed. by B. Gordon. "The Neolithic Taiwan Strait". Kaogu 6: 541–550, 569.

264 Jiao, Tianlong (2007). The neolithic of southeast China: cultural transformation and regional interaction on the coast. Cambria Press. pp. 89–90.

265 For more on the history of alcohol and drug use among Original People throughout prehistory, see Volume Three.

266 Abel, Ernest L. (1980). "Cannabis in the Ancient World". Marihuana: the first twelve thousand years. New York City: Plenum Publishers.

267 Ian Caldwell. (1997). A rock carving and a newly discovered stone burial chamber at Pasemah, Sumatra. In Bijdragen tot de Taal-, Land-en Volkenkunde 153, No. 2, 169-182.; See Bellwood, P., (1985), Prehistory of the Indo-Malaysian Archipelago, Sydney: Academic Press.

268 Van der Hoop, A.N.J. Th. à Th. van der, (1932), Megalithic remains in South-Sumatra, Zutphen: Thieme. p. 130.

269 Ian Caldwell. (1997).

270 Ian Caldwell. (1997).

271 Nicholas Wade. (2006).

272 Gollan, K. (1985). Prehistoric dogs in Australia: an Indian origin? In Recent Advances in Indo-Pacific Prehistory, V.N. Misra, and P. Bellwood, eds. Oxford, p. 439–443.

273 Dixon, R.M.W. (1980). The Languages of Australia. Cambridge University Press.

274 Alan Redd et al. (2002). Gene Flow from the Indian Subcontinent to Australia: Evidence from the Y Chromosome. www..ncbi.nlm.nih.gov/pubmed/11967156

275 Pardis C. Sabeti et al. Genome-wide detection and characterization of positive selection

in human populations Nature 449, 913-918 (18 October 2007) doi:10.1038/nature06250
276 Tishkoff SA, et al. (Jun-Jul 2001). Haplotype diversity and linkage disequilibrium at human G6PD: recent origin of alleles that confer malarial resistance. Science. 293(5529):455-62.
277 Alan J. Redd and Mark Stoneking. (1999). "Peopling of the Sahul: mtDNA Variation in Aboriginal Australian and Papua New Guinean Populations," American Journal of Human Genetics, 65, p. 808.
278 Peter Marsh. (2002). Polynesian Pathways. http://www.polynesian-prehistory.com/
279 Peter Marsh. (2002).
280 Dayton, Leigh. (Dec 12 1992). "Pacific Islanders Were World's First Farmers," New Scientist, p. 14.
281 J. Macmillan Brown. (1907). Maori and Polynesian: their origin, history and culture. Hutchinson and Co.
282 J. Macmillan Brown. (1907).
283 J. Macmillan Brown. (1907).
284 J. Macmillan Brown. (1907).
285 J. Macmillan Brown. (1907).
286 J. Macmillan Brown. (1907).
287 J. Macmillan Brown. (1907).
288 Vigne J-D, Carrère I, Briois F, and Guilaine J. (2011). The Early Process of Mammal Domestication in the Near East: New Evidence from the Pre-Neolithic and Pre-Pottery Neolithic in Cyprus. Current Anthropology 52(S4):S255-S271.; Vigne J-D, Guilaine J, Debue K, Haye L, and Gérard P. (2004). Early Taming of the Cat in Cyprus. Science 304(2668):259.; Vigne J-D, et al. (2009). Pre-Neolithic wild boar management and introduction to Cyprus more than 11,400 years ago. Proceedings of the National Academy of Sciences 106(38):16135-16138.
289 J. Macmillan Brown. (1907).
290 J. Macmillan Brown. (1924). Riddle of the Pacific. T. Fisher Unwin Ltd. p. 17.
291 Dan Vergano, (Dec 12 2009). "Did Easter Island get 'ratted' out?" USA Today, www.usatoday.com/tech/science/discoveries/2005-12-05-easter-island_x.htm
292 Rhett A. Butler, (Dec 2005). "Easter Island's demise caused by rats, Dutch traders says new theory," Mongabay, http://news.mongabay.com/2005/1206-easter_island.html
293 Quoted in Gladwin, Harold S. (1947) p. 94
294 Taylor, Thomas Griffith. (1937)., p. 189.
295 Francis Mazière, (1969). Mysteries of Easter Island, London: Collins, p. 207.
296 L Pauwels, J Bergier. (1968). The Morning of the Magicians. Avon Books, p. 172-173.
297 John Denison Baldwin. (1871).
298 John Denison Baldwin. (1871).
299 John Denison Baldwin. (1871).
300 A.L. Kroeber. (Apr-Jun 1921). Observations on the Anthropology of Hawaii. American Anthropologist, Vol 23, No 2.
301 Heckenberger, et al. (2008). "Pre-Columbian Urbanism, Anthropogenic Landscapes, and the Future of the Amazon,"Science 321, no. 5893: 1214-1217. www.sciencemag.org/cgi/content/full/321/5893/1214?ijkey=A7pIT4arhED8I
302 John Roach. (Aug 2008). "Ancient Amazon Cities Found; Were Vast Urban Network." http://news.nationalgeographic.com/news/2008/08/080828-amazon-cities_2.html
303 Gibbons, Ann. (1990). "New View of Early Amazonia," Science, 248:1488.
304 Mann, Charles C. (2000). "Earthmovers of the Amazon, Science, 287:786.
305 James L. Guthrie. (2001).
306 Martti Pärssinen, Denise Schaan and Alceu Ranzi. (2009). "Pre-Columbian geometric earthworks in the upper Purús: a complex society in western Amazonia," Antiquity Journal 83, no 322: 1084-1095. http://antiquity.ac.uk/ant/083/ant0831084.htm
307 David Biello. (Aug 2008). "Ancient Amazon Actually Highly Urbanized." Scientific American. http://www.scientificamerican.com/article.cfm?id=lost-amazon-cities
308 Shady Solís, Ruth (2005). Caral Supe, Perú : the Caral-Supe civilization : 5,000 years

of cultural identity in Peru. Lima: Instituto Nacional de Cultura.

309 Joseph F. Powell. (2005). The First Americans: Race, Evolution and the Origin of Native Americans. Cambridge University Press

310 R.W. Keatinge (Ed.). Peruvian Prehistory: An Overview of Pre-Inca and Inca Society.

311 James L. Guthrie. (2001). Guthrie writes: "Studies of mummies and coprolites [Google that!] have established the presence of tropical intestinal parasites, especially Ancylostoma duodenale, in ancient South America. They were present at Boqueirão do Sítio da Pedra Furada (Brazil) by 5000 B.C. (Ferreira, Araújo, and Confalonieri 1988), in coastal Peru by 2700 B.C. (Verano 1992), and in Minas Gerais (Brazil) by 2500 B.C. (Araújo 1980), originating almost certainly in Southeast Asia or Oceania (Fonseca 1970; Ferriera, Araújo, and Confalonieri 1982). Direct travel across either ocean by ancestors of people such as the Lengua of Paraguay (Fonseca 1970) seems to be the best explanation, because tropical parasites do not survive cold climates. Soper (1927) indicated Indonesia or Polynesia as the likely source of American Ancylostoma duodenale."

312 Haas, Jonathan; Winifred Creamer, Alvaro Ruiz (Dec 23 2004). "Dating the Late Archaic occupation of the Norte Chico region in Peru". Nature 432 (7020): 1020–1023.

313 Haas, Jonathan; Winifred Creamer, Alvaro Ruiz (2004).

314 Mann, Charles C. (2006). 1491: New Revelations of the Americas Before Columbus. Vintage Books.

315 Mann, Charles C. (2006).

316 Mann, Charles C. (2006).

317 "Archaeologists shed new light on Americas' earliest known civilization" (Dec 22 2004). (Press release). Northern Illinois University.

318 Latin America Herald Tribune. (2009). "Study Reveals DNA Links Between Ancient Peruvians, Japanese." www.laht.com/article.asp?ArticleId=325015&CategoryId=14095

319 Norman Totten, (1988). "Categories of Evidence for Old World Contacts with Ancient America," in The Book of Mormon: The Keystone Scripture, ed. Paul R. Cheesman Religious Studies Center, Brigham Young University, p. 187–205.

320 J. Bernard Davis. "Ancient Peruvian Skulls." PaleoBabble. www.michaelsheiser.com/PaleoBabble/On%20Ancient%20Peruvian%20Skulls.pdf

321 Thomas W. Whitaker, "Endemism and Pre-Columbian Migration of the Bottle Gourd, Lagenaria siceraria," in Man Across the Sea, p. 320–27.

322 C. R. Stonor and Edgar Anderson, (1949). "Maize Among the Hill Peoples of Assam," Annals of the Missouri Botannical Garden 36 no. 3: 355–405; W. R. Stanton and Frank Willett, (1963). "Archaeological Evidence for Changes in Maize Type in West Africa: an Experiment in Technique," paper 150, 63: 117–23. M. D. W. Jeffreys, (1967). "Pre-Columbian Maize in Southern Africa," Nature 215: 695–97.

323 Kolata, Alan L. (1993). The Tiwanaku: Portrait of an Andean Civilization. Wiley.

324 Michael E. Moseley. (2005). "The Maritime Foundations of Andean Civilization: An Evolving Hypothesis. In Pedro Trillo. (Ed.). Peru y El Mar: 12000 anos del historia del pescaria. Sociedad Nacional de Pesqueria.

325 Ponce Sanginés, C. and G. M. Terrazas, (1970), Acerca De La Procedencia Del Material Lítico De Los Monumentos De Tiwanaku. Publication no. 21. Academia Nacional de Ciencias de Bolivia.

326 Robinson, Eugene (1990). In Bolivia, Great Excavations; "Tiwanaku Digs Unearthing New History of the New World," (Dec 11 1990) The Washington Post: d.01

327 Protzen, Jean-Pierre; Stella Nair, (1997), Who Taught the Inca Stonemasons Their Skills? A Comparison of Tiahuanaco and Inca Cut-Stone Masonry: The Journal of the Society of Architectural Historians. vol. 56, no. 2, p. 146-167.

328 Jess McNall. (Sep 2010). "Ancient Nubians Made Antibiotic Beer." Wired. www.wired.com/wiredscience/2010/09/antibiotic-beer/

329 Justin Jennings, Brenda J. Bowser. (2008). Drink, Power, and Society in the Andes. The University Press of Florida. http://libarts.wsu.edu/anthro/pdf/DrinkintheAndesproofs.pdf

330 Terry G. Powis, et al. (Dec 2007). "Oldest chocolate in the New World." Antiquity Vol

81 Issue 314.
331 Browman, D. L. (1981). "New light on Andean Tiwanaku". New Scientist. vol. 69, no. 4, p. 408-419.
332 Carol A. Schultze. (2008). The Role of Silver Ore Reduction in Tiwanaku State Expansion Into Puno Bay, Peru. Unpublished dissertation, available via ProQuest.
333 Morell, Virginia (2002). Empires Across the Andes National Geographic, 201(6): 106
334 McAndrews, Timothy L. et al. (1997). Regional Settlement Patterns in the Tiwanaku Valley of Bolivia. Journal of Field Archaeology 24: 67-83.
335 Arnold D.E., et al. (2008). The first direct evidence for the production of Maya Blue: rediscovery of a technology. Antiquity 82(315):151-164.
336 McClintock, Jack. (2000). "The Nasca Lines Solution" Discover, p. 76.
337 Sunday Book Review. (Jul 16 2006). The New York Times.
338 John Neal, (2000). All Done With Mirrors: An exploration of measure, proportion, ratio and number, The Secret Academy, p. 199.
339 Simon Romero. (Jan 2012). "Once Hidden by Forest, Carvings in Land Attest to Amazon's Lost World." NY Times. www.nytimes.com/2012/01/15/world/americas/land-carvings-attest-to-amazons-lost-world.html
340 Martti Pärssinen, Denise Schaan and Alceu Ranzi (2009). "Pre-Columbian geometric earthworks in the upper Purús: a complex society in western Amazonia". Antiquity 83 (322): 1084–1095.
341 Thomas H. Maugh II. (Nov 2009). "Peru's Nazca culture was brought down with its trees." Los Angeles Times. www.latimes.com/news/nationworld/nation/la-sci-nazca2-2009nov02,0,2088132.story
342 "Nasca People Of Ancient Peru: Forest Clearances Sealed Civilization's Downfall." (Nov 2009). Science Daily. www.sciencedaily.com/releases/2009/11/091102212153.htm
343 A.H. Verrill. (1929). Old Civilizations of the New World, New Home Library, p. 301.
344 James L. Guthrie. (2001).
345 J.A. Rogers, (1961). Africa's Gift to America: The Afro-American in the Making and Saving of the United States. p. 14
346 John H. Bracey Jr., August Meier, and Elliot Rudwick (eds.). (1970). Black Nationalism in America. The Bobbs-Merrill Company, Inc. p. 100.
347 PBS. (2005). "The Story Of... Smallpox – and other Deadly Eurasian Germs." Variables. www.pbs.org/gunsgermssteel/variables/smallpox.html
348 Owen, Wayne (2002). "Chapter 2 (TERRA–2): The History of Native Plant Communities in the South." Southern Forest Resource Assessment Final Report. U.S. Department of Agriculture, Forest Service, Southern Research Station.
349 David L. Lentz, ed. (2000). Imperfect balance: landscape transformations in the Precolumbian Americas. Columbia University Press. p. 241–242.
350 Bancroft, Hubert Howe. (1883). The Native Races of the Pacific States. Vol. 3.
351 Goetz, Delia and Sylvanus G. Goetz. (1950). The Popol Vuh. Trans. Adrian Recinos. University of Oklahoma Press.
352 Goetz, Delia and Sylvanus G. Goetz. (1950).
353 Gomez, Ermilo Abreu. (1992). The Popol Vuh. Dante. p. 9-10.
354 Runoko Rashidi. "The African Roots of Humanity and Civilization."
355 Donnald K. Anderson. (1988). "H.Con. Res.331." www.senate.gov/reference/resources/pdf/hconres331.pdf
356 Ellsworth Huntington. (1924). Character of Races As Influenced by Physical Environment, Natural Selection and Historical Development. Ayer Publishing.
357 Smithsonian Institution, Bureau of American Ethnology. (1912). Handbook of American Indians North of Mexico: N-Z. U.S. Government Printing Office.
358 Jennings, Francis, ed. (1985). The History and Culture of Iroquois Diplomacy: An Interdisciplinary Guide to the Treaties of the Six Nations and Their League. Syracuse University Press.
359 Smithsonian Institution, Bureau of American Ethnology. (1912). Handbook of American Indians North of Mexico: N-Z. U.S. Government Printing Office.

360 Clark Wissler, D. C. Duvall. (1908). Mythology of the Blackfoot Indians, Volume 2, Parts 1-3. The Trustees.

361 Clark Wissler, D. C. Duvall. (1908).

362 Clark Wissler, D. C. Duvall. (1908).

363 Roberts, C.A.; Roberts, S. (2006). New Mexico. University of New Mexico. p. 24–26.

364 Washburn, Wilcomb E. (1996). The Cambridge history of the native peoples of the Americas, Part 1. Cambridge University Press. p. 371.

365 Gibson, Jon L. (2000). The Ancient Mounds of Poverty Point: Place of Rings. University Press of Florida.

366 S. McClintock, J. Kincheloe. "Cahokia." www.meredith.edu/nativeam/cahokia.htm

367 Bill Iseminger. (1997). "Monks Mound Updates: Long-Awaited Projects on Monks Mound to be Completed Summer 1998." http://cahokiamounds.org/explore/monks-mound-updates.pdf

368 Frank Joseph. (2010). Advanced Civilizations of Prehistoric America, Bear and Company. p. 35, 39.

369 Alex Whitaker. "The Pre-Columbian Americas." Ancient Wisdom: Prehistory at your Fingertips. www.ancient-wisdom.co.uk/americaprecolumbian.htm

370 George C. Daniels. "Ocmulgee Mounds." Lost Worlds. http://lostworlds.org/ocmulgee_mounds/

371 Pawlaczyk, George (Feb 16 2010), "Copper men: Archaeologists uncover Stone Age copper workshop near Monks Mound." News-Democrat.

372 Stephen Denison Peet; F.H. Reveell. (1895). The American Antiquarian and Oriental Journal, Vol. 17.

373 John Denison Baldwin. (1871). Ancient America, In Notes on American Archaeology. Harper and Brothers.

374 John Denison Baldwin. (1871).

375 Richard Thorton. (2010). "America's architectural heritage - Sapelo Island, Georgia." www.examiner.com/article/america-s-architectural-heritage-sapelo-island-georgia

376 Stone pages. (Apr 2004). "Oldest mound complex identified." www.stonepages.com/news/archives/000680.html

377 Anonymous. (Jan 10 1907). Nature, 75:255.

378 Anonymous. (1907).

379 Graham Connah. (2001). African Civilizations: An Archaeological Perspective (2nd ed). Cambridge University Press.

380 African World Heritage Fund. "Saloum Delta." www.awhf.net/?p=735

381 Luz Evelia Martín Del Campo-Hermosillo. (2010). Genderscape: The Ecology Of A Gendering Landscape. Unpublished doctoral dissertation. University of Florida. http://etd.fcla.edu/UF/UFE0041553/martindelcampo_l.pdf

382 Saturno, WA; Stuart D, Beltran B (Mar 3 2006). "Early Maya writing at San Bartolo, Guatemala". Science 311(5765): 1281–3.

383 Michael D. Coe, (1987). The Maya, London: Thames and Hudson, p. 161.

384 de Garay, Alfonso, Lourdes Cobo de Gallegos and James Bowman. 1975. Relaciones Familiares en el Pedigree de los Lacandónes de México. Anales del INAH.

385 Luz Evelia Martín Del Campo-Hermosillo. (2010). Genderscape: The Ecology Of A Gendering Landscape. Unpublished doctoral dissertation. University of Florida. http://etd.fcla.edu/UF/UFE0041553/martindelcampo_l.pdf

386 Krupp, Edward C. (Feb 1999). "Igniting the Hearth." Sky & Telescope. p. 94.

387 Peterson, Frederick. (1959). Ancient Mexico. G.P. Putnam's Sons, p. 50.

388 Personal communication, quoted in Jordan, Keith M. "The African Presence in Ancient America: Evidence from Physical Anthropology." Van Sertima, Ivan. Ed. (1987). African Presence in Early America. Transaction Publishers, p. 139

389 "Yale research on Maya murals presented to Mexican anthropologists." (May 24 2002). Yale Bulletin and Calendar, 30(30) http://www.yale.edu/opa/arc-ybc/v30.n30/story3.html

390 Stephanie Pappas. (May 2012). "Nevermind the Apocalypse: Earliest Mayan Calendar Found." www.livescience.com/20218-apocalypse-oldest-mayan-calendar.html

391 Harold G. Lawrence, (Jun-Jul 1962). "African Explorers of the New World," The Crisis, p. 322.

392 Koenig, Seymore H. (2005). Acculturation in the Navajo Eden: New Mexico, 1550-1750. YBK Publishers.

393 McDonald, D.S. (1998). "Intimacy and Empire: Indian-African Interaction in Spanish Colonial New Mexico, 1500-1800". American Indian Quarterly 22(1/2): 134-156.

394 Ekkehart Malotki. (2000). Kokopelli: The Making of an Icon. Univ of Nebraska Press.

395 Leo Wiener. (1921). Africa and the Discovery of America, Vol. 3. p. 258.

396 Haas, Jonathan; Winifred Creamer, Alvaro Ruiz (Dec 23 2004). "Dating the Late Archaic occupation of the Norte Chico region in Peru". Nature 432 (7020): 1020–1023.

397 Thomas J. Sienkewicz. (2001).

398 Thomas J. Sienkewicz. (2001).

399 Quoted in Carolyn Tate (ed.). (1995). The Olmec World: Ritual and Rulership. p. 65.

400 Alexander von Wuthenau, (1970). The Art of Terracotta Pottery in Pre-Columbian Central and South America. Crown Publishers, Inc., p. 79.

401 "A Link Between Chinese and American Cultures?: The Olmec and the Shang." National Paleolithic Society. www.natlpaleo.org/articles/xu/new_xu.htm

402 Thomas J. Sienkewicz. (ed.). (2001). "Olmecs." Encyclopedia of the Ancient World. Salem Press.

403 Wiercinski, A. (1971), "Affinidades raciales de algunas poblaines antiquas de Mexico", Anales de Instituto Nacional de Antropología e Historia, 7a epoca, tomo II, p. 123-143; Wiercinski, A. (1972). "Inter- and Intrapopulational Racial Differentiation of Tlatilco, Cerro de Las Mesas, Teothuacan, Monte Alban and Yucatan Maya", XXXIX Congreso Intern. de Americanistas, Lima 1970, Vol. 1, p. 231-252; Wiercinski,A. (1972). "An anthropological study on the origin of 'Olmecs'", Swiatowit, 33:1972, p. 143-174.

404 Haydenblit R. (Jun 1996). "Dental variation among four prehispanic Mexican populations." Am J Phys Anthropol 100, no 2: 225-46, www.ncbi.nlm.nih.gov/pubmed/8771313

405 Susan T. Evans, David L. Webster. (2009). Archaeology of Ancient Mexico and Central America: An Encyclopedia. Routledge.

406 R.A. Diehl. (2004). The Olmecs. Thames & Hudson, p. 25.

407 J.E. Cark and M.E. Pye. (2000). Olmec Archaeology in Mesoamerica. p. 234.

408 Richard G. Lesure. (Ed.) (2011). Early Mesoamerican Social Transformations: Archaic and Formative Lifeways in the Soconusco Region. University of California Press.

409 TG. Powis, et al. (Dec 2007). "Oldest chocolate in the New World." Antiquity 81(314).

410 Michael Balter. (Mar 25 2009). "Early Chinese May Have Eaten Millet Before Rice." Science. http://news.sciencemag.org/sciencenow/2009/03/25-01.html

411 Nicholas Bakalar. (Mar 2 2006). "Corn, Arrowroot Fossils in Peru Change Views on Pre-Inca Culture." National Geographic News. http://news.nationalgeographic.com/news/2006/03/0302_060302_peru_corn.html

412 James L. Guthrie. (2001).

413 Foster, Mary LeCron. (1999). The Transoceanic Trail: The Proto-Pelagian Language Phylum. Pre-Columbiana 1(1/2):88-113.

414 Arthur Evans. (1901). "The Palace of Minos." Vignaud Pamphlets: Crete. p. 436

415 Lancaster, Andrew (2009). "Y Haplogroups, Archaeological Cultures and Language Families: a Review of the Multidisciplinary Comparisons using the case of E-M35". Journal of Genetic Genealogy 5(1).

416 Rene Verneau. (1906). Les Grottes de Grimaldi, Vol. II., Monaco.

417 Boule, M. & Vallois, H.V. (1957). Fossil Men. Dryden Press. p. 291-292.

418 Fleure, H.J. (1945). The distribution of types of skin color, Geographical Review, 35, 580-595.

419 This "Mediterranean complexion" is usually referred to in the early literature with such terms as "ruddy," "reddish" "dark red" "reddish-brown," "brunet," "bronze," "copper-colored," "swarthy," and in rare instances, "brown."

420 Diop, Cheikh Anta. (1989). p. 131. In the same work, Diop professed; "the so-called

brown Mediterranean race is none other than the Negro race."
421 Giuseppe Sergi. (1901). p. 252.
422 Donald A. Mackenzie. (1917). Crete and Pre-Hellenic Europe: Myths and Legends, The Gresham Publishing Co. p. 147.
423 Angelo Mosso. (1910). The Dawn of Mediterranean Civilisation. Baker & Taylor. p. 405.
424 Angelo Mosso. (1910). p. 405-6.
425 Haddon, A. C. (1924). The races of man and their distribution. p. 24-25
426 Haddon, A. C. (1924). p. 24-25
427 Haddon, A. C. (1924).
428 Albert Churchward. (1913). Signs and Symbols of Primordial Man. Allen.
429 Albert Churchward. (1913).
430 Diop, Cheikh Anta. (1989). p. 264.
431 Sir Harry Hamilton Johnston. (1910). The Negro in the New World. p. 27
432 Sir Harry Hamilton Johnston. (1910). p. 27
433 W.E.B. Du Bois. (1904). Some Notes on Negro Crime, Particularly in Georgia. Atlanta University Press. p. 15.
434 John Denison Baldwin. (1869). p. 40-41.
435 Plato. (360 BC). Timaeus. Translated by Benjamin Jowett. Available at http://classics.mit.edu/Plato/timaeus.html
436 Wesley John Gaines. (1897). p. 12.
437 Martin Bernal. (1987). Black Athena: Afroasiatic Roots of Classical Civilization. Rutgers University Press. p. 77.
438 H. L. Taylor. (Jul 1930). "The Origin and Development of Lenses in Ancient Times." British Journal of Physiological Optics.
439 Donald A. Mackenzie. (1917). p.187.
440 James Baikie. (1910). The Sea-Kings of Crete. A. and C. Black. p. 144.
441 H.R. Hall. (1923). Rhind Lectures. p. 25-26.
442 Arthur Evans. (1921). The Palace of Minos, Vol. 1. MacMillan and Co. p. 16
443 Donald A. Mackenzie. (1917). p. 163.
444 H.R. Hall. (1923). p. 27.
445 Vigne J-D, Carrère I, Briois F, and Guilaine J. (2011). The Early Process of Mammal Domestication in the Near East: New Evidence from the Pre-Neolithic and Pre-Pottery Neolithic in Cyprus. Current Anthropology 52(S4):S255-S271.; Vigne J-D, Guilaine J, Debue K, Haye L, and Gérard P. (2004). Early Taming of the Cat in Cyprus. Science 304(2668):259; Vigne J-D, et al. (2009). Pre-Neolithic wild boar management and introduction to Cyprus more than 11,400 years ago. Proceedings of the National Academy of Sciences 106(38):16135-16138.
446 K. Kris Hirst. "Shillourokambos: PrePottery Neolithic Site in Cyprus." About. http://archaeology.about.com/od/shthroughsiterms/qt/Shillourokambos.htm
447 Alonso S, Flores C, Cabera V. (2005). The place of Basque in the European y-Chromosome diversity landscape, European Journal of Human Genetics, 13, p.1293-1302.
448 David MacRitchie. (1893). Fians, Fairies, and Picts. Two Horizons Press (In Production).
449 Harold Peake, (1922). The Bronze Age and the Celtic World. Benn Brothers. p. 29
450 Grafton Elliot Smith. (1911). The Ancient Egyptians. Harper & Brothers. p. 58.
451 James Owen. (2007). Stonehenge Settlement Found: Builders' Homes, "Cult Houses." National Geographic News. http://news.nationalgeographic.com/news/2007/01/070130-stonehenge_2.html
452 Thomas Moore, (1835). The History of Ireland Vol. 1. Orme, Brown, Green and Longmans, p. 38
453 Geoffry of Monmouth. (republished 1904).Histories of the Kings of Britain, (trans. Sebastian Evans). Available at www.sacred-texts.com/neu/eng/gem/gem09.htm
454 Kurt Mendelssohn. (1974). The Riddle of the Pyramids. Book Club Associates.

455 David MacRitchie. (1884). Ancient and Modern Britons, Vol. I, p.14

456 Godfrey Higgins. (1836). p. 59.

457 Albert Churchward. (1913). p. 197

458 Alexander Winchell. (1878). Adamites & preadamites: A popular discussion concerning the remote representatives of the human species & their relation to the Biblical Adam. J.T. Roberts.

459 Alexander Winchell. (1878).

460 Andra Jackson. (Feb 15 2011). "Womaddicts to sample ancestral electronica." The Sydney Morning Herald.

461 Charles Isaac Elton. (1882). Origins of English history. B. Quaritch. p. 138-162.

462 Charles Isaac Elton. (1882).

463 Idris Llewelyn Foster, Glyn Edmund Daniel. (1965). Prehistoric and early Wales. Routledge and K. Paul. p. 157.

464 Charles Isaac Elton. (1882).

465 Greg Noonan. (2009). An Seanchas: A study of ancient Irish origin stories by Gregory. http://www.anseanchas.com/

466 Charles Isaac Elton. (1882).

467 Stokes, Whitley (ed. and trans.). (1908). "The Training of Cúchulainn." Revue Celtique 29, p. 109-147. Later in this legend, Cú Chulainn seeks a woman's hand in marriage, whose father is a "big man" described in the following way: "Black as coal was every joint of him, from sole to crown." The father doesn't want Chulainn marrying his daughter, but Cú Chulainn trains as a warrior and comes back, killing the father and his men to abduct his daughter.

468 Greg Noonan. (2009).

469 James Mooney. (1888). "The Funeral Customs of Ireland." Proceedings of the American Philosophical Society, Vol. 25, p. 248.

470 James Mooney. (1888).

471 James Mooney. (1888).

472 Luke, Don. (1985). "African Presence in the Early History of the British Isles and Scandinavia." In Ivan Van Sertima. (Ed.). African Presence in Early Europe. Transaction Press. p. 223-44.

473 John Adams. (1802). A New History of Great Britain from the Invasion of Julius Caesar to the Present Time. T.N. Longman & O. Rees, p. 13.

474 Joseph Ritson. (1827). Memoirs of the Celts or Gauls. Payne and Foss, p. 114.

475 David MacRitchie. (1884). Ancient and Modern Britons: a retrospect, Vol. 2. Kegan Paul, Trench & Co., p. 157.

476 Charles Isaac Elton. (1882).

477 Charles Isaac Elton. (1882).

478 J.A. Rogers. (1980). Nature Knows No Color Line. Helga M. Rogers, p. 71.

479 Wesley John Gaines. (1897). p. 11.

480 Wesley John Gaines. (1897). p. 11.

481 Hakim Bey. "Manifesto of the Black Thorn League." http://hermetic.com/bey/blackthorn.html

482 Art MacDonald. (2011). "How the Irish Became White." Available at racism.org

483 Charles Isaac Elton. (1882).

484 David MacRitchie. (1884). p. 187.

485 Joseph Ritson, (1828). Annals of Caledonian, Picts, and Scots. Vol. II, Edinburgh: Ward D. Laing, footnote p. 7, 27.

486 John Rhys. (1902). The Welsh People, p. 618

487 Glanville Price. (2000). The Languages in Britain and Ireland, John Wiley & Sons

488 Charles Squire (1905). Celtic Myth and Legend. Available at www.sacred-texts.com/neu/celt/cml/cml07.htm

489 Editor. (Oct 1875). "Current Literature." The Academy and Literature, 8(182), p. 451.

490 William Chambers, Robert Chambers. (1884). Chambers's information for the people. W. & R. Chambers, p. 4.

491 "North Africans may have beaten Celts to Ireland." (May 28 2000). The Sunday Times; See also Morris-Jones, J. (1900). "Pre-Aryan syntax in insular Celtic'.' In Rhys, John and Brynmor-Jones, David (eds), The Welsh People, 617–41; and Pokorny, J. (1926-1930). "Das nicht indo-germanische Substrat im Irischen'.' Zeitschrift für celtische Philologie, 16:95–144, 231–66, 363–94; 17 (1927–8):373–88; 18 (1929–30):233–48.

492 Roger Blench. (1999). Archaeology and Language IV: Language Change and Cultural Transformation. Taylor & Francis.

493 Hakim Bey. "Manifesto of the Black Thorn League." http://hermetic.com/bey/blackthorn.html

494 Patrick T. English, (Jan-Oct 1959). Cushites, Colchians, and Khazars, Journal of Near Eastern Studies, Vol. 18.

495 John Colarusso. Nart Sagas from the Caucasus: Myths and Legends from the Circassians, Abazas, Abkhaz, and Ubykhs. Princeton University Press.

496 The Nart Sagas are available in Russian at www.kolhida.ru Google Translate can help convert most of the content to English.

497 Patrick T. English, (1959).

498 Patrick T. English, (1959).

499 Kesha Fikes and Alaina Lemon. (2002). African Presence in Former Soviet Space. Annual Review of Anthropology, Vol. 31. p. 517.

500 "Roman remains in York are 'elite' African woman." (Feb 2010). BBC News. http://news.bbc.co.uk/2/hi/uk_news/england/north_yorkshire/8538888.stm

501 "Roman remains in York are 'elite' African woman." (Feb 2010).

502 David MacRitchie. (1884). p. 157.

503 Lusane, Clarence (2003). Hitler's Black Victims: The Historical Experiences of European Blacks, Africans and African Americans During the Nazi Era. Routledge.

504 "Hitler Jewish? DNA Tests Show Dictator May Have 'Had Jewish And African Roots.'" (May 2011). Huffington Post. www.huffingtonpost.com/2010/08/25/hitler-jewish-dna-tests-s_n_693568.html

505 Cerezo M, Achilli A, Olivieri A et al. (May 2012). "Reconstructing ancient mitochondrial DNA links between Africa and Europe". Genome Res. 22 (5): 821–6.

506 Cerezo M. et al. (2012). The Moors came thousands of years later, carrying a different lineage, E1b1a, which evolved after E1b1b.

507 Quoted in Jean-Pierre Hallet. (1973). Pygmy Kitabu. Random House. p. 14.

508 John Iliffe. (2007). p. 12

509 Richard A. Lovett. (Jul 2006). "Bigger Cities Causing Stronger Summer Storms, Experts Say," National Geographic News, http://news.nationalgeographic.com/news/2006/07/060726-rain-cities.html

510 Chris Scarre (Ed.) (2003). Past Worlds Atlas of Archaeology. Borders Press.

511 Chris Scarre. (2003).

512 Underhill and Kivisild. (2007). "Use of Y Chromosome and Mitochondrial DNA Population Structure in Tracing Human Migrations". Annu. Rev. Genet. 41 (1): 539–64.

513 Ricaut FX, Waelkens M (Oct 2008). "Cranial discrete traits in a Byzantine population and eastern Mediterranean population movements". Human Biology 80 (5): 535–64.

514 John Illife. (2007). p. 10.

515 Batini et al. (2011). Signatures of the pre-agricultural peopling processes in sub-Saharan Africa as revealed by the phylogeography of early Y chromosome lineages.

516 Supreme Understanding. (2009). Rap, Race and Revolution: Solutions for Our Struggle. Supreme Design Publishing.

517 Steve Taylor. (2005). The Fall: The Evidence for a Golden Age, 6,000 Years of Insanity, and the Dawning of a New Era. O Books.

518 Steve Taylor. (2005).

519 Kurt Mendelssohn. (1974). The Riddle of the Pyramids. Book Club Associates.

520 John Wilford, (Jan 31 2007). "Wooden counterpart of Stonehenge found." NY Times.

521 Kalb, Philine, (Sep 1 1996). Megalith-building, stone transport and territorial markers; evidence from Vale de Rodrigo, Evora, south Portugal. Antiquity.

522 Kalb, Philine. (1996).
523 Gabriel Cooney. (2000). Opening the ground: archaeology and education in Ireland Antiquity. Vol. 74, No. 283, p. 199–203.
524 Kalb, Philine, (1996).
525 Giuseppe Sergi. (1901). p. 71
526 Bahn, Paul G. (1985). "Megalithic Recycling in Brittany," Nature, 314:671.
527 Geoffry of Monmouth. (republished 1904).Histories of the Kings of Britain, (trans. Sebastian Evans). Available at http://www.sacred-texts.com/neu/eng/gem/gem09.htm
528 Chris Scarre, (2010) "Rocks of Ages: Tempo and Time in Megalithic Monuments," European Journal of Archaeology 13(2):175- 193.
529 Dan Vergano, (Aug 2010). "Europe's Prehistoric Tombs Built in Bursts," USA Today. http://content.usatoday.com/communities/sciencefair/post/2010/08/barrow-tombs-of-prehistoric-europe-built-in-bursts/1
530 Anonymous; (Jan 1 1978). "Saudis Seek Experts to Solve a Desert Mystery," Kayhan International, p. 7.
531 T.E. Peet, (1912). Rough Stone Monuments and their Buiders, p. 36
532 Milburn, Mark. (1981). "Multi-Arm Stone Tombs of Central Sahara," Antiquity, 55:210.
533 Elizabeth Allo Isichei. (1997). A History of African Societies to 1870.
534 UNESCO. (1981). General History of Africa: Methodology and African prehistory.
535 Debra Black. (Oct 11 2012). "Bronze Age axe heads reveal secrets behind Stonehenge." The Toronto Star. www.thestar.com/news/world/article/1269131
536 Stan Lehman, (2006). "Another 'Stonehenge' Discovered in Amazon," NBC News. http://www.msnbc.msn.com/id/13582228/#.T9D907UmXIU
537 J. Macmillan Brown. (1907).
538 Stocks, Denys A. (2001). "Testing Ancient Egyptian Granite-Working Methods in Aswan, Upper Egypt," Antiquity, 75:89.
539 Martin Bernal. (1987).
540 Keita S.O.Y. (2005) Early Nile Valley farmers from El-Badari, aboriginals or "European" Agro-Nostratic Immigrants? Craniometric affinities considered with other data. Journal of Black Studies, 36:191-208.; See also Keita S.O.Y., Boyce, A.J. (2005).
541 Blench R (2006). Archaeology, Language, and the African Past. Rowman Altamira.
542 Ehret C., Keita S.O.Y., Newman P. (2004). The Origins of Afroasiatic: A response to Diamond and Bellwood (2003) in the Letters of Science 306, no. 5702, p. 1680.
543 Ehret C. (1995). Reconstructing Proto-Afro-Asiatic (Proto-Afrasian). University of California Press. Also see Ehret C (2002), The Civilizations of Africa: A History to 1800. James Currey Publishers; and Ehret C (2002) Language family expansions: broadening our understandings of cause from an African perspective, in Bellwood and Renfrew (Eds). Examining the Farming/Language Dispersal Hypothesis. Macdonald Institute for Archaeological Research.
544 Ofer Bar-Yosef and Anna Belfer-Cohen. (1998).
545 Nicholas Wade. (May 2000). "The Human Family Tree: Ten Adams and Eighteen Eves," New York Times.
546 Shlush, L.I. et al. (2009). "The Druze: A Population Genetic Refugium of the Near East." PLoS ONE 3(5): e2105.
547 Nicholas Wade. (2006).
548 M.D. Brown et al. (1998). mtDNA haplogroup X: an ancient link between Europe/Western Asia and North America?'American Journal of Human Genetics, v. 63, p. 1852-61, www.pubmedcentral.nih.gov
549 "Shawnee Mythology" Archived at www.bigorrin.org/archive123.htm
550 Bengston, John D. (2008), "Materials for a Comparative Grammar of the Dene–Caucasian (Sino-Caucasian) Languages." Aspects of Comparative Linguistics, 3, RSUH Publishers, p. 45–118.
551 M D Brown, S H Hosseini, A Torroni, H J Bandelt, J C Allen, T G Schurr, R Scozzari, F Cruciani, and D C Wallace. (Dec 1998). "mtDNA haplogroup X: An ancient link

between Europe/Western Asia and North America?" Am J Hum Genet 63, no. 6: 1852–1861. www.ncbi.nlm.nih.gov/pmc/articles/PMC1377656/

552 Donald N. Yates. (2009). Anomalous Mitochondrial DNA Lineages in the Cherokee. http://dnaconsultants.com/announcements/anomalous-mitochondrial-dna-lineages-in-the-cherokee

553 Hrdlicka, Ales. (1935). Pueblos, with Comparative Data on the Bulk of the Tribes of the Southwest and 460.

554 Stubbs, Bryan D. (1998). A Curious Element in Uto-Aztecan Linguistics. Epigraphic Society Occasional Papers 23:109-40.

555 Mary Ritchie Key. (1994). American Indian Languages Before Columbus. NEARA Journal 28(3,4):103-12.

556 Gordon, Cyrus Herzl. (1991). New Directions in the Study of Ancient Middle Eastern Cultures. Bulletin of the Middle Eastern Cultural Center in Japan 5:53-65.

557 Smithsonian Institution, Bureau of American Ethnology. (1912). Handbook of American Indians North of Mexico: N-Z. U.S. Government Printing Office.

558 Samy Swayd. (1998). The Druzes: An Annotated Bibliography. ISES Publications.

559 Sorenson, John L., and Martin H. Raish, comps. (1996.) Pre-Columbian Contact with the Americas across the Oceans, 2nd ed., 2 vols. Research Press.

560 Matt Kaplan, (Nov 8 2010). "Early Cities Spurred Evolution of Immune System?" National Geographic. http://news.nationalgeographic.com/news/2010/11/101108-cities-immune-system-tuberculosis-tb-evolution-dna-genetics-science

561 See ""The Black Man is the 7 in the Center of the Universe" in Supreme Understanding. C'BS Alife Allah. (2012). The Science of Self, Volume One: Man, God, and the Mathematical Language of Nature. Supreme Design Publishing.

562 Sonia R. Zakrzewski. (2003). "Variation in Ancient Egyptian Stature and BodyProportions." American Journal of Physical Anthropology 121:219–229

563 Angelo Mosso. (1910). p. 405-6.

564 Thomas Huxley. (1865). "On the Methods and Results of Ethnology" The Huxley Files: Collected Essays VII. http://aleph0.clarku.edu/huxley/CE7/M-REthn.html

565 Thomas Huxley. (1865).

566 Anne-Lyse Ducrest, Laurent Keller, Alexandre Roulin, (Sep 2008). Pleiotropy in the melanocortin system, coloration and behavioural syndromes, Trends in Ecology & Evolution, 23(9), p. 502-510.

567 J. Philippe Rushton, Donald I. Templer, (Jul 2012). Do pigmentation and the melanocortin system modulate aggression and sexuality in humans as they do in other animals? Personality and Individual Differences, 53(1), p. 4-8.

568 See The Science of Self, Volume One for details.

569 Chancellor Williams. (1987). The Destruction of Black Civilization, p. 31-32

ALSO FROM OUR COMPANY

How to Hustle and Win, Part 1: A Survival Guide for the Ghetto

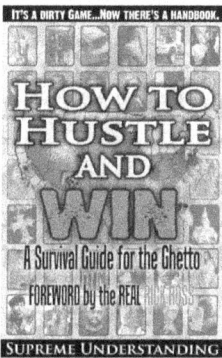

By Supreme Understanding
Foreword by the Real Rick Ross

This is the book that started it all. Now an international bestseller, this book has revolutionized the way people think of "urban literature." It offers a street-based analysis of social problems, plus practical solutions that anyone can put to use.

CLASS	PAGES	RETAIL	RELEASE
I-1	336	$14.95	Jun. 2008

ISBN: 978-0-9816170-0-8

How to Hustle and Win, Part 2: Rap, Race, and Revolution

By Supreme Understanding
Foreword by Stic.man of Dead Prez

Seen here in its original green cover, the controversial follow-up to *How to Hustle and Win* digs even deeper into the problems we face, and how we can solve them. Part One focused on personal change, and Part Two explores the bigger picture of changing the entire hood.

CLASS	PAGES	RETAIL	RELEASE
I-1	384	$14.95	Apr. 2009

ISBN: 978-0-9816170-9-1

Knowledge of Self: A Collection of Wisdom on the Science of Everything in Life

Edited by Supreme Understanding, C'BS Alife Allah, and Sunez Allah, Foreword by Lord Jamar of Brand Nubian

Who are the Five Percent? Why are they here? In this book, over 50 Five Percenters from around the world speak for themselves, providing a comprehensive introduction to the esoteric teachings of the Nation of Gods and Earths.

CLASS	PAGES	RETAIL	RELEASE
I-2	256	$14.95	Jul. 2009

ISBN: 978-0-9816170-2-2

The Hood Health Handbook, Volume One (Physical Health)

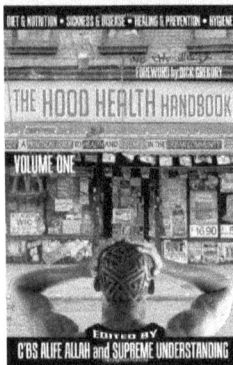

Edited by Supreme Understanding and C'BS Alife Allah, Foreword by Dick Gregory

Want to know why Black and brown people are so sick? This book covers the many "unnatural causes" behind our poor health, and offers hundreds of affordable and easy-to-implement solutions.

CLASS	PAGES	RETAIL	RELEASE
PH-1	480	$19.95	Nov. 2010

ISBN: 978-1-935721-32-1

The Hood Health Handbook, Volume Two (Mental Health)

Edited by Supreme Understanding and C'BS Alife Allah

This volume covers mental health, how to keep a healthy home, raising healthy children, environmental issues, and dozens of other issues, all from the same down-to-earth perspective as Volume One.

CLASS	PAGES	RETAIL	RELEASE
MH-1	480_	$19.95	Nov. 2010

ISBN: 978-1-935721-33-8

A Taste of Life: 1,000 Vegetarian Recipes from Around the World

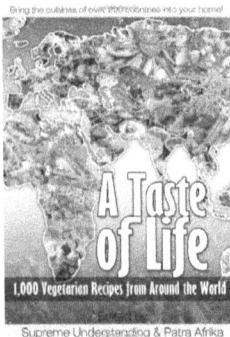

Edited by Supreme Understanding and Patra Afrika

This cookbook makes it easy to become vegetarian. In addition to over 1,000 recipes from everywhere you can think of, plus over 100 drink and smoothie recipes, this book also teaches how to transition your diet, what to shop for, how to cook, as well as a guide to nutrients and vitamins.

CLASS	PAGES	RETAIL	RELEASE
W-1	400	$19.95	Jun. 2011

ISBN: 978-1-935721-10-9

La Brega: Como Sobrevivir En El Barrio

By Supreme Understanding

Thanks to strong demand coming from Spanish-speaking countries, we translated our groundbreaking How to Hustle and Win into Spanish, and added new content specific to Latin America. Because this book's language is easy to follow, it can also be used to brush up on your Spanish.

CLASS	PAGES	RETAIL	RELEASE
0-1	336	$14.95	Jul. 2009

ISBN: 978-0981617-08-4

Locked Up but Not Locked Down: A Guide to Surviving the American Prison System

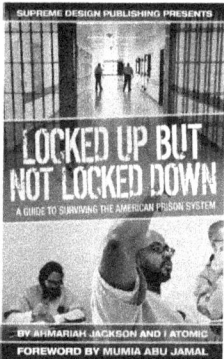

By Ahmariah Jackson and IAtomic Allah
Foreword by Mumia Abu Jamal

This book covers what it's like on the inside, how to make the most of your time, what to do once you're out, and how to stay out. Features contributions from over 50 insiders, covering city jails, state and federal prisons, women's prisons, juvenile detention, and international prisons.

CLASS	PAGES	RETAIL	RELEASE
J-1	288	$14.95	Jul. 2012

ISBN: 978-1935721-00-0

The Science of Self: Man, God, and the Mathematical Language of Nature

By Supreme Understanding and C'BS Alife Allah

How did the universe begin? Is there a pattern to everything that happens? What's the meaning of life? What does science tell us about the depths of our SELF? Who and what is God? This may be one of the deepest books you can read.

CLASS	PAGES	RETAIL	RELEASE
I-4	360	$19.95	Jun. 2012

ISBN: 978-1935721-67-3

The Science of Self: Man, God, and the Mathematical Language of Nature (Hardcover Edition)

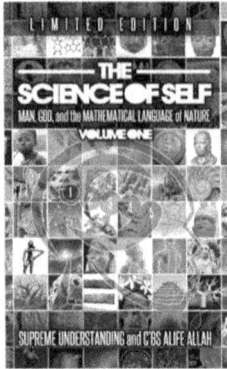

By Supreme Understanding

A beautiful hardcover edition of the bestselling work, *The Science of Self*. Under the full-color dust jacket is an embossed clothbound hard cover. Autographed and numbered as part of a special limited edition series, this book also includes the 16 full-color inserts found in the paperback edition.

CLASS	PAGES	RETAIL	RELEASE
I-4	360	$34.95	Jun. 2012

Only available direct from publisher.

365 Days of Real Black History Calendar (2012 Edition)

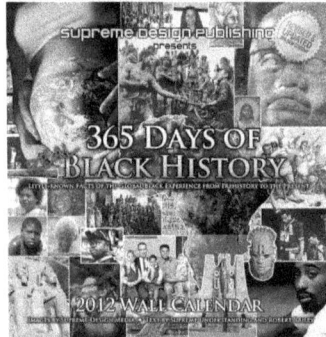

By Supreme Understanding and Robert Bailey

A calendar that'll never be out-dated! Over 365 important facts and quotes covering little-known, but important, moments in Black history. Written in brief chunks and easy language for all audiences.

CLASS	PGS	PRICE	RELEASE
I-2	26	$2.95	2011

Only available direct from publisher.

365 Days of Real Black History Calendar (2013 Edition)

By Supreme Understanding

Our 2013 calendar and planner was also designed to be timeless, as it's a beautifully-designed companion to *When the World was Black*. You'll find dozens of striking full-color images that help tell the stories of global Black history.

CLASS	PAGES	PRICE	RELEASE
I-2	26	$4.95	2012

Only available direct from publisher.

When the World was Black, Part One: Prehistoric Cultures

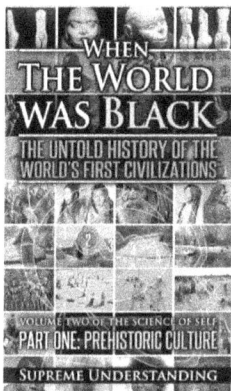

By Supreme Understanding
Foreword by Runoko Rashid

When does Black history begin? Certainly not with slavery. In two volumes, historian Supreme Understanding explores over 200,000 years of Black history from every corner of the globe. Part One covers the first Black communities to settle the world, establishing its first cultures and traditions. Their stories are remarkable.

CLASS	PAGES	RETAIL	RELEASE
I-3	400	$19.95	Feb. 2013

ISBN: 978-1-935721-04-8

When the World Was Black, Part Two: Ancient Civilizations

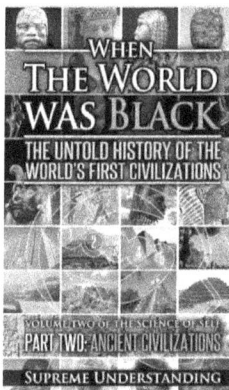

By Supreme Understanding

Part Two covers the ancient Black civilizations that gave birth to the modern world. Black people built the first urban civilizations in Africa, Asia, Europe, and the Americas. And every claim in these books is thoroughly documented with reputable sources. Do you want to know the story of your ancestors? You should. We study the past to see what the future will bring.

CLASS	PAGES	RETAIL	RELEASE
I-3	400	$19.95	Feb. 2013

ISBN: 978-1-935721-05-5

When the World was Black, Parts One and Two (Hardcover)

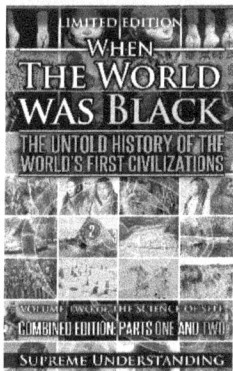

By Supreme Understanding

An incredible limited edition that combines Part One and Part Two into a single book, cased in an embossed clothbound hardcover and dust jacket. Autographed and numbered, this collector's item also includes both sets of full-color inserts.

CLASS	PAGES	RETAIL	RELEASE
I-3	800	$19.95	Dec. 2013

Only available direct from publisher.

Black Rebellion: Eyewitness Accounts of Major Slave Revolts

Edited by Dr. Sujan Dass

Who will tell the stories of those who refused to be slaves? What about those who fought so effectively that they forced their slavers to give up? Black Rebellion is a collection of historical "eyewitness" accounts of dozens of major revolts and uprisings, from the U.S. to the Caribbean, as well as a history of slavery and revolt.

CLASS	PAGES	RETAIL	RELEASE
P-3	272	$14.95	May 2010

ISBN: 978-0-981617-04-6

The Heroic Slave

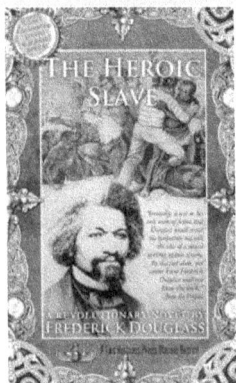

By Frederick Douglass

Most people don't know that Douglass wrote a novel...or that, in this short novel, he promoted the idea of violent revolt. By this time in his life, the renowned abolitionist was seeing things differently. This important piece of history comes with *David Walker's Appeal*, all in one book.

CLASS	PAGES	RETAIL	RELEASE
P-3	160	$14.95	Apr. 2011

ISBN: 978-1-935721-27-7

David Walker's Appeal

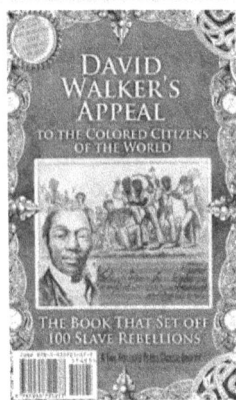

By David Walker

This is one of the most important, and radical, works ever published against slavery. Rather than call for an end by peaceful means, Walker called for outright revolution. His calls may have led to over 100 revolts, including those described in *Black Rebellion*. This important piece of history comes with Douglass' *The Heroic Slave*, which it may have helped inspire.

CLASS	PAGES	RETAIL	RELEASE
P-3	160	$14.95	Apr. 2011

ISBN: 978-1-935721-27-7

Darkwater: Voices from Within the Veil, Annotated Edition

By W.E.B. Du Bois

This book makes Du Bois' previous work, like *Souls of Black Folk*, seem tame by comparison. *Darkwater* is revolutionary, uncompromising, and unconventional in both its content and style, addressing the plight of Black women, the rise of a Black Messiah, a critical analysis of white folks, and the need for outright revolution.

CLASS	PAGES	RETAIL	RELEASE
I-4	240	$14.95	Jun. 2011

ISBN: 978-0-981617-07-7

The African Abroad: The Black Man's Evolution in Western Civilization, Volume One

By William Henry Ferris

Who would think a book written in 1911 could cover so much? Ferris, chairman of the UNIA, speaks up for the Black man's role in Western civilization. He discusses a wealth of history, as well as some revolutionary Black theology, exploring the idea of man as God and God as man.

CLASS	PAGES	RETAIL	RELEASE
I-5	570	$29.95	Oct. 2012

ISBN: 978-1935721-66-6

The African Abroad: Volume Two

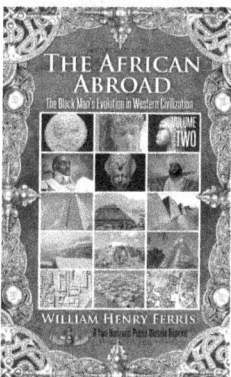

By William Henry Ferris

The second volume of Ferris' epic covers important Black biographies of great leaders, ancient and modern. He tells the stories of forty "Black Immortals." He also identifies the African origins of many of the world's civilizations, including ancient Egypt, Akkad, Sumer, India, and Europe.

CLASS	PAGES	RETAIL	RELEASE
I-5	330	$19.95	Oct. 2012

ISBN: 978-1-935721-69-7

From Poverty to Power: The Realization of Prosperity and Peace

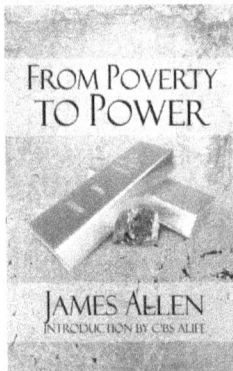

By James Allen

Want to transform your life? James Allen, the author of the classic *As a Man Thinketh,* explores how we can turn struggle and adversity into power and prosperity. This inspirational text teaches readers about their innate strength and the immense power of the conscious mind.

CLASS	PAGES	RETAIL	RELEASE
I-3	144	$14.95	May 2010

ISBN: 978-0-981617-05-3

Daily Meditations: A Year of Guidance on the Meaning of Life

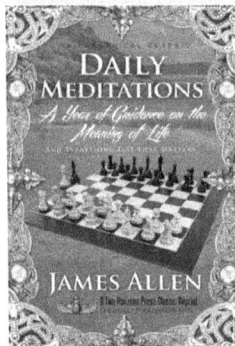

By James Allen

Need a guidebook to a productive and healthy year? This is it. James Allen delivers another great work in this book, this time offering 365 days of inspiration and guidance on life's greatest challenges. This book includes sections for daily notes.

CLASS	PAGES	RETAIL	RELEASE
C-3	208	$14.95	Apr. 2013

ISBN: 978-1-935721-08-6

The Kybalion: The Seven Ancient Egyptian Laws _

By the Three Initiates

Thousands of years ago, the ancients figured out a set of principles that govern the universe. In *The Kybalion*, these laws are explored and explained. This edition includes research into the authorship of the book, and where the laws came from.

CLASS	PAGES	RETAIL	RELEASE
C-4	130	$14.95	Oct. 2012

ISBN: 978-1-935721-25-3

Real Life is No Fairy Tale (w/ Companion CD)

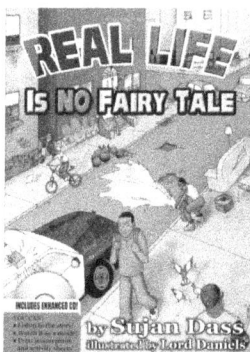

By Sujan Dass and Lord Williams

Looking for a children's book that teaches about struggle? Written for school age children, this full-color hardcover book is composed entirely in rhyme, and the images are as real as they get. Includes a CD with an audio book, animated video, review questions, and printable worksheets and activities.

CLASS	PGS	RETAIL	RELEASE
CD-4	36+	$16.95	Jun. 2010

ISBN: 978-0-9816170-2-2

Aesop's Fables: 101 Classic Tales and Timeless Lessons

Edited by Dr. Sujan Dass

What's better to teach our children than life lessons? This easy-to-read collection of classic tales told by an African storyteller uses animals to teach valuable moral lessons. This edition includes dozens of black-and-white images to accompany the timeless fables. Color them in!

CLASS	PAGES	RETAIL	RELEASE
CD-3	112	$14.95	Feb. 2013

ISBN: 978-1-935721-07-9

Heritage Playing Cards (w/ Companion Booklet)

Designed by Sujan Dass

No more European royalty! This beautiful deck of playing cards features 54 full-color characters from around the world and a 16-page educational booklet on international card games and the ethnic backgrounds of the people on the cards.

CLASS	PGS	RETAIL	RELEASE
CD-2	16+	$6.95	May 2010

UPC: 05105-38587

Black God: An Introduction to the World's Religions and their Black Gods

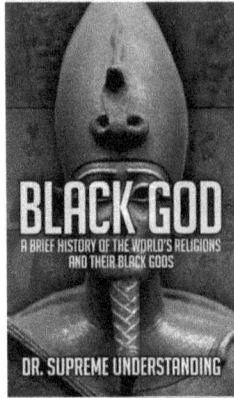

By Supreme Understanding

Have you ever heard that Christ was Black? What about the Buddha? They weren't alone. This book explores the many Black gods of the ancient world, from Africa to Europe, Asia, and Australia, all the way to the Americas. Who were they? Why were they worshipped? And what does this mean for us today?

CLASS	PAGES	RETAIL	RELEASE
C-3	200	$19.95	Jan. 2014

ISBN: 978-1-935721-12-3

Black People Invented Everything

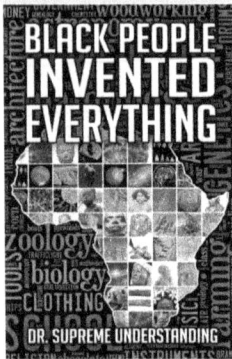

By Supreme Understanding

In *The Science of Self* we began exploring the origins of everything that modern civilization depends on today. In this book, we get into specifics, showing how Black people invented everything from agriculture to zoology, with dozens of pictures and references to prove it!

CLASS	PAGES	RETAIL	RELEASE
I-3	180	$14.95	Feb. 2014

NOT YET PUBLISHED

The Yogi Science of Breath: A Complete Manual of the Ancient Philosophy of the East

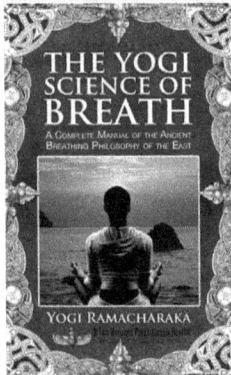

By Yogi Ramacharaka

A classic text on the science of breathing, one of the most ignored, yet important, aspects of our physical and emotional health. This book has been used by both martial arts experts and legendary jazz musicians. This edition explores the "secret science" of breath, and where its mysterious author learned such teachings.

CLASS	PAGES	RETAIL	RELEASE
PH-4	112	$14.95	Apr. 2012

ISBN: 978-1-935721-34-5

How to Get Our Books

To better serve our readers, we've streamlined the way we handle book orders. Here are some of the ways you can find our books.

In Stores

You can find our books in just about any Black bookstore or independent bookseller. If you don't find our titles on the shelves, just request them by name and publisher. Most bookstores can order our titles directly from us (via our site) or from the distributors listed below. We also provide a listing of retailers who carry our books at www.bestblackbooks.com

Online (Wholesale)

Now, you can visit our sites (like www.supremeunderstanding.com or www.bestblackbooks.com) to order wholesale quantities direct from us, the publisher. From our site, we ship heavily discounted case quantities to distributors, wholesalers, retailers, and local independent resellers (like yourself – just try it!). The discounts are so deep, you can afford to GIVE books away if you're not into making money.

Online (Retail)

If you're interested in single "retail" copies, you can now find them online at Amazon.com, or you can order them via mail order by contacting one of the mail order distributors listed below. You can also find many of our titles as eBooks in the Amazon Kindle, Nook, or Apple iBooks systems. You may also find full-length videobook or audiobook files available, but nothing beats the pass-around potential of a real book!

By Mail Order

Please contact any of the following Black-owned distributors to order our books! For others, visit our site.

Afrikan World Books
2217 Pennsylvania Ave.
Baltimore, MD 21217
(410) 383-2006

Lushena Books
607 Country Club Dr
Bensenville, IL 60106
(800) 785-1545

Special Needs X-Press
3128 Villa Ave
Bronx, NY 10468
(718) 220-3786

About the Publishers

Two Horizons Press is an imprint of Supreme Design, LLC. **Two Horizons Press** is a publisher of educational content that may go back more than 100 years. By republishing classic works that have gone ignored for political reasons, THP brings timeless information back to the public eye.

Supreme Design is the parent company for Supreme Design Publishing, Two Horizons Press, and Proven Publishing. Supreme Design was founded as a media firm in 2006 to improve society and eliminate oppression through transformative content and targeted delivery.

As an independent publisher of cutting-edge educational materials for urban families, **Supreme Design Publishing** engages difficult issues like racial justice and capitalism in the language of modern hiphop culture. Visit www.supremedesignonline.com to learn more!

Proven Publishing, another subsidiary of Supreme Design, offers our low-cost and high-quality publishing services to authors looking for greater control of their content. Proven Publishing provides the "proven" body of best practices that bring books from both Supreme Design Publishing and Two Horizons Press to life.

Visit www.provenpublishing.com to learn more!

These independent, family-run, community-based businesses are built and run according to the principles of honor and ethics of the **#360Movement**. For explanations of this cultural change campaign and its many manifestations, visit www.the360movement.com